Anonymous

A new Display of the Beauties of England

Vol. 1, Third Edition

Anonymous

A new Display of the Beauties of England
Vol. 1, Third Edition

ISBN/EAN: 9783337772208

Printed in Europe, USA, Canada, Australia, Japan

Cover: Foto ©Thomas Meinert / pixelio.de

More available books at **www.hansebooks.com**

A NEW DISPLAY

OF THE

Beauties of England,

OR

A Description of the moſt Elegant or Magnificent

PUPLIC EDIFICES, ROYAL PALACES,

NOBLEMEN'S and GENTLEMEN'S SEATS,

and other CURIOSITIES, Natural or Artificial,

in the different parts of the Kingdom.

ADORNED WITH

a Variety of COPPER PLATE CUTS, neatly Engraved.

VOLUME the FIRST.

The THIRD EDITION.

LONDON:

Printed for R. GOADBY; and Sold by J. TOWERS, at
Nº 111, in Fore Street, near Cripplegate; & R. BALDWIN,
Nº 47, in Pater-noſter Row.
MDCCLXXVI.

As the principal defign of this Work was to give defcriptions of the moft elegant and magnificent Public Edifices, Royal Palaces, and Noblemens and Gentlemens Seats in England, it was judged not improper to begin with that part of the Kingdom, which is within the diftance of about twenty miles round London, where a

greater

greater number of thefe are to be found, than in any other diftrict of the fame extent. And as the greateft part of our firft Volume is employed in defcribing this diftrict, it was found moft convenient not to attend to the divifion of the Counties. But in the fecond Volume, wherein remoter parts of the Kingdom are given an account of, the places defcribed have been exactly claffed under their refpective Counties.

A defcription of a greater number of Noblemens and Gentlemens Seats is to be found in this Work, than can be met with in any other publication; as this was

our

our capital object. And of thefe a very unufual number of engraved views are given. But in order to render the Work more compleat, fome account is alfo given of all the cities and market-towns in the kingdom, LONDON excepted, a defcription of which could not have been comprehended within our intended limits.

It is prefumed, that this Work will be found an agreeable companion for thofe who may occafionally vifit different parts of England, in order to take a view of the many fine palaces and feats with which this kingdom abounds. And thofe who may not have an

oppor-

opportunity of perfonally vifiting thofe delightful retreats, may yet receive no inconfiderable degree of fatisfaction, from thofe accounts and views of them, which are given in this Work.

A

NEW DISPLAY

OF THE

BEAUTIES OF ENGLAND.

NOTHING is more natural than a defire of being acquainted with whatever is moſt beautiful, remarkable, or curious in our own country. If we are pleaſingly gratified with deſcriptions of foreign countries, ſurely the curioſities of our native land cannot be leſs worthy our attention. ENGLAND is not only endeared to us by our connection with it, but has a juſt claim to our regard from the great variety of natural and artificial curioſities with which it abounds. It is the favourite reſidence of plenty and of freedom, of wealth, and of commerce; and the many advantages and excellencies with which nature has liberally endowed it, have been aided by the indefatigable induſtry of the inhabitants; which is ſufficiently evinced by the high degree of cultivation which appears in almoſt every part of the kingdom.

Though the air of England is for the moſt part thick and heavy, and the weather very precarious, and often extremely

foggy;

foggy; yet even this variety of weather is attended with considerable advantages. For, in the firſt place, it ſecures the iſland from thoſe extremes of heat and cold, to which other nations, though within the ſame degree of latitude, are annually expoſed; and it is in a great meaſure owing to this moderation of the climate, that the inhabitants of this iſland live to as great an age as in any part of Europe whatſoever. And that perpetual verdure for which England is remarkable, and for which it is greatly admired by all foreigners who come hither, is occaſioned by the refreſhing ſhowers and the warm vapours of the ſea.

With reſpect to the climate of England, there is an obſervation concerning it that was made by King Charles the Second, as we are informed by Sir William Temple, that deſerves to be remembered. 'I muſt needs add one thing (ſays
' Sir William) in favour of our climate, which I heard the
' King ſay, and I thought new and right, and truly like a
' King of England, that loved and eſteemed his own country.
' 'Twas in reply to ſome company, that were reviling our cli-
' mate, and extolling thoſe of Italy and Spain, or at leaſt of
' France. He ſaid, "He thought that that was the beſt cli-
" mate, where he could be abroad in the air with pleaſure, or at
" leaſt without trouble or inconvenience, the moſt days of the
" year, and the moſt hours of the day; and this he thought he
" could be in England, more than in any country he knew in
" Europe." And I believe (adds Sir William) it is true, not
' only of the hot and the cold, but even among our neighbours
' in France and the Low Countries themſelves, where the heats
' or the colds, and changes of ſeaſons, are leſs treatable than
' they are with us.'

It has been juſtly obſerved, that no country in the world can equal the cultivated parts of England for the great number of beautiful ſcenes with which it is adorned. The variety of high-lands and low-lands, the former gently ſwelling, and both of them forming proſpects equal to the moſt luxuriant imagination, the corn and meadow ground, the intermixtures of incloſures and plantations, the noble ſeats, comfortable houſes, chearful villages, and well-ſtocked farms, often riſing in the neighbourhood of populous towns and cities, decorated with the moſt vivid colours of nature, afford an inexpreſſible pleaſure.

Before we proceed to treat of the more diſtant parts of the kingdom, we ſhall give ſome account of the palaces, moſt elegant
gant

The Garden Front of the Royal Palace at Kew.

gant country feats, and other curiofities, within the diftance of
about twenty miles round London. And we fhall begin with
KEW, as that place is at prefent honoured with being the refidence of his Majefty.

The palace of KEW is a neat, plain building; but by no
means fuitable to the dignity of a King of Great Britain. The
principal court of the palace is in the middle; the ftable court
on the left hand; and the kitchen courts on the right. As you
enter the houfe from the principal court, a veftibule leads to the
great hall, which occupies two ftories in height, and receives
its light from windows in the upper ftory. It is furnifhed with
full-length portraits, reprefenting King William III. Queen
Mary, the prefent King of Pruffia, the late Emperor of
Germany, the prefent hereditary Prince of Brunfwick, the late
Elector of Cologne, and that famous Statefman Lord Treafurer Burleigh. Befides which there is a very good hunting
piece by Mr. Wootton, wherein are reprefented the late Frederick Prince of Wales, Lord Baltimore, Lord Cholmondeley,
Lord Bofton, Colonel Pelham, and feveral of his Royal Highnefs's attendants. In this room are likewife two large vafes of
ftatuary marble, on which are cut in baffo relievo the four feafons of the year.

From the hall a paffage leads to the garden, and on the right
hand of this paffage is their Majefties apartment, confifting of
an anti chamber, a drawing-room, a cabinet, and a gallery, with
waiting rooms, and other conveniencies for attendants. The
anti-chamber is hung with tapeftry, and over the doors are two
portraits, the one of the late Lord Cobham, the other of the
late Earl of Chefterfield.

The drawing room is likewife hung with tapeftry. Over the
doors are the portraits of King George I. and the late prince
of Wales, father to his prefent Majefty. There is alfo another picture in the room with three heads, being the portraits
of the late Princefs of Orange, and the Princeffes Amelia and
Caroline.

The cabinet is furnifhed with pannels of Japan; the cieling
is gilt; which, together with the chimney-piece, was defigned by the late ingenious Mr. Kent. The gallery, with
all its furniture, is entirely executed from defigns of the fame
artift. The colour of the wainfcotting is blue, and the ornaments are gilt. Over the chimney is a portrait of the late
Princefs of Orange, in a riding drefs; and on each fide of it
is a very fine picture by the celebrated Mr. Wootton; the

2   one

one reprefenting a ftag at bay, and the other a return from the chace. The fcene of both is Windfor foreft, and the perfons reprefented are the late Prince of Wales, the late Duke of Marlborough, Mr. Spencer, the Duke of Chandois, the Marquis of Powis, Lord Jerfey, and feveral other noblemen, gentlemen, and attendants.

On the left of the paffage which leads to the garden, are the apartments of the bed-chamber women. In their drawing-room is a very large collection of portraits of illuftrious perfons of both fexes; none of them very finely painted, yet curious and very entertaining. The cieling is executed from a defign of Mr. Kent's; as are likewife the cieling, chimney-piece, and all other parts of their dining-room.

The cieling of the great ftaircafe was alfo defigned by Mr. Kent. The principal floor is diftributed into one ftate apartment for their Majefties, and into lodging rooms for their children and attendants. The ftate apartment confifts of a gallery, a drawing room, a dreffing room, an anti-chamber, a bed room, and clofets.

The walls of the gallery are adorned with grotefque paintings, and children in theatrical dreffes, by the late Mr. John Ellis. The chimney-piece and all the furniture, are from defigns of Mr. Kent; and on the piers between the windows are four large painted looking glaffes from china.

The cieling of the drawing-room was defigned and painted by Mr. Kent, with grotefque ornaments, in party colours and gold. The center compartment reprefents the ftory of Leda. The room is hung with green filk, and furnifhed with a very pretty collection of pictures, by Domenichino, Paul Veronefe, Albano, Claude Lorrain, Cornelius Janfen, &c.

The Dreffing Room is richly furnifhed with Japan cabinets, and a great variety of curious works in Drefden porcelain, amber, ivory, &c. and there are alfo in it two large pictures, the one by Dupan, reprefenting the children of the royal family at play; and the other, the late Princefs Dowager of Wales, with his prefent Majefty, the late Duke of York, and the Princefs of Brunfwick, all in their infancy, attended by Lord Bofton, Lady Archibald Hamilton, and Mrs. Herbert.

Their Majefties bed-chamber is hung with tapeftry; the cieling and chimney-piece were defigned by Mr. Kent. The anti-chamber and clofets contain nothing remarkable, excepting an hygrometer of a very curious conftruction, invented and executed by the ingenious Mr. Pullein, one of the Chaplains to the late Princefs Dowager.

The

The GARDENS OF KEW are not very advantageously circumstanced with respect to their situation; as it is low, and commands no prospect. Originally the ground was one continued flat; the soil was in general barren, and without either wood or water. With so many disadvantages, it was not easy to produce any thing even tolerable in gardening. But with great expence and labour, all difficulties were at length overcome ; and what was once a desart, is now a kind of Eden. And the judgment with which art hath been employed to supply the defects of nature, and to cover its deformities, hath excited general admiration.

On entering the garden from the palace, and turning towards the left hand, the first building which appears is *the Orangery, or Green-House*; which was designed by Mr. Chambers, (now Sir William Chambers) and built under his inspection in the year 1761. The front extends one hundred and forty-five feet ; the room is one hundred and forty-two feet long, thirty-six wide, and twenty-five high. In the back shed are two furnaces to heat flues, laid under the pavement of the orangery, which are found very useful, and indeed very necessary in times of hard frost.

What is called *the Temple of the Sun*, is situated in an open grove near the orangery, and in the way to the physic garden. Its figure is of the circular peripteros kind, but without an attic ; and there is a particularity in the entablature, of which the hint is taken from one of the temples of Balbec. The order is Corinthian, the columns fluted, and the entablature fully enriched. Over each column on the frize are basso relievos, reprefenting lyres and fprigs of laurel ; and round the upper part of the cell are fufpended feftoons of fruits and flowers. The infide of the cell forms a faloon richly furnifhed and gilt. In the center of its cove is reprefented the fun, and on the frize, in twelve compartments, furrounded with branches of laurel, are reprefented the figns of the zodiac in baffo relievo. This building was alfo erected by Sir William Chambers.

The *Phyfic or Exotic Garden* contains a prodigious variety of curious plants collected with great diligence and judgment by the late Dr. Hill ; whofe abilities as a Botanift are well known. Several ftoves have been built for the cultivation of thefe plants ; and, amongft others, one very large one, its extent from eaft to weft being one hundred and fourteen feet.

Contiguous to the exotic garden is *the Flower Garden*; of which the principal entrance, with a ftand on each fide of it for rare flowers, forms one end. The two fides are enclofed

with high trees, and the end facing the principal entrance is occupied by an aviary of a vaſt depth, in which is kept a numerous collection of birds both foreign and domeſtic. The parterre
is divided by walks into a great number of beds, in which all kinds
of beautiful flowers are to be ſeen, during the greateſt part of the
year; and in its center is a baſon of water ſtocked with gold
fiſh.

From the flower-garden a ſhort winding walk leads to *the
Menagerie*. It is of an oval figure; the center is occupied by
a large baſon of water, ſurrounded by a walk; and the whole is
encloſed by a range of pens, or large cages, in which are kept
great numbers of Chineſe and Tartarian pheaſants, beſides many
ſorts of other large exotic birds. The baſon is ſtocked with
ſuch water-fowl as are too tender to live on the lake, and in the
middle of it ſtands a pavilion of an irregular octagon plan, deſigned by Sir William Chambers, in imitation of a Chineſe open
Ting, and built in the year 1763.

Near the Menagerie ſtands the *Temple of Bellona*, which was
alſo erected by Sir William Chambers. And paſſing from the
Menagerie towards the lake, in a retired ſolitary walk on the
left, is the *Temple of the God Pan*, which is of the monopteros
kind, but cloſed on the ſide towards the thicket, in order to make
it ſerve for a ſeat. It is of the Doric order; the profile imitated
from that of the theatre of Marcellus at Rome. Not far from
hence on an eminence, ſtands the *Temple of Eolus*. The order
is compoſite, in which the Doric is predominant. Within the
columns is a large ſemicircular nich, ſerving as a ſeat, which
revolves on a pivot, and may with great eaſe be turned by
one hand to any expoſition, notwithſtanding its ſize. The
Temple of Solitude is ſituated very near the ſouth front of the
palace.

At the head of the lake, and near the Temple of Eolus,
ſtands a Chineſe octagon building of two ſtories, built many
years ago; and which is commonly called the *Houſe of Confucius*. The lower ſtory conſiſts of one room and two cloſets,
and the upper ſtory is one little ſaloon, commanding a very
pleaſant proſpect over the lake and gardens. Its walls and
cieling are painted with groteſque ornaments, and little hiſtorical
ſubjects relating to Confucius, with ſeveral tranſactions of the
Chriſtian miſſions in China. In a thicket near the houſe of
Confucius, is erected the engine which ſupplies the lake and
baſons in the gardens with water. It was contrived by Mr.
Smeaton, and executed under his direction in the year 1761.

It

It anfwers perfectly well, raifing by means of two horfes, upwards of 3600 hogfheads of water in twelve hours.

From the Houfe of Confucius a covered clofe walk leads to a grove, where is placed a femi-octagon feat. A winding walk, on the right hand of the grove, leads to an open plain, on one fide of which, backed with thickets, on a rifing ground, is placed a Corinthian colonnade, defigned and built by Sir William Chambers in the year 1760, and called the *Theatre of Augufta.*

The next building which offers itfelf to view, is the *Temple of Victory*. It ftands on a hill, and was built in commemoration of the fignal victory obtained, on the 1ft of Auguft, 1759, at Minden, by the allied army, under Prince Ferdinand of Brunfwick, over the French army, commanded by the Marfhal de Contades. The cell, which commands a pretty profpect towards Richmond, and likewife over Middlefex, is neatly finifhed with ftucco ornaments. Thofe in the cieling reprefent ftandards, and other French trophies.

The upper part of the garden compofes a large wildernefs, on the border of which ftands a Morefque building, commonly called *The Alhambra.* This confifts of a faloon, fronted with a portico of coupled columns, and crowned with a lanthorn.

On an open fpace, near the center of the fame wildernefs, is erected the Tower commonly called *The great Pagoda.* This was begun under Sir William Chambers's direction, in the autumn of the year 1761, and covered in the fpring of the year 1762. The defign is an imitation of the Eaftern temples, and particularly of the Chinefe *Taa.* The bafe is a regular octagon, forty-nine feet in diameter ; and the fuperftructure is likewife a regular octagon in its plan, and its elevation compofed of ten prifms, which form the ten different ftories of the building. The loweft of thefe is twenty-fix feet in diameter, exclufive of the portico which furrounds it, and eighteen feet high ; the fecond is twenty-five feet in diameter, and feventeen feet high ; and all the reft diminifh in diameter and height, in the fame arithmetical proportion, to the ninth ftory, which is eighteen feet in diameter, and ten feet high. The tenth ftory is feventeen feet in diameter, and, with the covering, twenty feet high ; and the finifhing on the top is feventeen feet high : fo that the whole ftructure, from the bafe to the top of the fleuron, is one hundred and fixty-three feet. Each ftory finifhes with a projecting roof, after the Chinefe manner, covered with plates of varnifhed iron of different colours ; and round each of them there is a gallery enclofed with a rail. All the angles of the roof are adorned with large dragons, being eighty in number, covered with a kin l of thin glafs of various colours, which produces a moft dazzling reflexion; and the whole ornament at the top is double gilt. The walls of the building are compofed of very hard bricks; the outfide of well-coloured and well matched grey-ftocks, neatly laid, and with fuch care, that there is not the leaft crack or fracture in the whole ftructure, notwithftanding its great height, and the expedition with which it was built. The ftair-cafe, which leads to the different ftories, is in the center of the building.

Notwithftanding the ground on which this ftructure is erected lies low, we have, on a clear day, a very fine profpect from the top of this elegant building; whence we may fee northward, the hills of Harrow, Hampftead, and Highgate, fouthward to Banftead-downs and Epfom, taking in all that fine profpect of the county of Surrey, including Efher, Epfom-courfe, Wimbleton, Richmond park, Putney heath, with the whole county away to Carfhalton and Croydon, &c. Eaftward we have a fine view of the river up to London, with the beautiful feats and pleafant villages on each fide, as far as Blackheath and Shooter's hill, which bound the profpect on this fide. In the fame manner the Thames affords a fine profpect weftward, of Hampton-court, and all the delightful country feats and villages along the river to Maidenhead-bridge, Windfor, &c. &c. In fhort, there is not, perhaps, another place in the world, from which fo beautiful, populous, and well cultivated a fpot can be feen, as from the top of the Pagoda in Kew-gardens.

Near the great Pagoda, on a rifing ground, backed with thickets, ftands *The Mofque*; which was defigned and built by Sir William Chambers in the year 1761. The body of the building confifts of an octagon faloon in the center, flanked with two cabinets, finifhing with one large dome, and two fmall ones. The large dome is crowned with a crefcent, and its upright part contains twenty-eight little arches, which give light to the faloon. On the three front fides of the central octagon are three doors, giving entrance to the building; over each of which there is an Arabic infcription, which may be thus tranflated :

" Let there be no force in religion."
" There is but one God."
" Do not make any image or reprefentation of the Deity."

The minarets are placed at each end of the principal buildings.

ing. In the design of them, as well as in the whole exterior decoration of the building itself, Sir William Chambers has endeavoured to collect the principal particularities of the Turkish architecture. With regard to the interior decoration, he has not so scrupulously adhered to their style in building, but has aimed at something uncommon, and at the same time pleasing. At the eight angles of the room are palm trees modelled in stucco, painted and varnished with various hues of green, in imitation of nature; which at the top spread, and support the dome, represented as formed of reeds, bound together with ribbons of silk. The cove is supposed to be perforated, and a brilliant sunny sky appears, finely painted by Mr. Wilson of Covent-garden, the celebrated landscape painter.

In the way from the Mosque towards the palace, there is a Gothic building, designed by Mr. Muntz, the front representing a cathedral. The *Gallery of Antiques* was designed by Chambers, and executed in the year 1757. Continuing your way from the last mentioned building towards the palace, near the banks of the lake, stands the *Temple of Arethusa*, a small Ionic building of four columns. Near it there is a bridge thrown over a narrow chanel of water, and leading to the island in the lake. The design is, in a great measure, taken from one of Palladio's wooden bridges. It was erected in one night.

In various parts of the garden are erected covered seats; and besides the other buildings that have been mentioned, there is also the *Temple of Peace*. This was erected in commemoration of the late peace, which was as much applauded by the partizans of the court, as it was execrated by the bulk of the nation. The portico is Hexastyle Ionic; the columns fluted; the entablature enriched, and the tympan of the pediment adorned with basso relievos. The cell is in the form of a Latin cross, the ends of which are closed with semi-circular sweeps, wherein are niches for statues. It is richly finished with stucco ornaments, allusive to the occasion on which it was erected. But in truth this edifice had better have been omitted, as it is not very well adapted to excite any pleasing sensations; but is rather calculated to fill the breast of every Englishman who views it with disgust and indignation. The unparalleled series of victories and successes which attended the British arms during the last war, afforded the most glorious opportunity that ever offered, of humbling the House of Bourbon, and concluding such a treaty of peace as would have been an immortal honour to this nation. But in order to promote some private views of those in power, an ill-judged and inadequate peace was precipitated, to the great joy of our enemies, and the extreme regret of every Englishman who had a sincere regard for the honour and interest of his native country. However, an edifice has been erected at Kew to commemorate this treaty of peace, though, from the circumstances under which it was concluded, it will for ever reflect disgrace on every British minister who was concerned in its negociation.

The *Ruin* at Kew was designed and built by Sir William Chambers in the year 1759, in order to make a passage for carriages and cattle over one of the principal walks of the garden. His intention was to imitate a Roman antiquity, built of brick, with an incrustation of stone. The design is a triumphal arch, originally with three apertures, but two of them now closed up, and converted into rooms, to which you enter by doors made in the sides of the principal arch. Both the fronts of the structure are rustic. The north front is confined between rocks, overgrown with briars and other wild plants, and topped with thickets, amongst which are seen several columns, and other fragments of buildings; and at a little distance beyond the arch is seen an antique statue of a muse. The central structure of the ruin is bounded on each side by a range of arches. There is a great quantity of cornices, and other fragments, spread over the ground semingly fallen from the buildings; and in the thickets on each side are seen several remains of piers, brick walls, and other ruins.

The gardens of Kew undoubtedly are, upon the whole, extremely pleasing; but it has been thought, and not without reason, that with regard to the ornaments and buildings therein, a fondness for Turkish and Chinese chequer-work has too much prevailed, in preference to the more beautiful models of Grecian and Roman architecture.

The village of *Kew* is situated on the banks of the Thames, in the county of Surrey, opposite to Old Brentford. Here is a chapel of case, erected at the expence of several of the nobility and gentry in the neighbourhood, on a piece of ground that was given for that purpose by Queen Anne. In 1758, an act of parliament was passed for building a bridge across the Thames, opposite to Kew-green; and a bridge was accordingly erected, consisting of eleven arches. The two piers, and their dependant arches on each side next the shore, are built of brick and stone; but the intermediate arches, which are seven in number, are entirely wood. The centre arch is fifty feet wide, and the road over the bridge is thirty feet wide.

vide. Several gentlemen have elegant country-houses on Kew Green.

RICHMOND.

At a little distance from Kew, and about twelve miles from London, is the village of *Richmond*, which is esteemed the finest village in the British dominions. It was anciently the seats of our monarchs, and the palace, from its splendor, was called *Shene*, which in the Saxon tongue signifies bright or shining. Here died King Edward III. so much celebrated in the English annals ; and here also died Queen Anne, the wife of Richard II. who first taught the English women the use of the side saddle ; for before her time they used to ride astride. Richard was so afflicted at her death, that it gave him such a dislike to the place where it happened, that he defaced the fine palace. But it was repaired and beautified afresh by King Henry V. who, had he lived, intended to have made it his summer residence ; but during the long wars between the houses of York and Lancaster, it was greatly neglected, and at last consumed by fire in the year 1497. It did not, however, remain long in ruins ; for Henry VII. caused it to be rebuilt according to the best rules of architecture in that age, and commanded that the name of the village should be changed from Shene to Richmond ; he having borne the title of Earl of Richmond, before he obtained the crown by the defeat and death of Richard III. Henry VII. died here ; and here also his grand-daughter Queen Elizabeth breathed her last.

The late palace, which was finely situated, was a very plain edifice built by the Duke of Ormond, who received a grant of a considerable space of land about Richmond, from King William III. as a reward for his military services ; but it devolved to the crown on that nobleman's attainder, in the beginning of the reign of King George I. His late Majesty took great delight here, and made several improvements in the palace, while Queen Caroline amused herself at her Royal dairy-house, Merlin's-cave, the Hermitage, and other improvements which she made in the park and gardens of this pleasing retreat. And the present King has chiefly resided here, during the summer season, almost ever since his accession to the throne : but since the death of the late Princess Dowager of Wales, he has removed to Kew. And the palace here has just been pulled down, and a new one is begun to be erected.

A3

As to the gardens at Richmond, they are extremely fine without offering a violence to nature ; and Pope's advice with respect to planting, has been considered as a very accurate description of the beauties to be found here.

> " To build, to plant, whatever you intend,
> " To rear the column, or the arch to bend ;
> " To swell the terrace, or to sink the grot,
> " In all let nature never be forgot.
> " Consult the genius of the place in all,
> " That tells the waters or to rise or fall ;
> " Or helps th' ambitious hill the heavens to scale,
> " Or scoops in circling theatres the vale ;
> " Calls in the country, catches op'ning glades,
> " Joins willing woods, and varies shades from shades ;
> " Now breaks, or now directs th' intending lines ;
> " Paints as you plant, and as you work, designs."

In short, almost every thing in Richmond gardens has an agreeable wildness, and a pleasing irregularity, that cannot fail to charm all who are in love with nature, and afford a much higher and more lasting satisfaction, than the stiff decorations of art, where the artist loses sight of nature, which alone ought to direct his hand.

On entering these rural walks, you are conducted to the dairy, a neat but low brick building, to which there is an ascent by a flight of steps ; in the front is a handsome angular pediment, which has a fine effect on the eye of the spectator. The walls on the inside are covered with stucco, and the house is furnished suitable to a royal dairy, all the vessels for holding the milk being of the finest china, and the most beautiful patterns.

On a mount near one side of the dairy, is a temple, on the top of which is a circular dome and ball, being supported by pillars of the Tuscan order. Near the river is a wood, through which there is a walk to an elegant structure, called the Queen's Pavillion, and near it is a small summer house. The great summer-house is situated near the borders of the wood, and is a fine light airy building, having lofty windows, from which there is a most delightful prospect over the river to Sion-house, the seat of the Duke of Northumberland. In this edifice are two good pictures, representing the taking of Vigo by the Duke of Ormond.

Merlin's Cave, a gothic building, covered with thatch, is near a pond at the end of a labyrinth ; and in it is a library,
con-

confifting of a well-chofen collection of the works of modern authors, neatly bound in vellum. Merlin is reprefented like one of the ancient Britifh bards, and Queen Elizabeth in the drefs mentioned by ancient authors to have been worn by the Amazons : both thefe are waxen figures.'

On leaving this edifice, which has an antique and venerable appearance, you come to a large oval of about 500 feet in diameter, called the Foreft oval ; and turning from hence you have a view of the *Hermitage*, a grotefque building, which feems as if it had ftood many hundred years ; though it was only built by order of the late Queen Caroline. It has three arched doors, and the middle part which projects forward, is adorned with a kind of ruinous angular pediment ; the ftones of the whole edifice appear as if rudely laid together, and the venerable look of the whole is improved by the thicknefs of the folemn grove behind, and the little turret on the top with a bell, to which you may afcend by a winding walk. The infide is in the form of an octagon with niches, in which are the bufts of five celebrated men, who have been juftly numbered among the greateft ornaments of this country ; namely, Sir Ifaac Newton, Mr. Locke, Mr. Woolafton, Dr. Samuel Clarke, and Mr. Robert Boyle.

Leaving this feat of contemplation, you pafs through fields cloathed with grafs, and alfo through corn fields, and a wild ground interfperfed with broom and furze, which afford excellent fhelter for hares and pheafants ; of which laft there are here great numbers very tame. From this pleafing variety, in which nature appears in all her forms of cultivation, and of barren wildnefs, you come to an amphitheatre formed by young elms, and a diagonal wildernefs, through which you pafs to the foreft walk, which extends about half a mile, and then paffing through a fmall wildernefs, you leave the gardens ; to the weft of which are feen the fine houfes of feveral of the Nobility and Gentry. We fhall conclude our remarks relative to the gardens, with obferving, that the grand terras, which overlooks the river, is admired by all foreigners.

Richmond Green is extreamly pleafant, it being levelled and enclofed in a handfome manner. It is alfo furrounded with lofty elms, and adorned on each fide with the houfes of perfons of diftinction. A fun dial is here affixed in a pretty tafte, encompaffed with feats : this, and the railing-in of the green, were at the fole expence of the late Queen Caroline.

The village of Richmond, (or town, as it is frequently
called)

called) extends a full mile up the hill from the Thames, skirted and mingled with gardens. It is now a flourishing place; and a theatre has lately been erected here, where, during the summer season, dramatic entertainments are performed on the stage, by some of the best actors from London: for many people of fashion reside here, and in the neighbourhood. Great numbers from London are also constantly visiting the gardens, some going in parties by water, and others in the stage or their own carriages.

The summit of *Richmond Hill* affords a most enchanting prospect of towns, villages, bridges, woods, groves, gardens, fields, and an incredible number of delightful villas along the banks of the river Thames, which winds with a serpentine course through this delicious vale from Kingston to London. The tide before the building of Westminster bridge, used to rise as high as Richmond, but now falls short of it. It still, however, reaches sixty miles from the sea; which is a greater distance than the tide is carried by any other river in Europe.

There is here an alms-house, which was built by Dr. Duppa, bishop of Winchester, in the reign of King Charles II. for the support of ten poor widows, pursuant to a vow made by that prelate during that prince's exile. There is also another alms-house, endowed with above 100l. a year, which, since its foundation, has been considerably encreased by John Mitchell, Esq. Here are likewise two charity-schools, one for fifty boys, and the other for fifty girls.

Richmond Park, sometimes called the New Park in Surry, is one of the best parks in England. It was made in the reign of King Charles I. and enclosed with a brick wall, said to be eleven miles in compass. In this park there is a little hill cast up, called King Henry's mount, from which is a prospect of six counties, with a distant view of the city of London, and of Windsor-castle. The new lodge in this park, built by the late Sir Robert Walpole, Earl of Orford, is a very elegant edifice. It is built of stone in a square form, with wings on each side of brick. It stands on a rising-ground, and commands a very good prospect of the park. This park is the largest of any within the environs of London, except that of Windsor, and the finest too; for though it has little more than a wild variety of natural beauties to shew, yet these are such as cannot fail to please those who are as much delighted with views in their rudest appearance, as in all the elegance of art and design.

SION-

The West Front of Sion House.

S I O N - H O U S E.

Directly oppofite to the royal gardens at Richmond, though on the other fide of the river and in another county, ftands *Sion-houfe*, one of the feats of the Duke of Northumberland. It is called Sion from a monaftery of the fame name, which was founded by Henry V. in 1414, very near the place where the houfe now ftands, and which was endowed with one thoufand marks a year, for the maintenance of fixty nuns, including the abbefs and twenty-five men. The prefent edifice was erected by the Duke of Somerfet, Protector, and uncle to King Edward the Sixth; who began to build it about the year 1547; but many and great additions and improvements have been fince made to it, and efpecially by the prefent Duke of Northumberland. Sion Houfe is built on the very fpot where the church belonging to the monaftery formerly ftood, and is a very large, venerable, and majeftic ftructure, built of white ftone, in the form of a hallow fquare; fo that it has four external, and as many internal fronts; the latter of which furround a fquare court in the middle. The roof is flat, covered with lead, and furrounded with indented battlements, like the walls of a fortified city. Upon every one of the four outward angles of the roof, there is a fquare turret, flat-roofed, and embattled like other parts of the building. The houfe is three ftories high, and the eaft front, which faces the Thames, is fupported by arches, forming a fine piazza. The great hall was finifhed in the manner in which it at prefent appears by Inigo Jones; who was alfo employed to new face the inner court, and to make fome alterations in feveral of the apartments.

The gardens at Sion were firft laid out and finifhed in a very grand manner by the Protector Somerfet; but being made at a time when extenfive views were judged to be inconfiftent with that folemn referve and ftately privacy affected by the great, they were fo fituated as to deprive the houfe of every beautiful profpect which the neighbourhood afforded : at leaft none of them could be feen from the lower apartments. To remedy this inconvenience, the prefent Duke of Northumberland caufed a high triangular terras, which the Protector had raifed at a great expence, to be removed; the walls of the old gardens were alfo taken down, and the ground before the houfe levelled, and it now forms a fine lawn, extending from Ifleworth to Brentford. By thefe means a beautiful profpect is not only opened into the royal gardens at Richmond, but alfo up and down the river Thames. Towards the Thames the lawn is bounded by an ha-ha, and a meadow; which his Grace ordered to be cut down into a gentle slope, so that the surface of the water may now be seen even from the lowest apartments and the gardens. In consequence of these improvements, the most beautiful pieces of scenery imaginable is formed before two of the principal fronts, for even the Thames itself seems to belong to the gardens.

The house stands nearly in the middle point of that side of the lawn which is the furthest from the Thames, and communicates with Isleworth and Brentford, either by means of the lawn or a fine gravel walk, which in some places runs along the side, and in others through the middle of a beautiful shrubbery; so that even the most retired parts of this charming maze, where the prospect is most confined, almost the whole vegetable world rises up as it were in minature around you, and presents you with every foreign shrub, plant, and flower, which can be adopted by the soil of this climate.

The present Duke of Northumberland has not only thus improved the ground where the old gardens stood, but has also made a very large addition to it, and separated the two parts by making a new serpentine river. It communicates with the Thames, is well stored with all sorts of river fish, and can be emptied and filled by means of a sluice, which is so contrived as to admit the fish into the new river, but to prevent their returning back into the Thames. His Grace has also built two bridges, which form a communication between the two gardens, and has erected in that, which lies near Brentford, a stately Doric column; upon the top of which is a fine proportioned statue of Flora, so judiciously placed as to command as it were a distinct view of the situation over which she is supposed to preside.

The Kitchen gardens are very large, lie at a proper distance from the house, and contain every thing necessary or convenient, as a hot house, fire-walls, &c. The green house is a very neat building, with a Gothic front, designed by his Grace in so light a style, as to be greatly admired. The back and end walls of it are the only remains of the old monastery. This building stands near a circular bason of water, well stocked with gold and silver fish; and in the middle of the bason is a spouting fountain, which is well supplied, and plays without intermission.

Among the most remarkable particulars at Sion-house is the great gallery, which extends the whole length of the east-front

over

The Garden Front of the Earl of Harrington's Seat at Petersham in Surry.

over the arcades. There is also an immense quantity of old china vases, of different forms and sizes, crowded together in almost every apartment. And the Pedigree picture here is one of the greatest curiosities of its kind in England, and exhibits the noble and royal connections of the Percies; all which were united in the late Dutchess of Northumberland. We may also remark, that many fine prospects may be seen from the leads at the top of the house; for they command a view of the country to the distance of thirteen or fourteen miles, and consequently the greatest part of London may be seen from them. To these observations we may add, that the gardens, when viewed from the top of the house, form a finer landscape than can easily be conceived.

P E T E R S H A M.

This is a small village in Surrey, near the New Park, and a little to the south of Richmond Hill, Here stood a delightful seat built by the Earl of Rochester, Lord High Treasurer in the reign of King James II. But this fine house was burnt down in the year 1720, so suddenly, that the family, who were all at home, had scarcely time to save their lives. By this accident, the curious collection of paintings, and the whole library, of the Earl of Clarendon, author of the History of the Civil War, were wholly consumed. But on the ground where this house stood, another was erected after one of the designs of the Earl of Burlington, for the Earl of Harrington, who now resides in it. The front next the court is very plain, and the entrance to the house not very extraordinary; but the south front next the garden, is bold and regular, and the apartments on that side chiefly designed for state, are extremely elegant. The gardens were formerly crowded with plantations near the house; but they are now laid out in lawns of grass. The kitchen garden, before situated on the east side of the house, is removed out of sight; and the ground converted to an open slope of grass, leading up to a terrace of great length; from which is a prospect of the river Thames, the village of Twickenham, and of all the fine seats round that part of the country. On the other side of the terrace, is a plantation on a rising ground; and on the summit of the hill is a fine pleasure house, which on every side commands a prospect of the country for many miles.——Petersham gives the title of Viscount to the Earl of Harrington.——It appears from ancient records to have been a place of great antiquity; and formerly it was possessed of great privileges; so that no person could

C 2   be

be arrested in it, and no officer was permitted to come through it with any person in his custody whom he had arrested elsewhere.——The Earl of Dysart has a handsome seat at *Ham*, near this place, which was formerly in the possession of the Duke of Lauderdale. It is close by the river, and King Charles II. used to be frequently at this pleasant seat, being much delighted with it.

T W I C K E N H A M.

On the opposite side of the river, in the county of Middlesex, stands the pleasant village of *Twickenham*, which is particularly memorable for having been the residence of Mr. Pope. That celebrated poet purchased a house here in the year 1715, and took great delight in improving his house and gardens. And the improvements which he made were so elegant, that his seat became an object of general admiration, as well as its owner. The house and gardens have, however, been considerably enlarged since, by the late Sir William Stanhope, who purchased them after the death of Mr. Pope.

One of the chief ornaments of this agreable retreat, was the grotto, the improvement of which was one of the favourite amusements of Mr. Pope's declining years; so that not long before his death, by enlarging and increasing *it* with a number of ores and minerals of the richest and rarest kinds, he made it one of the most elegant and romantic retirements. Toward the beautifying of his gardens and grotto, Mr. Pope was assisted by presents of various kinds, from several of his friends, procured from the various quarters of the globe ; and among others who made him presents for this purpose, was the late Frederic Prince of Wales ; who often testified a great regard for men of genius and learning, though they did not prostitute their talents to gratify the Court, and who always appeared to be a real friend to the liberties of the people.

Our readers will, we presume, not be displeased with the following description which Mr. Pope himself gave of this romantic retreat, in a letter to a friend, long before it received the last and principal improvement. " I have," says he, " put the last hand to my works of this kind, in happily fi-" nishing the subterranean way and grotto: I there found a " spring of the clearest water, which falls in a perpetual rill, " that echoes through the cavern day and night. From the " river Thames you see through my arch up a walk of the " wilderness, to a kind of open temple, wholly composed of " shells

A View of Twickenham in the County of Middlesex.

" shells in the ruftic manner; and from that diftance, under
" the temple, you look down through a floping arcade of trees,
" and fee the fails on the river pafling fuddenly and vanifhing,
" as through a perfpective glafs. When you fhut the doors of
" this grotto, it becomes on the inftant, from a luminous room,
" a *camera abfcura*; on the walls of which all the objects of the
" river, hills, woods, and boats, are forming a moving pic-
" ture in their vifible radiations. And when you have a mind
" to light it up, it affords you a very different fcéne; it is fi-
" nifhed with fhells, interfperfed with pieces of looking glafs
" in regular forms; and in the cieling is a ftar of the fame ma-
" terial, at which, when a lamp (of an orbicular figure of thin
" alabafter) is hung in the middle, a thoufand pointed rays glit-
" ter and are reflected over the place. There are connected to
" this grotto, by a narrow paffage, two porches, one towards
" the river of fmooth ftones full of light and open; the other
" towards the garden, fhadowed with trees, rough with fhells,
" flints, and iron ore. The bottom is paved with fimple pebble,
" as is alfo the adjoining walk up the wildernefs to the temple,
" in the natural tafte, agreeing not ill with the little dripping
" murmur, and the aquatic idea of the whole place. It
" wants nothing to compleat it but a good ftatue with an
" infcription, like that beautiful antique one which you know
" I am fo fond of:

  " Hujus nympha loci, fecri cuftodia fontis,
    " Dormio, dum blandæ fentio murmur aquæ.
  " Parce meum, quifquis tangis cavo marmora, fomnum
    " Rumpere; fi bibas, five lavare, tace."

  " Nymph of the grot, thefe facred fprings I keep,
  " And to the murmurs of thefe waters fleep;
  " Ah, fpare my flumbers, gently tread the cave!
  " And drink in filence, or in filence lave."

" You'll think I have been very poetical in this defcription, but
" it is pretty near the truth."
  This letter was written in 1725. But afterwards, when it
was in its more perfect ftate, Mr. Pope wrote the following
fhort poem upon it.

  " Thou who fhalt ftop where Thames' tranflucent wave
  " Shines a broad mirror, thro' the fhadowy cave; .
  " Where ling'ring drops from min'ral roofs diftil,
  " And pointed chryftals break the fparkling rill,
                                                    " Un-

" Unpolifh'd gems no ray on pride beflow,
" And latent metals innocently glow :
" Approach.   Great nature ftudioufly behold !
" And eye the mine without a wifh for gold.
" Approach : But awful ! Lo ! the Ægerian grot,
" Where, nobly penfive, Sr. John fat and thought ;
" Where Britifh fighs from dying Wyndham ftole,
" And the bright flame was fhot thro' Marchmont's foul.
" Let fuch, fuch only, tread this facred floor,
" Who dare to love their country and be poor."

It hath been juftly obferved, that Mr. Pope's modefty is very confpicuous in thefe admirable lines.   He warns an awful approach to his grotto, on account of the reverence due to his friends, who fat and thought there ; without faying one word of himfelf.   But what renders it truly venerable, is its having been the feat of his own ftudy and meditation, which will afford inftruction and entertainment to the lateft pofterity.—It may be here remarked, that Mr. Pope erected in his garden a fmall pyramid to the memory of his mother, which is ftill remaining.

In th s pleafing retreat Mr. Pope (to borrow the words of Lord Orrery) " treated his friends with a politenefs that charmed, " and a generofity that was much to his honour.   Every gueft " was made happy within his doors.   Pleafure dwelt under his " roof, and elegance prefided at his table."   This fine feat is now in the poffeffion of Welbore Ellis, Efq. who married the daughter of the late Sir William Stanhope.

The ingenious Mr. Horace Walpole, well known in the republic of letters for his feveral elegant publications in polite literature, has alfo a delightful feat near Twickenham, known by the name of Strawberry Hill.   This romantic edifice, which is built in an agreeable retirement, appears to the eye like the fhattered outfide of an ancient priory.   The entrance is by a cloifter which is low, narrow, and obfcure, and humid ; upon the walls are to be feen epitaphs, and a variety of funeral infcriptions brought from Italy.   The manner in which the houfe is laid out anfwers to its entry.   A refactory, chapter, dormitory, chapel ; in fhort, all the fame as in a religious houfe ; and from the manner in which it is conftructed, from the furniture, the glaffes, the paintings, and the ornaments, one would take it to be a monaftery of the thirteenth century.   The library unites all the embellifhments which architects have endeavoured to give to this kind of building : the roof divided
into

Strawberry Hill, the Seat of Mr Horace Walpole.

The Seat of the late Sir George Pocock, formerly Governor Pitts at Twickenham

Marble Hall, Seat of the Earl of Buckinghamshire, late the Countess of Suffolk's.

into ogees is loaded with that fpecies of wreathed fhells, which the Gothic architecture feems to have borrowed from the ftalactites fufpended in thofe grottoes that held fo diftinguifhed a place in natural hiftory. The books are contained in feveral preffes, the pannels of which, made after the manner of glafs cafements of churches, are of the moft precious fort of wood, and of the 'fineft workmanfhip, upon the moft antique models. The fea's, the tables, and defks, difcover the fame regularity and tafte. The windows are of old painted glafs. It has been juftly obferved, that great delicacy and precifion were neceffary to give tafte to thofe fantaftic forms, fo widely deviating from the prefent fafhions.

The Earl of Buckinghamfhire has alfo a fine feat at Twickenham, called *Marble Hall*, which was fome years ago in the poffeffion of the Countefs of Suffolk. There are likewife feveral other fine feats here, particularly that of Sir George Pococke, which formerly belonged to Governor Pitt.

The church at Twickenham is a modern edifice, rebuilt by the contributions of the inhabitants, and is a handfome Doric ftructure. Mr. Pope's father and mother, as well as himfelf, were buried here in the fame vault; to whofe memory he erected a monument with the following infcription, written by himfelf.

D. O. M.

Alexander Pope, viro innocuo, probo, pio;

Qui vixit an. 75. ob. 1717.

Et Edithæ conjugi inculpabili, pientiffimæ;

Qui vixit annos 93. ob. 1733.

Parentibus bene merentibus

Filius fecit.

Et fibi. Obiit an. 1744. ætatis 56.

The laft line was added after Mr. Pope's own death, in purfuance of his will; but the reft was done after the death of his parents. However, Mr. Warburton, the prefent Bifhop of Gloucefter, has fince erected a very handfome monument in Twickenham church to the memory of this juftly celebrated Poet, whereon is his head in a kind of medallion, and underneath the following infcription:

ALEXANDRO POPE,

H. M.

Gulielmus Epifcopus Gloceftrienfis

Amicitæ caufa fac cur.

MDCCLXI.

And

And a little lower are the following lines :
POETA LOQUITUR.
For one who would not be buried in Westminster-
Abbey.

Heroes and Kings your diſtance keep,
In peace let one poor Poet ſleep :
Who never flatter'd folks like you,
Let Horace bluſh and Virgil too.

On the outſide of Twickenham church, there is alſo a ſtone
erected by Mr. Pope himſelf, whereon is the following inſcription :

To the Memory of
M A R Y   B E A C H,
Who died Nov. 5, 1725, aged 78.
ALEX. POPE, whom ſhe nurſed in his infancy,
And conſtantly attended for thirty-eight years,
In gratitude to a Faithful Servant,
Erected this ſtone.

I S L E W O R T H.

Iſleworth, or as it is ſometimes called Thiſtleworth, is a very
pleaſant village, finely ſituated on the banks of the Thames,
about two miles from Twickenham. Richard, King of the
Romans, had a palace here, which was burnt down by the Londoners in an inſurrection. Between this place and a ſmall village
called Worton, there was a mill in the reign of Queen Elizabeth, for the manufacture of copper and braſs, which were melted and forged out of the ore brought up from Mendip-hill in
Somerſetſhire. Here is an handſome church, and two charity-
ſchools. Several perſons of diſtinction have ſeats here, particularly the Earl of Shrewſbury.

B R E N T F O R D.

This town, which is about eight miles from London, receives its name from a brook, called Brent, which riſes about
Finchley Common, and runs through the weſt part of the
town, called Old Brentford, into the Thames. As it is a great
thoroughfare to the weſt, it has a conſiderable trade, particularly in corn, both by land and by the Thames ; and it is extremely full of inns and public-houſes. The market-houſe
ſtands in that part of the town called New Brentford, where
there is a church ; and there is alſo another in Old Brentford.
The market is held on Saturday, and there is alſo an annual
fair on the tenth of Auguſt. There are two charity-ſchools
here

The late Earl of Burlingtons Seat at Chiswick, seen from the Garden.

here. Old Brentford is situated upon a fine rising bank close
to the Thames, and is naturally capable of being made a very
beautiful spot. The opposite side of the river is Kew Green,
which appears from hence to advantage.—The Earl of Holder-
nesse has an handsome seat near Brentford.—At the Butts on the
north of New Brentford, is the place for the election of members
for the county of Middlesex.

CHISWICK.

This is a pleasant village in Middlesex, situated on the banks
of the Thames, about six miles from London. Here are several elegant seats, but the most remarkable is that of the late Earl
of Burlington, which now belongs to the Duke of Devonshire.
Lord Burlington had before a plain, commodious building,
with good offices about it; but a part of the old edifice being
some years ago destroyed by fire, his Lordship erected near it
the present beautiful villa, which, for elegance of taste, is
supposed to surpass every thing of its kind in England. The
court in the front, which is of a proportionable size with the
building, is gravelled, and constantly kept very neat. On each
side are yew hedges in pannels, with *Terminii* placed at a proper
distance; and in the front of these hedges are two rows of cedars
of Libanus, which, at a small distance, have a fine effect; the
dark shade of these solemn ever-greens affording a pleasing con-
trast to the whiteness of the elegant building that appears between them, the view of which from the road surprizes the
spectator in a most agreeable manner.

The ascent to the house is by a noble flight of steps, on one
side of which is the statue of Palladio, and on the other that of
Inigo Jones. The portico is supported by six fine fluted columns of the Corinthiaan order, with a pediment very elegant,
and the cornice, frize, and architrave, as rich as possible. This
magnificent front strikes all who behold it with uncommon pleasure and admiration.

The octagonal saloon finishing at top in a dome, through which
it is enlightened, is also very elegant. The other rooms are extremely beautiful, and are finely finished with pictures of the
greatest masters. Though the other front towards the garden
is plainer, yet it is in a very bold, noble, and masterly stile, and
has at the same time a pleasing simplicity, as has also the side
front towards the serpentine river, which is different from the
two others. If this edifice has any fault, it is its being too
small for so magnificent a design.

D

The

The inside of this structure is finished with the utmost elegance; the cielings are richly gilt and painted, and the rooms adorned with some of the best pictures in Europe. In the gardens, which are very beautiful, the villos are terminated by a temple, obelisk, or some such ornament, which produces a most agreeable effect.

The gardens are laid out in the finest taft; on descending from the back part of the house, you enter a verdant lawn planted with clumps of ever-greens, between which are two rows of large stone vases. At the ends next the house are two wolves in sione, done by the celebrated Scheemaker, the statuary; at the farther end are two large lions, and the view is terminated by three fine antique statues, dug up in Adrian's garden at Rome, with stone seats behind them, and behind a close plantation of ever-greens.

On turning to the house on the right hand, an open grove of foreft-trees affords a view of the orangery, which is seen as perfectly as if the trees were planted on the lawn; and when the orange-trees are in flower, their fragrance is diffused over the whole lawn to the house. These are separated from the lawn by a fossee, to secure them from being injured by the persons admitted to walk in the garden.

On leaving the house to the left, an easy slope covered with short grafs leads down to the serpentine river, on the side whereof are clumps of ever-greens, with agreeable breaks, between which the water is seen; and at the farther end is an opening into an inclosure, where are a Roman temple, and an obelisk, with grafs slopes, and in the middle a circular piece of water.

From hence you are led to the wilderness, through which you may ramble near a mile in the shade. On each side the serpentine river, are verdant walks, which accompany the river in all its turnings. On the right hand of this river is a building that is the exact model of the portico of the church of Covent Garden; on the left is a wilderness laid out in regular walks; and in the middle is a Palladian wooden bridge over the river.

With the earth dug from the bed of this river, Lord Burlington raised a terrace, that affords a prospect of the adjacent country; which, when the tide is up, is greatly enlivened by the view of the boats and barges passing along the river Thames.

2   Among

View of the back part of the Casina, & Serpentine River in Chiswick Gardens.

Among the variety of fine paintings which are in the different apartments of Chiswick House, the following may deserve particular notice; viz. In the Saloon, Lord Burlington and three of his sisters, Elizabeth, Juliana, and Jane, by Sir Godfrey Kneller; the Morocco Ambassador, in the reign of Charles II. the figure by Sir Godfrey Kneller, and the back ground and horse by Wyke; King Charles I. his Queen, and two children, by Vandyke. In the Red Velvet Room, a Madonna della Rosa, by Domenichino; Painting and Designing by Guido Rheni; the Holy Family, by Carlo Maratti; King Charles I. by Cornelius Johnson; the Duchess of Somerset, by Vandyke; the first Countess of Burlington, by the same artist; a portrait by Rembrandt; Mr. Killigrew, by Vandyke; the first Earl of Burlington, by the same; Mary, Queen of Scotland, by Fred. Zuchhero; and the Procession of the Dogesse, by Paolo Veronese. In the Blue Velvet Room; a Chymist's Shop, by David Teniers; a landscape and figures by Gaspar Poussin; Lord Sandwich in a round, by Sir Peter Lely; a woman frying fritters, by Schalcken; the Holy Family, by Carlo Maratti; the Flight into Egypt, by Nicolo Poussin; and Inigo Jones in a round, by Dobson. In the Red Closet, next the Blue Room; a landscape and ruins by Viviano, the figures by Mich. Angelo; Fishermen, by Rubens; a man hawking, by Inigo Jones; Temptation of St. Anthony, by Annibal Caracci; the Samaritan woman, by Paolo Veronese: a boy's head, by Holbein; and Cleopatra, by Leonardo da Vinci. In the Green Velvet Room; Mars and Venus, by Albano; our Saviour in the Garden, by Guercino; Rembrandt in his painting room, by Gerrard Dow; Bellisarius, by Vandyke; and the Earl of Pembroke and his sister, by the same artist. In the Bed Chamber; the Earl of Cumberland, in a round; Lady Burlington, in a round; and Mr. Pope, also in a round; by Kent. In the Gallery; Lord Clifford and his family, painted in 1444, by John Van Eyk, called John of Burges; Lady Dorothy Boyle, in crayons, by Lady Burlington; a head, by Holbein; a Venus sleeping; Henry IV. of France, in Mosaick; and the Ascension, by Albano. In the New Dining Room, the finding of Moses, by Seb. Ricci; a portrait, by Rubens; the first Lady Halifax, by Sir Peter Lely; the Marriage of Cupid, &c. by Andrea Schiavone; Mars and Venus, by Le Fevre; the woman taken in adultery, by Allesandro Veronese; and Liberality and Modesty, after Guido.

D 2

GUN-

GUNNERSBURY.

Gunnerfbury Houfe, which is fituated between Acton and Old Brentford, is an elegant ftructure, firft built by Mr. Web, fon-in-law to the famous Inigo Jones. It was fome years fince the feat of Henry Furnefe, Efq; but is now the refidence of the Princefs Amelia. This building, which is at once remarkable for majeftic boldnefs and fimplicity, is fituated on a rifing ground; and the approach to it from the garden is extremely fine.

The grand portico at the back front, which is fupported by ftately columns, has a heautiful appearance at a diftance, and commands a fine profpect of the county of Surrey, the river Thames, and of all the meadows on its banks for fome miles, and in clear weather of even the city of London.

The apartments are extremely convenient and well contrived. The hall, which is large and fpacious, is on each fide fupported by rows of columns, and from thence you afcend by a noble flight of ftairs to a faloon, which is a double cube of twenty-five feet high, and moft elegantly furnifhed. This fine room has an entrance into the portico on the back front : and from the finenefs of the profpect over the Thames, is a delightful place to fit in, during the afternoon in the fummer feafon. For it being contrived to face the fouth eaft, the fun never fhines on it after two o'clock; but extending its beams over the country, enlivens the beautiful landfcape that lies before this part of the edifice. On entering the garden from the houfe, you afcend a noble terace, which affords a delightful view of the neighbouring country; and from this terrace, which extends the whole breadth of the garden, you defcend by a beautiful flight of fteps, with a grand baluftrade on each fide. But it has been objected, that the gardens are laid out too plain, having the walls in view on every fide.

Acton is a confiderable village about feven miles from London, in which there is an handfome church, and feveral gentlemen's feats.—That part of it which is called *Eaft-Acton* has been of note for the wells near it on *Old Oak Common*, which ufed to be much frequented in May, June, and July, for their purging waters. At a fmall diftance from hence is what is called *Friars Place*, which is fuppofed to have been formerly a monaftery; and at a farm-houfe in it, there is

an

Vol. 1.

Gunnersbury House, the Seat of the Princess Amelia.

an orchard, which, in old writings, is called the Devil's orchard.

About three miles from the laft-mentioned place, is the village of *Kilborne*, or *Kilburn*, which is in the parifh of Hampftead. Here was formerly an hermitage, and afterwards a nunnery, to which the manor belonged, as did alfo fome lands and tenements in Knightfbridge; but after the diffolution of the monafteries, the fite of this nunnery was given by Edward VI. to John Dudley, Earl of Warwick. A fpring of medicinal waters was found out here a few years fince.

At a fmall diftance from hence is *Belfyfe*, which though now decayed, was formerly a fine feat of Lord Wotton, and afterwards of the Earl of Chefterfield. Here was alfo a chapel, and a deer-park. This place was of fpecial note in 1720, the famous South Sea year, when it was turned into an academy for mufic, dancing, and play; and not a little frequented by reafon of its neighbourhood to London.

H A M P S T E A D.

This is a fine village in Middlefex, fituated near the top of a hill, about four miles on the north weft fide of London. On the fummit of this hill is a heath of about a mile every way, that is adorned with feveral pretty feats, in a moft irregular, romantic fituation; and has a moft extenfive profpect over the city, into the counties all around it, viz. Bucks and Hertfordfhire, and even Northamptonfhire, Effex, Kent, Surrey, Berks, &c. with an uninterrupted view of Shooter's-hill, Barnfted Downs, and Windfor-caftle. Its chapel was anciently a chapel of eafe to Hendon, till about 1478, when it was feparated from it by the abbot and convent of Weftminfter, then patrons of the rectory of Hendon, who made a curacy or donative of it in their gift, as it remained till the fuppreffion of the monafteries, at which time King Henry VIII. fettled it on his new-made bifhopric of Weftminfter; but King Edward VI. diffolving that fee, granted the manor and chapel of Hampftead to Sir Thomas Wroth, for his fervices to the crown. After this it belonged to the Earls of Gainfborough; but it has fince been the property of feveral other perfons.

This village ufed to be much reforted to for its mineral waters; but they have lately been neglected. There is here a fine affembly room; and the old church, which was a chapel belonging to the Lord of the Manor, was fome years ago pulled down, and a new one erected in its room. There

is

is alfo an handfome chapel near the wells, built by the contributions of the inhabitants, who are chiefly citizens and merchants of London; and there is here alfo a meeting-houfe. Though this place is now fo crowded with good buildings, yet it is obfervable, that in the reign of Henry the Eighth, it was chiefly inhabited by the laundreffes who wafhed for the Londoners.

HIGHGATE.

At a fmall diftance eaftward of Hampftead is *Highgate*, a very large and populous village, a little above four miles north of London. It receives its name partly from its high fituation, overlooking London, and great part of Kent, Effex, and Hertfordfhire; and partly from a gate fet up there above four hundred years ago, to receive toll for the Bifhop of London, when the old miry road from Gray's Inn Lane to Barnet was turned through the Bifhop's Park. This toll was farmed by Queen Elizabeth at forty pounds a year. Where the chapel ftands, which is a very ancient edifice, was formerly an hermitage, and one of the hermits caufed a caufey to be made between Highgate and Iflington, by gravel dug out of the top of the hill, where is now a pond. The Bifhop of London prefented the hermits, the laft of whom was William Forte, prefented to the hermitage, in 1531, by Bifhop Stokefley. Near the chapel, in 1562, a free fchool was built and endowed by Lord Chief Baron Cholmondeley, at his own private expence; but it was enlarged, in 1570, by Edwin Sandys, Bifhop of London, and a chapel added to it. One William Pool, yeoman of the crown, alfo founded an hofpital here, below the hill, in the reign of King Edward the Fourth.

On that fide of Highgate which is next London, the finenefs of the profpect over the city, as far as Shooter's-Hill, and below Greenwich, has occafioned feveral handfome edifices to be built; particularly a very fine houfe erected by the late Sir William Afhhurft.——It is remarkable, that moft of the public-houfes in Highgate have a large pair of horns placed over the fign; and that when any of the country people ftop for refrefhment, a pair of large horns fixed to the end of a ftaff, is brought to them, and they are earneftly preffed to be fworn. If they confent, a kind of burlefque oath is adminiftered; that they will never eat brown bread when they can get white; never drink water when they can get wine, or fmall beer when they can get ftrong;

never

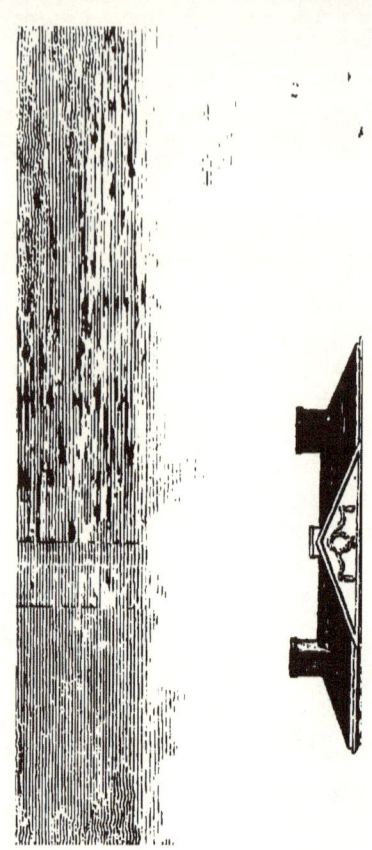

never kiſs the maid, when they can kiſs the miſtreſs; and abundance of other things of the ſame kind, which they repeat after the perſon who brings the horns, with one hand fixed upon them. This ridiculous ceremony is altered according to the ſex of the perſon who is ſworn; who is allowed to add to each article, " except I like the other better." The whole being over, he or ſhe muſt' kiſs the horns, and pay a ſhilling for the oath, to be ſpent among the company, to which he or ſhe belongs.——At a ſmall diſtance from Highgate is *Cane Wood*, where Earl Mansfield, the preſent Chief Juſtice of the King's Bench, has a fine ſeat, the ſituation of which is extremely rural.

On the eaſt-ſide of Highgate is *Muſwell Hill*, which took its name from a ſpring or well on the hill, near a houſe built by Alderman Roe, which afterwards came to the late Earl of Bath. By this well, which was eſteemed holy, was a chapel with an image of our Lady of Muſwell, to which great numbers went in pilgrimage. Both the manor and chapel were ſold in the reign of Queen Elizabeth, to Mr. William Roe, in whoſe family they continued, till Sir Thomas Roe, the ambaſſador, ſold them in the laſt century. The manor-houſe was afterwards converted into an houſe of public entertainment.

Not far from hence is the village of *Hornſey*, which is five miles north of London. Its church, whereof Highgate is a hamlet, is ſuppoſed to be built with the ſtones that came from Lodge-hill, the Biſhop of London's hunting ſeat in his park here; it having been his manor from the moſt ancient times. *Hornſey-wood*, which is nearer London, is a coppice of young trees, at the entrance of which is a genteel public houſe, to which great numbers of perſons reſort from the city. This houſe being ſituated on the top of a hill, affords a delightful proſpect of the neighbouring country.

TOTTENHAM HIGH CROSS.

This is a village in Middleſex on the weſt ſide of the river Lea, five miles north-eaſt from London.——David, King of Scotland, being poſſeſſed of this manor, after it had belonged to the Earls of Northumberland and Cheſter, gave it to the monaſtery of the Trinity in London; but King Henry VIII. granted it to William Lord Howard of Effingham, who being afterwards attainted, it reverted again to the King, who

then

then granted it to the Dean and Chapter of St. Paul's, to whom it still belongs. The church stands on a hill, which has a little river called the Mosel at the bottom, to the west, north, and east.

The parish is divided into four wards, viz. 1. Nether Ward, in which stands the parsonage and vicarage. 2. Middle Ward, comprehending Church-end, and Marsh-street. 3. High Cross Ward, containing the Hill, the Mill, Page-green, and the High Cross. And, 4. Wood Green Ward; which comprehends all the rest of the parish, and is larger than the three other wards put together.

The *Cross*, which gives name to the place, was once much higher than it is at present, and upon that spot Queen Eleanor's corpse was rested, when it was brought from Lincolnshire, where she died, to London. Of St. Loy's well, in this parish, it is said, that it is always brimful, but never runs over; and of the Bishop's Well the people report many strange cures.

In the middle of a circular tuft of elms, at the end of Page-green, which are called the *Seven Sisters*, there stood many years a walnut-tree always flourishing, yet never grew bigger nor taller. The seven trees which go under the denomination of *the Seven Sisters*, are said to have been planted by seven sisters; and one of the trees being crooked, the country people very gravely add this marvellous circumstance, that the female who planted this tree was crooked, though all her sisters were straight; and her obliquity, it seems, communicated itself to the tree which she planted.

There was a very great wood formerly, of four hundred acres, on and about the hill, on the west side of the parish.—In 1596, an alms-house was founded here by one Zancher, a Spaniard, the first confectioner ever known in this kingdom. Here are also a free-school, and a charity-school for twenty-two girls, who are cloathed and taught.——In the reign of Henry VIII. George Heningham, Esq; one of that prince's favourites, founded an alms house here for three poor widows. ——There are many pretty country houses and gentlemens seats in this neighbourhood; and, among others, Alderman Townsend has a very handsome seat here, known by the name of *Bruce Castle*. It is in a very pleasing situation, and the building has at once an air of neatness, grandeur, and antiquity.

WAL-

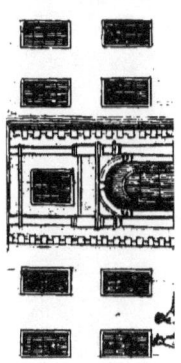

WALTHAMSTOW.

This is a confiderable village in the county of Effex, fituated on the river Lea, about fix miles from London. The greateft part of this parifh, in Edward the Confeffor's reign, belonged to Waltheof, a nobleman of great eminence, who fubmitted to William the Conqueror, and was thereupon reftored to his honours and paternal eftates. William alfo conferred on him the earldoms of Northumberland, Northampton, and Huntingdon, and gave him his niece Judith in marriage. Notwithftanding which, Waltheof engaging in a confpiracy to depofe William, was beheaded at Winchefter, about the year 1075.

The river here divides Effex from Middlefex as far as Leabridge. There are feveral ancient feats and handfome houfes, belonging to perfons of diftinction, at Walthamftow. The moft remarkable of which was that of Higham Hall, pleafantly fituated upon Higham-hill, a rifing ground, about half a mile north from Clay-ftreet, juft above the river Lea, overlooking the counties of Middlefex and Hertfordfhire, and commanding a moft delightful and extenfive profpect. It has been a magnificent and fpacious fabric, and in antient times when the Lords refided upon their royalties, no place could be more admirably fituated than this manfion, erected at the top of the hill of Higham, and having within its view the whole extent of its jurifdiction: but there are now hardly any traces of its ancient grandeur remaining.

Walthamftow church, which is dedicated to the Bleffed Virgin, is a large edifice fituated upon a hill, and confifts of three ifles, that on the north fide built by Sir George Monox, Knt. Alderman and Lord Mayor of London in the reign of Henry the Eighth, is called Monox's ifle; and that on the fouth fide bears the name of Thorne's ifle, from a Citizen and Merchant Taylor of that name, who was probably at the expence of building it. In this church are a great number of monuments.

Sir George Monox alfo built alms-houfes on the north-fide of the church-yard for thirteen poor people, eight men and five women; with an apartment for a free-fchool. And for their maintenance fettled on truftees an eftate in Mark-lane, London. Mr. Henry Maynard, a merchant of London, was alfo a great benefactor to this parifh.

Anthony Bacon, Efq; has a good houfe, ftanding in a paddock, about a mile and a half eaft from the church. And

E   Thomas

Thomas Grofvenor, Efq; has a fine old houfe, half a mile weft from the church.

Walthamftow contains feveral ftreets or hamlets, but which are not clofely joined or connected together, but are fituated as follows ; Shanhall-ftreet, an hundred yards weft from the church ; Hare-ftreet, a quarter of a mile fouth-eaft ; Woodford-ftreet, half a mile eaft ; and March-ftreet, three quarters of a mile weft of the church.

W A N S T E D.

This is a very pleafant village, at the diftance of fix miles from London. The parifh of Wanfted joins to that of Walt-hamftow. Wanfted is in a delightful fituation, the greateft part of it ftanding on an hill, from which is commanded a beautiful profpect of the city of London, and its environs ; the fine hills of Kent ; the river Thames ; and rich views of the neighbour-ing parifhes. It is fuppofed that there was here a Roman villa, or fome little ftation : for in the year 1715, as Sir Richard Child's gardeners were digging holes for planting an avenue of trees in the park, on the fouth-fide of the lower part of the gar-dens, they difcovered a teffelated Roman pavement. The owner would not permit it to be laid quite open ; but by the fragments thrown up, they obferved, that it confifted of fmall fquare Tef-feræ of brick of divers colours, from one inch to a quarter of an inch fquare. Round it there was a border of about a foot broad, compofed of red dies about three quarters of an inch fquare; within which were feveral ornaments wove in wreaths, and in the middle the figure of a man riding, holding fomething in his right hand. The pavement was fituated on a gentle gravelly afcent, towards the north ; and, at a fmall diftance from the fouth end of it, was a fpring, or well, of fine water, now abforbed into a great pond. From this well the ground rofe gently towards the fouth, till it came to an exact level, which reaches a great way. On the very brink of this level, and about three hundred yards directly fouth from the before faid well and pavement, were the ruins of fome brick foundations. Some years afterwards, upon making further improvements, the work-men found feveral fherds of broken pots, or fragments of urns, of different kinds of earth, fome brown, fome white, &c. but all of a coarfe clay; many pieces of bricks, which proved that there had been a building there ; and many calcined human bones, teeth, &c. A filver medal ; a copper one of the empe-

ror

ror Valens ; and another of copper, generally efteemed to be of the Conftantine age, were likewife found here. Smart Lethieulier, Efq; was of opinion, that this was the maufoleum of fome private family, whofe villa perhaps ftood on the more elevated ground where Wanfted now ftands.

The church here, which is dedicated to St. Mary, ftands near Wanfted-houfe, and was new built, chiefly at the expence of the late Richard Earl Tylney. Among other monuments, in this church, there is a very fumptuous one erected to the memory of Sir Jofias Child, a very eminent merchant, and well known for his excellent treatife on trade. This gentleman purchafed the manor of Wanfted, from whom it came to his defcendant, the prefent poffeffor, John, Vifcount Caftlemain, and Earl of Tylney.

There are at Wanfted, and in its neighbourhood, feveral fine feats of the nobility, gentry, and wealthy citizens ; but their luftre is greatly eclipfed by WANSTED HOUSE, the magnificent feat of Earl Tylney. This noble feat was prepared by Sir Jofias Child, who added to the advantage of a fine fituation, a vaft number of rows of trees, planted in avenues and viftas leading up to the fpot of ground where the old houfe ftood. The late Lord Tylney, before he was enobled, laid out the moft fpacious pieces of ground in gardens, that are to be feen in this part of England. The green-houfe is a very fuperb building, furnifhed with ftoves and artificial places for heat, from an apartment which has a bagnio, and other conveniences, that render it both ufeful and pleafant.

The houfe was built fince thefe gardens were finifhed, by the late Earl of Tylney, and defigned by Colonel Campbell, and is certainly one of the nobleft houfes not only near London, but in the kingdom. It is two hundred and fixty feet in length, and feventy in depth, fronted with Portland ftone. It confifts of two ftories, the ftate and ground ftory. This latter is the bafement, into which you enter by a door in the middle underneath the grand entrance, which is in a noble portico of fix Corinthian columns fupporting a pediment, in which are the arms of Lord Tylney. To this you afcend by a flight of fteps, and pafs into a magnificent faloon, richly decorated with painting and fculpture, through which you pafs into the other ftate rooms, which are fuitably furnifhed with pictures, gilding, velvet, tapeftry, and other rich hangings. Before this houfe is an octangular bafon,

E 2   which

which feems equal to the length of the front. On each fide as you approach the houfe, are two marble ftatues of Hercules and Venus, with obelifks and vafes alternately placed. The garden front has no portico, but a pediment with a bafs relief fupported by fix three quarter columns.

The fore front of the houfe has a long vifta that reaches to the greaf road at Leighton Stone, and from the back front facing the gardens is an eafy defcent that leads to the terrace, and affords a moft beautiful profpect of the river, which is formed into canals; and beyond it the walks and wildernefs extend to a great diftance, rifing up the hill, as they floped downwards befoie; fo that the fight is loft in the woods, and the whole country, as far as the eye can reach, appears one continued garden.

The grand hall in Wanfted Houfe is fifty-three feet long, by forty-five broad; the ornaments confift chiefly of two large antique ftatues, on marble pedeftals, Livia and Domitian; and three large pictures by Cafali, Coriolanus, Porfenna, and Pompey taking leave of his family. The Ball Room, which runs the whole length of the houfe, is feventy-five feet by twenty-feven; and is very elegantly fitted up with gilded ornaments of all kinds. One of the dining rooms is ornamented with three large pictures by Cafali; Alexander directing Apelles to paint Campafpe, who is fitting naked in a chair; the continence of Scipio; and Sophonifba taking poifon.

The manor of *Cannons-Hall*, or *Cann-Hall*, lies about a mile fouth-weft of Wanfted church. It anciently belonged to the prior and canons of the Holy Trinity, in London. It is now the property of William Colgrove, Efq;—A good houfe in this parifh, pleafantly fituated, and having thirty acres of gardens, was built in 1690, by Sir Francis Dafhwood; and from him the eftate paffed to Sir Orlando Bridgman; but is now the property of Humphrey Bowles, Efq.

WOODFORD.

This village is eight miles from London; and derives its name from the ford in the wood, or foreft, where now is Woodford Bridge. This was one of the 17 lordfhips with which Earl Harold endowed his abbey of Waltham holy-crofs, and was confirmed to that monaftery, with all its lands and appurtenances, and liberties, by King Edward the Confeffor, in his charter, in 1062. The cuftom of the manor of Woodford is *Borough-Englifh*; by which the youngeft fon inherits. The origin of this cuftom has been

The Prospect House at Woodford Row in Essex, the Seat of Robert Hucam Esqr.

been a subject of much difpute; but it appears to have prevailed greatly in the kingdom of the Eaft Saxons. Dr. Plot has conjectured, ' that it was introduced by the Lord of the ma-' nor's claiming the right of enjoying the bride, daughter of ' his tenant, on the wedding-night; therefore the villain, or ' flave, doubting whether the eldeft fon was his own, made the ' youngeft heir.' But as there feems not to be fufficient evidence, that this ever was an eftablifhed practice, the Doctor's conjecture has been fuppofed not to be well founded.

At *Woodford Row*, Richard Warner, Efq; has a fine garden, with a labyrinth, adorned with feveral Greek infcriptions, and other curiofities. And Robert Moxam, Efq; has an exceeding good houfe here, called the *Profpect-houfe*, a name which it derives from its fituation, which is remarkably pleafant.——Woodford Wells were formerly in repute, as purgative, and good for many diforders, but are now entirely neglected.

About a mile from Woodford is the parifh of *Chingford*, in which there is an eftate of 24l. per ann. holden of the rector. Upon every alienation, the owner of the eftate, with his wife, man-fervant, maid-fervant, each fingle on a horfe, come to the parfonage; where the owner does his homage, and pays his relief in the following manner. He blows three blafts with his horn; carries a hawk on his fift; his fervant has a greyhound in a flip; both for the ufe of the rector for that day. He receives a chicken for his hawk, a peck of oats for his horfe, and a loaf of bread for his greyhound. They all dine, after which the mafter blows three blafts with his horn, and they all depart.

C H I G W E L L.

This is a pleafant village in Effex, about ten miles from London. This parifh, as well as the neighbouring ones, is moft delightfully fituated; on which account, and from its convenient diftance, it is much frequented by perfons from the metropolis, it being one of the moft pleafing rides within the like diftance. The village is neat and agreeable, and has good accommodations for travellers; but carries on no manufacture; it being rather a place for receiving thofe who are fond of fhort excurfions into the country, than a place of much commerce. From Chigwell-row is a fine view extending upwards of thirty miles, and comprehending a great part of the river Thames, bounded by the
pleafant

pleasant hills of Kent ; by Danbury-spire in Essex ; by the forest
of Henhault ; and an exceeding rich country around.

In Chigwell church, there is a fine large plate of brass, with
the whole length portraiture of Samuel Harsnett, archbishop of
York, engraved thereon in a very curious manner. This prelate, who had been vicar of this parish, founded here two free
schools, one called the Grammar, and the other the English
school. At the west end of the church is a wooden belfrey, built
of chesnut, containing five bells; and over the belfrey is a handsome spire, shingled.——About a mile and a quarter south-west
of the church, in a bottom, washed by the river Roding, is
Luxborough, a fine seat belonging to John Raymond, Esq;—The
manor of *Barringtons*, now called *Rolls*, is about half a mile
north-east from the church. The mansion-house to it is an elegant modern building, with extensive offices, and every conveniency suitable to render it a very commodious and agreeable seat.
It stands upon the declivity of a large hill, and is enriched with
a fine prospect.

The *Forest of Henhault*, in this neighbourhood, is supposed
to have been so named from its having been well stocked with
deers from Henhault in Germany. Within this forest stands the
remarkable large oak called *Fair-lop*, measuring upwards of fifteen yards in bulk : it is not an over-tall tree, but is singularly
beautiful and curious, on account of the boughs spreading from
top to bottom in a regular circle ; and being level underneath,
about ten feet from the ground, so as to represent an umbrella.
A custom prevailed among many of the Londoners, to come
yearly to eat beans and bacon, dressed under the boughs of this
tree, which are supposed to extend eighty feet from the body all
around. It at last became so remarkable, that a fair was held
under it called *Fair-lop Fair* ; which fair some years ago was ordered to be discontinued by Lord Tylney and the Verdurer, on
account of its being a nuisance ; for besides the riots which frequently happened there, the deer suffered much.

Lamborn is a pleasant parish, adjoining to Chigwell. The
houses herein are scattered at a distance from each other, some
of which are neat, and the residence of gentlemen of fortune ;
particularly Deux-hall, the seat of R. Lockwood, Esq; which
commands an extensive prospect ; and Bishop's-hall, the seat
of William Waylet, Esq. The latter derives its name from
its having been formerly the habitation of Henry Spencer, bishop
of

Barrington Hall, at Hatfield-Broad-Oak, in Essex.

Belvedon Hall, in Essex, the seat of Jn.º Wright Esq.º

I. Olive del.

of Norwich, in the reign of King Richard II. a prelate more celebrated for his military exploits, than his learning and piety. The foil here is fruitful, and of various kinds, and hufbandry alóne feems to be the employ of the inhabitants. Lamborn church appears to be a very ancient edifice.

At a little diftance from hence, in the parifh of Stapleford Abbots, Sir Anthony Thomas Abdy, Bart. member of parliament for Knarefborough, in Yorkfhire, has a fine feat, known by the name of ALBYNS. It is fituated about half a mile north from Stapleford church, and is furrounded by a fmall park. It is a large ftately edifice, and by fome thought to be erected by Inigo Jones; but Mr. Horace Walpole is of opinion that this is a miftake.—Knowle, otherwife Knowle's hill, a mile fouthweft from the church, is a pleafant fpot in this parifh, where Henry Spencer, bifhop of Norwich, of whom we juft made mention, had alfo a feat. A piece of ground here, being a wood of twelve acres, is ftill called Bifhop's Moat, where is a moat, reported to have been paved with marble.

In the adjoining parifh of Naveftock, ftands NAVESTOCK HALL, the feat of the Earl of Waldegrave. It is fituated a little way north from the church, is a handfome regular brick building, and has fo many advantages and decorations, both of nature and art, as renders it a very pleafing and elegant feat. The gardens and grounds around it have been much improved by Lord Waldegrave.

The parifh of *Kelvedon Hatch* adjoins to Naveftock; it is but a fmall one, but has two feats in it belonging to perfons of figure in the county. One of which, belonging to John Wright, Efq; and known by the name of KELVEDON HALL, is a very elegant new-built brick-houfe, with proper offices belonging to it; and likewife pleafant gardens, fome pieces of water, and other decorations; but what contributes in the greateft meafure to render this fpot delightful, is the rich and extenfive profpect that it commands; in which a part of London, although full twenty miles diftant, is to be feen on a fine clear day by the naked eye.—John Luther, Efq; one of the members of parliament for the county of Effex, has alfo a feat here called MILES's, about a mile diftant from the church.—On a tomb ftone in the church here, is a plate with the following infcription:

" Fratres in unum.
" Here lies Richard and Anthony Luther, Efqrs. fo
" truly loving brothers, that they lived near forty years
" joint

" joint houfe-keepers together at Miles's, without any
" accompt between them."

In a neighbouring parifh, *Theydon Mount*, is a fine feat known
by the name of HILL HALL, which for elegance, and the finenefs of its profpects, is efteemed inferior to few in the county of
Effex. This edifice was built by Sir Thomas Smith, fecretary of
ftate in 1548. It is quadrangular, with very thick and lofty
walls, adorned with columns in imitation of ftone. The entrance to it is northward, along a ftately avenue of great length
and fuitable breadth, on each of which are rows of ftately elms,
and other plantations. Great alterations were made in it by Sir
Edward Smith in the laft century, and more have been made by
its prefent owner, Sir Charles Smith.—The church here, which
is dedicated to St. Michael, is pleafantly fituated. It was burnt
by lightning, and was rebuilt by Sir William Smith, of brick,
tiled. In the chancel of this church are feveral coftly monuments, the moft ancient of which is that erected to the memory
of Sir Thomas Smith, whom we have juft mentioned, and who
was not only an able ftatefman, but one of the moft learned
men of the age in which he lived, and a great promoter of the
ftudy of the Greek language.

Theydon Gernon is a very pleafant parifh, which lies upon the
weft fide of Theydon Mount. It is frequently called *Cooperfale*,
from a capital feat about two miles north of the church. The
houfe ftands upon the declivity of a hill, on the right hand fide
of the road leading to Epping. Around the houfe are a variety
of beautiful lawns, viftoes, and other agreeable objects, but the
profpect is very much confined. The village is but fmall, and
confifts chiefly of a few fhops, and houfes of artificers. But this,
with fome of the neighbouring parifhes, may with propriety be
called *the garden of Effex*, from the pleafing variety of the hills
and vales, the fertility of the foil, the goodnefs of the roads, the
neatnefs of the buildings, and the many additional ornaments
they receive from the number of noblemens and gentlemens
feats with which they abound; infomuch that a traveller cannot
pafs through this part of the county without being ftruck with its
beauty, and the variety of noble and pleafing profpects which
in different places prefent themfelves to its view.

At a fmall diftance from hence is the parifh of *Loughton*,
which is about thirteen miles from London, and in a very
healthy fituation. The village is fmall and neat, but carries
on little or no traffic. In this parifh are feveral very good
houfes,

houfes, particularly that in which Captain Williams refides, on the left hand fide of the road leading to London; one belonging to Sackville Boyle, Efq; at the bottom of Bucket-green; and another to Alexander Hamilton, Efq; upon Dedden-green. Richard Lomax Clay, Efq; late high-fheriff of this county, has an excellent houfe upon the fummit of Golden-hill, which commands an exceedingly rich and extenfive profpect, in which the greateft part of the city of London is included. And Loughton-hall, though it is not a regular, is a large handfome building, furrounded by a variety of beautiful profpects. The parifh of Loughton was one of the feventeen Lordfhips whherewith Earl Harold endowed his monaftery of Waltham; and in that monaftery it continued till the fuppreffion, when it came to the crown. It is faid that in 1688, the Princefs of Denmark, afterwards Queen Anne, retired to Loughton-hall, when fhe faw how things were going on with her imprudent father. Loughton church is very agreeably fituated, having a fine profpect all around it.

WALTHAM-ABBEY, or WALTHAM-HOLY-CROSS.

This is a town in Effex, on the eaft fide of the river Lea, which here dividing, inclofes fome iflands with fine meadows, and parts Effex from Hertfordfhire, and this village from Waltham Crofs, or Weft Waltham. The firft mention which is made of this place by antient writers, is about the latter times of the Saxons; when it appears that Tovi, a man of great wealth and authority, ftandard-bearer to King Canute, induced by the abundance of deer, built a number of houfes here, and peopled them with fixty-fix inhabitants. King Edward the Confeffor, into whofe hands it afterwards came, beftowed this village upon his brother-in-law Harold, fon to Earl Godwin, who built an abbey here, from whence the place derives its prefent name. Tovi had begun a church here for two priefts, and committed to their keeping a miraculous *Crofs*, faid to have been difcovered in a vifion to a carpenter far weftward, and brought hither in a manner unknown; which was reported to work many wonders. On account of that crofs, this place is faid to have obtained the name of *Holy Crofs*.

After Harold became poffeffed of it, in the year 1062, he founded here a college for a dean, and eleven fecular canons, in memory of King Edward, his Queen Ædith, his father and

F   mother,

mother, and all his other relations; and endowed it with Weſt Waltham, and ſixteen other manors. Many other very conſiderable grants were afterwards made to this monaſtery, and it was alſo endowed with very great and ſpecial privileges and immunities. However, it appears that the foundation for a dean and canons was of no longer continuance than from the year 1062 to 1177. For the court of Rome having formed the deſign of introducing into all convents *monks* inſtead of *ſeculars*, under pretence that the latter lived more irreligiouſly and carnally than the others, King Henry II. converted this college into a monaſtery for an abbot, and ſixteen monks of the order of St. Auguſtine. His principal motive for ſo doing, appears to have been, the ſaving his money; for, in order to pacify the Pope, having vowed to erect an abbey for canons regular, to the honour of God and St. Thomas à Becket, for the expiation of his ſins, it was much cheaper for him to make a ſmall change in this, than to erect a new one. However, from this time till the diſſolution of the monaſteries, it continued an abbey for Auſtin monks. Its abbots, who were mitred, and had the 20th place in parliament, lived in a moſt ſplendid, but hoſpitable manner; and were frequently viſited by King Henry III. when he was reduced, and obliged to carry his family about for a dinner. The abbey was at the diſſolution beſtowed by King Henry VIII. on Sir Anthony Denny, one of his favourites, and gentleman of his bed-chamber; but the manor of Waltham is at preſent in the poſſeſſion of Sir William Wake, Bart.

This abbey was a curious, large, and antique ſtructure; the whole front a few years ago was entirely rebuilt with brick and ſtone, after a modern and beautiful form by Charles Wake Jones, Eſq; and on each ſide front it had a wing. The hall was exceedingly handſome, being remarkable for its curious wainſcotting and excellent paintings. In length it meaſured ſixteen yards and a half; in breadth eight yards and a half; and in height nine yards and one foot. It was encompaſſed with many fertile paſtures, and pleaſant meads and marſhes. The ſpacious garden belonging to it was ſurrounded by a beautiful canal: the garden, which was very delightful, contained a variety of plants, and fruits, fine groves and walks; and in ſhort, every thing that was neceſſary to render it agreeable. But the fine tulip-tree that is here muſt not be forgotten, it being eſteemed the largeſt that ever was ſeen. This tree is ſtill left, and is encompaſſed

Waltham Abbey Church.

compaffed by a paling. But the houfe was pulled down in 1770, and the gardens are now let to a gardener.

Waltham-abbey-church is a Gothic edifice, rather large than neat, firm than fair, and very dark. The great pillars are wreathed with indentings, which are faid to have been formerly filled up with brafs. To the fouth fide of the church adjoins a chapel, now converted into a fchool; and formerly called *our Lady's*, becaufe there was founded in it a chantry of that name; and under it is a very fair arched charnal-houfe. The whole was formerly well leaded, but is now tiled. In the middle ftood the tower, cathedral-wife. Part of it falling down foon after the furrender of the abbey, probably in pulling down the chancel and choir, a wall was run up at the eaft end of the church; and a handfome tower was erected at the weft end, 86 feet in height from the foundation to the battlements. This was begun in the year 1558, at the charge of the parifhioners; and three years were employed in the building it. Every year's work is difcernible by the difference in the ftones; and the parifh was obliged, in order to raife money to complete the building, to fell their bells, which before hung in a wooden frame in the church-yard. So that Waltham, which had formerly bells without a fteeple, had for fome time a fteeple without bells. There are now fix bells.

The founder, King Harold, was buried in this church, with his two brothers, Girth and Leofwine. Since the demolition of the chancel, or of a chapel thereto adjoining, the place of his fepulchre is within the garden of the Lord of the Manor. Over his grave laid a grey marble ftone, with a crofs carved upon it, and a Latin epitaph, which has been thus tranflated:

" A fierce foe thee flew; thou a King, he a King in view:
" Both peers, both peerlefs; both fear'd, and both fearlefs:
" That fad day was mixt, by Firmin and Calixt;
" Th' one help'd thee to vanquifh, t'other made thee to languifh.
" Both now for thee pray, and thy requiem fay;
" So let good men all, to God for thee call."

The laft account we have of this tomb-ftone, is, that it was at Waltham-mill, and feen there by Dr. Uvedell of Enfield. Towards the end of Queen Elizabeth's reign, King Harold's coffin was difcovered by one Tomkins, gardener to Sir Edward Denny, being of a hard ftone, and covered with another; wherein the bones lay in proper order, with-

out

out any kind of dirt but upon the touch mouldered into duſt.

A decent meeting-houſe was erected here in 1729, for Proteſtant Diſſenters. There are alſo here four alms-houſes, founded for four widows by Mr. Green, purveyor to King James I.
with an orchard-and a barn adjoining, the rent of which is pay-
able to the ſaid widows. Upon the alms-houſes is the following
inſcription, the ſentiments of which deſerve to be attended to,
whatever may be thought of the poetry.

" Birth is a pain, life, labour, care, toil, thrall;
" In old age ſtrength fails, laſtly, death ends all.
" Whilſt ſtrong life laſt, let virtuous deeds be ſhown,
" Fruit of ſuch trees are thereby hardly ſeen or known.
" To have reward with laſting joys for ay,
" When vicious actions fall to ends decay.
" Of wealth o'erplus, land, money, ſtock, or ſtore,
" In life that will relieve aged, needy, poor,
" Good deeds defer not till the fun'ral rite be paſt;
" In life-time what's done, is made more ſure, firm, faſt;
" So ever after it ſhall be known and ſeen
" The leaf and fruit ſhall ever ſpring freſh and green. 1626,

In the eaſtern extremity of the pariſh, partly in it, and partly
in that of Epping, by the ſide of Copped Hall Park, is a fine
old camp, incloſing 11 acres, 2 roods, and 20 perches, commonly called Amber's-bank. The new road from Debdon-
green to Epping goes through it. Mr. Morant is of opinion,
that the deciſive battle between Boadicea and the Romans was
fought hereabouts.—Harold's Park, ſo named from Earl Harold, part of whoſe demeſnes it was, and given by him to Waltham-abbey, is about three miles north-eaſt of the church.

The town of Waltham-abbey is built moſtly of timber; it
is very irregular and inconvenient, and makes but a mean appearance; the chief houſe in it is that of James Barwick, Eſq,
The market-place is ſmall, and the market, which is held on
Tueſdays, is well provided with grain, and noted for fine veal,
pork, and pigs. Here are two fairs annually; one on the 14th
of May; and the other on September 25, 26; which laſt was
formerly held for ſeven days. On the one ſide of the town are
large and beautiful meadows, ſome of which are uſed in common
to the town. Theſe meadows in the time of King Alfred, in
the year 876, laid under water, which great water was
then navigable. That truly great King (who really was, what
                                                          ſome

some later Kings have only pretended to be, the father of his people) divided the grand streams of the river Lea into several rivulets, by which means some Danish ships which lay here for security, became water-bound, and their mariners were obliged to shift for themselves over-land; which proved a great check to the ravages of the Danes.

A new navigable river hath lately been cut here. It takes its rise at a place called Ives's ferry, in Hertfordshire, where it is supplied from the old river Lea, and extends through part of the town of Waltham-abbey, Endfield, Edmonton, and Hackney-marshes, Bromley, Limehouse, and Dick-shore, emptying itself into the Thames. The chief utility of which is, that the navigation to Waltham-abbey is shortened about ten miles, and the expensive delay of the craft in the Thames by easterly winds, is in a great measure avoided. These rivers afford plenty of fish, some salmon-trouts, eels, carp, tench, pike, perch, craw-fish, and many others.

Near the town, on one of these rivers, are several curious gun-powder-mills, upon a new construction, worked by water, the old ones having been worked by horses. These are reckoned the most compleat in England, and will make near an hundred barrels weekly for the service of the government, each barrel containing one hundred weight. They are now the property of Bouchier Walton, Esq.—On the north side of the town callico-printing is carried on with great spirit. The wool-combing business is also carried on here still; but not in so extensive a manner as it was formerly.

The learned Dr. Joseph Hall, afterwards Bishop of Exeter and Norwich, was minister of this parish; as was also Dr. Thomas Fuller, author of the Church History of Britain, the Worthies of England, &c. and who was so famous for the extraordinary strength of his memory.

About two miles from Waltham-abbey, in the road to Epping, is a beautiful seat, named WARLEYS, lately in the possession of Mr. Carter, but now belonging to his two daughters. The house is situated in a bottom; but the park and other objects about it rise to the view, and form a pleasing prospect.—Edward Parker, Esq; has also a good house about a quarter of a mile east from the town.

WEST-WALTHAM, or WALTHAM-CROSS.

This is a small town on the west side of the river Lea, in Middlesex and Hertfordshire. It is a post-town, and good thoroughfare in the Ware road, about twelve miles from London.

London. It has its name of Crofs, from that erected here by order of King Edward I. in memory of its being one of the refting places for the corpfe of his Queen, when fhe was brought from the north to be interred at Weftminfter. That princefs's effigies are placed round the pillar with the arms of her confort, and thofe of her own, viz. England, Caftile, Leon, and Poictou, which are ftill in part remaining, though greatly defaced.

E P P I N G.

This town lies eaft-north-eaft of Waltham-abbey, and is about fixteen miles from London. It is divided into two parts; namely, *Upland*, where the church is fituated; and *Townfide*, where the town ftands. It confifts chiefly of inns and publichoufes, the fhops being few in number, juft fufficient to fupply the town and neighbourhood with common neceffaries. It is near a mile in length, extending almoft due eaft and weft. A market is held here weekly on Fridays, and its principal commodities are fowls and butter, it being particularly famous for the latter, much of which is carried from hence to London. The buildings in the town are but indifferent; and here is a church and a brick chapel, the latter in a miferable condition, at which and the church, divine fervice is performed alternately. Here is a Diffenting-meeting houfe, and alfo a Quakersmeeting. The church ftands pleafantly on a rifing ground, is of one pace with the chancel, and of an uncommon length. It has of late been repaired and beautified, and is extremely neat.

Copped Hall, or *Copt Hall*, the feat of John Conyers, Efq; member for the county, is in the parifh of Epping. This is an elegant and convenient modern edifice, and is very agreeably fituated. The gardens belonging to it are well laid out, and here is a large park. In the old houfe here was a ftately gallery fifty-fix yards long, erected by Sir Thomas Heneage, which was blown down in November, 1639, by a violent hurricane. At this feat was formerly a chapel, wherein was placed the fine painted glafs window from Newhall chapel, and which John Conyers, Efq; fold to the parifhioners of St. Margaret's, Weftminfter, by whom it has been put up in the chancel of that church.

Epping-Foreft, which is a royal chace, and which reaches many miles from the town of Epping towards London, was anciently called the Foreft of Effex, and then of Waltham; and was granted by Edward the Confeffor to his favourite

Ran-

Randolph Pepper-king, afterwards called Peverell; who having a beautiful lady to his wife, William the Conqueror fell in love with her, and had a fon by her, called William Peverell.

C H E P I N G   O N G A R.

This is a fmall town in the county of Effex, fituated on the river Roding, eight miles from Epping, and twenty from London. It confifts chiefly of one ftreet of pretty good houfes, but has been a market-town for many years, on which account here are fome good inns. The market is kept weekly on Saturdays. The traffic of this town, except on market-days, is but trifling, and at thofe times is not very confiderable. Here are two fairs annually, the one on Eafter Tuefday, the other the day after the feaft of St. Michael, both of which fairs are for toys and hiring of fervants.

This place in old records was called *Ongar ad Caftrum*, from a caftle built here by Richard de Lucy, who was intrufted with the office of lieutenant of the kingdom in the abfence of King Henry II. in Normandy*. This caftle was fituated at on the top of an artificial hill, and furrounded by a large moat; which, with feveral other moats, compofed the fortification; but the caftle growing ruinous, was taken down in Queen Elizabeth's reign, and an handfome brick edifice erected in its room. But this building was demolifhed by Edward Alexander, Efq; who in 1744 erected, inftead of it, a large handfome fummer-houfe, embattled. It ftands at a fmall diftance northeaft from the church, is furrounded by a deep and wide moat, and afcended by a fteep winding walk, arched over moft of the way with trees, fhrubs, &c. The room is roofed by a beautiful dome leaded, the top of which is afcended by a pair of fteps, and over the embattlement the fpectator is prefented with a beautiful profpect on all fides.

This place is fuppofed to have been of fome note before the Saxons were mafters here. The church is built partly of Roman brick; and feveral Roman foundations have been difcovered in this parifh, particularly in the church and churchyard.

* This Richard de Lucy was alfo Sheriff of Effex and Hertfordfhire in 1156, and conftituted Juftice of England in 1162. The priory of Lefnes in Kent was of his founding, where he entered himfelf a canon regular, and died there in 1179.

At a little distance from hence is the parish of *Greenstead*, wherein David Robotier, Esq; has an handsome seat, called Greensted-Hall, which is situated a little way east from the church. The church is a very uncommon antique building; for the walls are of timber, not framed, but trees split, or sawn asunder, and set into the ground.

BRENTWOOD, or BURNTWOOD.

This is a post-town, in Essex, about eighteen miles from London, it is situated pleasantly upon a hill, affords a pleasing prospect to the inhabitants, and of late is greatly improved in its buildings. As it is on the high road from London to Harwich, it is a great thoroughfare, and has some good inns in it. One of these, the Crown Inn, deserves to be distinguished for its antiquity. Mr. Simmonds, in his collections says, he was informed by the master, who had writings in his possession to prove it, that it had been an inn for three hundred years with this sign; that a family named Salmon held it two hundred years, and that there had been eighty-nine owners, amongst which were an Earl of Oxford, and an Earl of Sussex.

Here is a good market weekly on Thursdays, and two fairs yearly for cattle and horses, one on the 18th of July, and the other on the 15th of October. Here is a grammar-school, which was founded in 1557, by Sir Anthony Brown; in which all boys of this parish, or any other parish within three miles of the school-house, are taught grammar-learning gratis. Sir Anthony also founded five alms-houses, for five single poor persons, three men and two women.

A chapel was founded at Brentwood about the year 1221, which was dedicated to Thomas a Becket; and the perquisites of the chaplain chiefly arose from travellers upon the road, and such as came out of devotion to *Saint* Thomas, as that ambitious and turbulent priest was stiled in an age of ignorance and superstition. From hence it arose, that a gate in this parish, in the way from Ongar, still retains the name of *Pilgrim's Hatch*. Divine service is now kept up in this chapel for the conveniency of the inhabitants of Brentwood, the parish church being near two miles distance.

Brentwood stands in the parish of *South Weald*, which is very extensive, and contains some very handsome gentlemen's seats. Sir Thomas Parker, late Lord Chief Baron of the Exchequer, but now retired from public business, has a pleasant seat here. Thomas Towers, Esq; Lord of the Manor, **has**

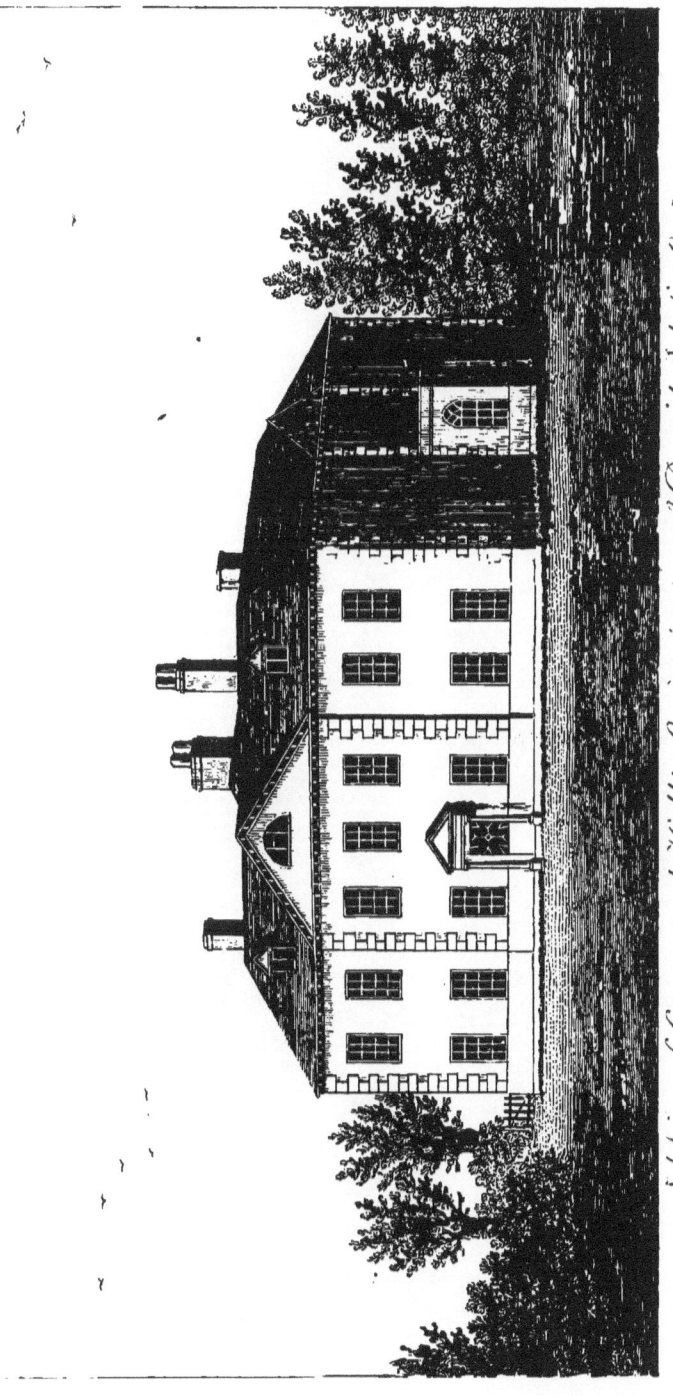

A View of Greenstead Hall in Essex, the Seat of David Rebow Esq.

has alfo a very elegant feat near the church, adorned with rich plantations, handfome gardens, a good park, &c. in which latter is built a profpect houfe, in the form of a tower, embattled, affording a moft delightful view. The Hon. Captain Hamilton has alfo an agreeable feat here. And on Weald Side Common is a feat called *Ditchley's*, the refidence of George Nicholls, Efq; adjoining to which is the feat of Anthony Wright, Efq. At Pilgrim Hatch is *Dounfell's*, the feat of Francis Manby, Efq. Befides thefe, there are many very good houfes, that cannot properly be called feats, but which are either the refidence or retirement of families of confiderable fortune.—On the London road is a bridge called *Puttal's*, fupported by Thomas Towers, Efq; and at the bottom of Wealdfide common is another bridge, called *Wright's*; through which bridges runs a rivulet, feparating Havering and Romford from this parifh.

South Weald church ftands on an hill, from whence is a fine profpect. It is an handfome building, confifting of two paces, fupported in the middle by five pillars of the Tufcan order. At the weft end there is a ftrong tower of confiderable height, embattled, in which are five bells. This tower was built in the beginning of King Henry the Seventh's reign.

The Saxon word *Weald*, fignifies *Wood*, and this place is fuppofed to have been one of the firft inhabited parts of Effex.—By the fouth fide of Weald-hall park there is a camp, inclofing about feventeen acres; it is circular, fingle ditched, and thought to have been a Roman fummer camp, or *Caftra Exploratorum*.—There are horfe races every year on Warley-common, which is at a little diftance from Brentwood.

HAVERING-AT-BOWER.

This place, which is about three miles from Romford, is faid to have derived its name from the following marvellous ftory, which may amufe our readers, though we prefume but few of them will give credit to it. We are told, that as the church of Clavering, in this county, was confecrating, and was to be dedicated to Chrift and St. John the Evangelift, King Edward the Confeffor riding that way, alighted, out of devotion, to be prefent at the confecration. During the proceffion, a *fair old man* came to the King, and begged alms of him in the name of God, and St. John the Evangelift. The King having nothing elfe to give, as his almoner was not at hand, took the ring from his finger, and gave it the

G

p.or

poor man. Some years after, two Englifh pilgrims having loft their way as they were travelling to the Holy Land, they faw a company cloathed in white, with two lights carried before them ; and behind them came *a fair ancient man*. The pilgrims joining them, the old man enquired who they were, and whence they came. After hearing their ftory, he brought them into a fine city, where was a room furnifhed with all manner of dainties ; when they had well refrefhed themfelves, and refted there all night, the old man fet them again in the right way. And at parting, he told them he was John the Evangelift ; adding, as the Legend goes on ; " Say ye unto Ed- " ward your King, that I greet him well by the token that he " gave to me this ring with his own hands at the hallowing of " my church, which ring ye fhall deliver him again. And fay " ye to him, that he difpofe his goods, for within fix months " he fhall be in the joy of heaven with me, where he fhall have " his reward for his chaftity, and for his good living." At their return home the two pilgrims waited upon the King, who was then at this bower, and delivered to him the meffage, and the ring, from which circumftance this place is faid to have received the name of Have-ring. This relation, however ridiculous, gained fo great credit in that age, as to occafion the whole ftory to be wrought in baffo relievo in the chapel at Weftminfter, where Edward the Confeffor lies buried, on the back of the fkreen that divides it from the altar. The ftatues of the king and the pilgrims are alfo over the courts of king's bench and common pleas, in Weftminfter Hall ; and over the gate going into Dean's-yard. His picture was alfo on the glafs of the eaft window of the fouth ifle of Romford chapel, with two pilgrims, and under it, *Johannes per peregrino mifit Regis Edwardo*. A good picture of him is now on the glafs of the chancel window of that chapel ; renewed in 1707. The ring pretended to have been given by him, as above, to St. John, was depofited among other reliques in his Abbey at Weftminfter.

This was anciently a retiring place for feveral of our Saxon kings : particularly of Edward the Confeffor, who took great delight in it, on account of its gloomy and folitary afpect, it being at that time woody, and therefore he thought it fuited well his private devotions. This place has been very productive of extraordinary ftories ; and accordingly the legend fays, it abounded fo with warbling nightingales, that they difturbed King Edward the Confeffor in his devotions, infomuch

much that he earneſtly prayed for their removal; ſince which
time, according to many of the ſage people of this neighbourhood, no nightingales have ever been heard to ſing in the park,
as in other places; but that many were heard without the pales.
Near the remains of the royal houſe ſtands Havering chapel,
dedicated to St. John the Evangeliſt. It is a ſmall building of
one pace with the chancel, the whole tiled.—Beſides the place
of Havering Bower, here was another at Pirgo, which belonged to the Queens of England; where they reſided at their own
conveniency, or perhaps during their widowhood, Havering being uſually part of the queen's jointure.—Lord Archer is owner
of the fine ſeat at *Pirgo*; the houſe is an antient venerable
ſtructure, within a conſiderable park. Here is a ſmall chapel
belonging to this ſeat.

R O M F O R D.

This town is ſix miles from Brentwood, and twelve from
London. It is pretty large, and conſiſts chiefly of one ſtreet,
near half a mile in length, at the upper part of which is held a
market every Tueſday for live calves; on each Wedneſday a
general market, and in the winter ſeaſon, on Mondays, a market for live hogs. Here is a fair annually, upon Midſummer
Day, for cattle and horſes. About the middle of the town
ſtands a good market-houſe, and a town-hall. This is a poſt-
town, and the greateſt thoroughfare in the county. Here is a
chapel which ſtands nearly in the center of the town, and is a
ſpacious ſtone building. In Romford-ſtreet near the turnpike,
is a charity ſchool, which was erected by ſubſcription in 1710.
It is a neat brick building, in which forty boys and twenty girls
are educated.

About half a mile out of Romford, on the road leading to
Brentwood, ſtands *Geddy-Hall*, the ſeat of Richard Benyon,
Eſq; formerly Governor of Fort St. George. It is a noble
manſion, and is ſurrounded by a pleaſant park and beautiful
gardens, plentifully watered by a fine canal.

About four miles from Romford is the pariſh of *Cranham*,
wherein General Oglethorpe, famous for ſettling the colony
of Georgia, has a ſeat. The houſe, which is a large antique
building, is named *Cranham Hall*. This place is ſuppoſed to
have derived its name of *Cranham* from a reſort of cranes
here, the hawking of which was an ancient ſport. And if
we were to judge from the bills of fare into which cranes
came, and the price of proviſions, remarked by our hiſtorians,

G 2   in

in the time of King Edward I. we muſt imagine the ſtomachs of the people of that fighting age to be of a ſtrange tone. For when a gooſe ſold for four-pence, a crane ſold for twelve-pence; and King William Rufus is ſaid to have turned off his major-domo, for ſetting before him a *crane* half roaſted.

In the pariſh of *Dagenham*, at the diſtance of fifteen miles from London, the late Henry Muilman, Eſq; had an hand-ſome ſeat. The building is of brick, ſpacious, ſurrounded by a park, and commanding an agreeable proſpect.—*Dagenham Breach* was made here upwards of fifty years ago, by the Thames, which overflowed one thouſand acres of rich land; but, after near ten years inundation, during which the works were ſeveral times blown up, it was at laſt ſtopped by Captain Perry, who had been employed ſeveral years in the Czar of Muſcovy's works at Veronitza; but the expence attending this amounted to more than forty thouſand pounds.

B,ERKING.

This is the neareſt market-town in the county of Eſſex to London, from which it is only eight miles diſtance, and ſeven from Romford. The town is of conſiderable extent, and chiefly inhabited by fiſhermen, whoſe boats, called ſmacks, lie at the mouth of the river Thames, from whence their fiſh is ſent up to Billingſgate. The market is held on Saturdays; and a fair is held here annually on the 22d of October, for horſes. It was to this place that King William the Conqueror retired, ſoon after his coronation, till he had erected forts in London to awe the inhabitants of that city.

At this place Erkenwald, the fourth biſhop of London, founded the ſecond nunnery of the Saxons in England*, in the year 666. It was of the order of St. Benedict, and dedicated to the Virgin Mary and St. Ethelburga, the firſt abbeſs, (ſiſter to the founder) who, with her ſucceſſor, was canonized. It ſtood on the north ſide of the church-yard. One gate, and part of the wall is ſtill remaining.

The manor of Berking, in the reign of Queen Elizabeth, belonged to Sir William Hewett, who was Lord Mayor of London in 1589, and concerning whom the following ſtory

* Folkſtone nunnery was the firſt, which was founded thirty-ſix years before.

is

is related. Sir William lived upon London-bridge, and had an infant daughter. One of his maids playing with this child out of a window over the river Thames, by chance dropped her in, almost beyond expectation of being saved. A young gentleman, named Edward Osborne, then apprentice to Sir William, at this calamitous accident leaped in boldly, and saved the child. In memory of which deliverance, and in gratitude, her father afterwards bestowed her in marriage to the said Mr. Osborne, with a very great dowry. Several persons of quality courted the young lady, and particularly the Earl of Shrewsbury. But Sir William Hewett said, " Osborne saved " her, and Osborne should enjoy her." This Mr. Osborne was ancestor to the present Duke of Leeds.

The parish of Berking is large, and so much improved, by lands recovered from the Thames and the river Roding, that the great and small tithes are computed at above 600l. a year.— A little beyond the town, towards Dagenham, stood a great old house, where the gunpowder plot is said to have been contrived.—About four miles north from Berking church, Charles Raymond, Esq; who was high sheriff for the county in 1771, has a fine seat, named *Valentines*, which has been termed a cabinet of curiosities. The house is one of the neatest, and best adapted to its size, of any modern one in the county : its ornaments are well chosen, and the grounds belonging to it laid out with great judgment and taste.—Bamber Gascoyne, Esq; has also a good house about a quarter of a mile south-east from the church, named *Biffrons*, which commands a fine prospect, and behind it is a pretty park.

LITTLE ILFORD.

The village of Little Ilford is three miles from Berking ; it is but small, consisting only of one street, which on Sundays many citizens of London and others resort to for an airing ; and the little traffic occasioned thereby is the chief support of its inhabitants.—Little Ilford church is small, but neat; and at the north-west corner of it the Lethieuller family has erected a very neat room, about fifteen feet square, separated from the church by an iron gate. It has a fire place, and every convenience to accommodate the family when they attend divine service. The pavement is of free-stone, and beneath it is the family vault. Along the north side of this room is a capital, supported by columns of the Doric order ; it is ascended by two steps ; and between the columns is a

very

very neat altar-tomb of black and white marble, supporting a beautiful marble urn of various colours. This monument is in memory of John Lethieuller, Esq. There are several other monuments here to persons of the same family, but the only one that we shall particularly mention, is that erected to the memory of Smart Lethieuller, Esq; a gentleman much distinguished for his skill in antiquities: and we shall insert the inscription on his tomb, because it is remarkable for propriety and elegance. It is as follows:

In memory of
SMART LETHIEULLER, Esq;
A Gentleman of polite Literature and elegant Taste,
An Encourager of Art and ingenious Artists,
A studious Promoter of Literary Enquiries;
A Companion, and a Friend, of learned Men;
Judiciously versed in Science of Antiquity,
And richly possessed of the curious productions of Nature.
But
Who modestly desired no other Inscription on his
Tomb, than what he had made the Rule of his Life;
To do justly,
To love Mercy,
And to walk humbly with God.
He was born Nov. 3, 1701.
And deceased without issue Aug. 27, 1760.

The most elegant simplicity runs through every part of this place, which is so well calculated to inspire serious contemplation, that few edifices of the kind are equal to it.

LEYTON.

This is a straggling village by the river Lea, about six miles from London. There are several handsome seats in the parish, belonging to wealthy citizens and other gentlemen, particularly Goring-house, also called the Forest-house, which is loftily situated fronting Epping-forest, and is the property of Samuel Bosanquet, Esq. The manor-house of Leyton, which is a fine seat, is the property of Thomas Blaydon, Esq.— About a quarter of a mile north-east from the church Thomas Oliver, Esq; has a beautiful seat, which formerly belonged to Sir Fisher Tench. It is a modern structure, adorned with large and delightful gardens, with plantations, walks, groves, mounts, and canals, stocked with fish and fowl. The seat of Henry More, Esq; near half a mile west from the church,

is

is also very agreeably situated. The house is large and hand-some, and the gardens and decorations belonging to it are suit-able.

One part of this parish is called *Leyton-stone*, which is in a pleasant and healthy situation; and the number of inhabitants here being greatly increased, a chapel of ease has been built for their convenience. It is somewhat singular that the parish of Walthamstow should have a piece of ground about fifty yards wide, which runs directly in a straight line through this parish. —Here seems to have been a Roman villa, or some summer camp or station; for between the manor-house and the canal, where the garden now is, in digging were found old foundati-ons, with a great many Roman bricks, intermixed with others, and several medals. And in enlarging the horse-pond, huge foundations were discovered six feet under ground; and a large arched gate with mouldings nine or ten feet high, and five or six broad, the top of which was also six feet under ground. The walls were four feet thick or more. A very large urn, with ashes and bones, was taken up in the church-yard in digging a deep grave. Several urns, with ashes in them, have been also found on the south side of Blind-lane, near Rockholts, in dig-ging for gravel.

There are several very handsome monuments In Leyton church and church-yard.—That indefatigable antiquarian, Mr. John Strype, was vicar of this parish. The famous Sir Tho-mas Roe, ambassador to the Great Mogul, the Grand Signior, and several European princes, in the reign of King James I. was born in this parish. In this great man the accomplish-ments of the scholar, the gentleman, and the statesman, were eminently united. During his residence in the Mogul's court, he zealously promoted the trading interest of this kingdom, for which the East India Company is indebted to him to this day. In his embassy to the Grand Signior, he collected many valua-ble Greek and oriental manuscripts, which he presented to the Bodleian library, to which he left his valuable collection of coins. The fine Alexandrian M.S. of the Greek Bible was procured by his means.

W E S T - H A M.

This parish, which joins to Leyton, is four miles distant from London. It includes *Stratford*, anciently surnamed *Lang-thorne*, and is parted from Middlesex on the south, and from St. Mary Stratford-le-Bow, by the river Lea, over which there are five bridges in this parish. Bow-bridge, which is

one

one of them, received the name of *Bow*, or *arched*, bridge, becaufe it was the firſt arched ſtone bridge in the county.   The
occaſion of its being built is thus related.   The ancient road
from this county to London was by *Old Ford* ; that is, through
the ford there without a bridge.   But that paſſage being difficult and dangerous, and many perſons loſing their lives, or being thoroughly wetted, which happened to be the caſe with
Maud, Queen to King Henry I. ſhe turned the road from Old
Ford, to the place where it is now, and made the cauſeways,
and built the bridges at her own charge.   And for the keeping
of them in repair, ſhe gave to the abbeſs of Berking certain
manors, and a mill called Wiggan-mill.

The pariſh of Weſt-Ham is divided into four wards ; namely, *Churd-ward, Stratford Langthorns, Plaiſtow-ward*, and
that of *Upton*.   Its ſituation is not high, nor yet very low, but
in general healthy ; and at the lower part of Plaiſtow affords a
beautiful view of the river Thames, and the county of Kent
for many miles.—This pariſh is divided from the county of
Kent by the river Thames.—From its vicinity to the metropolis, and from the conveniency which it has of water-carriage, a
number of wealthy merchants, traders, and induſtrious artiſts
have choſen it for their reſidence ; by which means of late
years the buildings have been much increaſed ; particularly by
the addition of two ſmall new-built hamlets, if they may be
thus called, on the Foreſt-ſide.   Theſe are Maryland-point
and the Gravel-pits ; one facing the road to Epping, and that
to Chelmsford.   *Maryland-point* is a cluſter of houſes near
Stratford ; the firſt of them were erected by a merchant, who
had got a fortune in that colony, from whence they took their
name.—*Stratford*, (i. e. the *ſtreet at the ford)* is a very large and
conſiderable hamlet in this pariſh ; and diſtinguiſhed from the
other adjoining, Stratford at Bow, lying on the weſt ſide of
Bow-bridge, in the county of Middleſex, by the appellation
of *Langton*, or *Langthorn*.   *Plaiſtow hamlet* lies ſouth of the
church, and Upton north of the ſame.

About half a mile ſouth-ſouth-weſt from the church, are
the remains of *Stratford-abbey*, once a conſiderable monaſtery
here, and part of the old gate of which is ſtill ſtanding.   This
monaſtery was founded about the year 1134, by William
Montfichet, for the monks of the Ciſtertion order, and dedicated to the Virgin Mary, and All Saints.   Its demeſnes in this
pariſh comprehend 1500 acres.—Weſt-ham church, which is
dedicated to All Staints, is large ; both church and chancel

3   having

having north and fouth ifles: there are feveral monuments in it, two of which are ancient.

EAST-HAM.

The fituation of this parifh is rather low, and its foil gravelly, except in the marfhes. Several wealthy citizens and other gentlemen refide in it, on which account it has feveral good houfes in it.——A tradition prevails here, that the houfe called *Green-ftreet*, (late the feat of Sir Nicholas Gerard, and now belonging to Mrs. Whitefide) was once the habitation of an Earl of Weftmoreland, and probably of Lady Latimer.—— Tradition likewife fays that Queen Anne Boleyn was confined in a tower ftill ftanding near the faid houfe.——One of the moft remarkable particulars here is, the fpring called *Miller's Well*, the water of which is efteemed to be extremely good, and has not ever been known to be frozen, or to have varied in its height, either in fummer or in winter.——A part of Kent, in the parifh of Woolwich, lies on this fide the river, and divides this parifh from the Thames.

DEPTFORD.

This is a large and populous town in the county of Kent, about four miles and an half from London. It was anciently called Weft Greenwich; and is faid to have received its prefent name, from its having a deep ford over the little river Ravenfbourn, near its influx into the Thames, where it has now a bridge. It is divided into Upper and Lower Deptford, which contain together two churches, feveral meetinghoufes, and about 1900 houfes. It is moft remarkable for its noble dock, where the royal navy was formerly built and repaired, till it was found more convenient to build the larger fhips at Woolwich, and other places, where there is a greater depth of water; but notwithftanding this, the yard is enlarged to more than double its former dimenfions, and a vaft number of hands are conftantly employed. It has a wet dock of two acres for fhips, and another of an acre and an half, with vaft quantities of timber and other ftores, and extenfive buildings, as ftore-houfes, and offices, for the ufe of the place; befides dwelling-houfes for thofe officers who are obliged to live upon the fpot, in order to fuperintend the works. Here the royal yachts are generally kept; and near the dock is the feat of Sir John Evelyn, called Says Court, where that juftly celebrated Prince, Peter the Great, Czar of Mufcovy, refided for fome time; and in this yard completed his knowledge and skill in the practical part of naval architecture.

In this town are two hospitals, one of which was incorporated by King Henry VIII. in the form of a college, for the use of seamen, and is commonly called *Trinity House* of Deptford Strond: this contains twenty-one houses, and is situated near the church. The other, called *Trinity Hospital*, has thirty-eight houses fronting the street. This is a very handsome edifice, and has large gardens well kept belonging to it. Though this last is the finest structure, yet the other has the preference, on account of its antiquity; and as the Brethren of the Trinity hold their corporation by that house, they are obliged, at certain times, to meet there for business. Both these houses are for decayed pilots, or masters of ships, or their widows; the men being allowed twenty shillings, and the women sixteen shillings, a month.

Trinity House was founded in the year 1515, by Sir Thomas Spert, Knight, commander of the great ship Henry Grace de Dieu, and comptroller of the Navy, for the regulation of seamen, and the convenience of ships and mariners on our coast, and incorporated, as we we before observed, by Henry VIII. who confirmed to them not only the antient rights and privileges of the company of mariners of England, but their several possessions at Deptford; which, together with the grants of Queen Elizabeth, and King Charles II. were also confirmed by letters patent of the first of James II. in 1685. The master, wardens, assistants, and elder brethren of this corporation, are by charter invested with the power of examining the masters of his Majesty's ships, and also the mathematical children of Christ's hospital; of appointing pilots to conduct ships in and out of the river Thames; and of amercing all such as shall presume to act as masters of ships of war, or pilots, without their approbation. It is their business also to settle the several rates of pilotage, and erect lighthouses, and other sea-marks, upon the several coasts of the kingdom, for the security of navigation; to which light-houses all ships pay one halfpenny a ton. They are likewise impowered to grant licences to poor seamen, not free of the city, to row on the river Thames for their support, in the intervals of sea-service, or when past going to sea; and to prevent aliens from serving on board English ships, without their licence, upon the penalty of 5l. for each offence. They are likewise authorised to punish seamen for desertion, or mutiny, in the merchants service; and to hear and determine the complaints

plaints of officers and feamen in the merchants fervice; but
fubject to an appeal to the Lords of the Admiralty, or the
judge of the Court of Admiralty. To this company belongs
the Ballaft-Office for clearing and deepening the river Thames,
by taking from thence a fufficient quantity of ballaft for the
fupply of all fhips that fail out of that river; in which fervice
fixty barges, with two men in each, are conftantly employed,
and all fhips that take in ballaft pay them 1s. a ton, for which
it is brought to the fhips fides.——We have been the more
particular in enumerating the powers, and the bufinefs, of this
corporation, becaufe its authority and powers are of fo extenfive a nature, and of fo much importance to us as a maritime
ftate. We fhall, therefore, further obferve, that there are
annually relieved by this company about 3000 poor feamen,
their widows, and orphans; and this, as it is faid, at the expence of about 6000l. They meet frequently at their houfe
in Water-lane, Thames-ftreet, generally on Wednefdays and
Saturdays; but their courts are not conftantly fixed to a fet
time. Their houfe in Water-lane has been twice burnt down,
once at the fire of London, and the laft time in the year
1718. Among the curiofities preferved in the hall of this
building, is a flag taken from the Spaniards by the famous Sir
Francis Drake, whofe picture is alfo there; a large and exact
model of a fhip entirely rigged, and two large globes; and
in the parlour are five large drawings, curioufly performed by
the pen, of feveral engagements at fea in the reign of Charles
the Second.

GREENWICH.

This town, which is chiefly famous for its fine hofpital
and park, is faid to contain upwards of 1300 houfes. Its
parifh church, which has been lately rebuilt by the commiffi-
ners for erecting the fifty new churches, is a very handfome
ftructure, dedicated to St. Alphage, Archbifhop of Canterbury, who is faid to have been flain by the Danes in the year
1012, on the fpot where the church now ftands. There is
a college at the end of the town, fronting the Thames, for
the maintenance of twenty decayed old houfekeepers, twelve
out of Greenwich, and eight who are to be alternately chofen
from Snottifham and Caftle Rifing in Norfolk. This is called
the Duke of Norfolk's College, though it was founded, and
endowed, in 1613, by Henry Howard, Earl of Northampton,
the Duke of Norfolk's brother, and by him committed to the
care of the mercers company. There is a chapel belonging

ing to this College, in which the Earl's body is laid, which, as well as his monument, was removed hither a few years ago, from the chapel of Dover caftle, of which he was conftable. In the year 1560, Mr. John Lombard, author of the Perambulation of Kent, alfo built and founded an hofpital here, for twenty-two perfons, called Queen Elizabeth's College. This is faid to be the firft hofpital founded by an Englifh Proteftant. There are likewife two charity-fchools in this parifh, one founded by Sir William Boreman, and the other by John Roan. A market was erected in this town in the year 1737, the direction of which is in the governors of the Royal Hofpital, to which the profits arifing from it were appropriated. The market days are Wednefdays and Saturdays.

Greenwich has been the refidence of feveral of our Monarchs. King Henry VIII. and the Queens Mary and Elizabeth, were born here; and that excellent young Monarch, Edward VI. died here. The palace was firft erected by Humphry, Duke of Gloucefter, who named it Placentia. King Edward IV. beftowed confiderable fums of money in enlarging and beautifying it, in which he was followed by King Henry VII. But it was completed by Henry VIII. who often kept his Chriftmas, and other great feftivals, at this place, with magnificent joufts and tournaments: and the ground, which was called the Tilt-yard, is the fpot on which the Eaft wing of the Royal hofpital is built. But this palace being afterwards fuffered to run to ruin, was pulled down by King Charles II. who began another, a moft magnificent edifice, and lived to fee the firft wing finifhed. But this was afterwards converted into a part of the Royal Hofpital: and that which is properly the palace here now, is an edifice of no great extent, and is at prefent converted into apartments for the governor of the hofpital, and the ranger of the park.

The park is well ftocked with deer, and affords a noble and delightful view of the Hofpital, the river Thames, and the city of London. This park was enlarged by King Charles II. who walled it round, planted it, and caufed a royal obfervatory to be erected on the top of the fteep of the hill. This edifice his Majefty erected for the ufe of the celebrated Mr. John Flamftead, and it ftill retains the name of that eminent aftronomer. King Charles likewife furnifhed it with mathematical inftruments for aftronomical obfervations, and a deep dry well for obferving the ftars in the day time.

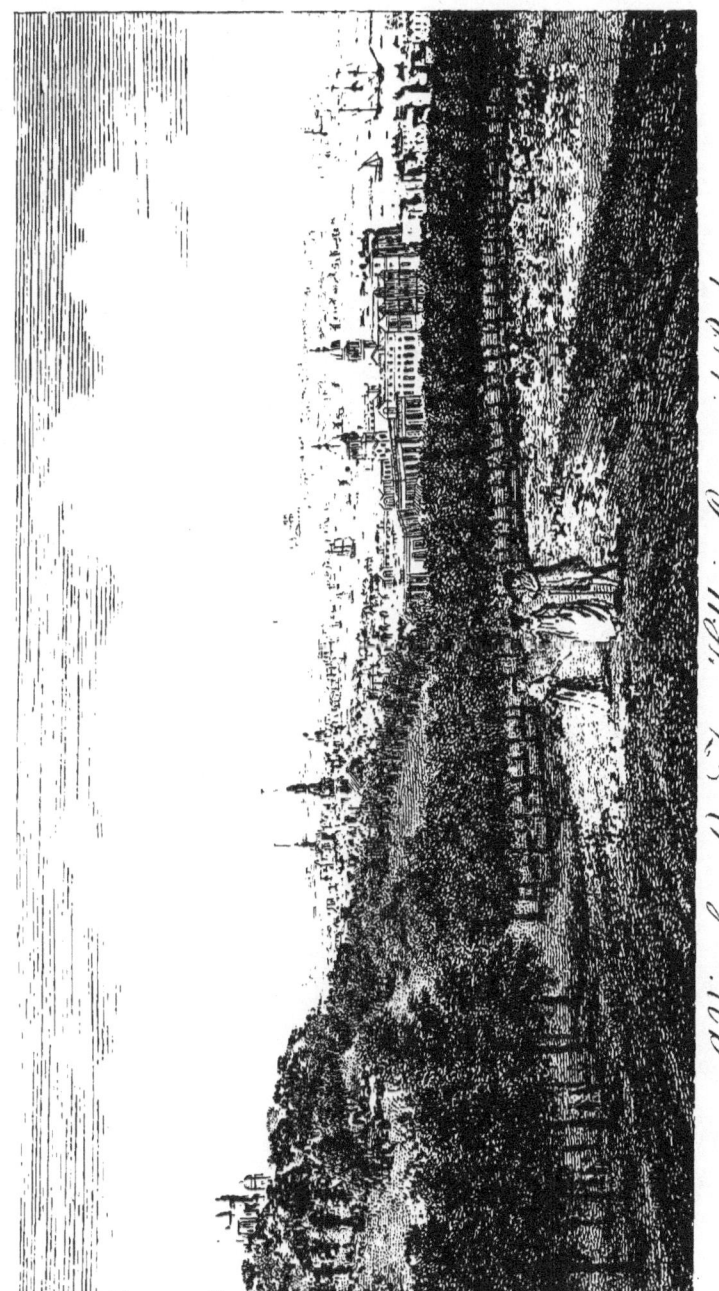

A View from One-Tree Hill in Greenwich Park.

N.1.

time.—This park is much reforted to in the Eafter and Whit-
fun holidays, by young men and women from London and the
neighbourhood, who divert themfelves by running down the
hills, and other rural fports.

The *Royal Hofpital* at Greenwich is fo magnificent a ftructure, that it can fcarcely be taken for any thing lefs than the
palace of a great monarch. Indeed, the wing which King
Charles the Second defigned for the Palace, is now the firft
wing of the hofpital towards London. For King William the
Third being very defirous of promoting the commerce, navigation, and naval ftrength of this kingdom, by inviting great
numbers of his fubjects to betake themfelves to the fea, gave
this noble palace, and feveral other edifices, with a confiderable
fpot of ground, for the ufe of thofe Englifh feamen and their
children, who by age, wounds, and other accidents, fhould be
difabled from farther fervice at fea; and for the widows and
children of fuch as were flain at fea, fighting againft the enemies
of their country. King William alfo by his letters patent, in
1694, appointed commiffioners for the better carrying on his
public-fpirited and laudable defign, in which he defired the affiftance of his fubjects, as the neceffities of his affairs did not permit him to advance fo confiderable a fum towards this work as
he defired, and as was requifite for the purpofe. In compli-
ance with this requeft, many benefactious were made to this
noble charity, both in that and the fucceeding reigns; which,
according to the tables hung up at the entrance of the hall, a-
mount to 58,209l. And afterwards the eftate of the Earl of
Derwentwater, which was forfeited by that nobleman's being
concerned in the rebellion in 1715, and which amounted to
6000l. per annum, was given by parliament to this hofpital.
The firft range had coft King Charles II. 36,000l. and another was ordered to be built on the fame model. This has been
completed with equal magnificence, and the whole ftructure
entirely finifhed.

The front to the Thames confifts of thefe two ranges of
ftone buildings, with the Governor's houfe at the back part
of the center, behind which the park, well planted with
trees, rifes with a noble afcent. Thefe buildings, between
which is a large area, perfectly correfpond with each other, and
each range is terminated by a very noble dome. In each front
to the Thames, two ranges of coupled Corinthian columns,
finely wrought, fupport their pediments, and the fame order is
continued in pilafters along the building. In the center of each

part,

part, between thefe ranges of Corinthian columns, is the
door, which is of the Doric order.   The buildings which are
continued from thofe of which we have juft been fpeaking,
and which face the area, correfpond with them, though in a
more fine and elegant manner.   In the center of both is a range
of columns fupporting a pediment, and at each corner a range
of Corinthian pilafters.   The front is rufticated, and there are
two feries of windows.   The domes at the end, which are
one hundred and twenty feet high, are fupported on coupled
columns, as are the porticoes below ; and under one of thefe
is the chapel, which is adorned on the infide with the utmoft
elegance and beauty.   On the fides of the gate which opens
to thefe buildings from the park, are placed a large celeftial
and terreftrial globe ; and in the center of the area is fixed
on a pedeftal, a ftatue of our late excellent Monarch, King
George II.

The Hall of this Hofpital, which is very noble, is finely
painted by Sir James Thornhill. At the upper end of it are reprefented, in an alcove, the late Princefs Sophia, King George
I. King George II. Queen Caroline, the Queen Dowager of
Pruffia, Frederic, Prince of Wales, the late Duke of Cumberland, and the five Princeffes, the daughters of his late Majefty.
On the cieling over the alcove are Queen Anne and Prince
George of Denmark : and on the cieling of the Hall are King
William and Queen Mary, with feveral fine emblematical figures.   All ftrangers who fee this hall pay two-pence each, and
this income is applied to the fupport of the mathematical fchool,
for the fons of failors.

In the year 1705, an hundred difabled feamen were the firft
that were received into this hofpital ; but it at prefent contains
near two thoufand difabled feamen, and an hundred boys, the
fons of feamen, who are inftructed in navigation, and bred up
for the fervice of the royal navy ; but there are no out-penfioners, as at Chelfea.   Each of the mariners has a weekly allowance of feven loaves, weighing fixteen ounces each ; three
pounds of beef, two of mutton ; a pint of peafe ; a pound and
a quarter of cheefe ; two ounces of butter ; fourteen quarts of
beer ; and one fhilling a week tobacco money.   The tobacco
money of the boatfwains is 2s. 6d. a week each ; that of their
mates 1s. 6d. and that of the other officers in proportion to their
rank.   Befides which each common penfioner is completely
cloathed once in two years.

For the better fupport of this hofpital, every feaman in the
Royal

Royal Navy, and in the fervice of the merchants, pays 6d. a month. This is ftopped out of the pay of all failors, and delivered at the fixpenny receiver's Office on Tower-hill. And therefore a feaman who can produce an authentic certificate of his being difabled, and rendered unfit for the fea-fervice, by defending any fhip belonging to Britifh fubjects, or in taking any fhip from the enemy, may be admitted into this hofpital, and receive the fame benefit from it, as if he had been in the immediate fervice of the government. The hofpital has about an hundred Governors, compofed of the Nobility, great Officers of ftate, and perfons in confiderable pofts under the King.

On the fouth fide of Greenwich lies *Blackheath*, a large plain fo called from the blacknefs of its foil. It is much admired for the beauty of its fituation, and its excellent air; and has been rendered memorable by being the theatre of feveral remarkable tranfactions. It was here the Danifh army lay a confiderable time encamped in the year 1011, and it was here that the famous Wat Tyler, the Kentifh rebel, muftered 100,000 men. Jack Cade alfo, who ftiled himfelf John Mortimer, and laid claim to the crown, pretending that he was kinfman to the Duke of York, encamped on this heath for a month together in this and the neighbouring counties, in 1451. And the following year King Henry VI. pitched his royal pavilion here, having affembled troops to withftand the force of his coufin, Edward, Duke of York, who was afterwards King Edward IV. And here againft that King did the baftard Falconbridge likewife encamp. And in 1497, the Lord Audley, Flemmock, an Attorney, and Jofeph the Blackfmith, encamped on this place, in the rebellion they raifed againft King Henry VII. And here that politic and warlike Prince routed them, killing above 2000 on the fpot, and taking about 14000 prifoners.

In 1415, the Lord Mayor and Aldermen of London, with 400 citizens in fcarlet, and with red and white hoods on, came to Blackheath, where they met that victorious Prince, King Henry the Vth, who had juft returned from France, after the famous battle of Agincourt; and from Blackheath they conducted his Majefty to London. And in 1474, the Lord Mayor and Aldermen, attended by 500 citizens, alfo met King Edward IV. here, on his return from France. It appears alfo to have been ufal formerly to meet foreign Princes,

and

and other perfons of high rank, on Blackheath, on their arrival in England. On the 21ft of December, 1411, Maurice,
Emperor of Conftantinople, who came to folicit affiftance
againft the Turks, was met here with great magnificence by
King Henry IV. And in 1416, the Emperor Sigifmund was
met here and from hence condufted in great pomp to London. In 1518, the Lord-Admiral of France, and the Archbifhop of Paris, both Ambaffadors from the French King,
with above 1200 attendants, were met here by the Admiral
of England, and above 500 gentlemen. And the following
year Cardinal Campejus, the Pope's legate, being attended
hither by the gentlemen of Kent, was met by the Duke of
Norfolk, and many Noblemen and Prelates of England ; and
here in a tent of cloth and gold, he put on his Cardinal's
robes richly ermined, and from hence rode to London. And
here alfo King Henry VIII. met the Princefs Ann of Cleves,
in very great ftate and pomp, and was foon after married to
her.

On the Eaft-fide of Blackheath ftands *Morden College*, erected for the fupport of poor decayed Merchants, by Sir John
Morden, Bart. a Turkey-merchant, feveral years before his
death, which happened in the year 1708. It confifts of a
large brick building, with two fmall wings, ftrengthened at
the corners with ftone ruftic. The principal entrance, which
is in the center, is decorated with Doric columns, feftoons,
and a pediment on the top, over which rifes a turret, with
a dial; and from the dome, which is fupported by fcrolls,
rifes a ball and fane. To this entrance there is an afcent
by a flight of circular fteps ; and having afcended them,
and paffed through this part of the building, we enter an
inner fquare furrounded with piazzas. The chapel is neatly
wainfcotted, and has a coftly altar-piece; and it has a burying-place adjoining, for the members of the college. The
founder, by his own defire, was buried in a vault under the
communion table of the chapel. Sir John Morden erected
his college at a fmall diftance from his own habitation, in a
place called Great Stone Field, and endowed it, after his Lady's
deceafe, with his whole real, copyhold, and perfonal eftate,
to the value of about 1300l. per annum. He placed in this
hofpital twelve decayed Turkey merchants in his life time ;
but, after his deceafe, the Lady Morden, finding that the
fhare allotted her by Sir John's laft will, was not fufficient for
her decent fupport, fome parts of the eftate not anfwering fo

3   well

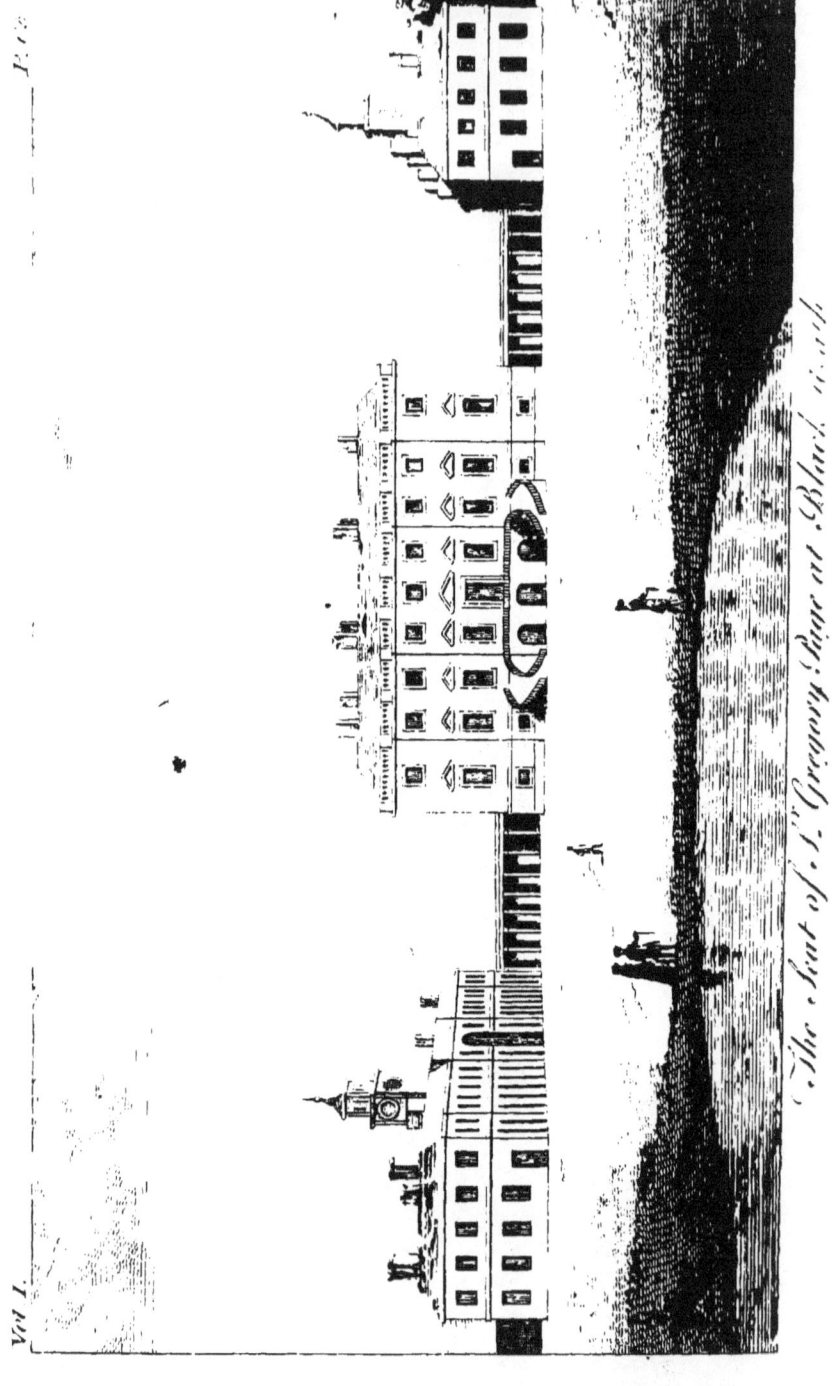

The Seat of S.t Gregory Page at Blach ..... th

well as had been expected, she was obliged to reduce the number to four. But upon her death the whole estate coming to the college, the number was encreased, and there are at this time thirty-five poor gentlemen; and the number not being limited, it is to be encreased as the estate will afford ; for the building will conveniently hold forty. The treasurer is allowed 40l. a year ; and the chaplain, who reads prayers twice a day, and preaches twice every Sunday, had at first a salary of 30l. per annum, which the Lady Morden doubled at her death. The present chaplain is the Rev. Mr. Moses Brown, author of the Sunday Thoughts, Piscatory Eclogues, and other pieces. Lady Morden was in several respects a benefactress to the college, and as she put up her husbands' statue in a niche over the gate, the trustees have put up hers in another niche, adjoining to that of her husband. The treasurer, chaplain, and pensioners, are obliged to reside in the college ; and, except in case of sickness, no other persons are to reside, live, or lodge there ; but no person can be admitted as a pensioner, who cannot make it appear that he is above sixty years of age. The pensioners have each 20l. a year, and at first wore gowns, with the founders badge ; but this badge has not been worn for some years. They have a common table in the hall to eat and drink together at meals ; and each has a convenient apartment, with a cellar. Seven Turkey merchants have the direction of this hospital, and the nomination of the persons to be admitted into it ; to them the treasurer is accountable, and whenever any of these die, the surviving trustees chuse others in their stead.

There are several noblemens and gentlemens seats on Blackheath ; and in particular, those of the Earl of Chesterfield, and the Earl of Dartmouth. And not far from Morden College is a noble house built by Sir Gregory Page, Bart. This is a very magnificent edifice, built in the modern taste, consisting of a basement, state, and attic story. The wings contain the offices and stables, which are joined to the body of the house by a colonade. It stands in the midst of a park; with a large piece of water before it. The back front has an Ionic portico of four columns, but having no pediment does not make so agreeable a figure as might be wished. This is one of the finest seats in England belonging to a private gentleman ; and the gardens, park, and country around, render it a most delightful seat : yet this fine edifice was begun, raised, and covered, in the space of eleven months. It is adorned with many capital paintings ; among which are the following ;

Sampfon and Dalilah, by Vandyke; Juno and Ixion, by Rubens; Rubens and his miftrefs, by Rubens himfelf; David and Abigal, by Rubens; the woman taken in Adultery, by Paul Veronefe; Mofes and Pharaoh's daughter, by the fame; a counfellor, his wife, and daughter, by Titian; and a Venus, Cupid, and fatyrs, by Nich. Pouffin.

Two fairs are held on Blackheath annually, one on the 12th of May, and another on the 11th of October, for bullocks, horfes, and toys.

On the fouth fide of Blackheath, and weft of Sir Gregory Page's park, lies the pleafant village of *Lee*; at the eaft end of which, next Lee Green, is a pleafant houfe and gardens of Henry Pelham, Efq. and in the ftreet of Lee are the houfes of the honourable Henry Roper and of David Papilion, Efq. and of feveral other perfons of fafhion; and on the north fide of the ftreet, is an old feat of the Boone family, with the remains of a grove, and a pleafant piece of water in the ground adjoining. The ftrait road from London to Maidftone is through Lee village. Between the parifh of Lee, Eltham and Chiflehurft, is a hamlet called Modingham, in which is a fmall feat of Lord Apfley, now lord chancellor, with pleafant grounds about it; the beauty of the whole is owing to his lordfhip's improvements; and here is alfo a very old manfion which belonged to the ancient family of the Stoddards.

Between the village of Lee, and the fummit of the hill, next Blackheath, are the elegant gardens and pleafure grounds belonging to the villa of the late Sir Samuel Fludyer, Bart. now, or lately inhabited by Harry Verelft, Efq. fome time governor of Bengal. The houfe is not large, but hath a very handfome apartment upon the firft floor, towards the gardens and pleafure grounds; and the profpects from thefe rooms to Shooter's hill, Eltham, and Lee village, and into Sir Gregory Page's beautiful grounds and park, with the woods of Greenwich park fkirting the view to the north, are moft picturefque and beautiful. The front of the houfe commands the Dulwich hill, with Lewifham church placed in the very center of the view below them. On the fummit of the hill next the heath ftands the ancient church of Lee, very fmall. The churchyard is neat, and much ornamented with coftly monuments of ftatuary and black marble. The great aftronomer Dr. Edmund

Hal-

Halley lies buried here under a plain table tomb, with an in-scription of some length in Latin. In the church, on the north of the communion table, is a stately arched monument of ala-baster, supported with columns of black marble of the Corin-thian order. The rectory house, and that of Thomas Edlyne, Esq; on the eminence near the church, command from every side of them very pleasing views, the adjacent ground being high-ly improved, and the near and distant prospects enriched with feats, farm-houses, towns and villages; the Kentish and Dul-wich hills in the front, and Blackheath and Greenwich park behind, with an extensive view, over London and Westmin-ster, of the Middlesex hills, which bound the horizon to the north west.

Shooter's Hill, which is near Blackheath, was formerly used as a butt for archers, and was in great repute among the neigh-bouring people, till King Henry the VIIIth's time; from whence some say it took its name. But others tell us, though this ap-pears less probable, that it received its name from the frequent robberies that were committed here. It was common, it is said, for thieves to lie lurking in the woods about here, in or-der to shoot passengers, and then rifle them. And in the sixth year of King Richard II. an order was made for enlarging the high-road here, according to the statute of King Edward the Ist. And King Henry IV. granted leave to Thomas Chap-man, to cut down and sell the wood here, that it might not be an harbour for thieves; and to lay out the money raised there-by, for the improvement of the highways. And in July, 1739, a very good design was begun to be put in execution on Shooter's Hill, a number of hands being employed in cutting a new road, wide enough for three carriages to pass a-breast, on the eastern descent of the hill, which was formerly so narrow, that it was impossible for a passenger, if way-laid, to escape falling into a ruffian's hands, which was the cause of many rob-beries here.

King Henry VIII. and his Queen Katharine, once came in very great splendor, on a May-day, from Greenwich to Shoot-er's Hill; and here they were received by 200 archers clad all in green, with one personating Robin Hood as their captain, who first shewed the King the skill of his archers in shooting, and then leading the ladies into the wood, gave them a fine en-tertainment of venison and wine, in green arbours, and booths adorned with fine pageants, and all the efforts of romantic gal-lantry.

Shooter's

Shooter's Hill affords a moft noble and extenfive profpect, not only into almoft all parts of this county, but into Suffex, Surrey, and Effex; and alfo of the cities of London and Weftminfter, and both up and down the river Thames, where the continual paffage of numerous fhips, veffels, and boats of all kinds, yields a moft pleafing and delightfull appearance. A defign was fome time fince formed of building a town here, but it feems now to be laid afide.

CHARLTON.

This is a pleafant and well-built village, on the north fide of Blackheath. It is particularly famous for a diforderly fair held in its neighbourhood on the 18th of October, St. Luke's Day; when the mob, who wear horns on their heads, ufed to take all kind of liberties, and the lewd and vulgar women who attended there gave a loofe to all manner of indecency; but thefe irregularities have of late years been much reftrained. This is called *Horn Fair*, and there are fold at it rams' horns, horn toys, and wares of all forts. Of this whimfical fair, a vulgar tradition gives the following origin. It is faid that King John, who had a palace at Eltham, in this neighbourhood, being out a hunting near Charlton, which was then a mean hamlet, was feparated from his attendants; when entering a cottage, he found the miftrefs of it alone, who being handfome, the King became enamoured of her, and as fhe was not the moft modeft of her fex, he found means to debauch her. But, in the mean time, her hufband came in, and caught them in the fact; and threatening to kill them both, the King was forced to difcover himfelf, and to purchafe his fafety with gold. Befides which, he gave the hufband all the land, from thence as far as the place now called Cuckold's Point, and alfo beftowed on him the whole hamlet; eftablifhing a fair, as a condition of his holding his new demefne, in which horns were both to be fold and worn. A fermon is preached on the fair day in the church: which is one of the handfomeft in the county. It was beautified and repaired by Sir Adam Newton, Bart. who was tutor to King James the Firft's fon, Prince Henry: this manor being granted by this monarch to that gentleman. At the entrance of the village ftands the antient Manor-Houfe built by Sir Adam Newton. The two laft Earls of Egmont inhabited this manfion fome years ago; but it is now in the poffeffion of Mr. Jones, who married the heirefs of it. It is a ftately Gothic ftructure, with four turrets on the top; the court before the houfe is

fpa-

A View of the Manor House at Charlton, built by Sire Adam Newton.

A View of Woolwich.

ſpacious ; and there are two large Gothic piers to the gates ; and on the outſide of the wall is a long row of ſome of the oldeſt cypreſs trees in England. Behind the houſe are large gardens, and beyond theſe a ſmall park, which joins to Wool-wich common.

WOOLWICH.

This is a market-town in Kent, about nine miles from London, and three from Greenwich, ſituated on the banks of the river Thames, and wholly taken up by, and in a manner raiſed from, the yards and docks erected there for the naval ſervice. In the reign of King Edward I. Woolwich was in the poſſeſſion of Gilbert de Mariſco ; and he held it, as half a Knight's fee, of Warren de Monchenſie, Baron of Swanſ-combe. But Queen Elizabeth, when the buſineſs of the navy increaſed, built here larger ſhips than were uſually employed before ; new docks and launches were erected, and places pre-pared for building and repairing ſhips of the largeſt ſize ; be-cauſe here was a greater depth of water, and a freer channel, than at Deptford. This is reckoned the mother-dock of the royal navy, and is ſaid to have furniſhed as many ſhips of war as any two docks in England.

All the buildings and yards belonging to the dock, are en-compaſſed with an high wall, and are very ſpacious and con-venient, and ſo prodigiouſly full of all ſorts of ſtores, of tim-ber, plank, maſts, pitch, tar, and other naval proviſions, as can hardly be conceived. Beſides the building-yard, here is a large rope-walk, where the biggeſt cables are made for men of war ; and on the Eaſt, or lower part of the town, is the Gun-yard, commonly called, *the Warren*, or *the Gun Park* ; where there is a vaſt quantity of cannon of all ſorts, for the ſhips of war, every ſhip's guns a-part, heavy cannon for batteries, and mortars of all ſorts and ſizes ; inſomuch that here have been laid up at one time, between ſeven and eight thouſand pieces of ordinance, beſides mortars and ſhells, almoſt beyond num-ber. Here is alſo the houſe where the firemen and engineers prepare their fire-works, and charge bombs, carcaſſes, and grenadoes, for the public ſervice.

The town has been of late years much enlarged and beau-tified, ſeveral fine docks, rope yards, and capacious magazines added ; and the royal foundery for cannon repaired and im-proved. The regiment of the royal train of artillery com-monly lies here ; and is an academy for inſtructing them in the art of gunnery. The Thames is here near a mile over

at high water, and the water falt upon the flood ; and as the
channel lies ftrait Eaft and Weft for about three miles, the
tide runs very ftrong, and the river is entirely free from fhoals
and fands, and has feven or eight fathom water ; fo that the
largeft fhips may ride here with fafety, even at low water.
The parifh-church of Woolwich is one of the fifty new churches, and is a very handfome edifice.   A weekly market is
kept in this town on Fridays.—There is a fortification near
Woolwich, on the river Ravenfbourn, the area of which is
enclofed with treble ramparts and ditches, very high and deep,
near two miles in compafs ; which is fuppofed to be a work of
the Romans.

Between Woolwich and Dartford is a village named *Erith,*
fituated on the banks of the Thames.   And on the brow of a
hill near this place, is a very agreeable feat, belonging to Sir
Sampfon Gideon, Bart.   It is called BELVEDERE HOUSE,
and commands a vaft extent of a fine country many miles beyond the Thames, which is about a mile and an half diftant.
This river and its navigation add greatly to the beauty of this
fcene,   which exhibits to the eye of the fpectator a moft pleafing
and delightful landfcape.   The innumerable fhips employed in
the immenfe trade of London, are beheld continually failing
up and down the river.   On the other fide are profpects not
lefs beautiful, though of another kind.   The proprietor of this
feat has very judicioufly laid out his grounds, and made many
beautiful viftas.   The houfe is but fmall, though an addition has been made of a very noble room ; this and two
others are finely furnifhed with a valuable collection of pictures by the greateft mafters ; among which are the following:
a portrait of Sir John Gage, by Hans Holbein ;   St. Catherine,
by Leonardo da Vinci ;   Rembrandt painting an old woman, by
himfelf ;   Snyders with his wife and child, by Rubens ;   Boors
at cards, by Teniers ;   the Marriage in Cana of Galilee, by
Paul Veronefe ;   the genealogy of Chrift, by Albert Durer ;
Herod confulting the wife men, by Rembrandt ;   and Mars and
Venus, by Paul Veronefe.

D A R T F O R D.

This is an handfome large town, fixteen miles from London.
But it is more properly called *Darentford,* from its being fituated on the river Darent, which runs through it, and at a fmall
diftance falls into the Thames.   On this river the firft paper-
mill in England was erected by Sir John Spilman, who obtained

Belvidere House, the Seat of Sir Sampson Gideon Bar.t

tained a patent, and 200l. a year from K. Charles I. to enable him to carry on that manufacture : and on this river was
also the first mill for flitting iron bars for making wire. The
town is full of inns and other public houses, on account of
its being a great thoroughfare to Canterbury and Dover. Here
is a harbour for barges, and the town is finely watered by two
or three good springs. King Edward III. had a general tournament performed here by his Nobles, and also here founded
a convent, whose Abbess and Nuns were, for the most part,
of the noblest families in this kingdom ; and this convent King
Henry VIII. turned into a palace. King Henry VI. founded
an alms-house here for five poor decripid men. There is a
market here on Saturdays, which is generally well stored with
corn, and other provisions; and much frequented by corn-
chandlers and meal-men. Here is also an annual fair on the
2d of August for horses and bullocks. There is a large gunpowder mill here ; and it is very remarkable, that though it
has been blown up four times, between the years 1730 and
1738, yet no one ever received any personal damage by these
misfortunes. This town gives the title of Viscount to the Earl
of Jersey.

Crayford is a small town near Dartford, which obtained its
name from its having anciently a ford over the river Cray, or
Crouch, a little above its influx into the Thames. This place
is famous for a battle fought near it, between the Britons and
Saxons, commanded by Hengist, A. D. 457, in which the Britons were overthrown. In the adjacent heath and fields, are
several caves, supposed to have been formed by the Saxons as
places of security and shelter for their wives, children, and effects, during their wars with the Britons.

There are also several villages in Kent, which take their
names from the small river Cray, on the banks of which they
are situated. This stream rises a little to the south-west of St.
Mary Cray, runs by that town, and passing by Paul's Cray,
Foot's Cray, and North Cray, runs into the Darent, near its
conflux with the Thames at Dartford creek, opposite to Pur-
fleet. The principal of these places is St. Mary Cray, about
which are many woods of Birch, from which the broom-makers in Kent-street, Southwark, are supplied.

At *Foot's Cray*, which is about twelve miles from London,
Mr. Harene has a very fine seat, which was built by the late
Bouchier Cleeve, Esq; after a design of Palladio, of the Ionic
order,

order, and is very elegant. The original defign had four porticos, three of which are filled up in order to gain more room.
The hall is octagonal, and has a gallery round which conveys
you to the bed-chambers. It is enlightened from the top, and is
very beautiful. The edifice is built of ftone, but the offices,
which are on each fide at fome diftance, are brick. The houfe
ftands on a rifing ground, with a gradual defcent from it till
you come to the water, which from the houfe appears to be a
fmall river gliding along through the whole length of the
ground : and in that part of the water which is oppofite to the
houfe, there is a fine cafcade conftantly flowing out of it. But
this water, which appears to be fuch a pretty natural ftream,
and which has fo pleafing an effect, is in reality artificial, and
is brought from the river Cray, which runs juft by. When the
canal or cut, which is made through the ground to receive the
water from the river, is full, it forms the cafcade before the
houfe, by flowing over in that place, and the furplus water being inftantly buried in the ground, is again conveyed under this
cut or canal to the main ftream. The chief beauty of the
ground about the houfe confifts in its fimplicity, it being entirely
without ornament, and the whole of it a kind of lawn, having
little befides the plain turf. The fituation is pleafant, and the
profpect from the houfe very good. The difpofition of the
rooms within the houfe appears to be very convenient, and the
feveral apartments are elegantly finifhed. The gallery, which
extends the whole length of the North front of the houfe, is a
very grand room, and is filled with pictures by the moft eminent mafters.

Near the road from Dartford (of which we have lately
fpoken) to Gravefend, is a large common called *Dartford
Brink*, where Edward III. held a folemn tournament in the
year 1331. The conteft between the families of York and Lan-
cafter began here, when Richard Plantagenet, Duke of York,
&c. A. D. 1452, brought together on this fpot an army of ten
thoufand men. At prefent it is the theatre of more peaceful
fcenes, as appears by the booths erected on a part of it, in
which the fpectators behold the great cricket-matches that are
played on this agreeable fpot.

About half a mile to the left of the road, between Dartford
and Gravefend, is the venerable church of *Stone*, which has in
it feveral ancient monuments. The manfion called Stone-caftle
is to the right of the road : the ancient ftructure is gone to
ruins, and a modern building erected in its place, which is
now

A View of Foots-Cray Place, in the County of Kent.

A View of Gravesend in the County of Kent.

A View of the River Thames near Northfleet.

now the habitation of John Talbot, Efq. Greenhithe is a romantic fituation on the bank of the Thames; on the left, are a number of large pits, from which are fhipped innumerable tons of chalk and lime. Beyond the eighteenth mile ftone, on the left hand, is the feat of the late John Calcraft, Efq. one of the reprefentatives of the city of Rochefter. The houfe is very convenient, and the gardens beautifully romantic: from a fpacious and elegant room at the weft end of the houfe, as well as from various parts of the gardens, the eye is entertained with views of the river, and the whole Effex fhore, that are perfectly enchanting: and upon the whole it is one of the moft delightful fpots on the bank of the Thames.

The country about Greenhithe and Swanfcomb is famous for being the rendezvous of the Danifh free-booters, who drew their fleet into the inlet or rivulet that formerly was pretty deep between the hills, on which Northfleet and Swanfcomb are fituated: the latter place derives its name from a captain of thofe barbarians, called Swein's camp. There remain ftill feveral fmall hills caft up by thefe free-booters, and called fconces, being ftations for a fmall number of men employed as centinels, when the camp was here.—Swanfcomb is alfo faid to be the place, where the Kentifh men, fheltered with boughs in their hands like a moving wood, furprized William the Conqueror, and, throwing down their boughs, threatened battle, if they had not their ancient cuftoms and franchifes; which he thereupon granted them.— There is a fair held here on *Whit-Tuefday.*

The afcent from this valley to Northfleet is lately made very eafy, and much improved. Between the road and the Thames is the feat of Thomas Chiffinch, Efq. pleafantly fituated.—The village of *Northfleet* is on an eminence near Gravefend, and is very ancient, for it is found recorded in Domefday book. The church contains feveral ancient monuments.

G R A V E S E N D.

This town, which is twenty-two miles from London, is a flourifhing and populous place; but the ftreets are narrow, and the pavement bad. Gravefend has changed its fituation fince the great increafe of trade in this nation, and approached nearer the river, as the chief fupport of its inhabitants. It was incorporated, together with Milton, which is at a fmall diftance from hence, in the 10th year of Queen Elizabeth's reign, by the name of the port-reeve, (which has been changed to that of Mayor) jurats, and inhabitants of the towns of Gravesend and Milton. Gravesend is situated on the river Thames, opposite to Tilbury Fort, and is a vast thoroughfare between London and Dover. Here is seated one of the block-houses for securing the passage of the Thames up to London; and this being the usual landing place for all strangers and seamen, occasions a great resort of all degrees of people; for whose accommodation there are held here two large weekly markets, on Wednesdays and Saturdays, well stored with all forts of provisions. Here all outward bound ships must stop and come to an anchor, when a searcher of the customs comes on board, and looks after the several cockets, which contain the entries of the several parts of the cargo, if of divers forts; and this is called *Clearing*.

In the reign of King Richard II. this town was burnt and plundered by the French; who, to make reprisals upon the English, for the ravage and plunder made in France by the English army, under the Lord Nevil, came up the Thames with their ships, and burnt and plundered this and several other towns, and carried away many of the inhabitants. But to enable the town of Gravesend to recover this loss, the Abbot of St. Mary le Grace, on Tower-hill, whom King Richard had granted a manor belonging to Gravesend, obtained that the inhabitants of Gravesend and Milton should have the sole privilege of carrying passengers by water from hence to London, at 2d. a head, or 4s. the whole fare; but the fare is now raised to 9d. a head in the tilt boat, and 1s. in the wherry. The former must not take in above forty passengers, and the latter no more than ten. The watermens company are by act of Parliament obliged to provide officers at Billingsgate and at Gravesend, who at every time of high water, by night and day, are at their respective places to ring publickly a bell set up for that purpose, for fifteen minutes, to give notice to the tilt-boats and wherries to put off; and coaches ply at Gravesend at the landing of people from London, to carry them to Rochester.

Gravesend being burnt down in the year 1727, the Parliament in 1731, granted 5000l. for rebuilding its church, which stood near the high road, but is now nearer the river, and is a new and elegant building. Here is a very handsome charitable foundation, Mr. Henry Pinnock having in 1624, given twenty-one dwelling houses, and a house for a master-weaver to employ the poor: and a good estate is
also

alfo fettled for repairs.——In the reign of Queen Elizabeth, the Lord-mayor, aldermen, and companies of the city of London, were ordered by her Majefty to receive all eminent ftrangers and foreign ambafladors at Gravefend, in their formalities, and fo to attend them up to London in their barges, if they came by water. If they came by land, they met them at Shooter's Hill, or on Blackheath, on horfe-back.

Within a few years paft, great improvements have been made in the lands near this town, by turning them into kitchen gardens, with the produce of which Gravefend not only fupplies the neighbouring places for feveral miles round, but alfo fends great quantities to the London markets. There are two annual fairs held here, one on the 23d of April, and the other on the 24th of October, for horfes, cloathes, toys, and other goods.

Tilbury Fort, which is in the county of Effex, oppofite to Gravefend, is a regular fortification, planned by Sir Martin Beckman, chief engineer to Charles II. with baftions, the largeft of any in England. It has a double moat; the innermoft of which is 180 feet broad, with a good counterfcarp, a covered way, ravelins and tenailles, and a platform, on which 106 cannon are placed, from 24 to 46 pounders each, befides fmaller ones planted between them, and the baftions and curtains, alfo planted with guns; and here is a high tower, called the Block Houfe, which is faid to have been built in the reign of Queen Elizabeth. On the land fide are two redoubts of brick; and there it is able to lay the whole level under water. The four proconfular ways made in Britain by the Romans croffed each other here. Great part of the land in this level, which is formed of thofe unhealthy marfhes, called the *Three Hundreds*, is held by the farmers, cowkeepers, and grazing butchers of London, who generally ftock them with Lincoln-fhire and Leicefterfhire weathers, which they buy in Smith-field, in September and October, and feed them here till Chrift-mas or Candlemas; and this is what the butchers call right Marfh mutton.

BROMLEY.

This is a fmall town, fituated on the river Ravenfbourn, in Kent, at the diftance of ten miles from London. The Bifhop of Rochefter has a palace here. King Edgar is faid to have given this manor to the Bifhops of that fee in the

year

year 955. Here is an Hofpital erected by Dr. Warner, Bifhop of Rochefter, in the reign of King Gharles II. for twenty poor Clergymen's widows, with an allowance of 20l. a year each, and 50l. a year to the chaplain. There is a mineral fpring here, the water of which has been found, by a chemical analyfis, to contain the fame qualities as the Tunbridge water, in a greater degree. A market is kept here every Thurfday, and two annual fairs, one on the 3d of February, and the other on the 5th of Auguft, for horfes, bullocks, fheep, and hogs.

Chefilhurft, or *Chiflehurft*, which is about three miles from Bromley, is famous for being the retirement of our celebrated Camden, who refided here for feveral years, and here com-. pofed the greateft part of the Annals of the reign of Queen Elizabeth. He died here in 1623, but his body was carried to London, and buried in Weftminfter-abbey. At this place alfo that great ftatefman, Sir Francis Walfingham, was born.

E L T H A M.

This is a pleafant town, feven miles from London, in the midway between Bromley and the Thames. It is full of good houfes, and fome families of rich citizens inhabit here. There was formerly a royal palace here, which fome fay was built by Anthony Beck, Bifhop of Durham, who beftowed it upon Queen Eleanor, the wife of Edward I. but others fay there was formerly a royal palace here before that time. However, King Edward II. conftantly refided in this palace, and his fon being born here, was on that account called John Eltham. The palace here was much enlarged by the fucceeding Kings, who when the court was kept at Greenwich, often retired hither. There are, however, no traces of the palace now remaining. Here are two charity fchools. The feat of Sir John Shaw is at a fmall diftance from Eltham.

L E W I S H A M.

This is a pleafant village upon the Tunbridge road, near three miles from Eltham, and fouth weft of Blackheath; and a little beyond the five mile ftone upon that road, on the eaft of the village, lie the pleafant gardens of Mr. Blackwel, banker: they take in the valley, and the hill above it, to which the afcent is through a beautiful fhrubbery; and from
the

the summit of the hill you command a very rich prospect on all sides, with the public Tunbridge road at a quarter of a mile distance in the bottom. Upon the declivity of Blackheath, next Lewisham, is the free school, for the benefit of several parishes in the hundred of Blackheath. It is situated upon a very healthy spot. It is now, and hath long since been a considerable board-ing school, preserving at the same time the original institution. It was founded in the last century by Abraham Colfe, vicar of Lewisham, who bequeathed other charities to the parish of Lewisham.

DULWICH.

This is a very pleasant village in Surry, on the borders of Kent, five miles from London, in which and about the neigh-bourhood are many very agreeable country houses. Here are some very fine prospects, especially near the house of entertain-ment called the Green Man. In particular, the fine walk op-posite to this house, where from under a tree distinguished by the name of *the Oak of Honour*, you have a view as in a fine piece of painting, of the houses as well as churches, and other public edifices, from Putney Down to Chelsea, with all the adjacent villages, together with Westminster, London, Dept-ford, and Greenwich, and over the metropolis, as far as High-gate and Hampstead.

Dulwich is noted for the medicinal waters in its neighbour-hood, called *Sydenham Wells*; but more particularly for its college. This was founded and endowed in 1619, by Mr. William Alleyn, who named it, *The college of God's gift*. This gentle-man was a comedian, and a principal actor in many of Shake-speare's plays; and the cause which induced him to found this college is said to have been the following. He was once person-ating the devil, in some theatrical exhibition; and on this occa-sion, we are told, he was so much terrified, at the opinion of his seeing a real devil upon the stage, that he from that mo-ment quitted the theatre, devoted the remainder of his life to religious exercises, and formed the resolution of founding this col-lege. But the whole of this tale appears to be without foundation; and there is great reason to believe, that Mr. Alleyn was induced to the erection of this charitable foundation by much better and more rational motives. However, this college was founded for a master and warden, who were always to be

of

of the name of Alleyn, or Allen; with four fellows, three of whom were to be divines, and the fourth an organist; and for fix poor men, as many poor women, and twelve poor boys, to be educated in the college by one of the fellows as fchool-mafter, and by another as ufher. In this original endowment, he excluded all future benefactions to it, and conftituted for vifitors the church-wardens of St. Giles's, Cripplegate, St. Saviour's, Southwark, and St. Botolph, Bifhopfgate; who, upon any difagreement among them, were to appeal to the archbifhop of Canterbury, before whom all the members were to be fworn at their admiffion. To this college belongs a chapel, in which the founder himfelf, who was feveral years mafter, lies buried. The mafter of this college is lord of the manor, for a confiderabe extent of ground, and enjoys all the affluence and eafe of the Prior of a monaftery. Both he and the Warden, muft be unmarried, and are for ever debarred the privilege of entering that ftate, on pain of being excluded the college; but as the Warden always fucceeds upon the death of the Mafter, great intereft is conftantly made, by the unmarried men of the name of Allen, to obtain the poft of Warden.

The original edifice is in the old tafte; but part of it has been lately pulled down, and rebuilt with greater elegance, out of what has been faved from the produce of the eftate. The Mafter's rooms are richly adorned with very noble old furniture, which he is obliged to purchafe on his entering into that ftation; and for his ufe there is a library, to which every Mafter generally adds a number of books. The college is alfo accommodated with a very pleafant garden, adorned with walks, and a great profufion of fruit trees and flowers.

It appears that Mr. Alleyn, the founder of this college, was one of the beft actors of the age in which he lived; and is celebrated by Ben Jonfon as fuperior to the ancient Rofcius. He was mafter of the Fortune play-houfe near Whitecrofs-ftreet, in London, which was erected by himfelf. He is faid to have been diftinguifhed by his moral qualities as a man, as well as by his abilities in his profeffion. Befides being a player himfelf, and mafter of a play-houfe, he was alfo keeper of the King's wild beafts, or mafter of the royal bear garden. But after the erection of this college, it is obferved by an old writer, that " this famous man was fo e-" qually mingled with humility and charity, that he became

" his

" his own penfioner; humbly fubmitting himfelf to that pro-
" portion of diet and cloathes, which he had beftowed on
" others."

There is a fair held at Dulwich on the 25th and 26th
of May for toys.—Not far from hence is *Norwood*, which ufed
to be noted for the refidence of certain gypfies here, to whom
many credulous perfons reforted for the purpofe of having their
fortunes told.

Stretham is a village in this neighbourhood, at the diftance
of fix miles fouth weft of London, and three miles to the
north of Croydon, which ufed to be much frequented for
its medicinal waters. It has a charity-fchool, and a feat
belonging to the Duke of Bedford, who is Lord of the
manor.

C R O Y D O N.

This is a large and populous town in Surry, fituated on the
edge of Banfted Downs, ten miles and a half from London:
'Tis faid there was once a royal palace in this place, which was
given with the manor to the Archbifhops of Canterbury, who
converted it into a palace for themfelves; but is now much decayed. Archbifhop Whitgift founded an hofpital here, which he
endowed with farms for the fupport of a warden, and twenty-
eight men and women, decayed houfe keepers of Croyden and
Lambeth, with a fchool for ten boys, and as many girls, with
20l. a year, and a houfe for the mafter, who muft be a clergyman. The church, which is efteemed the fineft and largeft in
the county, has feveral ftately monuments, particularly one for
Archbifhop Grindall, another for Archbifhop Sheldon, and another for Francis Tyrell, a grocer in London, who generoufly
gave 200l. to build the market houfe. Here is a great corn
market on Saturdays, chiefly for oats and oatmeal for the fervice
of London; and the adjacent hills being well covered with
wood, great quantities of charcoal are made and fent to
this city.—Croydon has two fairs, held on the 5th of July,
and the 2d of October, for horfes, bullocks, fheep, and
toys.

BEDDINGTON, which is at a little diftance from Croydon,
.; is the feat and manor of the ancient family of the Carews.
It is a noble edifice; but the wings are too deep for the body
of the houfe; for they fhould either have been placed at a
greater

greater diſtance, or not have been ſo long. The court before them is fine, as is the canal in the park, which lies before this court, and has a river running through it. All the flat part of the park is taken up with very fine gardens, which extend in viſtas two or three miles. It is ſaid that the orange-trees, which formerly grew here in the open air, have been killed by too great care to preſerve them. They had originally only moving houſes, to ſhelter them in winter, from the ſeverity of the weather; but ſome years ago, the owner was at the expence of erecting a fine green-houſe, with ſaſhes in front, ſince which time the trees began to decay, though they ſtood here in the open ground above an hundred years, and annually produced great quantities of fruit. The pleaſure houſe, which was built by Sir Francis Carew, has the famous Spaniſh Armada painted on the top of it, and under it is a cold bath. The church is a beautiful ſmall Gothic pile, built of ſtone, in the north and ſouth iſles of which are ſeveral ſtalls after the manner of cathedrals : and here is alſo two charity ſchools, one for boys, and the other for girls.

Carſhalton, which is on the ſouth-weſt ſide of Croydon, near Banſted-downs, lies among innumerable ſprings which all together form a river in the very ſtreet of the town, and joining other ſprings that flow from Croydon and Beddington, form one ſtream called the Wandell. Though this village is ſituated among ſprings, it is built upon firm chalk, and one of the moſt beautiful ſpots on that ſide of London, on which account it has many fine houſes belonging to the citizens of London, ſome of them built with ſuch grandeur and expence, that they might be rather taken for ſeats of the nobility, than the country houſes of citizens and merchants. Mr. Scawen intended to build a magnificent houſe here in a fine park which is walled round, and vaſt quantities of ſtone and other materials were collected by him for this purpoſe; but the deſign was never carried into execution. Here alſo Dr. Ratcliff built a very fine houſe, which afterwards belonged to Sir John Fellows, who added gardens and curious water works. It is at length paſſed into the poſſeſſion of the Lord Hardwicke, who ſold it to the late William Mitchell, Eſq. In levelling the road near this place, to make an avenue to a gentleman's ſeat, a large quantity of human bones was found.

Woodcote,

Woodcote, or *Woodcote-warren*, which is three miles fouth-weft of Croydon, is thought to have been anciently a city. Dr. Gale, who narrowly examined it, tells us, that there are found much rubbifh of buildings, the foundations of houfes, plain marks of ftreets and lanes, fquared ftones, many wells, at fmall diftances from each other, befides other marks of antiquity. Camden takes this to have been the Noviomagus of Ptolemy; becaufe it agrees exactly with the diftances from London and other places.

B L E C H I N G L E Y.

This is a fmall antient parliamentary borough by prefcription, having had that privilege ever fince parliaments had a being; yet has no market, but has fairs on June 11, and November 2. It is twenty miles from London. The town ftands on a hill, on the fide of Holmfdale, with a fine profpect as far as the South Downs and Suffex. Here is an alms-houfe and a free-fchool. It has an handfome church, which had a fpire, but in 1608 was confumed by lightning, and all the bells melted.

Godftone, which is a village two miles north-eaft of Blechingley, is famous for its quarries of excellent ftone. A part of this village lies in the road leading to Eaft-Grinftead; but the other part, as well as the church, ftands upon an eminence at a confiderable diftance.

Tandridge, which is a village three miles eaft of Blechingley, was once fo confiderable as to give name to the hundred in which it ftands, and had a priory of black canons, of the order of St. Auguftine, founded by Odo de Dammartin, in the reign of King Richard I. It was appointed for three priefts, and for the fupport and maintenance of the fick and poor, and the hofpitable entertainment of travellers.

G A T T O N.

This place is eighteen miles from London, and was formerly a confiderable town, but it has at prefent no market, though it fends two members to parliament. It is a very ancient place, and fome are of opinion that it was a Roman ftation, from the coins and other antiquities that have been difcovered here: and where the manor-houfe ftands, it is faid there was once a caftle. The river Mole rifes in this parifh, which is alfo noted for a quarry of white free ftone, which

L   is is foft, and endures the fire admirably well in winter, but neither fun nor air. 'Tis much ufed by chymifts, bakers, and glafs houfes.

B A N S T E D.

This is a village noted for abundance of walnut trees, but more for its neighbouring Downs, one of the moft delightful fpots in England. It is particularly rendered fo by the agreeable feats around it; and by its fine carpet-ground, covered with fhort herbage, perfumed with thyme and juniper, which makes the mutton of this tract, though fmall, remarkably fweet. There is here a fine profpect of feveral counties on both fides the Thames, including a view of the Royal Palaces of Windfor, Hampton Court, and alfo of London, from the Tower to Weftminfter, it being a tract of no lefs than thirty miles, extending from Croydon to Farnham, though under different appellations. There is a four mile courfe here, which, in the feafon of horfe-races, is much frequented, as all Banfted Downs are, throughout the whole fummer, for their wholefome air.

E P S O M.

This is a well-built and handfome town in Surrey, fixteen miles from London. It abounds with many genteel houfes, which are principally the retreats of the merchants and citizens of London. It is extremely pleafant, and lies open to Banfted Downs. Its mineral waters, which come from a fpring near Afhted, were difcovered in 1618, and foon became extremely famous; but though they are not impaired in virtue, they are far from being in the fame repute as formerly; however, the falt made of them is valued all over Europe. It has been obferved, that there are here fo many fields, meadows, orchards, and gardens, that a ftranger would be at a lofs to know whether this was a town in a wood, or a wood in a town. A fair is held here on the 5th of Auguft, for toys.—In Hudfon's-lane here was Epfom-court, that ancient Saxon feat, long fince converted into a farm.

Adjoining to Epfom is *Durdans*, a fine feat belonging to the Earl of Guilford.——About two miles from Epfom is a village named *Ewell*, near which a magnificent palace was erected by King Henry the Eighth, that obtained the name of *Nonfuch* from its unparalleled beauty. The learned Hentzer, a German, who wrote his Itinerarium in the reign of Queen Elizabeth, fpeaking of this palace, fays, it was built

with

with an excefs of magnificence and elegance, even to oftentation. " One would imagine, fays he, that every thing in the power of architecture to perform, was employed in this work ; there are every where fo many ftatues that feem to breathe fo many miracles of confummate art, fo many cafts that rival even the perfection of Roman antiquity, that it may well claim and juftify its name of Nonfuch. The palace is fo encompaffed with parks, with deer, with delightful gardens, groves, and walks fo embrowned by trees, that it feems to be a place pitched upon by Pleafure herfelf, to dwell in along with Health. In the pleafure gardens, are many columns and pyramids of marble, and two fountains which fpout water : one has a pyramid, upon which are perched fmall birds that ftream water out of their bills. In the grove of Diana is the other fountain, where Acteon is reprefented turned into a ftag, as he was fprinkled by the Goddefs and her nymphs. There is, befides, another marble pyramid, filled with concealed pipes, which fprinkle all that come within their reach." Such is the defcription which Hentzer gave of this palace and gardens ; but the palace was afterwards fuffered to fall to decay ; and King Charles the Second giving it to one of his miftreffes, the Duchefs of Cleveland, fhe pulled it down and fold the materials, with which a new houfe was built by the Earl of Berkeley, and which afterwards came into poffeffion of the Earl of Guilford, and was named Durdans, of which we have juft made mention.

Mitcham, which is nine miles from London, is a well-inhabited village, much frequented by the citizens of London. Here is a fair on the 12th of Auguft, for cattle and toys.—At a little diftance from hence are two villages of the name of Towting, fituated near each other, and diftinguifhed by the epithets Upper and Lower. Upper Towting ftands in the road from Southwark to Epfom, and has an alms-houfe, founded in 1709, by the mother of Sir John Bateman, Lord Mayor of London, for fix poor alms-women, to be nominated by the heir of the family. This village is adorned with feveral fine feats belonging to gentlemen and citizens of London. Lower Towting is a mile and a half to the fouth-eaft of the former.

Martin, a village about a mile fouth-weft of Towting, is a place of great antiquity ; for here Kenulph, one of the Weft Saxon Kings, was flain in the houfe of his favourite miftrefs. Here was a magnificent abbey, founded by King

Henry

Henry the First, for canons of the order of St. Augustine, and dedicated to the Virgin Mary. The prior of this abbey sat in the House of Lords, and the abbey itself was endowed with great privileges, and very considerable revenues.

P E C K H A M.

This is a pleasant village in Surrey, in the parish of Camberwell. Here is the seat of the late Lord Trevor, built in the reign of King James the Second, by Sir Thomas Bond, who being deeply engaged in the pernicious schemes of that arbitrary and imprudent prince, was obliged to leave the kingdom with him, when the house was plundered by the populace, and became forfeited to the Crown. The front of the house stands to the north, with a spacious garden before it, from which extends two rows of large elms, of considerable length, through which the Tower of London terminates the prospect. But on each side of this avenue you have a view of London; and the masts of vessels appearing at high water, over the trees and houses up to Greenwich, greatly improve the prospect. The village of Peckham, which lies on the back side of the gardens, is shut out from the view by plantations. The kitchen garden and the walls were planted with the choicest fruit trees from France, and an experienced gardener was sent for from Paris to have the management of them; so that the collection of fruit trees in this garden has been accounted one of the best in England. After the death of the late Lord Trevor, this seat was purchased by a private gentleman.——There are also at Peckham several other villas, and neat houses of retirement, inhabited by the tradesmen of London, and those who have retired from business. It principally consists of one long street, and has a Dissenting meeting-house. Here is a fair on the 21st of August for toys.—*Peckham Rye* is a village on the south side of Peckham.

Camberwell is a pleasant village, situated about a mile to the northward of Peckham, and two miles from Southwark, in the road to Croydon. It has several pretty houses belonging chiefly to tradesmen of London, and a fair on the 18th of August for toys.

Clapham is a very agreeable village, three miles from London, and contains many pleasant houses. There is a small fair held here on the 27th of August.—On an hill near the road side stands the church, and there is an handsome school-house built by the parish, for teaching the children of the poor of the village.

Ken.

Lambeth Palace?

Kennington is a village near Lambeth, and is one of the eight precincts of that parish. Near it is Kennington Common, a small spot of ground on the side of the road to Camberwell, and about a mile and an half from London. Upon this spot is the gallows for the county of Surrey.

L A M B E T H.

This is a village in Surrey, situated on the Thames, between Southwark and Battersea. It is particularly famous for its containing, for several ages, the palace of the Archbishop of Canterbury. This structure was originally formed by Baldwin, Archbishop of that see, in the year 1188; who first intended to have raised a superb structure at Hackington, near this place; but the Monks, with whom he was at variance, obtained the Pope's mandate against it; when, taking down what he had erected, he removed the best of the materials to Lambeth, with which he built the palace, a college, and church, having before purchased the ground of the Bishop and Convent of Rochester, by a fair exchange.

In the year 1250, Boniface, Archbishop of Canterbury, having, by his arrogance, rendered himself hateful to the citizens of London, retired, for the security of his person, to this palace; and finding it in a ruinous condition, within the space of three years rebuilt the whole north side, the archiepiscopal apartments, the library and cloysters, the guard chamber, the chapel, and Lollards tower.

From that time this palace became the residence of the greatest persons of the church, and was soon enlarged by many additional buildings; Cardinal Pole built the gate, which, for that time, is a noble structure. The Lollards tower, which is thus named from a room in it prepared for the imprisonment of the followers of Wickliff, the first English reformer, who were called Lollards, was finished by Chichely, and remains a lasting memorial of his cruelty, and anti-christian spirit. It is a small room, twelve feet broad and nine long, planked with elm, and there still remain eight rings and staples, to which pious men were chained, for presuming to differ in opinion from that prelate. The spacious hall was erected by Juxon, and the brick edifice between the gate and this hall was begun by Archbishop Sancroft, and finished by the immortal Tillotson.

From the present structure being thus erected at different periods, it is not at all surprising that it has but little appearance of uniformity; but the edifice, though old, is in most

parts

parts strong; the corners are faced with rustic, and the top surrounded with battlements; but the principal apartments are well proportioned, and well enlightened: the Gothic work about it is irregularly disposed, and it is in itself irregular. Some of the inner rooms are too close and confined; but there are many others open and pleasant in themselves, with the advantage of being convenient, and of affording very agreeable prospects. For as this palace is situated on the banks of the Thames, it affords a fine view up and down the river, and from the higher apartments, a prospect of the country way.—The palace, with the rows of trees before it, and the church of Lambeth adjoining, when viewed from the Thames, make a very pretty picturesque appearance.

In this palace is a very fine library founded in the year 1610, by Archbishop Sancroft, who left by will all his books for the use of his successors in the archiepiscopal see of Canterbury. This library has been greatly increased by the benefactions of the Archbishops Abbot, Sheldon, and Tennison, and consists of 617 volumes of manuscript, and above 14500 printed books.

The church, which stands by the palace, is a very antique structure, dedicated to St. Mary. It has a square tower, and both that and the body of the church, are crowned with battlements. In this parish are eight precincts, denominated the Archbishop's, the Prince's, Vauxhall, Kennington, the Marsh, the Wall, Stockwell, and the Dean's precinct.—It is remarkable, that at Lambeth Wall is a spot of ground, containing an acre and nineteen poles, named Pedlar's acre, which has belonged to the parish from time immemorial, and is said to have been given by a pedlar, upon condition that his picture, with that of his dog, be perpetually preserved in painted glass in one of the windows of the church, which the parishioners caused to be performed in the south-east window of the middle isle.

This is a very large parish, and contains many hundred houses. There is a school here, which was founded by Richard Laurence, citizen and merchant of London, in the year 1661, for educating twenty poor children of the Marsh and Wall liberties of this parish, for which purpose he endowed it with 35l. per ann. And by the road side, from Vauxhall to Kingston, is an alms-house for seven poor women, built in 1618 by Caron the Dutch Ambassador, who resided in England 28 years.

In

In the Marſh and St. George's Fields, ditches were made when London was beſieged by the Daniſh King Canute, who turned the courſe of the Thames from about the King's barge-houſe to a place beyond the bridge; and it was here that Prince died in his cups.

VAUXHALL is one of the eight precincts of the pariſh of Lambeth; but is particularly famous for the pleaſantneſs of the gardens, which have been for many years converted into a place of elegant entertainment, during the ſpring and ſummer ſea-ſons. They were the beſt of the kind perhaps in the world: in the midſt of the garden is a ſuperb orcheſtra, containing a fine organ, and a band of muſic, with ſome of the beſt voices, and the ſeats or boxes are diſpoſed to the beſt advantage with re-ſpect to hearing the muſic. In moſt of the boxes are pictures painted from the deſigns of Mr. Hayman, on ſubjects admirably adapted to the place. But there are in the grand pavilion four pictures of his own hand, from the hiſtorical plays of Shake-ſpeare, that are univerſally admired for the deſign, colouring, and expreſſion. And in the ball-room there are ſome very fine hiſtorical pieces by Mr. Hayman, chiefly relating to the ſuc-ceſſes of the late war. The trees in theſe gardens are ſcattered here with a pleaſing confuſion. At ſome diſtance are ſeveral noble viſtas of very tall trees, where the ſpaces between each are filled up with neat hedges, and on the inſide are planted flowers and ſweet ſmelling ſhrubs. Some of theſe viſtas termi-nate in a view of ruins, and others in a proſpect of the adjacent country, and ſome are adorned with the painted repreſentation of triumphal arches. There are here alſo ſeveral ſtatues, and in particular a good one in marble by Mr. Roubiliac, of the late Mr. Handel, playing on a lyre in the character of Orpheus. As Ranelagh has its rotunda, ſo here alſo is a rotund and ball room, finely illuminated, in which is an orcheſtra with an or-gan, where, if the weather proves rainy, the company may be ſafely ſheltered and entertained. Some of the principal walks have alſo lately been covered in a very elegant manner. And when it grows dark the garden near the orcheſtra is illumina-ted, almoſt in an inſtant, with about 1500 glaſs lamps, which glitter among the trees, and render it exceeding light and brilli-ant: and ſoon after a very extraordinary piece of machinery has of late been exhibited, on the inſide of one of the hedges near the entrance into the viſtas: by removing a curtain is ſhewn a very fine landſcape illuminated by concealed lights; in which

the

the principal objects that strike the eyes are the cascade or waterfall, and a miller's house. The exact appearance of water is seen flowing down a declivity, and turning the wheel of the mill: it rises up in foam at the bottom, and then glides away. This moving picture, attended with the noise of the water, has a very pleasing and surprising effect both on the eye and ear. Every thing is provided in these gardens in the most elegant manner, for such company as chuse to stay and sup here.

NEWINGTON BUTTS.

This is a village extending from the end of Blackman-street, to Kennington Common, and is said to have received the name of Butts, from the exercise of shooting at Butts, much practised both here and in most other parts of England, in the reign of Henry VIII. to fit men to serve in the army as archers. The Drapers and Fishmongers company have alms-houses here. In the church-yard an handsome monument has lately been erected to the memory of Mr. Allen, a young man who was murdered in St. George's Fields by some of the foot-guards, when they were wantonly sent out to inflict military execution on an unarmed mob, at the time that Mr. Wilkes was confined in the King's Bench Prison. Several other persons were infamously butchered at the same time, under the pretence of suppressing a riot; for the Ministry rather chose to endeavour to intimidate the people, by these violent methods, and thereby bring them to a tame submission to every arbitrary measure, than to regulate their own conduct by the principles of law, and of the constitution.

BATTERSEA.

This is a village in Surrey, situated on the river Thames, four miles from London. It gives the title of baron to Lord Viscount Bolingbroke. The manor was given to that nobleman's ancestors, together with Wandsworth, by King Charles I. and Sir Walter St. John founded a free-school here for twenty poor boys, and endowed it with 200l. of which the interest was to put one or more of them apprentice; and the lady St. John also gave 100l. the interest of which was likewise to put a poor boy or girl apprentice every year. The gardens about this place are noted for producing the finest asparagus. A bridge has been lately erected from hence to Chelsea, on the opposite side of the Thames.

Two

Two miles to the fouth-weft of Batterfea is *Wandfworth*, a village that has feveral handfome houfes belonging to the gentry and citizens of London, and is faid to have obtained its name from the river Wandle, which paffes through it, under a bridge into the Thames. There are here copper-works, faid to have been firft erected by certain Dutchmen, and a fair held on Monday, Tuefday, and Wednefday, in Whitfunweek.

P U T N E Y.

This is a village fituated on the Thames, to the north-weft of Wandfworth, and oppofite to Fulham, to which it is joined by a bridge. Here is an old church, erected after the fame model with that of Fulham; and they are both faid to have been built by two fifters. That part of Putney which joins to the heath, commands a fine view, both up and down the river Thames; and here the citizens of London have many pretty feats. In the church, which ftands near the Thames, are feveral handfome monuments, moft of them modern. In this village was born the famous Thomas Cromwell, Earl of Effex, in the reign of King Henry the Eighth, whofe father was a blackfmith here.

Fulham is a village on the other fide of the Thames, in the county of Middlefex, four miles from London. In William the Conqueror's time this was held of the King by the canons of St. Paul's; and there is an ancient houfe here, which is moated about, and belongs to the Bifhop of London. King Henry the Third often lay in it. There is a toll paid for paffing over the wooden bridge from hence to Putney, not only for horfes, coaches, and all carriages, but even by foot-paffengers.

W I M B L E T O N.

This is a village in Surrey, three miles fouth of Putney church, where Ethelbert King of Kent was defeated in a battle by Ceaulin the Weft Saxon, in the year 568. Wimbletonhoufe ftands about half a mile fouth from the road, on Wimbleton-common. It was built by Sir Thomas Cecil, fon of the Lord Treafurer Burleigh, in the year 1588; and was afterwards General Lambert's, who had here the fineft flowergarden in England. The manor of Wimbledon was purchafed by Sarah Churchill, Dutchefs Dowager of Marlborough; and is now the property of Lord Spencer, together with a fine feat

M   the

fhe built here, which is adorned with a grand terrace walk, that has a fine profpect to the fouth. Wimbleton-common or heath, which is fuppofed to be as high as Hampftead Heath, is about a mile each way, and is adorned on the fides with feveral handfome feats.

Rochampton is fituated between Putney Heath and Eaft-Sheen, and is one of the pleafanteft villages near London, having in it feveral fine houfes of merchants; but they are fcattered about, fo as not to refemble a ftreet, or regular town.

EAST-SHEEN.

This is a pleafant village, fituated a little to the fouth of Mortlake, where is the fine feat of the Lord Vifcount Palmerfton, the fucceffor of Sir William Temple. The gardens were laid out and compleated by Sir William Temple, who fpent much of his time here. This eminent man was an excellent judge of gardening, and was very fond of his garden; in which he fomewhat refembled Epicurus, whom in this refpect he admired, and concerning whom he thus expreffes himfelf, in his Effay on *Gardening*. ' Epicurus (fays he) paffed his life
' wholly in his garden; there he ftudied, there he exercifed,
' there he taught his philofophy; and indeed, no other fort of
' abode feems to contribute fo much, to both the tranquility of
' mind, and indolence of body, which he made his chief ends.
' The fweetnefs of air, the pleafantnefs of fmells, the verdure
' of plants, the cleannefs and lightnefs of food, his exercifes
' of working or walking, but above all, the exemption from
' cares and folicitude, feem equally to favour and im-
' prove, both contemplation and health, the enjoyments of
' fenfe and imagination, and thereby the quiet and eafe both of
' body and mind.'

Barnes is a village in Surrey, almoft encompaffed by the Thames. It lies between Mortlake and Barn Elms, and is feven miles from London, and five from Kingfton.—*Mortlake* is fituated on the Thames, between Putney and Richmond, about one mile weft of Barnes. Here are two charity-fchools, and a famous manufacture for weaving tapeftry hangings.

ESHER.

A View of Esher Place in Surry.

E S H E R.

This is a village in Surrey, about seventeen miles from London, situated near Walton-upon-Thames and Hampton-court, of which last it affords a fine prospect, as well as of the other parts of Middlesex.

Esher Place was the seat of the late Henry Pelham, Esq. The house is a Gothic structure, built of a brownish red brick, with stone facings to the doors, windows, &c. It stands upon almost the lowest ground belonging to it, and has the river Mole gliding close by it and through the grounds. This house was originally one of those built by Cardinal Wolsey; but the late Mr. Pelham rebuilt the whole, except the two towers in the body of the house, which are the same that belonged to the old building, and the whole is rebuilt in the same style of architecture it was before, which uniformity is certainly better than an unnatural mixture of Gothic and modern too often practised. There is a fine summer house built upon a hill on the left hand as you enter, which commands the view of the house, park, and country round on both sides the Thames for many miles. The park and ground in which the house is situated appears quite plain and unadorned; yet perhaps not a little art has been used to give it this natural and simple appearance, which is certainly very pleasing. But in one part of it there is a pretty wilderness laid out in walks, and planted with a variety of ever green trees and plants, with a grotto in it, and seats in different places. The wood in the park is well disposed, and consists of fine oak, elm, and other trees, and the whole country round appears finely shaded with wood.

The grand floor of the house is elegantly finished, and consists of six rooms. The great parlour is carved and gilt in a taste suitable to the style of the house, with curious marble chimney pieces and slab. In this room are the portraits of Mr. Pelham, Sir Robert Walpole, afterwards Earl of Orford, Lord Townshend, the Duke of Rutland, the late Duke of Devonshire, and the late Duke of Grafton; a picture of Lady Catharine Pelham and her son is over the chimney. In the drawing room over the chimney, there is a picture of King Charles II, when only eleven years old, by Vandyke. The library is curiously finished, and there is a good collection of books in it.

CLARE-

CLAREMONT.

This fine feat, which is a little beyond Efher, and which was the property of the late Duke of Newcaftle, is now the feat of Lord Clive. The houfe was defigned and built by the late Sir John Vanburgh, in a whimfical ftyle of architecture. It was afterwards purchafed of Sir John by the late Duke of Newcaftle, who was at a great expence in improving the place. The ftructure, though fingular, does not appear to be irregular. It is built of brick with a deal of variety in it, and of confiderable extent, but not much elevated. The Duke built a grand room for the reception of company when numerous, which makes the ends of the houfe not appear fimilar. The houfe has a lawn in the front, fhaded on each fide with trees, and the ground behind it rifing gradually fhews the trees there alfo, fo that the houfe appears to be embowered by them, except juft in the front; and the white fummer-houfe with four little pinnacles, one at each corner, built on the mount which gives names to the place, when viewed from before the front of the houfe, rifes up finely from behind the trees, and altogether forms a very pleafing appearance. The park in which it is fituated is diftinguifhed by its noble woods, lawns, walks, mounts, profpects, &c. The fummer-houfe called the Belvedere, at about a mile diftance from the houfe, on that fide of the park next Efher, affords a very beauiful and extenfive view of the country quite round, yet that from the fummer-houfe at Efher Place is perhaps no way inferior to it.

CHERTSEY.

This is a market town in Surrey, nineteen miles from London, and ftands upon the bank of the Thames, over which it has a bridge. The inhabitants trade much in malt, which is fent in barges to London. Here is an handfome freefchool, which was erected by Sir William Perkins, who had a feat here. There are annual fairs here on the firft Monday in Lent, and on May 3, July 26, and September 14. Here was once an abbey, by the ruins of which the ftreets are fomewhat raifed. Sir Nicholas Carew, mafter of the buck hounds to Charles the Second, built a fine houfe here with the ruins of the abbey.—This is the place to which our celebrated poet Cowley retired, in the latter part of his life, and where he died. And in this retreat, as Sprat expreffes it, ' fome few

2   ' friends

A View of the Cascade at Ham Farm.

' friends and books, a chearful heart, and an innocent con-
' fcience, were his conftant companions.'

WEYBRIDGE.

This is a village in Surrey, four miles fouth weft of Hampton-court, which derives its name from a bridge formerly erected here over the river Wey. About this village are feveral fine
feats, particularly thofe of the prefent Duke of Newcaftle, and
the Earl of Portmore.

OATLANDS is the feat of Henry, Duke of Newcaftle, and
Earl of Lincoln. The park is about four miles round. The
houfe is fituated about the middle of the terrace, the majeftic
grandeur of which, and the beautiful landfcape which it commands, words cannot defcribe, nor the pencil delineate, fo as
to give an adequate idea of this fine fcene.

The ferpentine river which you look down upon from the
terrace, though artificial, appears as beautiful as it could do
were it natural ; and a ftranger who did not know the place
would conclude it to be the Thames, in which opinion he
would be confirmed by the view of Walton bridge over that
river, which by a happy contrivance is made to look like a
bridge over it, and clofes the profpect that way finely.

HAM FARM is the feat of the Earl of Portmore. The houfe
is a large handfome ftructure, built regularly of brick, with a
fine lawn before the garden front. The grounds about it confift of about 500 acres, 130 of which are laid out for pleafure,
befides a paddock of about 60 acres. Here is a fine command
of water, there being two navigable rivers, the Thames, which
comes with a fine bending courfe by the fide of the terrace,
and the Wey, which runs directly through the grounds, and
joins the Thames at the terrace. There is a fwing bridge over
the Wey, which may be turned afide at pleafure, to let boats
and other veffels pafs. The Wey is navigable up to Guildford
and other places. The terrace next the Thames is beautiful ;
and though it lies upon a flat, there are fome good views from
it, and from other parts of the gardens. This place was firft
beautified by the Countefs of Dorchefter, in the reign of
James II.

WALTON UPON THAMES.

This is a village in Surrey, fituated on the Thames, oppofite to Shepperton in Middlefex. It is faid that the laft mentioned

tioned county once joined to this town, till about 300 years ago, the old current of the Thames was changed by an inundation, and a curch deftroyed by the waves.

At this place is a very curious bridge over the Thames, erected by the public fpirited Samuel Decker, Efq; who lived in this town, and who applying to parliament for that purpofe, obtained in the year 1747, an act to empower him to erect a bridge there, and this admirable ftructure was completed in Auguft 1750.

It confifts of only four ftone piers, between which are three large trufs arches of beams and joifts of wood, ftrongly bound together with mortifes, iron pins, and cramps; under thefe three arches the water conftantly runs; befides which are five other arches of brick work on each fide, to render the afcent and defcent the more eafy; but there is feldom water under any of them, except in great floods, and four of them on the Middlefex fide are ftopped up, they being on high ground above the reach of the floods.

The middle arch, when viewed by the river fide, affords an agreeable profpect of the country, beautifully diverfified with wood and water, which is feen through it to a confiderable diftance. The prodigious compafs of this great arch to a perfon below, occafions a very uncommon fenfation of awe and furprize; and his aftonifhment and attention are encreafed, when he proceeds to take notice, that all the timbers are in a falling pofition; for there is not one upright piece to be difcovered; and at the fame time confiders the very fmall dimenfions of the piers by which the whole is fupported.

In paffing over this bridge, when you have proceeded paft the brick-work, the vacant interftices between the timbers, yield, at every ftep, a variety of profpects, which, at the centre, are feen to a ftill greater advantage. But though each fide is well fecured by the timber and rails, to the height of eight feet; yet it affords only a parapet of wide lattice work, and the apertures feem, even to the eye, large enough to admit the paffage of any perfon to go through, provided he climbs, or is lifted up; and as the water is feen through every opening to a great depth below, thofe unufed to fuch views cannot approach the fide without fome apprehenfions.

It would, indeed, have been eafy to have clofed thefe openings between the braces and rails with boards, but they are purpofely left open to admit a free paffage for the air,

in

in order to keep the timbers the more found, and that the leaft decay may be the more eafily perceived and repaired.

From this admirable bridge the nobility and gentry in this neighbourhood find a very agreeable benefit, efpecially as the ferries are dilatory, dangerous, and at times impaffable; and its being erected has caufed the roads thereabouts, in both counties, efpecially on the Surrey fide, to be greatly improved.

KINGSTON UPON THAMES.

This is a town in Surrey, twelve miles from London, which received its name from its having been the refidence of feveral of our Saxon Kings, fome of whom were crowned on a ftage in the market place. It is a populous and well built place, and in the reigns of Edward the Second and Third, fent members to parliament. Here is a fpacious church with eight bells, in which are pictures of the Saxon Kings who were crowned here, and alfo that of King John, who gave the inhabitants of this town their firft charter. Here is alfo a wooden bridge of twenty arches over the Thames; a free-fchool erected and endowed by Queen Elizabeth; an alms-houfe built in 1670 by Alderman Clive, for fix men, and as many women, and endowed with land to the value of 80l. a year; and a charity fchool for thirty boys, who are all cloathed. The fummer affizes for this county are generally held here. There is a gallery on the top of a hill here, that overlooks the town. Befides the above bridge, there is another of brick over a ftream, that flows from a fpring which rifes four miles above the town, and within the diftance of a bow fhot from its fource, forms a brook that drives two mills. Here is a good market for corn, and the town carries on a confiderable trade.

Hircomb's Place here was one of the houfes of Richard Nevil, Earl of Warwick, who was furnamed *the King-maker*, becaufe he placed Edward the Fourth upon the throne, and afterwards, dethroning him again, reftored Henry the Sixth. This famous nobleman, in fortune, power, and influence, was the moft confiderable fubject who ever appeared in England. In the magnificence of his living, and his unbounded hofpitality, he excelled all his cotemporaries. Whether he refided in town, or in the country, he always kept open houfe. At his houfe in London, we are told, fix oxen were generally eaten daily for breakfaft. Every foldier might come into his kitchen, and take away whatever meat he could carry off

upon

upon the point of his dagger ; which is not a stronger proof of the hospitality of this Lord, than of the plain and simple manners of the age in which he lived. It is said by some writers, that no less than thirty thousand persons lived daily at his board, in the different manors and castles which he possessed in England.

HAMPTON COURT.

This royal palace is delightfully situated on the north bank of the river Thames, about two miles from Kingston, fourteen from London, and at a small distance from a village called Hampton. This magnificent structure was built with brick by Cardinal Wolsey, who here set up two hundred and eighty silk beds for strangers only, and richly stored it with gold and silver plate ; but it raised so much envy against him, that to screen himself from its effects, he gave it to King Henry VIII. who, in return, suffered him to live in his palace of Richmond. King Henry greatly enlarged it, and it had then five spacious courts adorned with buildings, which in that age were so greatly admired by all foreigners as well as the natives, that the learned Grotius says of this place :

Si quis opes nescit (sed quis tamen ille ?) Britannus,
    Hampton Curia, tuos consultat ille Lares ;
Contulerit toto cum sparsa palatia mundo,
    Dicet, Ibi Reges, hic habitare Deos.

That is,

If e'er a Briton what is wealth don't know; let him repair to Hampton Court, and then view all the palaces of the earth, when he will say, Those are the residence of Kings, but this of the Gods.

In order to give a more perfect idea of this grandeur, we shall give a description of the ornaments of this palace, as they appeared in the reign of Queen Elizabeth, from an author who describes what he himself saw.

" The chief area, says he, is paved with square stone; " in its center is a fountain that throws up water, covered " with a gilt crown, on the top of which is a statue of Ju- " stice, supported by columns of black and white marble. The " chapel of this palace is most splendid, in which the Queen's " close is quite transparent, having its windows of crystal. " We were led into two chambers called the audience, or " chambers of audience, which shone with tapestry of gold

" and

" and filver, and filk of different colours; under the canopy
" of ftate are thefe words embroidered in pearl, VIVAT
" HENRICUS OCTAVUS. Here is befides a fmall chapel
" richly hung with tapeftry, where the Queen performs her
" devotions. In her bed-chamber the bed was covered with
" very coftly coverlids of filk. At no great diftance from
" this room we were fhewn a bed, the teafter of which was
" worked by Anne Boleyn, and prefented by her to her
" hufband Henry VIII. All the other rooms being very
" numerous, are adorned with tapeftry of gold, filver, and
" velvet, in fome of which were woven hiftory pieces, in
" others Turkifh and American dreffes, all extremely na-
" tural.

" In the hall are thefe curiofities : a very clear looking
" glafs, ornamented with columns and little images of alaba-
" fter; a portrait of Edward VI. brother to Queen Elizabeth ;
" the true portrait of Lucretia ; a picture of the battle of Pa-
" via ; the hiftory of Chrift's paffion, carved in mother of
" pearl ; the portrait of Mary Queen of Scots ; the picture
" of Ferdinand Prince of Spain, and of Philip his fon ; that
" of Henry VIII. under which was placed the Bible, curioufly
" written on parchment ; an artificial fphere ; feveral mufi-
" cal inftruments : in the tapeftry are reprefented negroes
" riding upon elephants ; the bed in which Edward VI. is
" faid to have been born, and where his mother, Jane Sey-
" mour, died in childbed. In one chamber were feveral ex-
" ceffively rich tapeftries, which are hung up when the
" Queen gives audience to foreign ambaffadors ; there were
" many counterpanes and coverlids of beds lined with ermine.
" In fhort, all the walls of the palace fhine with gold and
" filver. Here is befides a certain cabinet called Paradife,
" where befides that every thing glitters fo with filver, gold,
" and jewels, as to dazzle one's eyes, there is a mufical in-
" ftrument made all of glafs, except the ftrings. After-
" wards we were led into the gardens, which are moft plea-
" fant." Such was the account given of the magnificence of
this palace, two centuries ago by Hentzner, the German.

This palace is, with the parks, encompaffed in a femi-
circle by the Thames. King William and Queen Mary were
fo greatly pleafed with its fituation, which rendered it capable of great improvements, and of being made one of the
nobleft palaces in Europe, that while the former was caufing
the old apartments to be pulled down, and rebuilt in the more

beautiful manner in which they now appear, her Majefty, impatient to enjoy fo agreeable a retreat, fixed upon a building near the river, called the Water Gallery, and fuiting it to her convenience, adorned it with the utmoft elegance, though its fituation would not allow it to ftand after the principal building was compleated.

Since the pulling down of the Water Gallery, which ftood before the fine ftone front that faces the river, the ground to the fouth weft has received confiderable improvements. This fpot is laid out in fmall inclofures, furrounded with tall hedges, in order to break the violence of the winds, and render them proper for the reception of fuch exotic plants as were moved thither in fummer out of the confervatories. Here are two bafons conftantly fupplied with water, for the fupport of thefe plants in dry weather; and as thefe are fituated near the great apartments, moft of the plants may be viewed from the windows.

At a fmall diftance to the weft, ftood a large hot-houfe, for preferving fuch tender exotic plants as require a greater fhare of warmth than is generally felt in this climate. Of this part of gardening Queen Mary was fo fond, that fhe allowed a handfome falary to Dr. Plukenet, a very learned botanift, for overlooking and regiftering the curious collection of plants fhe caufed to be brought into the garden; but fince her Majefty's death they have been much neglected, and very few of the moft curious plants are now to be found there.

The park and gardens, with the ground on which the palace now ftands, are about three miles in circumference. On a pediment at the front of the palace on this fide, is a bas relief of the triumphs of Hercules over Envy; and facing it a large oval bafon, anfwering to the form of this part of the garden, which is a large oval divided into gravel walks and parterres, laid out in an elegant manner, by thofe two eminent gardeners, London and Wife.

At the entrance of the grand walk, are two large marble vafes, of exquifite workmanfhip, one faid to be performed by Mr. Cibber, father to the poet laureat, and the other by a foreigner; thefe pieces are reported to be done as a trial of fkill; but it is difficult to determine which is the fineft performance. They are beautifully adorned with bas-relief; that on the right hand, reprefenting the triumphs of Bacchus, and the other on the left, Amphitrite and the Nereides. At the bottom of this walk, facing a large canal which runs into the park, are two other large vafes, the bas-relief on one repre-

　　　　　　　　　　　　　　senting

fenting the judgment of Paris; and that on the other Meleager hunting the wild boar.

In four of the parterres are four fine brafs ftatues. The firft is a gladiator, which formerly ftood in the parade of St. James's Park, at the foot of the canal, and was removed thither in the reign of Queen Anne. The original was performed by Agafias Defitheus of Ephefus, and is in the Borghefian palace at Rome. The fecond is a young Apollo; the third a Diana; and the fourth, Saturn going to devour one of his children: all after fine originals.

On the fouth fide of the palace is the privy garden, which was funk ten feet, to open a view from the apartments to the river Thames; in this garden is a fine fountain, and two grand terrace walks.

On the north fide of the palace is a tennis court: and beyond that a gate which leads into the wildernefs: farther on is the great gate of the gardens, on the fides of which are large ftone piers, with the lion and unicorn couchant, in ftone.

At the gates of the firft entrance into the palace, are four large brick piers, adorned with the lion and unicorn, each of them holding a fhield, whereon are the arms of Great Britain, with feveral trophies of war well carved on ftone.

Paffing through a long court yard, on each fide of which are ftabling for the officers of his Majefty's houfhold, we come next to the firft portal, which is ftrongly built of brick, and decorated by Wolfey with the heads of four of the Cæfars, Trajan and Adrian on one fide, and on the other Tiberius and Vitellius.

Thro' this portal we pafs into a large quadrangle, remarkable for nothing extraordinary, but its fpacioufnefs and uniformity. This leads to a fecond quadrangle, where over the portal is a beautiful aftronomical clock, made by the celebrated Tompion, on which are curioufly reprefented the twelve figns of the zodiac, with the rifing and fetting of the fun. the various phafes of the moon, and other ornaments, and indications of time.

On the left hand of this quadrangle is the great old hall, in which, by Queen Caroline's command, was erected a theatre, wherein it was intended that two plays fhould have been acted every week, during the time of the court's continuance there; but Mr. Colley Cibber obferves, that only feven plays were performed in it, by the players from Drury-lane, the

N 2   fummer

summer when it was raifed, and one afterwards for the entertainment of the Duke of Lorrain, afterwards Emperor of Germany. In the front is a portal of brick, decorated with four
Cæfars heads without names.

One the oppofite fide of this quadrangle is a ftone colonade
of fourteen columns, and two pilafters of the Ionic order, with
an entablature and baluftrade at the top, adorned in the middle
with two large vafes.

This leads to the great ftaircafe, adorned with iron ballu-
fters curioufly wrought and gilt, the whole erected on porphyry. From the cieling hangs, by a ftrong brafs chain, gilt,
a large glafs lanthorn which holds fixteen candles, and has an
imperial crown at the top. This ftaircafe, with the cieling,
were painted by Signor Verrio, an Italian, by order of King
William III.

At the top, on the left fide, are Apollo and the nine Mufes,
at whofe feet fits the God Pan with his unequal reeds, and a
little below them the Goddefs Ceres, holding in one hand a
wheat fheaf, and with the other pointing to loaves of bread ;
at her feet is Flora, furrounded by her attendants, and holding in her right hand a chaplet of flowers ; near her are the
two river Gods, Thame and Ifis, with their urns ; and a large
table in the middle, upon which is a quantity of rich plate, decorated with flowers.

On the cieling are Jupiter and Juno, with Ganymede riding on Jupiter's eagle, and offering the cup. Juno's peacock
is in the front : one of the Parcæ, with her fciffars in her
hand, feems to wait for Jove's orders to cut the thread of life.
Thefe figures are covered with a fine canopy furrounded with
the figns of the zodiac, and by feveral zephyrs, with flowers in
their hands ; and on one fide of them is Fame with her two
trumpets.

Beneath is a beautiful figure of Venus riding on a fwan, Mars
addreffing himfelf to her as a lover, and Cupid riding on another fwan.

On the right hand are Pluto and Proferpine, Cœlus and
Terra, Cybele crowned with a tower, and others. Neptune
and Amphitrite are in the front, and two attendants are ferv-
ing them with nectar and fruit. Bacchus is leaning on a
rich ewer, and, being accompanied by his attendants, places
his left hand on the head of Silenus, who fits on an afs that
is fallen down, he feeming to catch at a table, to which
Diana above is pointing. The table is fupported by eagles ; on
one fide of it fits Romulus, the founder of Rome, with a wolf ;

and

and on the other fide of it is Hercules leaning on his club. Peace in her right hands holds a laurel, and in her left a palm over the head of Æneas, who feems inviting the twelve Cæfars, among whom is Spurina the foothfayer, to a celeftial banquet. Over their heads hovers the genius of Rome with a flaming fword, the emblem of deftruction, and a bridle, the emblem of government; both in her right hand.

The next is the Emperor Julian writing at a table, while Mercury dictates to him.

Over the door at the head of the ftairs is a funeral pile, done in ftone colour; and under the abvoe paintings are thirty-fix pannels reprefenting trophies of war, and other decorations in the fame colour.——We fhall now proceed to give a particular defcription of the principal apartments of the palace, with their noble furniture and fine paintings.

The Guard Chamber.

From the ftair-cafe we pafs into the guard-chamber, which is very large and fpacious, it being upwards of fixty feet long, and forty feet wide. This room contains arms for five thoufand men, artfully difpofed in various forms. Fronting the door are three trophies of drums, hanging in an uniform manner under the windows five in each trophy. There are pilafters of pikes, bayonets, and bandaleers, on each fide fixteen pannels, which go round the room, with a great variety of decorations and figures, as mufkets in chequer work, ftars made of bayonets, fwords, &c. alfo circles, ovals, hexagons, and octagons; in the centers of fome are the famed Medufa's head, and of others Jupiter's thunder, and other devices carved upon a fhield: the fides are garnifhed with bandaleers.

The arms were thus difpofed by Mr. Harris, who was the perfon that firft contrived to place the arms in the fame beautiful order in the fmall armoury in the Tower of London, wich is univerfally admired, by people of all nations, who have curiofity to furvey them. This man was originally a common gunfmith, but after he had given fuch public proof of his ingenuity, he was allowed a penfion from the crown.

Over the chimney are the arms of England, &c. with the garter, and motto round them; and underneath is a neat cypher of a W, and over it the royal crown, curioufly carved in Walnut-tree.

On the right hand of the door as we enter, are the halbe ts

berts for the Yeomen of the guard, eighteen in number, and a little farther, fix large carbines, regularly placed on a table.

The King's first Presence-Chamber.

This room is hung with rich old tapeftry. The cieling is vaulted, and from the center hangs a fine lufture of nineteen branches. Fronting the door are the canopy and chair of ftate, which, as well as the ftools, are of crimfon damafk; on the back part of the canopy are the King's arms, and round the vallance, a crown and cypher embroidered in gold.

On the left hand of the entrance, behind the door is a fine picture about eighteen feet by fifteen, by Sir Godfrey Kneller, of King William III. who is in armour on a ftately grey horfe, trampling on the trophies of war, by which lies a flaming torch. At the top in the clouds Mercury and Peace fupport his helmet, decorated with laurel, and a Cupid holds a fcroll. On the bottom part of the picture appear Neptune and his attendants by the fide of a rock, welcoming the hero on fhore; and at a diftance is feen a fleet of fhips, their fails fwelled with the eaft wind. In the front ground Plenty with her cornucopia offers him an olive branch, and Flora prefents flowers.

Over the chimney is a whole length of the Marquis of Hamilton, Lord Steward of the houfhold to King Charles I. by Van Somer; and over the doors are two pieces of architecture, finely executed by Roffo.

The Second Presence-Chamber.

Over the chimney is a whole length of Chriftian VI. King of Denmark, by Van Somer. This picture, as moft of the large ones are, is decorated round the frame on the outfide with feftoons of fruits and flowers, beautifully carved in high-relief in lime wood.

Over all the doors are pieces of ruins and landfcapes by Roffo.

The hangings of this room are very antient tapeftry, but very rich, the lights being all gold, and the fhadows filk; the fubject of thofe on the left are Hercules and the Hydra; and thofe on the right Midas with his afs's ears.

The room is fpacious, with a vaulted cieling, from the center of which hangs a gilt chandelier of twelve branches. The chair of ftate and ftools are of crimfon damafk, fringed with the

fame

fame colour. Here are two tables of fine marble, which have pier-glaffes over them, with gilt ftands on each fide.

The Audience Room.

Over the chimney is a whole length of Elizabeth, queen of Bohemia, who was his late majefty's great grandmother, and the daughter of King James I. Her hufband, Frederick V. prince elector Palatine of the Rhine, and herfelf likewife, were driven out of their kingdom, for want of feafonable fupport of her father. She came over into England in the year after the reftoration of her nephew, King Charles II. and died about nine months after that in London, at the Lord Craven's in Drury-Lane, in the year 1662.

Over each of the doors in this room, is a madonna, by Dominico Fetti.

The tapeftry is fine ; the fubject on one fide, Abraham and Lot dividing their lands ; and on the other, God appears to Abraham in the front, and Abraham is purchafing a piece of ground for a burying-place.

The room is lofty : in the middle hangs a beautiful chandelier of filver, chafed, with fixteen branches. Between the windows are glaffes ; and under them tables, finely carved and gilt, ftand on each fide.

Here is a fine canopy of ftate, with window-curtains, chair, and ftools, of rich crimfon damafk, laced, and fringed with gold.

The Drawing Room.

Over the chimney-piece is a whole length of King Charles I. which is one of the fineft pieces of Vandyke ; and over the doors are two capital pictures ; the firft is David, with Goliath's head, by Fetti ; and the other, the holy family, by Corregio. The other furniture of this room confifts of a rich chair of ftate and ftools, two large marble tables between the windows, with pier glaffes up to the cieling, and two pair of fine gilt ftands : the window-curtains are tiffue, with a filver ground. There are fix filver fconces on the tapeftry, which is richly woven in with gold, but is very ancient ; the fubject, the fcripture-ftory of Abraham fending his fervant to get a wife for Ifaac.

The State Bed-Chamber.

Over the doors are two pieces of flowers, beautifully painted, by Baptift.

Over

Over the chimney is a whole length of the dutchefs of York, (daughter of the Lord Chancellor Hyde, and mother to Queen Mary and Queen Anne) painted by Van Somer; under which, and over the two doors, is a large collection of china, placed there by Queen Mary, who was peculiarly fond of that fort of ware.

The tapeftry is the hiftory of Jofhua, all round the room, which is very fpacious.

The cieling was painted by Verrio. The fubject of one part of it is Endymion and the moon: Endymion is lying with his head in Morpheus's lap, and Diana viewing him with the utmoft attention as he fleeps.

On another part of the cieling is a fine figure of Somnus, or fleep, with his attendants. In the border are four land-fcapes, and four boys, with bafkets of flowers, intermixed with poppies.

The bed is of crimfon velvet, laced with gold, and adorned with white plumes of feathers on the top. There are like-wife in this room, eight filver fconces chafed, with the judg-ment of Solomon upon them; a fine black and gold Indian fcreen; a large pier-glafs, ornamented with glafs, that is cut and tinged with blue; a marble table, and two gilt ftands: and in one corner, an eight day clock in a walnut-tree cafe.

The King's Dreffing-Room.

Over the doors are fine flower-pieces, by Baptift.

The cieling is painted by Verri; the fubject, Mars and Venus. Mars is fleeping in Venus's lap; feveral Cupids are ftealing away his armour; fome his coat, others his fhield, helmet, fword, and fpear; while others are binding him about his legs and arms with fetters of rofes. The border is em-bellifhed with jeffamine, orange-trees in pots, and feveral forts of birds.

The room is about twelve feet long, and fix wide; and in it are two windows, with rich window-curtains, a neat table between them, on which ftands a clock; and on the right hand is a curious weather-glafs. The hangings are of ftraw-coloured India damafk; the chair and fcreen are of the fame.

The King's Writing-Clofet.

Over each door is a piece of flowers, by Baptift, in a contraft tafte; and over the chimney is a fine picture by
Boug-

Bougdane of all forts of birds; the peacock in front, and the principal figure.

In the left hand corner is a curious weather-glafs; and in another part of the room, an Indian cabinet, filled at top with fine china, placed there by the late Queen Mary.

This clofet is of a triangular form, and has two windows. The hangings and ftools are of a pea green India damafk; there is a fine collection of china over the chimney, and a glafs there, fo placed, as to fhew all the rooms on that fide of the building at once.

Queen Mary's Clofet.

The hangings of this clofet are all needle-work, faid to be wrought with Queen Mary's own hand; there are alfo an eafy chair, four others, and a fcreen, all faid to be the work of that excellent Queen. The work is extremely neat; the figures are well fhadowed, perhaps equal to the beft tapeftry, and fhew great judgment in drawing. Over the chimney-piece is an old painting, faid to be Raphael's, reprefenting Jupiter's throne, by which is the thunder, and his eagle in the clouds.

The Queen's Gallery.

This is likewife called the tapeftry-gallery, and is about feventy feet long, and twenty-five feet wide. It is hung with feven beautiful pieces of tapeftry, reprefenting the hiftory of Alexander the Great, and done after the famous paintings of Le Brun; they are however not placed according to chronology, for fome of the laft actions of Alexander's life are placed before thofe which preceded them. Under that part of the tapeftry which reprefents the ftory of Alexander and Diogenes, and which is placed over the chimney-piece, is a very neat buft of a Venus in alabafter ftanding upon an oval looking-glafs, under which are two doves billing in baffo-relievo. Among the other furniture in this gallery, are two very fine tables of Egyptian marble.

The Queen's State Bed-chamber.

Overy the chimney piece is a whole length of King James I. painted by Van Somer.

On his right hand is Anne his royal confort, fecond daughter of Frederick, King of Denmark; and on his left, the Princefs Elizabeth, his daughter, who was afterwards Queen of Bohemia. Thefe were likewife both painted by Van Somer.

O   Over

Over the other door is a beautiful whole length, of that hopeful youth, Henry, Prince of Wales, eldest son of king James I. who died in the 19th year of his age, amidst the public rejoicings which were made for the reception of the Palsgrave, who was just come over into England, in order to solemnize his nuptials with the Princess Elizabeth.

The cieling of this bed-chamber was painted by the late Sir James Thornhill. The subject is, Aurora rising out of the ocean in her golden chariot, drawn by four white horses. In the cornice are four portraits, one on every side, 1. His late majesty King George I. 2. His late majesty King George II. 3. Her late majesty Queen Caroline. 4. His royal highness the late Prince of Wales.

In this chamber there is likewise a fine bed of crimson damask, two Indian sconces, and a glass lustre, with silver nozzles.

The Queen's Drawing-Room.

The cieling here was painted by Signior Verrio, in the middle of which is the figure of the late Queen Anne, representing Justice, with the scales in one hand, and the sword in the other; she is dressed in a purple robe, lined with ermine; and Neptune and Britannia are holding a crown over her head.

On the sides of the room are several other paintings of Verrio, representing the British fleet; Prince George of Denmark pointing to it; and the four parts of the world shewn by four figures; but these were thought so badly executed, that they are now quite concealed, and covered over with green damask hangings, upon which are placed nine pictures, three on each side, the length of the room, and three at the end; these pieces were formerly all in one, and of a prodigious length, as may be discerned by some parts of the figures, which have been cut asunder, some in one place and some in another. The whole is a triumph of Julius Cæsar, consisting of a long procession of soldiers, priests, officers of state, &c. at the end of which, that Emperor appears in his triumphant chariot, with Victory over his head, crowning him with laurel.

It is painted in water-colours upon canvas, by Andrea Montegna, who was a disciple of Jacobo Squarcoine.

The Queen's State Audience-room.

There are five whole length pictures in this room, all painted by Holbein. The first represents the Dutchess of Brunswick.

The

The second the Duke of Brunswick. The third the Marchioness of Brunswick, their daughter. The fourth the Dutchefs
of Lenox; and the laft, the Queen of Scots.

The canopy of ftate here is very rich; as are alfo the tapef-
try-hangings, the ftory of which is the children of Ifrael carrying the twelve ftones to the river Jordan, as related in the 4th
chapter of the book of Jofhua.

The Prince of Wales's Prefence-chamber.

Over one of the doors is Guzman, over another Gondamor,
two Spanifh Ambaffadors; over the third is Madame Chatillon,
the famous French Admiral's lady; and over the chimney
Lewis XIII. of France, with a walking-ftick in his hand, and
a dog by his fide; all four pictures by Holbein.

The tapeftry hangings are of green damafk, wherein is curioufly wrought the hiftory of Tobit and Tobias.

Here are two fine gilt ftands in the form of Termini, and a
canopy of ftate.

The Prince of Wales's Drawing-room.

This is hung with tapeftry, reprefenting Elymas the forcerer
ftruck with blindnefs; this is taken from one of the cartoons.
Over the chimney-piece is the Duke of Wirtemburgh; over
one of the doors is a whole length of the wife of Philip II. King
of Spain; and over the other, a whole length of Count Mansfield, general of the Spaniards in the Low Countries, all by
Holbein.

The Prince of Wales's Bed-chamber.

Over one of the doors, is a whole length of the Prince of
Parma, governor of the Netherlands; over the chimney-
piece is a whole length of the Duke of Lunenburgh; great
grandfather to his prefent majefty; over another door, Philip II.
King of Spain; and over a third, the Queen of Denmark,
confort of Chriftian IV. Thefe are likewife painted by Holbein.

The bed is of green damafk.

The private Dining-room.

Here are four pictures of the Spanifh armada, by Vander
Velde; and over the cimney, a very fine one by Van Dyke,

O 2

of

of the Lord Effingham Howard, Lord High Admiral of England.

The King's private bed-chamber is hung with fine tapeſtry, which repreſents the remarkable engagement at Solbay, in the year 1672.—In the *Cartoon gallery* were the celebrated cartoons of Raphael Urbin, ſo called from their being painted on paper. Theſe are ſeven pieces of ſacred hiſtory, taken from the New Teſtament, and were at fiſt deſigned only as patterns for tapeſtry. For theſe fine pieces Lewis the Fourteenth is ſaid to have offered 100,000 louis d'ors. The ſubjects of them are, 1. The miraculous draught of fiſhes; 2. The death of Ananias; 3. Elymas the ſorcerer ſtruck with blindneſs; 4. The lame man healed by Peter and John; Paul and Barnabas at Lyſtra; 6. Paul preaching at Athens; and 7. Chriſt's charge to St. Peter, commonly called the giving the keys. Theſe cartoons were the greateſt ornaments of Hampton-court; and attracted the admiration of foreigners, as well as natives of England; and it is ſuppoſed that ſome foreigners, lovers of the fine arts, have made voyages to England chiefly for the purpoſe of viewing them. But theſe admirable pieces have lately, with a *mean ſelfiſhneſs*, unworthy of a great Prince, been removed to Buckingham-houſe, or, as it is now ſtiled, the Queen's Palace, where they are concealed from the public eye. It is ſaid they were damaged by the removal; and it muſt be remembered, that they were not purchaſed by his preſent Majeſty, (which would have altered the nature of the caſe) but placed at Hampton Court by King William III. who built the cartoon gallery on purpoſe for their reception.

The Admirals Gallery.

In this Room are the Pictures of the following renowned Admirals.

1. Sir George Rooke.	9. Admiral Beaumont.
2. Sir Cloudeſly Shovel.	10. Sir Thomas Dilks.
3. Sir John Leake.	11. Admiral Benbow.
4. Lord Torrington.	12. Admiral Whetſtone.
5. Admirl Churchill.	13. Admiral Wiſhart.
6. Sir Stafford Fairborne.	14. Admiral Gradon.
7. Sir John Jennings.	15. Admiral Munden.
8. Sir Thomas Hopſon.	

All painted by Sir Godfrey Kneller, and Mr. Dahl.

The

The Queen's Stair-case

There is here a large picture, in a gold frame, painted by Vick, of King Charles II. and Katharine his Queen. The Duke of Buckingham is therein reprefented as Science, in the habit of a Mercury, and Envy is ftruck down by naked boys.

There are additional ornaments in the Mofaic tafte, on each fide of the ftair-cafe as well as the cieling, by Mr. Kent.

The New Quadrangle.

In the center of this fquare is a round bafon, and four large lamps on pedeftals of iron work; and on the right hand, over the windows, are the twelve labours of Hercules done in Frefco.

The Room of Beauties.

The firft is the Lady Pe-terborough,	6th. Lady Effex.
2d. Lady Ranelagh.	7th. Lady Dorfet.
3d. Lady Middleton.	8th. Queen Mary
4th. Mifs Pitt.	9th. The Dutchefs of Grafton.
5th. Dutch. of St. Alban's.	

Queen Mary was painted by Wiffing, and all the reft by Sir Godfrey Kneller.

We fhall conclude our account with obferving, that the whole palace confifts of three quadrangles. The firft and fecond are Gothic, but in the latter is a moft beautiful colonade of the Ionic order, the columns in couplets, built by Sir Chriftopher Wren. Through this you pafs into the third court or quadrangle, in which are the royal apartments, which were magnificently built of brick and ftone by King William.

PAIN's HILL.

This fine feat, which is near Cobham in Surrey, at the diftance of about twenty miles from London, belongs to the Hon. Mr. Charles Hamilton, who has made great improvements, by inclofing a large tract of barren land, which though fo poor as to produce nothing but heath and broom, he has fo well cultivated and adorned, that few places are equal to it. The whole

whole place is about five miles round : it is laid out in the modern taste, and planted with a beautiful variety of trees, plants, and flowers. The fine equalities of the ground give a perpetual variety to the prospects, especially on that side next the river Mole, which river though it lies lower than the level of the gardens by twenty feet, is brought into them by means of a wheel curiously contrived, which is turned by the river. Every time it turns round it takes up the water and conveys it through a spiral pipe from the circumference of the wheel to the center of it, from whence it is discharged into a trough, and from thence through pipes into the gardens, where by the joint assistance of nature and art, it is formed into a fine winding lake or piece of water, with an island in it, planted and laid out in walks with bridges over it of the most simple contrivance, and the whole surrounded with rising grounds, clumps of trees, and hanging woods, in as romantic and picturesque a manner as imagination can conceive. A collection of fine Italian and other paintings, brought from this elegant seat, have been just advertised to be sold.

S T A I N E S.

This is a market town, in the county of Middlesex, 17 miles from London, and derives its name from the Saxon word *Stana* which signifies a *Stone*, and was applied to this place from a boundary-stone, anciently set up here to mark the extent of the city of London's jurisdiction upon the Thames. It is a pleasant populous town, with several good inns, and has a bridge and a ferry over the river Thames; and being a lordship belonging to the crown, is governed by two constables and four headboroughs, who are appointed by his majesty's steward. Here is a market on Fridays, and a fair on the 28th of September. The church stands alone, almost half a mile from the town. From Stanes to Brentford, all that lies between thee high road along Hounslow, and the Thames, was called the Forest, or Warren of Stanes, till Henry III. disforested it.

On the south east side of Stanes is *Runny Mead*, celebrated for being the spot whereon King John was compelled by his barons to sign the famous charter of English liberties, stiled *Magna Charta*.

———*Near Thames's silver waters lies a mead*
Where England's barons, bold in freedom's, cause,
Compell'd their king to ratify her laws :

2 *With*

With conſtancy maintain'd the ſubjeĕt's right,
And ſerv'd a ſov'reign in his own deſpite.
On that fam'd mead, their honeſt claims to ſeal,
They riſk'd their private for the public weal;
Bravely reſolv'd to make the tyrant yield,
Or die, like heroes, on the glorious field.

Runny Mead is now divided into ſeveral encloſures, parcel of the demeſne of the manor of Egham.

E G H A M.

This town is ſituated on the Thames, in the county of Surry, eighteen miles from London, oppoſite to Stanes, and at the diſtance of four miles from Windſor. It is divided into four tithings, and being a thoroughfare from London to the weſt, has ſome very good inns. Here is an handſome charity ſchool, beſides alms-houſes, particularly one, built and endowed by Sir John Denham, one of the barons of the exchequer in the reign of King Charles II. for five poor old women, who have each an orchard. The parſonage houſe here was the ſeat of Sir John Denham, who rebuilt it, and who was the father of the celebrated poet of that name, who took great delight in it.

W I N D S O R.

This very agreeable town, which is twenty-two miles from London, in the county of Berkſhire, is ſuppoſed to derive its name from its *winding ſhore*, on the South ſide of the Thames. It is ſituated on a riſing ground: the principal ſtreet looks ſouthward over a long and ſpacious valley, chequered with corn fields and meadows, interſperſed with groves, and watered by the Thames, which glides through the proſpeĕt in a tranſfluent and gentle ſtream; and, fetching many windings, ſeems to linger in its way. On the other ſide, the country ſwells into hills, which are neither craggy nor over high, but riſe with a gradual aſcent that is covered with perpetual verdure where it is not adorned with trees.

This town was conſtituted a borough by King Edward I. with great privileges, ſuch as exemption from all tolls of bridges, markets, and fairs. It ſent members to parliament from the 39th of that prince's reign, to the 14th of Edward III. when it intermitted till the 25th of Henry VI. but has ſent two members ever ſince. It has charters from both King James I. and II. It is governed by a mayor, high ſteward, under-ſteward,
ward,

ward, a town clerk, two bailiffs, and twenty eight other perfons, chofen out of the moft fubftantial inhabitants, thirteen of
whom are called fellows or benchers of the Guildhall ; and of
thefe thirteen, ten are called aldermen ; from among whom
the mayor and bailiffs are annually chofen.   The members of
parliament are elected by the inhabitants paying fcot and lot,
who are computed to be in number about three hundred, and
the mayor is the returning officer.

The church here is a fpacious ancient building, fituated in
the high ftreet of the town, in which is alfo the town houfe, a
neat regular edifice, built in 1686, and fupported with columns
and arches of Portland ftone ; at the north end is placed in a
niche the ftatue of Queen Anne, in her royal robes, with the
globe and other regalia ; and underneath, in the freeze of the
intablature of the leffer columns and arches, is the following
infcription in gold letters :

Anno Regni VI*.
Dom. 1707.

Arte tua ,fculptor, non eft imitabilis ANNA ;
ANN*Æ vis fimilem fculpere? fculpe Deam.*
S. Chapman, *Prætore.*

And in another niche on the fouth fide is the ftatue of Prince
George of Denmark, her majefty's royal confort, in a Romam
military habit, and underneath is the following infcription :

Sereniffimo Principi
GEORGIA *Princpi* Daniæ.
Heroi omni fæculo venerando,
Chriftophorus Wren, *Arm.*
Pofuit. MDCC XIII.

In the area, underneath the town-hall, the market is kept every
Saturday, and is plentifully fupplied with corn, meat, fifh, and
all other provifions.

WINDSOR-CASTLE is the moft delightful royal palace in
England. It was firft built by William the Conqueror foon after his being eftablifhed on the throne of this kingdom, on account of its pleafant and healthful fituation, and as a place of fecurity ; was greatly improved by Henry I. who added many additional buildings, and furrounded the whole with a ftrong wall.
Our

Our fucceeding Monarchs refided in the fame caftle, till King Edward III. caufed the antient building to be taken down; erected the prefent ftately caftle, and St. George's chapel; inclofed the whole with a ftrong wall or rampart of ftone, and inftituted the order of the garter.

It may be proper to obferve, that William of Wykeham, afterwards Bifhop of Winchefter, was principally employed by Edward III. in building this caftle, and when he had finifhed it, he caufed this doubtful fentence to be cut on one of the towers.

THIS MADE WYKEHAM.

Which being reported to the King, as if that prelate had affumed to himfelf the honour of building this caftle, that Bifhop would probably have fallen under his Majefty's difpleafure, had he not readily affured his royal mafter, that he meant it only as an acknowledgment, that this building had *made him great* in the favour of his Prince; and had occafioned his being raifed to his prefent high ftation.

Great additions were in fucceeding times made to the caftle, by feveral of our monarchs, particularly by Edward IV. Henry VII. Henry VIII. Elizabeth and Charles II. This laft Prince, foon after his reftoration, entirely repaired the caftle, and though it had fuffered greatly by plunder and rapine, in the preceding times of national diforder, he reftored it to its ancient fpendor. As that prince ufually kept his court there during the fummer feafon, he fpared no expence in rendering it worthy the royal refidence; he entirely changed the face of the upper court; he enlarged the windows, and made them regular; richly furnifhed the royal apartments, and had them decorated with large and beautiful paintings, and erected a large magazine of arms.

In fhort, King Charles II. left little to be done to the caftle, except fome additional paintings in the apartments, which were added by his fucceffors James II. and William III. in whofe reign the whole was completed.

This ftately and venerable caftle is divided into two courts or wards, with a large round tower between them called the middle ward, it being formerly feparated from the lower ward by a ftrong wall and draw-bridge. The whole contains above twelve acres of land, and has many towers and batteries for its defence: but length of time has abated their ftrength.

The caftle is fituated upon a high hill, which rifes by a gentle afcent, and enjoys a moft delightful profpect around it:

VOL. I.   P   in

in the front is a wide and extensive vale, adorned with corn
fields and meadows, with groves on either side, and the calm
smooth water of the Thames running through it, and behind
it are every where hills covered with woods, as if dedicated by
nature for game and hunting.

On the declivity of the hill is a fine terrace, faced with a
rampart of free stone, 1870 feet in length. This may justly
be said to be one of the noblest walks in Europe, both with
respect to the strength and grandeur of the building, and the
fine and extensive prospect over the Thames, of the adjacent
country on every side, where from the variety of fine villas
scattered about, nature and art seem to vie with each other in
beauty.

When Queen Elizabeth resided at Windsor, she used to
walk on this terrace near an hour every day before dinner, if
not prevented by windy weather, to which she had a particular aversion. Wet weather was no interruption to her amuse-
ment there; for she took great delight in walking abroad when
the rain was only mild and calm, with an umbrella over her
head.—This noble walk is covered with fine gravel, and has
cavities, with proper drains, in order to carry off the rain, so
that let it fall never so heavy, none of it will lie upon the terrace; by which means it is dry, hard, and fit for walking on, as
soon as ever the storm is over.

From this terrace you enter into a beautiful park of the
finest green or lawn, which lies round this Royal Castle, and
is no small ornament to Windsor; it is called the Little or
House-Park, to distinguish it from another adjoining of much
larger extent; but this is computed to be four miles in circumference, and contains near 500 acres of land; it was enlarged
and inclosed by a brick-wall in the reign of the late King
William III. and is most delightful for its natural beauty, and
the many shady walks, especially that called Queen Elizabeth's
walk; which, on the summer evenings, is chiefly frequented
by the best company: the fine plain on the top of the hill, was
made level for bowling in King Charles IId.'s time, (an exercise
in which that Prince much delighted) and from hence is the
like extended prospect over the same most beautiful and well
cultivated country, and the river Thames. The lower part of
this park, under the terrace of the north side of the Castle, was
designed and laid out for a garden in the reign of Queen Anne;
but on the demise of that Princess, and in a country where
the beauties of nature are more attended to than the decorations
of art, this design was laid aside: in this park is constantly a
good

good ſtock of deer and other game, and the Keeper's Lodge at the farther end next the road ſide, is a delightful habitation. The preſent Keeper of this park is the Earl of Pomfret.

In the upper court of the caſtle, is a ſpacious and regular ſquare, containing on the north ſide the royal apartments, and St. George's chapel and hall; on the ſouth and the eaſt ſides are the royal apartments, thoſe of the Prince of Wales, and the great officers of ſtate; and in the centre of the area is an equeſtrian ſtatue in copper of King Charles II. in the habit of one of the Cæſars, ſtanding on a marble pedeſtal, adorned with various kinds of fruit, fiſh, ſhipping, and other ornaments.

The _Round Tower_, which forms the weſt ſide of this upper court, contains the governor's apartments. It is built on the higheſt part of the mount, and there is an aſcent to it by a large flight of ſtone ſteps; theſe apartments are ſpacious and noble, and among the reſt is a guard room, or magazine of arms. King Charles II. began to face this mount with brick, but only compleated that part next the court. The preſent governor of this caſtle is the Duke of Montague. His lodgings command a moſt extenſive view to London, and, as they ſay, into twelve counties. They alſo tell you, that in the guard-chamber, are the coats of mail of John, King of France, and David, King of Scotland, both priſoners h re at the ſame time. The royal ſtandard is raiſed on this tower on ſtate-holidays, or when the king or royal family reſide here. On the oppoſite corner of the royal buildings is _King John's Tower_, ſo named from its being the apartment aſſigned to that French monarch, when he was priſoner in England.

The _Royal Apartments_ are on the north ſide of this princely Caſtle, and commonly go under the name of the Star Building, from the garter and ſtar largely diſplayed in gold, and fixed in the middle of the building on the outſide next the terrace.

The uſal entrance into the apartments is from the upper court or ward, through a handſome Veſtibule, ſupported by pillars of the Ionic order, with ſome antique braſs buſtos in the ſeveral niches of no great account; and alſo figures of a Roman veſtal, and a ſlave in the action of picking a thorn out of his foot. The great ſtair caſe is finely painted with ſeveral fabulous ſtories from Ovid's Metamorphoſes, particularly the ſtory of Phaeton, who is repreſented on the dome petitioning Apollo for leave to drive the chariot of the ſun; and on the ſtair-caſe, in large compartments, are the transformation of

Phae-

Phaetan's fisters into poplars, their tears distilling amber from the trees, with this inscription, *Magnis tamen excidit Aufis, great events happen to the bold*: Also the story of Cycnus, K. of Liguria, who, being inconsolable for Phaeton's death, was transformed into a swan. Over these, and on the several parts of the cieling, supported by the winds, are represented the signs of the zodiac, with baskets of flowers, beautifully disposed, and at each corner are the elements of earth, air, fire, and water, expressed by Cornucopeas, birds, zephyrs, flaming censers, water nymphs with fishes, and a variety of other representations expressing each element; also Aurora, with her nymphs in waiting, giving water to her horses. In proper attitudes in several parts of this stair case, are also represented comedy, tragedy, musick, painting, and other sciences, and the whole stair-case is beautifully disposed and heightened with gold, and has a view to the back stairs, whereon is painted the story of Meleager and Atalanta. The painting of this stair-case was by Sir James Thornhill.—We now proceed to a particular description of the principal apartments.

The Queen's Guard Chamber.

This room, which is the first apartment into which you enter, is completely furnished with fire-arms, as guns, bayonets, pikes, bandaleers, &c. beautifully ranged and disposed into various forms, with the star and garter, the royal cypher, and other ornaments intermixed, cut in lime-wood. Over the chimney, is a full portrait of prince George of Denmark in armour on horseback, by Dahl, with a view of shipping, by Vandewell: on the cieling is Britannia, in the person of Queen Catharine of Portugal, consort to King Charles II. seated on a globe, bearing the arms of England and Portugal, with the four quarters of the world, viz. Europe, Asia, Africa, and America, and their respective symbols attended by deities, presenting their several offerings. The signs of the zodiack are on the outer part of this beautiful representation. In different parts of the cieling are Mars, Venus, Juno, Minerva, and other heathen deities, with zephyrs, cupids, and other embellishments properly disposed.

The Queen's Presence-Chamber.

On the cieling of this room Queen Catharine is represented attended by religion, prudence, fortitude, and other virtues: she is under a curtain spread by time, and supported by zephyrs, while fame founds the happinefs of Britain; below, Juftice is driving away envy, fediticn, and other evil genii. The room is hung with tapeftry, containing the hiftory of the beheading of St. Paul, and the perfecution of the primitive Chriftians; and adorned with the pictures of Judith and Holofernes; by Guido Reni; a magdalen, by Sir Peter Lely; and a Prometheus by young Palma.

The Queen's Audience Room.

On the cieling is Britannia reprefented in the perfon of Queen Catherine, in a car drawn by fwans to the temple of virtue, attended by Flora, Ceres, Pomona, &c. with other decorations heightened with gold. The canopy is of fine Englifh ve-vet, fet up by Queen Anne; and the tapeftry was made at Cob-lentz, in Germany, and prefented to King Henry VIII. The pictures hung up in this room, are, a Magdalen by moonlight, by Carracci; St. Stephen ftoned, by Rotterman; and Judith and Holofernes, by Guido Reni.

The Ball Room.

On the cieling King Charles II. is reprefented giving freedom to Europe by the figures of Perfeus and Andromeda; on the fhield of Perfeus is infcribed *Perfeus Britannicus*, and over the head of Andromeda is wrote *Europa Liberata*, and Mars attended by the celeftial deities, over the olive branch. On the coving of this chamber is the ftory of Perfeus and Andromeda, the four feafons, and the figns of the Zodiac, the whole heightened with gold. The tapeftry, which was made at Bruflels, and fet up by King Charles II. reprefents the feafons of the year; and the room is adorned with the following pictures, the Roman Charity, after Tintoret; Duns Scotus, by Spagnoletto; a Madona, by Titian; Fame by Palmegiani; the Arts and Sciences, alfo by Palmegiani; and Pan and Syrinx, by Stanick.

The Queen's Drawing Room.

On the cieling is painted the affembly of the Gods and Goddefles, the whole intermixed with cupids, flowers, &c. and eightened with gold. The room is hung with tapeftry re-fenting the twelve months of the year, and adorned with pictures of Lot and his daughters, after Angelo; Lady
Digby

Digby, wife of Sir Kenelm Digby, by Vandyke ; a sleeping
Venus, by Pouffin ; a family in the character of Mark Anthony and Cleopatra, by De Bray ; a Spanish family, after Titian ;
and a flower piece by Varellt.

The Queen's Bed-Chamber.

The bed of state is rich flowered velvet made in Spitalfields,
by order of Queen Anne, and the tapestry, which represents
the harvest season, was also made at London, by Peyntz. The,
cieling is painted with the story of Diana and Endymion, and
the room is adorned with the pictures of the holy family, by
Raphael ; Herod's cruelty, by Julio Romano ; and Judith
and Holofernes, by Guido.

The Room of Beauties.

This is so named from the portraits of the most celebrated
beauties in the reign of King Charles II. They are fourteen
in number, viz. Lady Offory, the Duchefs of Somerset, the
Duchefs of Cleveland, Lady Gramont, the Countefs of Northumberland, the Duchefs of Richmond, Lady Birons, Mrs.
Middleton, Lady Denham and her sister, Lady Rochefter, Lady
Sunderland, Mrs. Dawson, and Mrs. Knott. These are all
original paintings drawn to great perfection by Sir Peter Lely.

The Queen's Dreffing Room.

In this room are the following portraits ; Queen Henrietta
Maria, wife to King Charles I. Queen Mary, when a child,
and Queen Catherine ; these three are all done by Vandyke ;
the Duchefs of York, mother to Queen Mary and Queen Anne,
by Sir Peter Lely.

In this room is a clofet wherein are several paintings, and
in particular a portrait of the Countefs of Defmond, who is
faid to have lived to within a few days of one hundred and fifty
years of age ; also a portrait of Erafmus, and other learned
men.   In this clofet is likewife the banner of France annually
delivered on the fecond of Auguft by the Duke of Marlborough, by which he holds Blenheim-houfe, built at Woodftoc'
in Oxfordfhire, in the reign of Queen Anne, as a national r-
ward to that great General for his many glorious victories o'r
the French.

Green

Queen Elizabeth's, or the Picture Gallery.

This is richly adorned with the following paintings: King James I. and his Queen, whole lengths, by Vanfomer ; Rome in flames, by Julio Romano ; a Roman family, by Titian ; the holy family, after Raphael ; Judith and Holofernes, by Tintoret ; a portrait of Charles VI. Emperor of Germany, by Sir Godfrey Kneller ; the wife men making their offerings to Chrift, by Paulo Veronefe ; two ufurers, an admired piece, by the famous blackfmith of Antwerp ; Perfeus and Andromeda, by Schiavone ; Aretine and Titian, by Titian ; the Duke of Gloucefter, a whole length, by Sir Godfrey Kneller ; Prince George of Denmark, a whole length, by Dahl ; King Henry VIII. by Hans Holbein Vandenelli, an Italian ftatuary, Correggio ; the founders of different orders in the Romifh church, by Titian and Rembrandt ; a rural piece in low life, by Baffano ; a fowl piece, by Varelft ; the battle of Spurs near Terevaen, in France, in 1513, by Hans Holbein ; two views of Windfor caftle, by Wofterman, and two Italian maikets, by Michael Angelo. In this room is alfo a curious amber cabinet, prefented by the King of Pruffia to Queen Caroline.

There is here likewife Queen Caroline's china clofet, filled with a great variety of curious china elegantly difpofed, and the whole room is finely gilt and ornamented ; over the chimney are the pictures of Prince Arthur and his two fifters, the children of King Henry VII. by Holbein ; and in this clofet is alfo a fine amber cabinet, prefented to Queen Anne, by Dr. Robinfon, Bifhop of London, and plenipotentiary at the congrefs of Utrecht.

The King's Clofet.

The cieling of this is adorned with the ftory of Jupiter and Leda. Among the curiofities in this room is a large frame of needle work, faid to be wrought by Mary Queen of Scots, while a prifoner in Forthinghay caftle ; among other figures, fhe herfelf is reprefented fupplicating for juftice before the Virgin Mary, with her fon, afterwards King James I. ftanding by her ; in a fcroll is worked thefe words *Sapientiam amavi et exquifivi a juventute mea.* This piece of work, after its having lain a long time in the wardrobe, was fet up by order of Queen Anne. The pictures are, a Magdalen, by Carracci ;
a fleep-

a sleeping Cupid, by Correggio; contemplation, by Carracci; Titian's daughter, by herself; and a German Lady, by Raphael.

The King's Dressing Room.

The cieling of this is painted with the story of Jupiter and Danaë; and adorned with the pictures of the birth of Jupiter, by Julio Romano; and of a naked Venus asleep, by Sir Peter Lely.

The King's Bed Chamber.

This is hung with tapestry, representing the story of Hero and Leander; the bed of state, which was set up in the reign of King Charles II. is of fine blue cloth, richly embroidered with gold and silver; and on the cieling that Prince is represented in the robes of the garter, under a canopy supported by Time, Jupiter and Neptune, with a wreath of laurel over his head; and he is attended by Europe, Asia, Africa, and America, paying their obeisance to him. The paintings are, King Charles II. when a boy, in armour, by Vandyke; and St. Paul stoned at Lystra, by Paulo Veronese.

The King's Drawing Room.

On the cieling is King Charles II, riding in a triumphal car, drawn by the horses of the sun, attended by Fame, Peace, and the polite arts; Hercules is driving away rebellion, sedition, and ignorance; Britannia and Neptune, properly attended, are paying obeisance to the monarch as he passes; and the whole is a representation of the restoration of that monarch, and the introduction of arts and sciences in these kingdoms. In the other parts of the cieling are painted the labours of Hercules, with festoons of fruit and flowers, the whole beautifully decorated in gold and stone colour. The pictures hung up in this room are, a converted Chinese, by Sir Godfrey Kneller; the Marquis of Hamilton, after Vandyke, by Hanneman; Herodias's daughter, by Carlo Dolci; a Magdalen, by Carlo Dolci; and a Venetian Lady, by Titian.

The King's Public Dining Room.

On the cieling is painted the banquet of the gods, with a variety of fish and fowl. The pictures hung up here are, the portraits of his present Majesty, and the late Queen Caroline,

roline, whole lengths; Hercules and Omphale, Cephalus and Procris, the birth of Venus, and Venus and Adonis, the four laſt by Genario; a naval triumph of King Charles II. by Verrio; the marriage of St. Catherine, by Dawkers; nymphs and ſatyrs, by Rubens and Snyders; hunting the wild boar, by Snyders; a picture of ſtill life, by Girardo; the taking of the bears by Snyders; a night piece, being a family ſinging by candle light, by Quiſtin; a Bohemian family, by De Brie; divine love by an unknown hand; and Lacy, a famous comedian in King Charles the Second's time, in three characters, by Wright.

Many of the paintings in this room are beſt ſeen at noon by the reflection of the ſun; the carving of this chamber is very beautiful, repreſenting a great variety of fowl, fiſh and fruit, done to the utmoſt perfection on lime wood, by Mr. Gibbons, a famous ſtatuary and carver in the reign of King Charles II.

The King's Audience Chamber.

On the cieling is repreſented the eſtabliſhment of *pure religion* in theſe nations on the reſtoration of that *pious Prince*, Charles II. in the characters of England, Scotland, and Ireland, attended by Faith, Hope, Charity, and the Cardinal Virtues; Religion triumphs over Superſtition and Hypocriſy, which are driven by Cupids from before the face of the church; all which appear in proper attitudes, and the whole highly finiſhed. The paintings in this room are, Our Saviour before Pilate, by Michael Angelo; the Apoſtles at our Saviour's tomb, by Schiavoni; Peter, James, and John, by Michael Angelo; and the Dutcheſs of Richmond, by Vandyke. The canopy of this room is of green velvet, embroidered with gold, very rich, ſet up in the reign of King Charles II.

The King's Preſence Chamber.

On the cieling is Mercury, with an exceeding good original portrait of King Charles II. which he ſhews to the four quarters of the world, introduced by Neptune; Fame declaring the glory of that prince, and Time driving away Rebellion, Sedition, nd their companions. Over the canopy is Juſtice in ſtone colour, ſhewing the arms of Britain to Thames and his river nymphs, with the ſtar of Venus, and this label, *Sydus Corioli-ium*; at the lower end of the chamber is Venus in a ſea car,

drawn

drawn by Tritons and sea nymphs. This cieling is in all parts beautifully painted, and highly ornamented with gold and stone-colour. The painting in this room are, Henry Duke of Glou-cester, brother to King Charles II. by Vandyke ; the Countess of Dorset his governess, by ditto ; Father Paul the Venetian, by Tintoret ; the tapestry of this chamber, is the history of Queen Athaliah.

The King's Guard-Chamber.

In this spacious and noble room is a large magazine of arms, viz. pikes, pistols, guns, coats of mail, swords, halberts, bayonets, drums, &c. to the amount of some thousands, all beau-tifully disposed in colonades, pillars, circles, shields, and other devices in a most curious manner, ranged by Mr. Harris, late master-gunner of the castle, the same person who made that beautiful arrangement of the small arms in the great armoury in the Tower of London, and at Hampton Court, and whom we have before spoken of.

The cieling is painted in water-colours : in one circle is Peace and Plenty, and in the other Mars and Minerva. In the dome, is a representation of Mars, and the whole room is decorated with instruments of war adapted to the chamber. Over the chimney is a portrait, as large as life, of Charles XI. King of Sweden, on horseback, by Wyck. And over the door they shew the armour of Edward the Black Prince.

In this room the Knights of the Garter dine in great state at an Installation, in the absence of the Sovereign.

St. George's Hall.

This Hall is particularly set apart to the honour of the order of the Garter, and is one of the noblest rooms in Europe, both with regard to the building and the painting, which is here per-formed in the most grand taste. In a large oval in the centre of the cieling King Charles II. is represented in the habit of the or-der, attended by England, Scotland, and Ireland ; Religion and Plenty hold the crown of these kingdoms over his head ; Mars and Mercury, with the emblems of war and peace stand on each side. In the same oval, regal government is represented upheld by religion and eternity, with Justice attended by forti-tude, temperance and prudence, beating down rebellion and faction. Towards the throne is represented in an octagon St.

George's

George's crofs incircled with the garter, within a ftar or glory fupported by Cupids, with the motto,

HONI SOIT QUI MAL Y PENCE.

and befides other embellifhments relating to the order, the mufes are reprefented attending in full concert.

On the back of the ftate, or Sovereign's throne, is a large drapery, on which is painted St. George encountering the Dragon, as large as the life, and on the lower border of the drapery is infcribed,

VENIENDO RESTITUIT REM,

in allufion to King William III. who is painted in the habit of the order, fitting under a royal canopy, by Sir Godfrey Kneller. To the throne is an afcent by five fteps of fine marble, to which the painter has added five more, which are done with fuch perfection as to deceive the fight, and induce the fpectator to think them equally real.

This noble room is an hundred and eight feet in length, and the whole north fide is taken up with the triumph of Edward the Black Prince, after the manner of the Romans. At the upper part of the hall is Edward III. that Prince's father, the conqueror of France and Scotland, and the founder of the order of the garter, feated on a throne, receiving the Kings of France and Scotland prifoners ; the Black Prince is feated in the middle of the proceffion, crowned with laurel, and carried by flaves ; preceded by captives, and attended by the emblems of victory, liberty, and other enfignia of the Romans, with the banners of France and Scotland difplayed. The painter has given a loofe to his fancy by clofing the proceffion with the fiction of the Countefs of Salifbury, in the perfon of a fine lady, making garlands for the Prince, and the reprefentation of the merry wives of Windfor.

At the lower end of the hall is a noble mufic gallery, fupported by flaves, larger than the life, in proper attitudes, faid to reprefent a father and his three fons, taken prifoners by the Black Prince in his wars abroad. Over this gallery on the lower compartment of the cieling is the collar of the order of the garter fully difplayed. The painting of this room was done by Verrio, and is highly finifhed and heightened with gold.

The King's Chapel.

This chapel is decorated in a very gay and fplendid manner. On the cieling is finely reprefented our Lord's afcenfion ; and

the

the altar piece is adorned with a noble painting of the laſt ſupper. The north ſide of the chapel is ornamented with the repreſentation of our Saviour's raiſing Lazarus from the dead, his curing the ſick of the palſy, and other miracles, beautifully painted by Verrio; and in a group of ſpectators the painter has introduced his own effigy, with thoſe of Sir Godfrey Kneller, and Mr. Cooper, who affiſted him in theſe paintings. The eaſt end of this chapel is taken up with the cloſets belonging to his Majeſty and the Royal family. The canopy, curtains, and furniture are of crimſon velvet, fringed with gold; and the carved work of this chapel, which is well worthy the attention of the curious, is done by that famous artiſt Gibbons, in lime tree, repreſenting a great variety of pelicans, doves, palms, and other alluſions to ſcripture hiſtory, with the ſtar and garter, and other ornaments finiſhed to great perfection.

St. George's Chapel.

This ancient ſtructure, which is ſituated in the middle of the lower court, is in the pureſt ſtile of Gothic architecture, and was firſt erected by King Edward the Third, in the year 1337, ſoon after the foundation of the college, for the honour of the order of the garter, and dedicated to St. George, the patron of England; but however noble the firſt deſign might be, King Edward IV. not finding it entirely compleated, enlarged the ſtructure and deſigned the preſent building, together with the houſes of the dean and canons, ſituated on the north and weſt ſides of the chapel; the work was afterwards carried on by Henry VII. who finiſhed the body of the chapel, and Sir Reginald Bray, knight of the garter, and the favourite of that King, affiſted in ornamenting the chapel and compleating the roof.

The architecture of the inſide has always been eſteemed for its neatneſs and great beauty, and in particular the ſtone roof is reckoned an excellent piece of workmanſhip. It is an ellipſis ſupported by Gothic pillars, whoſe ribs and groins ſuſtain the whole ceiling, every part of which has ſome different device well finiſhed, as the arms of Edward the Confeſſor, Edward III. Henry VI. Edward IV. Henry VII. and Henry VIII. alſo the arms of England and France quarterly, the croſs of St. George, the roſe, portcullis, lion rampant, unicorn, &c. In a chapel in the ſouth iſle is repreſented in ancient painting, the hiſtory of John the Baptiſt, and in the ſame iſle are painted on large pannels of oak, neatly carved

and

and decorated with the feveral devices peculiar to each Prince, the portraits at full length of Prince Edward, fon to Henry VI. Edward IV. Edward V. and Henry VII.   In the north ifle is a chapel dedicated to St. Stephen, wherein the hiftory of that faint is painted on the pannels, and well preferved.   In the firft of thefe pannels St. Stephen is reprefented preaching to the people; in the fecond he is before Herod's tribunal; in the third he is ftoning; and the fourth he is reprefented dead.   At the eaft end of this ifle is the chapter houfe of the college, in which is a portrait at full length, by a mafterly hand, of the victorious Edward III. in his robes of ftate, holding in his right hand a fword, and bearing the crowns of France and Scotland, in token of the many victories he gained over thofe nations.   On one fide of this painting is kept the fword of that great and warlike Prince.

But what appears moft worthy of notice is the choir.   On each fide are the ftalls of the Sovereign and Knights companions of the moft noble order of the garter, with the helmet, mantling, creft, and fword, of each Knight, fet up over his ftall on a canopy of ancient carving curioufly wrought, and over the canopy is affixed the banner or arms of each Knight properly blazoned on filk, and on the back of the ftalls are the titles of the Knights, with their arms neatly engraved and blazoned on copper.   The Sovereign's ftall is on the right hand of the entrance into the choir, and is covered with purple velvet and cloth of gold, and has a canopy and compleat furniture of the fame valuable materials; his banner is likewife of velvet, and his mantling of cloth of gold.   The Prince's ftall is on the left, and has no diftinction from thofe of the reft of the Knights companions, the whole fociety, according to the ftatutes of the inftitution, being companions and collegues, equal in honour and power.

The altar piece was, foon after the reftoration, adorned with cloth of gold and purple damafk by King Charles II. but on removing the wainfcot of one of the chapels in 1707, a fine painting of the Lord's fupper was found, which being approved of by Sir James Thornhill, Verrio, and other eminent mafters, was repaired and placed on the altar piece.

Near the altar is the Queen's gallery, for the accommodation of the ladies at an inftallation.

In a vault under the marble pavement of this choir, are interred the bodies of Henry VIII. and Jane Seymour his Queen, King Charles I. and a daughter of the late Queen Anne.

Anne. In the fouth ifle, near the door of the choir, is buried Henry VI. and the arch near which he was interred, was fumptuoufly decorated by Henry VIII. with the royal enfigns and other devices, but they are now much defaced by time.

In this chapel is alfo the monument of Edward Earl of Lincoln, Lord High Admiral of England in the reign of Queen Elizabeth, erected by his Lady, who is alfo interred with him. The monument is of alabafter, with pillars of porphyry.

Another, within a neat fcreen of brafs work, is erected to the memory of Charles Somerfet, Earl of Worcefter, and Knight of the garter, who died in 1526, and his lady, daughter to William Earl of Huntingdon.

Alfo a ftately monument of white marble erected to the memory of Henry Somerfet, Duke of Beaufort, and Knight of the garter, who died in 1699. There are here alfo the tombs of Sir George Manners, Lord Roos; that of the Lord Haftings, Chamberlain to Edward IV. and feveral others.

The Tomb-Houfe.

This edifice, which is adjoining to the eaft end of St. George's Chapel, was erected by King Henry VII. for a burial place for himfelf and thofe who fhould fucceed him on the Throne of England: but this Prince afterwards altering his purpofe, began the more noble edifice at Weftminfter; and this fabric remained neglected till Cardinal Wolfey obtained a grant of it from Henry VIII. and then defigned and began here a moft fumptuous monument for himfelf, from whence this building obtained the name of *Wolfey's Tomb-houfe*; and fome have erroneoufly fuppofed, that at firft the whole building was erected by that famous Cardinal. Lord Bacon obferves, that this monument " far exceeded that of King Henry VII. in Weftminfter-Ab- " bey;" and at the time of the Cardinal's difgrace, and his lofs of the King's favour, the defign had been fo far executed, that four thoufand two hundred and fifty ducats had been paid to the ftatuary for executing that part of the work which was then done. But the Cardinal dying foon after his retirement from court, was privately buried in the chapel of Leicefter Abbey, and this monument remained unfinifhed; and at laft, in 1646, became the plunder of the parliamentarian foldiers. King James II. afterwards converted this building into a Popifh chapel,

chapel, and mafs was publickly performed here ; fince which it has been entirely neglected, and fuffered to run to ruin.

We fhall now proceed to fpeak of *Windfor Great Park*, which lays on the fouth fide of the town, and opens by a moft noble road, or *Long-Walk*, in a direct line, to the top of a delightful hill at the diftance of near three miles. This road, through a double plantation of trees on each fide, leads to the Ranger or Keeper's Lodge, the refidence of his Royal Highnefs the late Duke of Cumberland, who greatly improved the natural beauties of this park, and by large plantations of trees, extenfive lawns, new roads, fpacious canals, and rivers of water, made this villa a moft delightful habitation. This park is fourteen miles in circumference, and is well ftocked with deer, and variety of other game. The late Duke was fucceeded both in the rangerfhip of this park, as alfo in title by his royal nephew, the prefent Duke of Cumberland.

The late erected building, or *Belvidere*, on Shrub's Hill, over a beautiful verdure and young plantation of trees, is very elegant, and affords the moft delightful rural fcene ; the noble piece of water in the valley underneath, was effected at a large expence, and from a fmall ftream or current of water, was made a fpacious river, capable to carry barges and boats of pleafure, with freedom ; his Royal Highnefs alfo erected over this river, a bridge of a moft curious architecture, on a noble and bold plan, being a fingle arch, one hundred and fixty-five feet wide ; this piece of water was a great ornament to the park, and terminates in a grotto, and large cafcade or fall of water ; but has of late fuffered damage by the breaking up of the head bank.

Neither was the attention of his Highnefs confined to the park only, but extended in like manner to the adjoining Foreft, that fcene of rural diverfion, and place of refidence of the royal game. Among the improvements made here by that Prince, the new two miles courfe on Afcot Heath cannot be paffed unnoticed : This race ground was laid out and brought into the moft beautiful order at a large expence, and is one of the firft courfes in the kingdom. The foreft is of great extent, and was appropriated to hunting, and the habitation of the King's deer, by William I. who eftablifhed many laws and regulations which are at this time obferved for the prefervation of the royal game, and better regulation of the foreft. In this extenfive tract of land are feveral agreeable towns and villages,

of

of which Wokingham is the principal, and almost in the center
of the forest; and although the land is generally barren and un-
cultivated, it [affords great delight and pleasure in riding, by
beautiful hills and vales intermixed with fine lawns and herbage
for cattle, also by the many agreeable habitations of gentlemen,
whose

> *Pleasant* Villas *intervene,*
> *To grace the sweetly varied scene.*

And, if we consider the noble exercise of the chace which
this forest admits of the large verdures and shady plantations of
oak, beech, and other trees, that so frequently abound in this
delightful spot, it must be confessed that this park and forest are
peculiarly adapted by nature to rural pleasure and delight; and
that no just idea can be formed of the many beauties that here, on
every side, offer to our sight, by the best description in prose; our
great English poet, Mr. Pope, only can truly paint out these
sylvan scenes and delightful habitations; whose Muse, (whilst
himself resided in this Forest) produced one of the finest poems
in our language, on this subject, and which he thus elegantly
introduces,

> *The groves of* Eden, *vanish'd now so long,*
> *Live in description, and look green in song :*
> *These, was my breast inspir'd with equal flame,*
> *Like them in beauty, should be like in fame.*
> *Here hills and vales, the woodland and the plain,*
> *Here earth and water seem to meet again.*
> *Not* Chaos *like, together crush'd and bruis'd,*
> *But, as the world, harmoniously confus'd :*
> *Where order in variety we see,*
> *And where, tho' all things differ, all agree.*
> *Here waving groves a chequer'd scene display,*
> *And part admit, and part exclude the day ;—*
> *There, interspers'd in lawns and op'ning glades*
> *Thin trees arise, that shun each other's shades.*
> *Here in full light the russet plains extend ;*
> *There wrapt in clouds the blueish hills ascend*
> *Ev'n the wild health displays her purple dyes,*
> *And mid'st the desart, fruitful fields arise,*
> *That crown'd with tufted trees and springing corn,*
> *Like verdant isles the sable waste adorn.——*
> *Not proud* Olympus *yields a nobler sight,*
> *Tho' Gods assembled grace his tow'ring height,*

3

Than

Than what more humble mountains offer here,
Where, in their bleſſings, all thoſe Gods appear.

Cranbourne Lodge in this neighbourhood, belonged alſo to his late Royal Highneſs, as Ranger of the Foreſt. This lodge is moſt pleaſantly ſituated, and has an extenſive proſpect over a fine plain and country, forming a moſt beautiful landſcape. In a ſpacious chamber of the houſe are painted and regularly ranged in large pannels, the military dreſſes of the different corps in the armies of Europe. The Duke of Glouceſter is the preſent Ranger of the foreſt, and great improvements have been made to this lodge by his Highneſs. Oppoſite to the front of this lodge on the neighbouring plain, in the pariſh of *Wingfield*, is a hand- ſome building erected and endowed by the late Earl of Rane- lagh, ſome time Ranger of this foreſt, for the education of twenty boys and girls : on this pleaſing ſpot or part of the foreſt are the villas of the late Mr. Buckley, Lady Beauclerk, Mr. Mitford, and other gentlemen; and at a ſmall diſtance *Fern- Hill* offers to the ſight on a delightful eminence.

St. *Leonard's Hill* is adjoining to the Duke's lodge, and re- quires due notice, on account of the pleaſing ſeat of Lillye Aynſcombe, Eſq; and the large plantation of oak and beech, which here form the moſt agreeable variety or face of nature. On the ſummit of the hill the Counteſs of Waldegrave has lately erected a noble edifice, which commands a moſt extenſive and delightful proſpect over the river Thames, and a moſt beau- tiful fruitful country.

Sunning Hill which is at a ſmall diſtance, is a very delightful part of the foreſt, and many gentlemen of fortune have here pleaſing villas or lodgings for the ſummer ſeaſon, to drink the mineral waters, which in many caſes are deemed beneficial to health. The wells are deſigned with ſome taſte, and are neatly laid out: the aſſembly-houſe is handſome and ſpacious, with pleaſant gardens. Public breakfaſtings are here every Monday morning, and frequent aſſemblies of gentlemen and ladies are held for the benefit of agreeable converſation, and to partake of the pleaſing amuſements of the country.

Swinley Lodge, which is not far from Sunning Hill, be- longs to the maſter of the buck-hounds. Here is always a number of deer, under his care and direction, kept for the royal chaſe. He appoints the days of hunting, takes care of the foreſt deer, and the King's ſtag and buck-hounds; and

R

for

for this purpose has many inferior officers under him, who superintend the several parts of the forest, divided into different walks or appointments.—Many other villages also partake of the pleasures of the forest, and surround this royal castle, as Ingfield-green, Old-Windsor, Datchet, &c. where gentlemen of fortune have their country seats. In the neighbourhood of Ingfield-green, and on the decline of the plain, is Cooper's-Hill, long since celebrated by Sir John Denham.

Old Windsor was formerly a place of note, and the residence of several of our Saxon monarchs before the time of William I. who fixed upon the adjacent hill for his residence; and by this means, together with the Castle, in a short time was raised a new town, while this once royal residence went to decay, and retained little more than the honour of its antiquity, and giving name to the whole country around,

The Hon. Mr. Bateman, Lord Mulgrave, Lady Primrose, and Colonel Montague, have here their residence in the summer-season: the houses of the three first are most agreeably situated on the banks of the Thames, and have large walks and gardens. The seat of Colonel Montague, called Beaumont lodge, is on the hill, and commands a most extensive and delightful prospect of the river and country ; the gardens are large and extend to Ingfield Green, that lies behind. Mr. Bateman's House is a cabinet, or uncommon collection, of curiosities, chiefly antiques; by some approved, by others held too minute and inconsiderable. But upon the whole, this house and gardens are a most agreeable villa ; and the plantations, or yew tree's shade, round the Church, add to the pleasing scene, and together, form the most inchanting rural spot.

Datchet, also a pleasant village, lies higher up the river, and has the conveniency of a bridge built by Queen Anne, with an entrance into Windsor little park. The course of the river, and the road round the park wall is most agreeable, especially on summer evenings. This village has of late been much improved, and is inhabited by many gentlemen of fortune, on account of its pleasant situation and vicinity to Windsor.

E T O N.

Though Eton is in a different county, namely, Buckinghamshire, yet it may be said to be one and the same town with Windsor, by the ready communication of a bridge over
the

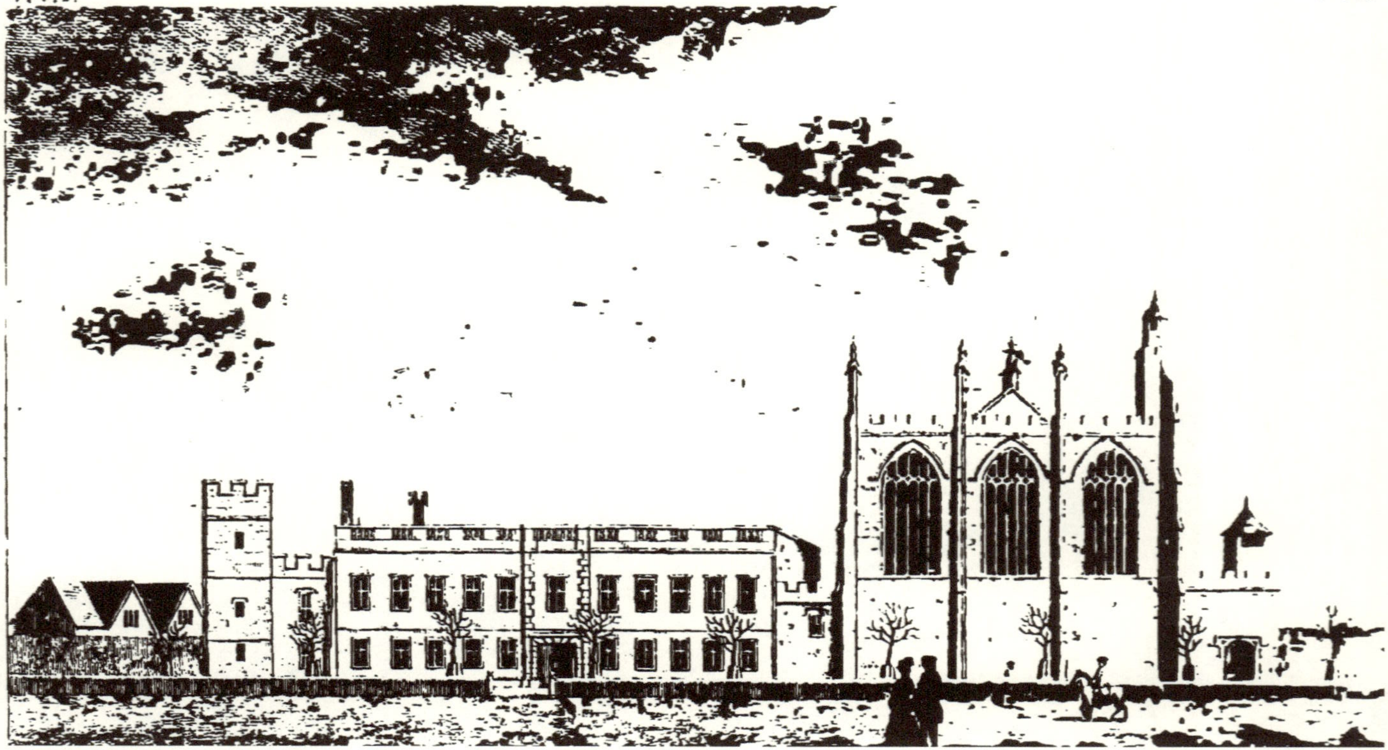

the river. It is pleasantly situated on the banks of the Thames, in a delightful valley, and is in a remarkable healthy soil. It has long been celebrated for the College here, which has produced a great number of eminent and learned men. *Eton College* was founded by Henry VI. for the support of a provost and seven fellows, one of whom is vice-provost, and for the education of seventy King's scholars, as those are called, who are on the foundation. These when properly qualified, are elected, on the first Tuesday in August, to King's College, Cambridge, but they are not removed, till there are vacancies in the College, and then they are called according to seniority; and after they have been three years at Cambridge, they claim a fellowship. Besides those on the foundation, there are seldom less than three hundred scholars, at this time there are many more, who board at the masters houses, or within the bounds of the College. The school is divided into upper and lower, and each of these into three classes. To each school there is a master and four assistants or ushers. The revenue of the College is about 5000l. a year. Here is a noble library enriched by a fine collection of books left by Dr. Waddington, Bishop of Chester, valued at 2000l. and Lord Chief Justice Reeves presented to this library the collection left him by Richard Topham, Esq; keeper of the records in the Tower. In the great court is a fine statue of the founder, erected at the expence of the late provost Dr. Goldolphin, Dean of St. Paul's. The chapel is in a good style of Gothic architecture. The schools and other parts, which are in the other style of building, are equally well, and seem like the design of Inigo Jones.

DITTON PARK.

The ancient and venerable mansion so called, which is situated in the parish of Datchet, was built by Sir Ralph Winwood, secretary of state to King James I. It came afterwards into the family of Montagu, and on the death of the late Duke, this house and manor of Datchet came to the Dutchess of Manchester, eldest daughter and joint heiress to that noble family. The house is built in the form of a castle, surrounded by a large moat of water, and in the middle of a pleasant park, well planted with timber; the apartments are large, and beautifully painted, and in the picture gallery is a good collection of paintings, many of them by the first masters. Lord Beaulieu married the Dutchess of Manchester, and has much improved the house and gardens.

R 2   There

There are alfo feveral other fine feats in this neighbourhood; particularly LANGLEY PARK, the feat of the Duke of Marlborough. The houfe is a noble edifice built by the late Duke, all of ftone, has commodious offices, and is moft agreeably defigned, fituated in a large park, with fhady walks, and has a beautiful lawn and canal : the banqueting-houfe on the rifing ground of the park, adds to the profpect from the terrace of Windfor Caftle.

At a fmall diftance is *Percy Lodge*, the feat of the Earl of Tankerville. This was the refidence of the late Dutchefs of Somerfet, after the deceafe of the Duke. The gardens and park are large, and beautifully defigned.

Langley-Green, Wexham, and *Stoke-Green* are in this neighbourhood. In the firft mentioned green, Lord Granard has lately built a commodious and elegant feat ; and in thefe villages are many agreeable houfes of gentlemen of fortune, who conftantly refide here : in the laft mentioned green General Howard has a moft pleafant feat and gardens.

Stoke-Houfe lately belonged to the Lady Cobham, but on her deceafe was purchafed by Mr. Penn, one of the proprietors and governors of Pennfylvania. It is an ancient and noble edifice, with a large and pleafant park ; and adjoining to the houfe is the parifh church of Stoke, and a neat hofpital, built and endowed by a Countefs of Huntingdon, for the fupport and maintenance of twelve old and indigent perfons of both fexes. The fcite of this ancient hofpital has of late been removed, and a new one built in an adjoining convenient part of the neighbourhood, by Mr. Penn.—*Baileys*, not far from hence, is an agreeable feat belonging to the Earl of Godolphin.

Farnham aud *Eaft-Burnham* are pleafant villages, and have many agreeable houfes and villas, particularly the elegant houfe and gardens of Mr. Charles Eyre. Near Burnham is *Hitcham-Houfe*, fituated in a valley, which was formerly the country refidence of that learned phyfician, Dr. Friend, to whofe family it at prefent belongs, but is now in the poffeffion of Lady Windfor. The gardens are large, and well defigned ; and in the hall is an original painting of the late Queen Caroline, which that Princefs prefented to Dr. Friend.

The village of *Taplœ*, which is not far diftant, is of fo pleafant a fituation, that it has caufed many gentlemen of fortune of late to refide here, who have built very agreeable houfes. The manor-houfe on the fummit of the hill is an

antient

A View of Chiefden House in Buckinghamshire

antient and noble building, and enjoys a moft beautiful profpect over the country, and the river Thames, which runs underneath. This houfe belongs to the Earl of Inchiquin, who refided here during the life of the late Prince of Wales; but on his highnefs's death, his lordfhip removed to Cliefden Houfe, in the neighbourhood.

C L I E F D E N - H O U S E.

This feat, which is in Buckinghamfhire, five miles northweft of Windfor, is remarkable, both on account of its moft beautiful fituation, and alfo becaufe it was the ordinary refidence of the late Prince of Wales, father to the prefent King. The houfe was built by George Villiers, Duke of Buckingham, in the reign of King Charles II. and came by marriage of the heirefs of that family to the late Earl of Orkney, who greatly improved both the houfe and gardens, which were alfo farther extended and enlarged by the late Prince of Wales, and made moft delightful, infomuch that in every part, or wherever the eye is turned, nothing offers to the fight but the moft agreeable avenues, parterres, and fine lawns, and thefe heightened by an extenfive view of the river Thames, and a moft beautiful and well cultivated country: the houfe is a ftately regular edifice, and the rooms fpacious and noble: in the grand chamber the tapeftry hangings reprefent the battles of the late Duke of Marlborough, wrought to great perfection, by order of the late Earl of Orkney, who was himfelf an officer of fuperior rank in thofe glorious campaigns; on the front of the houfe is raifed a moft noble terrace or walk, which is faid to be higher than the terrace of Windfor Caftle; it is certain, the profpect here is equally extenfive and beautiful.

DAWNEY COURT is the feat of Sir Charles Palmer, Bart. of the family of Roger Palmer, Earl of Caftlemain, who was fent by King James II. on the coftly embaffy to Rome in the year 1687; and the magnificent ftate-coach, made ufe of by that nobleman on that ignominious occafion, was many years kept here.

UNDERCOMBE is the agreeable feat of Thomas Eyre, Efq; and here are alfo the ruins of the antient nunnery of Burnham. It was of the order of St. Auftin, and confifted of an abbefs, and feven or eight nuns. It was founded by Richard, King of the Romans, in the year 1165, and dedicated to the Virgin Mary.

COLE-

COLEBROOK, or COLNBROOK.

This town, part of which is in Buckinghamshire, and part in Middlesex, is eighteen miles from London. It stands on four channels of the river Coln, over each of which it has a bridge. The principal support of the place are the inns, on account of its being in the Bath road. The market is on Wednesdays, and a fair is held here the third week in April. Here is a charity-school, and an ancient chapel, said to have been founded by King Edward III.

UXBRIDGE.

This is a town in Middlesex, in the road to Oxford, eighteen miles and an half from London. Though it is entirely independent, and is governed by two bailiffs, two constables, and four headboroughs, it is only a hamlet to Great Hillingdon. The river Coln runs through it in two streams, full of trout, eels, and other fish, and over the main stream is a stone bridge that leads into Buckinghamshire. The church, or rather chapel, was built in the reign of Henry VI. This town has many good inns, and is particularly distinguished by the whiteness of the bread, particularly their rolls. There are many corn mills at a small distance, and a considerable number of waggon loads of meal are carried from thence every week to London. Uxbridge gives the title of Earl to the noble family of Paget.

At the village of *Hillingdon*, which is a mile from Uxbridge, is a church wherein lies buried John Lord Strange, who married Jaquetta, sister to Elizabeth, Queen of England, wife of King Edward I.

RICKMANSWORTH.

This is a town in Hertfordshire, at the distance of nineteen miles from London. It is situated in a low moorish soil on the borders of Buckinghamshire, near the river Coln. It has a market on Saturday, and is governed by a constable and two headboroughs. The several mills on the streams near this town cause a great quantity of wheat to be brought to it. Here is a charity school for twenty boys and ten girls, with an almshouse for five widows, and another for four. In the neighbourhood is a warren hill, where the sound of a trumpet is repeated twelve times by the echo.

MOOR

Moor Park, near Rickmansworth, in Hertfordshire, the seat of the late Lord Anson.

MOOR PARK.

NEAR Rickmanfworth, on the left, is MOOR PARK, which was the feat of Lord Anfon, but at prefent belongs to Sir Lawrence Dundas, Bart. The park is not large, but is very beautiful, whether we confider it within itfelf or with regard to the fine and extenfive profpects from it. The houfe was originally built by Cardinal Wolfey, and, paffing through many hands, was afterwards in poffeffion of the Duke of Monmouth. Then it came into the hands of Mr. Stiles, who enlarged, repaired, and beautified it, under the direction of Sir James Thornhill. It ftands on a hill, not quite on the fummit. It is of ftone of the Corinthian order; and, if not in the higheft ftile of architecture, is yet very noble. The fouth, or principal front, has a portico and pediment of four columns. The offices are joined to the houfe by a beautiful circular colonade of the Ionic order, which terminates very elegantly with domes on each fide their entrance.

WATFORD.

THIS is a market-town in Hertfordfhire, fixteen miles from London. It is fituated upon the river Coln, where is has two ftreams that run feparately to Rickmanfworth. The town is very long, but confifts of only one ftreet, which is extremely dirty in winter, and the waters of the river at the entrance of the town, were frequently fo much fwelled by floods as to be impaffable; but in the year 1750, the road at the entrance of Watford was raifed by a voluntary contribution; by which means the river is now confined within its proper bounds. In the church are feveral handfome monuments; there are alfo a free-fchool and feveral alms-houfes belonging to the town.

CASHIOBURY PARK.

THIS is a little beyond Watford, on the left, and is faid to have been the feat of the Kings of Mercia, during the Heptarchy, till Offa gave it to the monaftery of St. Alban's. Henry VIII. beftowed it on Richard Morifon, Efq; from whom it paffed to Arthur Lord Capel, Baron of Hadham, and from him came by inheritance to be the manor of the Earls of Effex, who have here a noble feat in the form of an H, with a large park adorned with fine woods and walks; the gardens were

I planted

planted and laid out by Le Notre in the reign of King Charles II. The front and one side are of brick and modern, the other side is very old.

SAINT ALBAN's.

This is a large and very ancient town in Hertfordshire, twenty-one miles from London, and was so called from St. Alban, who suffered in the persecution under Dioclesian, and being afterwards canonized, and interred on a hill in the neighbourhood of this town, a monastery was erected and dedicated to him by King Offa. King Edward I. erected a magnificent cross here in memory of Queen Eleanor; and King Edward VI. incorporated this town by a charter, granting the inhabitants a mayor, a steward, a chamberlain, and ten burgesses; but the mayor and steward are here the only Justices of Peace. Here are three churches, besides the ancient cathedral called St. Alban's belonging to the monastery, which is now a parish church.

In this ancient edifice is a funeral monument and effigies of King Offa, its founder, who is represented seated on his throne; and underneath is the following inscription:

Fundator Ecclesiæ circa annum 793.
Quem male depictum, et residentem cernitis alte
Sublimem solio, MERCIUS OFFA fuit.

That is,
The founder of the church, about the year 793.
Whom you behold ill-painted on his throne
Sublime, was once for MERCIAN OFFA known.

on the east side stood the shrine of St. Alban, where the following short inscription is still to be seen;

S. ALBANUS VEROLAMENSIS, ANGLORUM PROTO-
MARTYR, 17 Junii 293.

In the south isle near the above shrine is the monument of Humphry, brother to King Henry V. commonly distinguished by the title of the good Duke of Gloucester. It is adorned with a ducal coronet, and the arms of France and England quartered. In niches on one side are seventeen Kings; but in the niches on the other side there are no statues remaining. The inscription, which alludes to the pretended miraculous cure of a blind man detected by the Duke, is as follows:

Piæ

Piæ Memoriæ V. Opt. Sacrum.
Hicjacet HUMPHREDUS, Dux ille Gloceſtrius olim,
HENRICI Sexti protector, fraudis ineptæ
Detector, dum ficta notat miracula cœci.
Lumen erat patriæ, columen venerabile regni,
Pacis amans, Muſiſque favens melioribus; unde
Gratum opus Oxonio, quæ nunc ſchola ſacra refulget.
Invida ſed mulier regno, regi, ſibi nequam,
Abſtulit hunc, humili vix hoc dignata ſepulcro.
Invidia rumpente tamen, poſt funera vivit.

Which has been thus tranſlated:

Sacred to the memory of the beſt of men.
Interr'd within this confecrated ground,
Lies he, whom HENRY his protector found:
Good HUMPHRY, Gloc'ſter's Duke, who well could ſpy
Fraud couch'd within the blind impoſtor's eye.
His country's light, the ſtate's rever'd ſupport,
Who peace and riſing learning deign'd to court;
Whence his rich library at Oxford plac'd,
Her ample ſchools with ſacred influence grac'd:
Yet fell beneath an envious woman's wile,
Both to herſelf, her King, and country vile;
Who ſcarce allowed his bones this piece of land;
Yet ſplte of envy ſhall his glory ſtand.

About fifty years ago in digging a grave, a pair of ſtairs were diſcovered that led down into a vault where a leaden coffin was found, in which his body was preſerved entire, by a kind of pickle in which it lay, only the fleſh was waſted from the legs, the pickle at that end being dried up. Many curious medals and coins are to be ſeen in the church, that have been dug out of the ruins of Old Verulam that ſtood on the other ſide of the river Ver, or Moore, which runs ſouth weſt of the town.

In the chancel of St. Michael's church in this town, there is a neat monument of white marble, erected to the memory of the famous Lord BACON, by Sir Thomas Meautys, who was his Lordſhip's ſecretary. This nobleman, though he had ſome conſiderable failings as a man, and as a ſtateſman, poſſeſſed one of the moſt comprehenſive underſtandings, and was one of the greateſt philoſophers, that have appeared in this, or in any other country. On his monument his Lordſhip is re-

preſented

prefented fitting in a chair, in a contemplative and his ufual pofture, one hand fupporting his head, the other hanging over the arm of the chair, and underneath the following infcription :

FRANCISCUS   BACON,
Baro de Verulam, Sancti Albani Vicecomes ;
Seu notioribus titulis,
Scientiarium Lumen, Facundiæ Lex,
Sic fedebat.

Qui poftquam omnia naturalis fapientiæ,
Et civilis arcana evolviffet,
Naturæ Decretum Explevit,
Compofita Solvantur ;
Anno Domini, M.DC.XXVI.
Ætatis LXVI.

Tanti Viri
Mem.
Thomas Meautys,
Superftitis Cultor,
Defuncti Admirator,
H. P.

Which may be thus translated :
FRANCIS BACON,
Baron of Verulam, Vifcount St. Alban's ;
Or by more confpicuous titles,
Of Lciences the Light, of Eloquence the Law,
Sat thus.

Who after all natural wifdom,
And fecrets of civil life he had unfolded,
Nature's law fulfilled,
Let Compounds be diffolved,
In the year of our Lord, M.DC.XXVI.
Of his age, LXVI.

To the Memory of fo Great a Man,
Thomas Meautys,
Living his Attendant,
Dead his Admirer,
Hath placed this Monument.

The

The town of St. Alban's is built in an irregular manner; but the situation is pleasant and healthy, and there are many good inns in the place for the accommodation of travellers, it being on the great north road to Coventry, Birmingham, Chester, Nottingham, Derby, &c. There was besides the abbey, a small nunnery in this town, with several chapels and chantries; but they are all entirely demolished. The late Dutchess of Marlborough built a fine house in the neighbourhood of this town, which now belongs to her great grandson, Earl Spencer. She likewise built some good alms-houses, and a charity school for children.

This town is a particular district of itself, and its jurisdiction extends over several towns and parishes, even as far as Barnet. It has sent members to parliament from the earliest times, and is governed by a mayor, high-steward, recorder, twelve aldermen, and twenty-four assistants. The weekly market is on Saturday, and here are three fairs annually, viz. on the 25th of March, on the 17th of June, and on the 29th of September.

GORHAMBURY, a little to the west of St. Alban's, was formerly the paternal estate of the great Lord Bacon, concerning whom we have lately spoken, and is now the seat of the Lord. Viscount Grimston.

H A T F I E L D

Is a town in Hertfordshire, nineteen miles from London, and was formerly called Bishop's Hatfield, from its belonging to the bishops of Ely. Here was once a royal palace, from whence both Edward VI. and Queen Elizabeth were conducted to the throne. It is a place of great antiquity; for it appears from our historians, that an ecclesiastical synod was held here in the year 681. The church is a venerable Gothic structure, built in the form of a cross; and at the end of the chancel is an antient chapel. On the west end is a tower, and in it a ring of five large bells. There are many curious monuments in this church, and the living is reckoned one of the richest in England.

The town does not contain any remarkable buildings, nor is it very populous; but here are two charity-schools, well endowed. Here is a weekly market on Thursday, and two annual fairs, one on the 23d of April, and another on the 18th of October.

The

The Earl of Salisbury has here a noble seat built by the great Lord Burleigh, called HATFIELD-HOUSE. The park and gardens, in which is a vineyard, is watered by the river Lea.

B A R N E T.

This town, which is eleven miles from London, is sometimes called *High Barnet*, from its situation on a hill ; and was also formerly called Chipping, or Cheaping-Barnet, from King Henry the Second's granting the monks of St. Alban's the privilege of holding a market here, the word *Cheap*, or *Chepe*, being an ancient word for a market. It is at present a great thoroughfare, being situated in the road to St. Alban's, and the first stage on the great north road. It has several good inns, with a great number of public houses; and many considerable farmers live in the neighbourhood.

The town is long, and the church, which stands in the middle of it, is a very ancient structure. Here is a free-school founded by Queen Elizabeth, and endowed partly by that Princess, and partly by Alderman Owen of London, whose additional endowment is paid by the fishmongers company. Here is also an alms-house founded and endowed by James Ravenscroft, Esq; for six widows. But what Barnet is most noted for at present is, its races in the month of August, which last three days, and are frequented by vast numbers of all ranks of people from London.

The weekly market at Barnet is on Monday, and it has two annual fairs, each of which holds three days ; the first is on the 8th, 9th, and 10th of April ; and the second on the 4th, 5th, and 6th of September, for Welch and Scotch cattle.

Barnet is famous for being the place where the decisive battle was fought between the houses of York and Lancaster, on Easter-day, 1471, in which the great Earl of Warwick, stiled the King-maker*, was slain, with many others of the principal nobility. The place supposed to be the field of battle, is a green spot, a little before the meeting of the St. Alban's and Hatfield roads ; and here, in the year 1740, an obelisk was erected by Sir Jeremy Sambrooke, on which is the following inscription :

* Vid. P. 95, 96.

Here

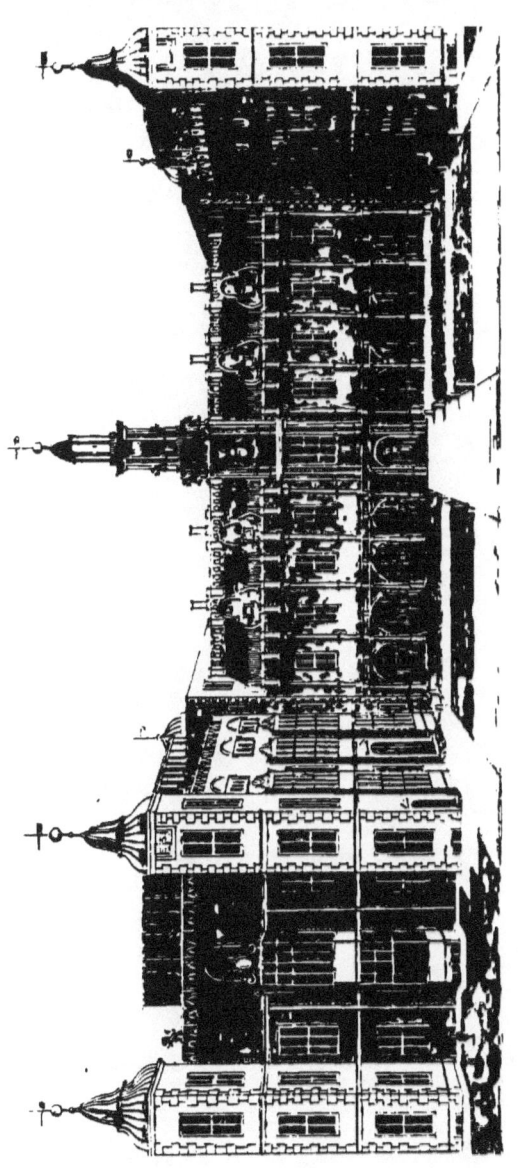

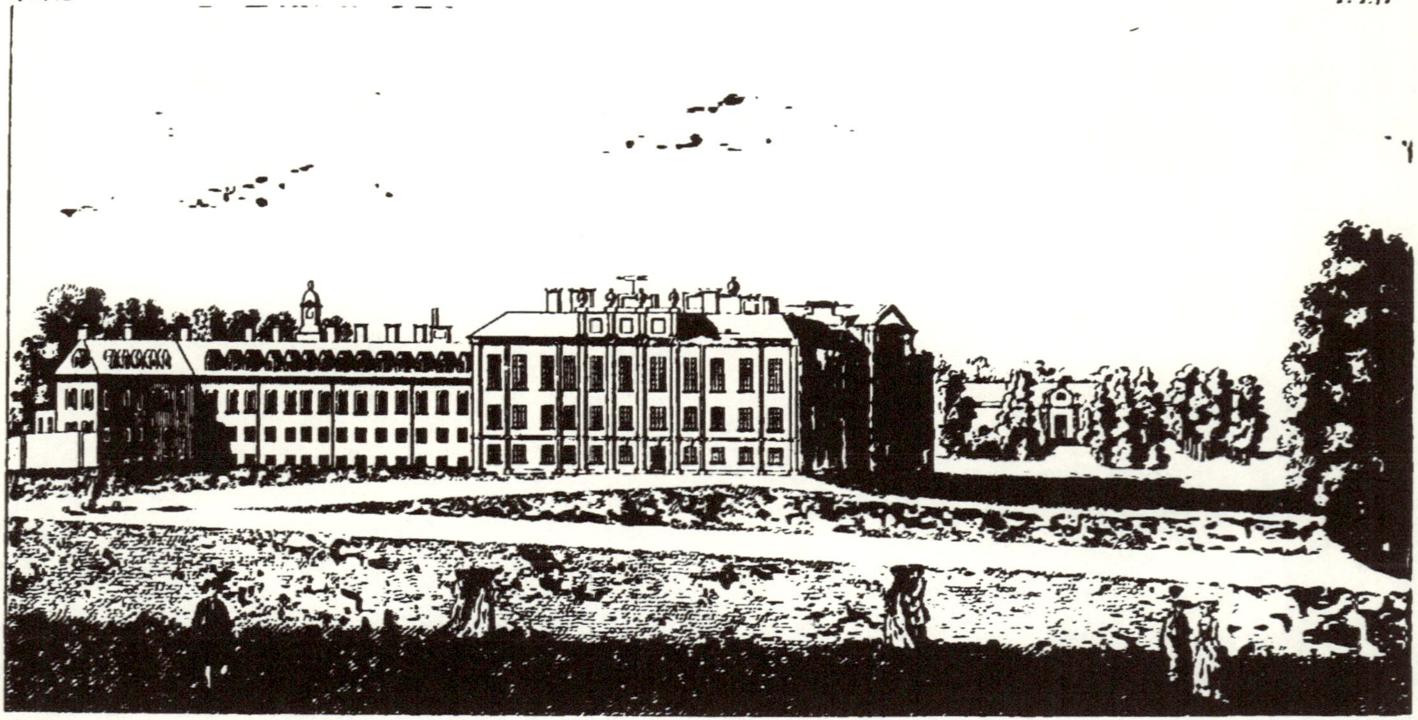

Here was
Fought the
Famous BATTLE
Between E D W A R D.
the 4th, and the
Earl of W A R W I C K,
April the 14th,
Anno 1471,
In which the Earl
was defeated,
and flain.

About two miles north-west from Barnet is *Derehams*, which was the seat of the late Earl of Albemarle.

Elstree, Idlestree or *Eaglestree*, (for it has been called by all these names,) a village near Barnet, upon the borders of Middlesex, is thought by Norden to have been the station of *Sulloniacæ*, mentioned by Antonius in his Itinerary, as at the distance of twelve miles from London: but Mr. Camden and Bishop Gibson think it was at Brockley-hill in this neigbourhood, many coins, urns, Roman bricks, and other antiquities, having been dug up there.

Totteridge has been adorned with fine seats belonging the citizens of London, from the time of King James I. The Saxons gave it the name from its situation on the top of a hill. There was anciently a monastery here.

Edgeware, which is a town eleven miles from London, in the road to St. Alban's, is situated on the very edge of the county of Middlesex. The old Roman way, called Watling-Street, passes by here from London.

Harrow on the Hill, is situated in the county of Middlesex, twelve miles north-west of London. It is famous for a free-school founded by Mr. John Lyons, in the reign of Queen Elizabeth; and every 4th of August a select number of the scholars, dressed in the habit of archers, come with their bows, and shoot at a mark for a silver arrow.

K E N S I N G T O N.

This is a large and populous village in Middlesex, about two miles from Hyde Park Corner, part of which is in the parish of St. Margaret's, Westminster. The palace, which

was

was the feat of the Lord Chancellor Finch, afterwards Earl of Nottingham, was purchased by King William, who greatly improved it, and caused a royal road to be made to it, through St. James's and Hyde Parks, with lamp posts erected at equal distances on each fide. Queen Mary enlarged the gardens; her fifter Queen Anne improved what Mary had begun, and was fo pleafed with the place, that fhe frequently fupped during the fummer in the green-houfe, which is a very beautiful one; but her late Majefty Queen Caroline compleated the defign, by extending the gardens from the great road in Kenfington to Acton; by bringing what is called the Serpentine river into them, and by taking in fome acres out of Hyde Park, on which fhe caufed a mount to be raifed, with a chair upon it, that could be eafily turned round, fo as to afford fhelter from the wind. This mount is furrounded with a grove of evergreens, and commands a fine view over the gardens to the fouth and weft. In fhort, thefe gardens, which are three miles and a half in compafs, are kept in great order, and in fummer-time are reforted to by great numbers of people. The palace indeed has none of that grandeur, which might be expected in the refidence of a Britifh Monarch; its nearnefs to the town makes it very convenient, but it is very irregular in point of architecture. However the royal apartments are grand, and fome of the pictures are very fine.

On paffing the bafe court, you enter through a large portico into a ftone gallery, that leads to the great ftair cafe, which is a very fine one, and confifts of feveral flights of black marble fteps, adorned with iron balufters finely wrought. The painting here affords the view of feveral balconies with groups of figures reprefenting yeomen of the guard, and fpectators, among whom are drawn Mr. Ulrick, commonly called the young Turk, in the Polonefe drefs in which he waited on his late Majefty King George I. Peter, the wild youth, &c. The ftair cafe is richly decorated and painted by Mr. Kent.

The firft room is hung with very fine tapeftry, reprefenting the goddefs Diana, hunting and killing the wild boar. Over the chimney is a picture in a grand tafte, reprefenting one of the Graces in the character of Painting, receiving inftructions from Cupid. This piece is faid to be done by Guido Reni. In one corner of the room is a marble ftatue of Venus, with an apple in her hand; and in another is the ftatue of Bacchus, whofe head is finely executed; but

the

the body, which is inferior to it, seems to be done by another hand.

The second room has its ceiling painted with Minerva, surrounded by the arts and sciences, by Mr. Kent. Over the chimney is a very fine piece representing Cupid admiring Pfyche, while she is asleep, by Vandyke. On each side of the room are hung several pictures, as King Henry VIII. and the Comptroller of his houshold, by Holbein: a three quarter picture of King Charles I. and another of his Queen, by Vandyke: the Duke and Duchess of York, by Sir Peter Lely: as also King William and Queen Mary, when Prince and Princess of Orange, over the doors by the same hand.

The third room, which was the late Queen's apartment, is adorned with very beautiful tapestry, representing a Dutch winter piece, and the various diversions peculiar to the natives of Holland, done by Mr. Vanderbank. Over the chimney is an admirable picture of King Charles II. King James II. and their sister the Princess of Orange, when children, by Vandyke.

In the fourth room is the picture of a battle or skirmish between the Germans and Italians, by Holbein. Another of Danæ descending in a shower of gold, and another of the widow Eliot finely executed by our countryman Riley.

In the fifth room is a picture of the crucifixion, and another of our Saviour laid on the cross, both by Titian: of our Saviour calling St. Matthew from the receipt of customs, by Annibal Caracci; and of his healing the sick in the temple, by Verrio: a picture of Henry IV. of France, by Titian: two heads of Queen Mary I. and Queen Elizabeth, when children, by Holbein: the late Queen Anne, when an infant, by Sir Peter Lely: and several heads by Raphael.

In the sixth room, or rather gallery, are the pictures of King Henry VIII. and Queen Katharine of Arragon, both by Holbein: King Philip of Spain, and Queen Mary, by the same hand: King James I. by Vandyke: King Charles II. the face by Sir Peter Lely: Queen Elizabeth in a Chinese dress, drawn when she was a prisoner at Woodstock: King James II. when Duke of York, and another of his Queen, both by Sir Peter Lely: King William and Queen Mary in their coronation robes, by Sir Godfrey Kneller. Sir Godfrey was knighted on his painting these pictures; King William being doubtless pleased with so fine a picture of his Queen. The next is Queen Anne, after Sir Godfrey Kneller;

ler: and a picture of Queen Caroline, which is but poorly exe-cuted. In this room is a curious amber cabinet, in a glafs cafe ; and at the upper end a beautiful orrery, likewife in a glafs cafe.

The feventh, which is called the Cupalo room, has a ftar in the center, and the ceiling all around is adorned with paintings in mofaic : round the room are placed at proper diftances, eight buftos of ancient poets, and fix ftatues of the heathen gods and goddeffes at full lengh, gilt.   Over the chimney piece is a curi-ous bas relief in marble, reprefenting a Roman marriage, with a bufto of Cleopatra, by Mr. Ryfbrack.

In the King's great drawing-room, over the chimney, is a very fine picture of St. Francis adoring the infant Jefus, held in the lap of the Virgin Mary, Jofeph attending, the whole per-formed by Sir Peter Paul Rubens.   In this room are alfo the holy family, finely painted by Paul Veronefe : three priefts, by Tintoret : a noble picture of St. Agnes over one of the doors, by Domenichino : St. John Baptift's head, Mary Magdalen, and a naked Venus, all by Titian : a Venus in a fupine pofture, ftealing an arrow out of Cupid's quiver, with beautiful orna-ments in the high gufto of the Greek antique, reprefenting Love and the Drama, by Jacoba da Puntormo ; upon the ori-ginal out-lines of the great Michael Angelo Buonaroti : a picture of Villiers, Duke of Buckingham, and his younger brother, when boys, one of the capital pieces of Vandyke : two large pictures by Guido Reni, one of Venus dreffing by the Graces ; the other of Andromeda chained to a rock : our Saviour in the manger, by Baffan ; and a picture of part of the holy family, by Palma, the elder.

The ceiling of this room, in which there is fuch a mixture of facred and prophane pieces, is painted with the ftory of Ju-piter and Semele.

In the ftate chamber, the bed is of crimfon damafk ; and over the chimney is a picture of our Saviour and St. John Baptift, by Raphael.

In the ftate dreffing-room the hangings are all of needle-work; a prefent from the Queen of Pruffia.   Here is a picture of Ed-ward VI. by Holbein ; of a young nobleman of Venice, by Tintoret : another young nobleman of the fame place, by Tin-toret ; and Titian's lady, painted by himfelf.

The painted gallery is adorned with many admirable pieces.
I   At

At the end is King Charles I. on a white horfe, with the Duke d'Efpernon holding his helmet ; the King is an auguft and noble figure, with fome dejection in his countenance ; the triumphal arch, curtain, and other parts of the back ground, are finely executed, and fo kept, that the King is the principal figure that ftrikes the eye ; and at a little diftance it has more of the life than a picture.

Fronting this picture, at the other end of the gallery, is the fame King with his Queen, and two children, King Charles II. when a child, and King James II. an infant, in the Queen's lap. The King's paternal tendernefs is finely expreffed, his fon ftanding at his knee; the Queen's countenance is expreffive of refpect towards his Majefty, and a fond care of her child, which fhe feems to defire the King to look on. The infant is exquifitely performed ; the vacancy of thought in the face, and the inactivity of the hands, are equal to life itfelf at that age. Thefe two admirable pieces were done by Vandyke.

One of the next capital pictures in this gallery is Efther fainting before King Ahafuerus, painted by Tintoret. All the figures are finely drawn and richly dreffed in the Venetian manner ; for the Venetian fchool painted all their hiftorical figures in their own habits, thinking them more noble and picturefque than any other.

The next piece is the nine mufes in concert, finely drawn by the fame mafter.

Midas preferring Pan to Apollo, is a fine piece, by Andrea Schiavone ; but it is a good deal hurt by time ; the figures however are well drawn and coloured ; and the affectation of judgment in Midas is finely expreffed.

The fhepherds offering gifts to Chrift, St. John in prifon, the ftory of the woman of Samaria, and John Baptift's head are fine pieces, by Old Palma.

Noah's flood, by Baffan, is a mafterly performance.

Over the chimney is a madona, by Raphael, which, though a fmall piece, gives a very high idea of that great mafter's abilities. There is alfo in this gallery a madona, by Vandyke, which is exquifitely performed.

The other pictures here are, the birth of Jupiter, a fine piece, by Julio Romano ; a Cupid whetting his arrow, by Annibal Caracci ; and a Venus and Cupid, by Titian.

T CHEL

C H E L S E A.

This is a very large and populous village, two miles from London, pleasantly situated on the banks of the Thames, and opposite to Battersea, to which it is joined by a bridge that has been lately erected. But what is most remarkable here is CHELSEA HOSPITAL, which is a noble edifice erected for the invalids in the land service. The original building on this spot was a college founded by Dr. Sutcliff, Dean of Exeter, in the reign of King James I. for the study of Polemic divinity, and was endowed to support a Provost and Fellows, for the instruction of youth in that branch of learning. The King, who laid the first stone, gave many of the materials, and promoted the work by a large sum of money, and the clergy were very liberal on the same occasion; but the sum settled upon the foundation by Dr. Sutcliff being far unequal to the end proposed, the rest was left to private contributions; and these coming in slowly, the work was stopped before it was finished, and therefore soon fell to ruin. At length the ground on which the old college was erected, becoming escheated to the crown, Charles II. began to erect the present hospital, which was carried on by James II. and compleated by William and Mary.

The whole edifice, which was built by the great Sir Christopher Wren, consists of a vast range of buildings. The front towards the north opens into a piece of ground laid out in walks for the pensioners; and that facing the south into a garden which extends to the Thames, and is kept in good order. This side affords not only a view of that fine river, but of the county of Surry beyond it. In the center of this edifice is a pediment supported by four columns, over which is a handsome turret, and through this part is an opening which leads through the building. On one side of this entrance is the chapel, the furniture and plate of which were given by King James I. and on the other side is the hall, where all the pensioners dine in common, the officers by themselves. In this hall is the picture of King Charles II. on horseback, with several other pieces as large as the life, designed by Signior Verrio, and finished by Mr. Cook. These were presented by the Earl of Ranelagh. The pavement of both the chapel and hall are black and white marble. The altar piece in the chapel is the resurrection, painted by Sebastian Ricci.

The wings, which extend east and west, join the chapel
and

The South Front of Chelsea Hospital.

and hall to the north, and are open towards the Thames, on the south; these are near 360 feet in length, and about 80 in breadth, they are three stories high, and the rooms are so well disposed, and the air so happily thrown in by means of the open spaces, that hardly any thing can be more pleasant. On the front of this square is a colonade extending along the side of the hall and chapel, over which upon the cornice is the following inscription in capitals:

In subsidium et levamen emeritorum senio, belloque fractorum, condidit CAROLUS II. *Auxit* JACOBUS II. *Perfecere* GU-LIELMUS *et* MARIA, *Rex et Regina,* MDCXC.

And in the midst of the quadrangle is the statue of King Charles II. in the antient Roman dress, somewhat bigger than the life, standing upon a marble pedestal. This was given by Mr. Tobias Rustat, and is said to have cost 500l.

There are several large buildings adjoining, that form two other large squares, and consist of apartments for the officers and servants of the house, for old maimed officers of horse and foot, and the infirmary for the sick.

An air of neatness and elegance is observable in all these buildings. They are composed of brick and stone, and which way soever they are viewed, there appears such a disposition of the parts as is best suited to the purposes of the charity, the reception of a great number, and the providing them with every thing that can contribute to the convenience and pleasure of the pensioners.

Chelsea Hospital is more particularly remarkable for its great regularity and proper subordination of parts, which is very apparent in the north front. The middle is very principal, and the transition from hence to the extremities, is very easy and delightful.

The expence of erecting these buildings is computed to amount to 150,000l. and the extent of the ground is above forty acres.

In the wings are sixteen wards, in which are accommodations for above 400 men, and there are besides in the other buildings, a considerable number of apartments for officers and servants.

These pensioners consist of superannuated veterans, who have been at least twenty years in the army; or those soldiers who are disabled in the service of the crown. They wear red coats lined with blue, and are provided with all other cloaths, diet, washing and lodging. The Governor has 500l. a year; the

Lieu-

Lieutenant Governor 250l. and the Major 150l. Thirty-six Officers are allowed 6d. a day: thirty-four light horsemen, and thirty ferjeants, have 2s. a week each; forty-eight corporals and drums have 10d. per week; and three hundred and thirty-six private men, are each allowed 8d. a week. As the house is called a garrifon, all the members are obliged to do duty in their respective turns; and they have prayers twice a day in the chapel, performed by two chaplains, who have each a falary of 100l. a year. The phyfician, fecretary, comptroller, deputy treafurer, steward, and surgeon, have alfo each 100l. per annum, and many other officers have confiderable falaries. As to the out-penfioners, who amount to between eight and nine thoufand, they have each 7l. 12s. 6d. a year.

These great expences are fupported by a poundage deducted out of the pay of the army, with one day's pay once a year from each officer and common foldier; and when there is any deficiency, it is fupplied by a fum raifed by parliament. This hofpital is governed by the following commiffions; the Prefident of the treafury, the Principal Secretary of ftate, the Pay-mafter general of the forces, the Secretary at war, the Comptrollers of the army, and by the Governor and Lieutenant Governor of the hofpital.

The Apothecaries Company have a fpacious and beautiful *phyfic garden* at Chelfea, which contains near four acres, and is enriched with a vaft variety of plants both domeftic and exotic. This was given by Sir Hans Sloane, Bart. on condition of their paying a quit-rent of 5l. per annum, and annually delivering to the prefident and fellows of the royal fociety, at one of their public meetings, fifty fpecimens of different forts of plants, well cured, and of the growth of this garden, till the number of fpecimens amounts to 2000.

There is alfo at Chelfea a place of public entertainment remarkable for its elegance, and well known by the name of RANELAGH GARDENS, fo called from their formerly belonging to the Earl of Ranelagh. There is no place of public pleafure of the kind equal to this in any other part of Europe; and it is the refort of people of the firft quality. Though its gardens are beautiful, it is more to be admired for the amph theatre. This is a circular building, the external diameter is one hundred and eighty-five feet, round the whole is an arcade,

3   and

and over that a gallery with a balluſtrade (to admit the company into the upper boxes) except where the entrances break the continuity. Over this are the windows, and it terminates with the roof. The internal diameter is one hundred and fifty feet, and the architecture of the inſide correſponds with the outſide, except that over every column, between the windows, termini ſupport the roof. In the middle of the area, where the orcheſtra was at firſt deſigned, is a chimney having four faces; in which is a fire, whenever the weather makes it neceſſary. The orcheſtra fills up the place of one of the entrances. The entertainment conſiſts of a fine band of muſic with an organ, accompanied by the beſt voices; and of late fireworks of the moſt ſplendid kind have been exhibited here. The company is regaled with tea and coffee.

P A N C R A S.

This is a ſmall hamlet in Middleſex, on the north-weſt ſide of London. It has a church dedicated to St. Pancras, and called St. Pancras in the Fields, an old plain Gothic ſtructure, with a ſquare tower without a ſpire. It is a vulgar tradition that this church is of greater antiquity than St. Paul's cathedral, of which it is only a prebend; but this ariſes from a miſtake; for the church of St. Pancras, termed the mother of St. Paul's, was ſituated in the city of Canterbury, and was changed from a Pagan temple to a Chriſtian church by Auſtin the monk, in in the year 598, when he dedicated it to St. Pancras.

Pancras church-yard is a general burying place for perſons of the Romiſh religion. There are a great number of tombs in it; and in particular a very elegant one erected to the memory of Lady Henrietta Beard, only daughter of James, Earl of Waldegrave, who was firſt married to Lord Edward Herbert, ſon to the Marquis of Powis, and afterwards to Mr. Beard, the celebrated ſinger, and who was alſo one of the managers of Covent-garden theatre. A very handſome monument has likewiſe been lately erected to the memory of Miſs Dorothea Dias de Faria, who was drowned on the 26th of June, 1772, in the fifth year of her age. And another in memory of a proteſtant young Lady, Mary Barſnet, who died in 1750, aged twenty-three years, on whoſe monument are the following lines:

" Go, ſpotleſs honour, and unſully'd truth,
" Go, ſmiling innocence, and blooming youth;

" Go,

" Go, female fweetnefs, join'd with manly fenfe,
" Go, winning wit, that never gave offence ;
" Go, foft humanity, that bleft the poor,
" Go, faint-ey'd patience, from affliction's door ;
" Go, modefty, that never wore a frown,
" Go, virtue, and receive thy heav'nly crown !
" Not from a ftranger came this heart-felt verfe,
" The friend infcrib'd thy tomb whofe tears bedew'd thy
" hearfe."

K E N T I S H   T O W N.

· This has arifen from a fmall village, to be a place of confiderable repute ; for the air being extremely healthy, many of
the citizens of London have built houfes in it ; and many others
who cannot afford that expence, take ready furnifhed lodgings
for the fummer, particularly thofe who are afflicted with con-
fumptions, and other diforders.   There is no parifh church in
the town, but they have a good chapel of eafe at a little diftance,
belonging to Pancras parifh.   In the town are fome genteel
boarding-fchools, and many public-houfes, it being much reforted to by the people of London.

I S L I N G T O N.

This is a confiderable village in Middlefex, on the north
fide of London : it has been fo much enlarged within thefe few
years by the addition of new buildings, that it almoft joins to
the capital.   It is a place of great antiquity, and appears to
have been built by the Saxons, and in the time of William
the Conqueror was called Ifendon or Ifledon.   By the fouth
weft fide of this village, is a fine refervoir called New River
Head, which confifts of a large bafon, into which the New
River difcharges itfelf ; part of the water is from thence conveyed by pipes to London, while another part is thrown by
an engine through other pipes up a hill to a refervoir, which
lies much higher, in order to fupply the higheft parts of London.

The church is one of the prebends of St. Paul's ; the old
Gothic ftructure lately taken down, was erected in the year
1503, and ftood till 1751, when it being in a ruinous condition, the inhabitants applied to parliament for leave to rebulid
it, and foon after erected the prefent ftructure, which is a
very fubftantial brick edifice, though it does not want an air
of lightnefs.   The body is well enlightened, and the angles
ftrengthened and decorated with a plain ruftic.   The floor
is

is raifed confiderably above the level of the church-yard, and the door in the front is adorned with a portico, which confifts of a dome fupported by four Doric columns ; but both the door and the portico appear too fmall for the reft of the building. The fteeple confifts of a tower, which rifes fquare to a confiderable height, terminated by a cornice fupporting four vafes, at the corners. Upon this part is placed an octangular balluftrade, from within which rifes the bafe of the dome in the fame form, fupporting Corinthian columns with their fhafts wrought with ruftic. Upon thefe refts the dome, and from its crown rifes the fpire, which is terminated by a ball and its fane. Though the body of the church is very large, the roof is fupported without pillars, and the infide is extremely commodious, and adorned with an elegant plainnefs.

This parifh is very extenfive, and includes Upper and Lower Holloway, three fides of Newington Green, and part of Kingfland. There are in Iflington two meeting-houfes and a charity-fchool founded in the year 1613, by Dame Alice Owen, for educating thirty children ; this foundation, together with that of a row of alms-houfes, are under the care of the Brewers company.

Iflington contains a vaft number of inhabitants, many handfome rows of very neat houfes having been lately built in it. And the number of public-houfes in it is very confiderable ; and there are feveral noted places of entertainment in the neighbourhood ; particularly the White Conduit Houfe ; the Shakefpeare and Jubilee Gardens, formerly known by the name of Dobney's ; New Tunbridge Gardens ; and Sadler's Wells, where, during the fummer feafon, people are amufed with balance-mafters, walking on the wire, rope-dancing, tumbling, dancing, finging, and pantomime entertainments. Indeed, houfes of diffipation of every kind, have of late years been greatly increafed in the neighbourhood of London, to a degree that would not have been fuffered, if the morals of the people were an object of any confideration to thofe who are invefted with the powers of government.

Near the New River, on the north of Iflington, is an antient edifice, called *Cannonbury-houfe* ; and near it feveral handfome houfes have been built within thefe few years. The old houfe is partly let out in lodgings, and partly ufed as a genteel public-houfe. At a little diftance from it is a farm and a public-houfe, called *Highbury Barn*, near which are the remains of ancient fortification, in a place known by the

name

name of Reedmoat, or fix acre field. Moft of our antiqua-
rians have fuppofed that this was the place where Paulinus,
the Roman General, fled with his men, when the Britons,
under the command of Queen Boadicea, murdered all the inhabitants of London, and fet fire to that city.

As the refervoir of the *New River* before mentioned, is near
Iflington, and as this is a work of great public utility, it may
not be improper here to give a more particular account of it.—
Various were the projects in the reigns of Queen Elizabeth and
King James the Firft, for fupplying the city of London with
a fufficient quantity of water for domeftic ufes; the former
granted an act of parliament, which gave the citizens liberty to
cut and convey a river from any part of Middlefex or Hertfordfhire to the city of London, within the limited time of
ten years; and the latter granted another act, in which they obtained the fame power, but without being confined to any limited 'time; nobody however began this great and important work, till at laft Sir Hugh Middleton undertook to bring a
river from Amwell in Hertfordfhire to the north fide of London near Iflington.

The work began on the 20th of September 1608, and was
attended with innumerable difficulties. The diftance from London is twenty miles, and he was obliged, in order to avoid the
eminencies and vallies in the way, to make it run a courfe of
thirty eight miles, three quarters and fixteen poles, and to carry
it over two vallies in long wooden frames or troughs lined with
lead; that at Buthill being 660 feet in length, and 30 in height;
under which, or the paffage of the land waters is an arch capacious enough to admit under it the largeft waggon laden with
hay or ftraw: the other near Highbury is 462 feet long and 17
in height, where it is raifed along the top of high artificial
banks, and at the bottom of the hollow fupported by poles, fo
that any perfon may walk under it. In fhort, over and under
this river, which fometimes rifes high, and at others is conveyed under ground, runs feveral confiderable currents of land waters, and both above and below it a great number of brooks,
rills, and water courfes have their paffage.

This river, which is of ineftimable benefit to London, was
by this truly great man, brought to the city within the fpace
of five years, and was admitted into the refervoir near Iflington on Michaelmas day 1613; on which day Sir Thomas
Mid-

Middleton, brother to the great Sir Hugh, was elected Lord Mayor for the enfuing year, who accompanying Sir John Swinnerton, then Lord Mayor, attended by many of the Aldermen, the Recorder, and other gentlemen, repaired to the bafon, now called New River Head, when about fixty labourers, handfomely dreffed, and wearing green caps, carrying fpades, fhovels, and pickaxes, marched, preceded by drums and trumpets, thrice round the bafon, when ftopping before the Lord Mayor, Aldermen, and other gentlemen, who were feated upon an eminence, one of the labourers addreffed himfelf to them in a long copy of verfes, which being ended, the fluices were opened, and the ftream ran plentifully into the refervoir, under the found of drums and trumpets, the difcharge of feveral pieces of ordnance, and the loud acclamations of the people.

Sir Hugh Middleton, to enable himfelf to complete this grand work, had at laft, after fpending his own fortune, been obliged to apply to King James I. who advancing him a fum of money, became entitled to a moiety of its profits; he was alfo obliged to fell many other fhares, and in fhort, was in a manner entirely ruined by a project that has been attended with unfpeakable benefit to this city: fince by the water of this river, a fpeedy ftop has been put to a great number of dreadful fires, and the health of the city has been remarkably preferved by the cleanlinefs it has introduced among us. Yet fo little were the advantages that might then, and are now derived from this river, at that time underftood, that for above thirty years, there were not divided above 5l. odd money, to each of the fhares, which are 72 in number.

This river now draws moft of its water from the Lee, which being the property of the city of London, that corporation, contrary to the intereft of the city in general, oppofed a bill brought into parliament for giving farther powers to the New River company, to take the advantage that might be obtained by the river Lee; but the oppofition was without effect, and in 1738-9 the bill paffed into a law.

The Governors of the New River company then agreed with the proprietors of the lands on the river Lee for a cut of two cubic feet of water from that river, at a certain rate; and after the agreement, told them they would double the price for a four foot cut, which the proprietors agreed to, not confidering the great difproportion between the two cuts; and this cut of the river Lee now supplies the largest share of the New River water.

In this river there are forty-three sluices, and over it two hundred and fifteen bridges. On its approaching the refervoir, called New River Head, there are feveral fmall houfes erected at a confiderable diftance from each other on its banks, into which the water runs, and is conveyed by pipes to the nearer parts of the metropolis. On its entering the above refervoir, it is there ingulphed by fifty-eight main pipes, each of feven inches bore; and here alfo an engine worked by horfes, throws a great quantity of water up to another refervoir, fituated on much higher ground, from which the water runs in pipes to fupply the higheft ground in the city, and its liberties. Many years ago 30,000 houfes were thus fupplied by this water, and fince that time feveral main pipes have been laid to carry it into the liberties of Weftminfter.

H O X T O N.

This is a very antient place, and in the Conqueror's furvey is named *Hochefton*. It was formerly a town, and had a weekly market; but that has been long fince difcontinued. It has been fo much encreafed in buildings, that it joins to the metropolis. The moft remarkable edifice here is AsKE's HOSPITAL, a handfome building erected by the Haberdafhers company in the year 1692, purfuant to the will of Robert Afke, Efq; who left 30,000l. for building and endowing it, in order to afford lodging and board for twenty poor men of that company, and for as many boys to be inftructed in reading, writing, and arithmetic. Each of the penfioners hath an apartment confifting of three rooms, with proper diet at a common table, and firing; the annual fum of three pounds, and a gown every fecond year; which, together with the falaries of the chaplain, clerk, butler, porter, and other domeftics, amount to about 800l. per annum.

A plan of the building was drawn by Dr. Hooke, a learned mathematician of Grefham College, and upon his model it was erected in an advantageous fituation, fronting the eaft, with grafs plats before it, adorned with rows of lime-trees and inclofed with a handfome wall and iron gates. On the piers of the great gates at the fouth end, are two ftone ftatues, reprefenting two of Afke's Hofpital men, in full proportion. The principal part of the building is only one ftory high with garrets; where a portico with twenty-one ftone pillars

lars extends on a line on each fide of the chapel, which is placed in the middle, and on each fide above thefe pillars is a range of twenty-two very fmall windows. The pillars of the chapel extend to the top of the firft ftory, and that edifice rifing confiderably above the reft of the building, is terminated by a handfome pediment; with a clock, under which is the effigies of the founder in ftone, cloathed in his gown, and holding in his hand a roll of parchment, which feems to be his laft will. Under him is the following infcription:

ROBERTO ASKE *Armigero, hujus Hofpitii Fundatori, Socie. Haberda. B. M. P. C.*

And on one fide of him is this infcription:

Anno Chrifti MDCLXXXII. *Societas Haberdafheorum* de London *hoc Hofpitium condiderunt, ex Legato & Teftamento* ROBERTI ASKE *Armigeri, ejufdem Societatis; ad viginti Senum Alimenta, & totidem Pueroi um Educationem.*

On the other fide this infcription:

The worfhipful Company of Haberdafhers built this Hofpital, purfuant to the gift and truft of R. ASKE, *Efq; a late worthy Member of it, for the relief of twenty poor Members, and for the Education of twenty Boys, fons of decayed Freemen of that company.*

Fronting the entrance of the chapel is a large pair of very handfome iron gates, and at each end of the Hofpital is an edifice of the fame height as the chapel.—There are fundry other alms-houfes at Hoxton, which have been erected for different charitable purpofes; and, among others, the alms-houfes erected and endowed by Mrs. Mary Weftby, of Bocking, in Effex, widow, in 1749, for fourteen poor women. Thefe are commonly called *the Old Maid's Alms-houfes*; though either maids or widows may be admitted; but they muft be Diffenters.

Kingfland is a hamlet in the parifh of Iflington, lying betwixt Hoxton and Newington; and between Kingfland and Shoreditch church are what are called the Ironmongers Almshoufes, which are very handfome, and have pleafant walks. They were founded by Sir Robert Geffryes, formerly Lord Mayor of London, who was a member of the Ironmongers

Com-

Company, and are appropriated for the reception and support of fifty-six decayed members of that Company. Each of them has a room, with part of a cellar, six pounds a year in money, and a gown. None are admitted under fixty years of age; but a wife may reside with her husband, and when he dies be elected in his room. They have a handsome chapel, where a clergyman reads prayers every day, and preaches on Sundays, for which he has a proper falary, with commodious apartments to reside in.

S T O K E   N E W I N G T O N.

This is a village three miles from London, which is very large and populous, great numbers of citizens having built houses in it, on account of its vicinity to the capital. The church is a small, low, Gothic structure, and belongs to the dean and chapter of St. Paul's; and there is also a dissenting meeting here. Behind the church is a pleasant grove, shaded with tall trees, and seats for the accommodation of such as frequent it, for the benefit of the air.

Newington Green, which is a village near Newington, and partly in the same parish, is a very agreeable place. The principal part consists of a handsome square, in the middle of which is an extensive and beautiful grass-plat, with gravel-walks, leading from each of the angles; and on the east side is an handsome meeting for Protestant Dissenters.

E D M O N T O N

Is eight miles from London, and although only a small village in former times, yet by the great increase of buildings is now become confiderable; but the houses are scattered up and down along the road, without any regular order, and few of them join together, being mostly separated by gardens and enclosures. There is an assembly-room here.

E N F I E L D

Is a town in Middlesex, about ten miles from London, which is supposed to have been anciently called *Enfen*, from its situation among fens, and in marshy ground. There was formerly a royal seat in it, supposed to have been built in the reign of King Henry VII. and in the last century it was noted for being the residence of a great number of tanners, but at present little of that trade is carried on here.

The

A View of the Marquis of Caernarvon's Seat at Southgate.

The town is pleasantly situated, and the church, which is a low Gothic structure, stands about the middle of it. There is also a meeting house here, and several rich citizens of London have their country-seats near the town.—There is a weekly market here on Saturday, and a fair held on the 25th of May, and another on the 29th of September.

Lord Lyttleton has informed us, on the authority of an ancient author, who lived in the reign of Henry II. that the citizens of London had a chase or forest, extending from that part of the city, called Hounsditch, above twelve miles north, and that it was the joint property of the whole corporation. In this forest the citizens enjoyed the diversion of hunting, and such other exercises as were common in those warlike times. As commerce and a love of industry encreased, these diversions were in a great measure neglected, the forest was gradually laid open, and at last became the property of private persons. *Enfield chace*, which is the only part now remaining of this extensive forest, has been for many years the property of the crown, and is at present annexed to the dutchy of Lancaster.

In the reign of King James I. when that prince resided at Theobalds, Enfield chace was well stocked with deer, the King being extremely fond of hunting; but the parliament army, during the civil war, destroyed all the game, cut down the trees, and let the ground out in small farms. It continued in that condition till the restoration, when young trees were planted, and the whole stocked with game; but it is far inferior to what it was formerly. The ranger, who is appointed by the crown, has a most elegant seat, called the Lodge, and there are many seats belonging to persons of quality, all along the borders of the chace, particularly at Southgate, where the Marquis of Caernarvon, son to the Duke of Chandos, has a most noble country house, in which his Lordship generally resides, during the summer.

CHESHUNT

Is a very agreeable village, in Hertfordshire, fourteen miles from London, and many of the citizens have their country seats here. The Ermine-street, or Roman military way, passes near it, and in a field to the north-west are the remains of a strong camp. It is raised in an oblong form with deep ditches, but most of them are now filled up. There was formerly a Benedictine nunnery here, dedicated to the Virgin Mary; and Edward III. gave this village the privilege

lege of keeping a weekly market, but it is now difcontinued.

THEOBALDS

Is a moft pleafant village, near Chefhunt, wherein are many fine feats belonging to the Citizens of London. The palace of Theobalds, in which King James I. much delighted, now belongs to the Duke of Portland, who lets it out in tenements. This palace, which was very magnificent, was originally built by the great Lord Burleigh; and Hentzner, who has given a defcription of it in his *Itinerarium*, fays, that the gallery was painted with the genealogy of the Kings of England, and from thence was a defcent into the garden, which was encompaffed with a ditch filled with water, and large enough to have the pleafure of rowing a boat between the fhrubs; it was adorned with a great variety of trees and plants, labyrinths made with much labour, a jet d'eau with its bafon of white marble, and with columns and pyramids. In the fummer houfe, the lower part of which was built femicirculary, were the twelve Roman Eemperors in white marble, and a table of touchftone; the upper part of it was fet round with leaden cifterns, into which water was conveyed through pipes. This feat the Lord Burleigh gave to his younger fon Sir Robert Cecil, in whofe time King James I. ftaying there for one night's refrefhment, as he was coming to take poffeffion of the crown of England, he was fo delighted with the place that he gave him the manor of Hatfield Regis in exchange for it, and afterwards enlarged the park, and encompaffed it with a wall ten miles round. The palace he often vifited, in order to enjoy the pleafure of hunting in Enfield Chace and Epping Foreft, and at laft died there. In the civil wars it was however plundered and defaced, it being the place from whence King Charles I. fet out to erect his ftandard at Nottingham; King Charles II. granted the manor to George Monk, Duke of Albermale; but it reverting again to the crown, for want of heirs male, King William III. gave it to William Bentick, whom he created Earl of Portland, from whom it defcended to the Duke his grandfon: the great park, a part of which was in Hertfordfhire, and a part in Middlefex, is now converted into farms.—— In this neighbourhood Richard Cromwell, who had been protector, but abdicated, paffed the laft part of his life in a very private manner.

HOD-

HODDESDON

Is a confiderable town, feventeen miles from London, in the county of Hertford. It is a confiderable thoroughfare, and a place of great antiquity. It is a confiderable market for all forts of corn. Queen Elizabeth, by charter granted a grammar-fchool to this town, and endowed it with certain privileges; and an alms-houfe was founded here in the reign of King Henry VI. by Richard Rich, fheriff of London, and anceftor to the late Earls of Warwick. Here are the ruins of an ancient chapel; but by whom it was built does not appear, only that it belonged to an hofpital for leprous perfons, which is now totally demolifhed. The weekly market is held on Thurfday, and here is a fair for toys on the 29th of July.

WARE

Is a town in Hertfordfhire, twenty-one miles from London, and fituated in a valley on the eaft-fide of the river Lea.—It is faid, that fome ftrolling parties of the Danes failed up this river from the Thames, in their fmall open boats, and infefted this part of the country. They likewife built a fort here, to fecure themfelves from the army of Alfred, and for its better defence, raifed the water fo high, by a great dam, or as they called it, a Weare, that it was with great difficulty the Englifh could diflodge them. And from this circumftance we are told the town received its name. This place is a confiderable thoroughfare, being one of the beft poft-towns on the north road. Ware was founded in the year 914, and began to be of fome note in the reign of King John, when the high road to the north, which before went through Hertford, was by the procurement of Sayer de Quincy, then lord of the manor, turned through this town.—It confifts of one ftreet, about a mile in length, with feveral back ftreets and lanes, well inhabited. The church is large, built in the form of a crofs, and has an handfome gallery, erected by the governors of Chrift's Hofpital in London, who fend feveral of the children of that hofpital hither, either for health or education. Befides a charity fchool, here are feven alms-houfes, well endowed. At the Bull inn in this town, there is a famous bed, much vifited by travellers from London and other places; it is faid to be twelve feet fquare, and

capable

capable of containing twenty couple. This town is a great market for corn and malt: 5000 quarters of malt are often sent in a week to London by the barges, which generally return with coals.—The market is on Tuesday, and here are two fairs held, one on the last Tuesday in April, and another on the Tuesday before St. Matthew's day.

Near Ware is a spot of ground called Lemon field, where three Roman wine vessels were dug up in 1729. These vessels were of a pale reddish earth, and of the form of the Roman amphora, with two handles, and pointed at the bottom, for the purpose of fixing them in the ground. They were eighteen inches below the surface, and full of earth and chalk-stones of the neighbouring soil. Many human bodies have been dug up hereabouts, but though the ground around them is black, they appeared not to have been burnt, and seemed by their shallow burial to have been the relics of a battle.—On the south of Ware is *Amwell*, where the New River, of which we have already spoken, takes its rise.

HERTFORD

Is at the distance of twenty-one miles from London, and was a place of some note in the time of the ancient Britons. The East Saxon Kings often kept their courts here, and upon the first division of the kingdom into counties, it was made a county town. It sent members to parliament in the reign of King Edward the first, but after the seventh of Henry the fifth, on the petition of the bailiff and burgesses to be excused, on account of their poverty, that privilege was discontinued till the twenty-second of James the first.

In the time of Henry the Seventh, the standard of weights and measures was fixed here, and Queen Mary made this a corporation, by the name of bailiffs and burgesses; and by her charter, the number of burgesses was to have been sixteen. In the twenty-fifth and thirty-fifth years of Queen Elizabeth, Michaelmas term was kept here, by reason of the plague at both times in London; and that Queen granted this town a new charter. King James the First afterwards granted it another charter, with the stile of mayor, burgesses, and commonalty, to have ten capital burgesses, and sixteen assistants, and the mayor to be chosen out of the burgesses, by both the burgesses and assistants; but now this town is governed by a mayor, a high steward, who is generally a nobleman, a recorder, nine aldermen, a town clerk, chamberlain,

berlain, ten capital burgeſſes, and ſixteen aſſiſtants, together with two ſerjeants at mace.

The town of Hertford ſtands pleaſantly in a ſweet air and dry vale : it is built after the figure of a Roman Y, and has a caſtle, placed between the two horns, in which is the ſeſſions-houſe for the county. It has alſo a county gaol, and formerly had five churches, which now are reduced to two, All Saints and St. Andrew's. All Saints is ſituated on the ſouth ſide of the town, and has a tall ſpire, covered with lead, and eight good bells, beſides an organ, and an handſome gallery for the mayor and aldermen of the borough, and for the governor of Chriſt church hoſpital in London, who have erected a good houſe in this town, to receive ſick and ſupernumerary children ; they have alſo built a large gallery in the church, in which 200 of their children may be accommodated. St. Andrew's is only remarkable for giving its name to one of the ſtreets. Here are three charity ſchools, and alſo a free grammar ſchool, founded by Richard Hale, Eſq; in the reign of King James the Firſt.

The chief commodities of this town are wheat, malt, and wool ; and it is ſaid to ſend no leſs than 5000 quarters of malt to London weekly, by the river Lea. It is however obſerved, that the magnificence of this town is much diminiſhed, ſince the north road from London, which went through it, was turned through the town of Ware.

The caſtle of Hertford was built by King Alfred, to defend the town and neighbourhood againſt the Danes, who came up in their light pinnaces from the Thames by the river Lea, as far as Ware, and erected a fort there, whence they made frequent ſallies to plunder and deſtroy the country.

The members of parliament for Hertford are choſen by the freemen in general, the mayor being the returning officer. The weekly market is on Saturday, and there are four annual fairs held here, namely, on the Saturday fortnight before Eaſter, the twelfth of May, the fifth of July, and the eighth of November.

HACKNEY.

This is a very large, populous, and pleaſant village, in Middleſex, on the north-eaſt ſide of London. It is ſo remarkable for the country ſeats of merchants and rich citizens, that it is ſaid there are not leſs than an hundred gentlemens coaches kept in it. The pariſh has ſeveral hamlets belonging to it, among which are Clapton on the north, Dorlefton and Shacklewell on the weft, and Hummerton, which leads to Hackney-marfh, on the eaft.

Hackney church is an antient Gothic ftructure; it was a diftinct rectory and vicarage in the year 1292, and dedicated to St. Auguftine; but the Knights Templars having obtained a mill and other poffeffions in the parifh, they were, upon the fuppreffion of their order, granted to the Knights Templars of St. John of Jerufalem, from which the church is fuppofed to have received the prefent appellation of St. John: however, it was not prefented to by that name till after the year 1660. The living is now only a vicarage, the great tithes being in lay hands.—There are two diffenting meeting-houfes here.—At the bottom of Hackney-marfh was difcovered, fome years ago, the remains of a great ftone caufeway, which by the Roman coins found there, appears to have been one of the famous highways made by the Romans.

It is from this place, that the coaches let to the people in London firft received their name; for in the laft century, many perfons of condition refiding in Hackney, and many people having gone on vifits to fee their friends there, it occafioned them often to hire horfes, or carriages; fo that in time it became a common name for fuch horfes, coaches, and chairs, as were let out to the people of London; and the name has now diffufed itfelf, not only through Great Britain, but likewife Ireland.

B E T H N A L - G R E E N.

This is a pleafant village near London, chiefly inhabited by merchants and citizens of London, and has been long noted for private mad-houfes. The church is one of the fifty appointed to be built by act of parliament, and ftands on the north of Spitalfields. It is a neat commodious edifice, built with brick, coped and coined with free-ftone; and the tower, which is not high, is of the fame materials. This village was one of the hamlets of Stepney, from which parifh it was feparated in the late King's reign.—The old Roman military way from the Weft, paffed with it to Lea Ferry, at Old Ford. —Within this hamlet, Bonner, Bifhop of London, had formerly a palace.

MILE-

MILE-END

Was fo called on account of its being a mile from Aldgate; fuch was its fituation in former times; but at prefent what is called Mile-end, extends above a mile in length; its fartheft extremity being bounded by Bancroft's Alms-houfes. There were in antient times feveral fmall hofpitals, here particularly one for lepers; but no remains of it are left. At prefent there are many good houfes at Mile-end, and more alms-houfes than are probably any where elfe to be met with, within the fame compafs of ground.

The firft that deferves our notice is that called TRINITY HOSPITAL, which was founded by the corporation of the Trinity Houfe. It is a very noble, and yet not a very expenfive edifice; but is rendered beautiful by its fituation, and the agreeable manner in which it is laid out. It confifts of two wings and a center, wherein is the chapel, which rifes confiderably higher than the other buildings, and has an afcent to it by a handfome flight of fteps fecured by iron rails; this chapel has large windows, and is adorned with a pediment; behind it rifes a turret, ornamented with a clock, and crowned with a fane. On each fide of the chapel, are two fets of apartments exactly refembling the wings.

The wings are low but neat buildings, with an afcent of feven fteps to each pair of doors, fecured by brick walls capped with ftone, and there are fix of thefe afcents to each wing, befides two in the front, and one on each fide the chapel. Between each of thefe afcents is a pump fixed clofe to the wall.

It is remarkable that all thefe afcents lead to the upper ftory; there are however rooms below, but thefe are under ground, and the windows upon a level with a broad ftone pavement, that furrounds the area next the houfes. In the centre of each wing is a handfome pediment, adorned with the company's arms, with the reprefentation of ropes, anchors, and fea weeds, in open work, fpread over the face of the pediments, and the area within confifts of handfome grafs-plats, divided by gravel walks, kept in excellent order, leading down the middle, and acrofs to the centre of the area, where is a ftatue in ftone of Mr. Robert Sandes, well executed. He has a bale of goods placed behind; he ftands with his right foot upon another bale, and near his left foot is a fmall globe, and anchor. On the pedeftal is the following infcription:

To

To the memory of CAPTAIN ROBERT SANDES, an elder brother, and deputy master of the corporation of Trinity House, who died in 1701, and bequeathed to the poor thereof one hundred pounds ; also the reversion (after two lives) of a freehold estate in the county of Lincoln of 147l a year, now in their possession.   This statue was erected by the corporation A. D. 1746.

The end of each wing next the road has an empty niché, and over it is a small pediment, on each side of which is placed a small ship.

The ground on which this hospital stands was given to the corporation of the Trinity-house by Capt. Henry Mudd, an elder brother, and the above beautiful and commodious building was erected by the company in the year 1695, for the reception of twenty-eight masters of ships, or their widows, each of whom receives 16s. per month, 20s. a year for coals, and a gown every second year.

Adjoining to the Trinity alms-houses are eight others, belonging to the Drapers company, for the widows of four freemen and four sailors, who have each an allowance of 1s. 8d. per week, with half a chaldron of coals at Michaelmas, and a gown every two years.

. There are are also near the same place twelve alms-houses, belonging to the Skinners company, for twelve widows, who have each an allowance of five pounds four shillings a year, with half a chaldron of coals.

Fuller's alms-houses, founded by a judge of that name, in 1592, for twelve poor men, are in that neighbourhood.   And there are also a few alms-houses, for the widows of ship-masters, founded by Capt. Fisher, who setttled upon it a freehold of forty pounds a year.

. But the most splendid foundation of the kind here, is BANCROFT's beautiful alms-houses, school, and chapel; which were erected by the Drapers company in the year 1735, pursuant to the will of Mr. Francis Bancroft, who bequeathed to that company the sum of 28,000l. and upwards, in real and personal estates, for purchasing a site, and building upon it an alms-house, with convenient apartments for twenty-four almsmen, a chapel, and school-room for one hundred poor boys, and two dwelling houses for the schoolmasters, and endowing the same. He also ordered that each of the alms-men should have 8l. and half a chaldron of coals yearly, and a

gown

gown of baize every third year; that the fchool boys fhould be cloathed and taught reading, writing, and arithmetic; that each of the mafters, befides their houfes, fhould have a falary of 30l. per annum, and the yearly fum of 20l. for coals and candles, for their ufe and that of the fchool; with a fufficient allowance for books, paper, pens and ink; that the committee of the court of affiftants fhould have 5l. for a dinner, at their annual vifitation of the alms-houfes and fchool; and that 3l. 10s. fhould be given for two half yearly fermons to be preached in the parifh churches of St. Helen and St. Michael, Cornhill, or elfewhere, in commemoration of this foundation, at which the alms-men and boys were to be prefent. To each of thefe boys, when put out apprentices, he gave 4l. but if they were put to fervice they were to have no more than 2l. 10s. to buy them cloaths.

The edifice is not only neat but extremely elegant, confifting of two wings and a center detached from both of them. In the middle of the front is the chapel, before which is a noble portico, with Ionic columns, and coupled pilafters at the corners, fupporting a pediment, in the plane of which is the dial. There is an afcent to the portico by a flight of fteps, and over the chapel is an handfome turret. On each fide of the portico, are two houfes like thofe in the wings. The conftruction of the wings is uniform, lofty and convenient; twelve doors in each open in a regular feries, and the windows are of a moderate fize, numerous, and proportioned to the apartments they are to enlighten. The fquare is furrounded with gravel walks, with a large grafs plat in the middle, and next the road the wall is adorned with handfome iron rails and gates. In fhort, the ends of the wings next the road being placed at a confiderable diftance from it, the whole is feen in a proper point of view, and appears to the greateft advantage.

It is worthy of remark, that this Bancroft, who left fo large a fum for erecting and endowing this fine hofpital, and even ordered two fermons to be annually preached in commemoration of his charity, was, according to the laft edition of Stow's Survey, one of the Lord Mayor's officers, and by informations and fummoning the citizens before the Lord Mayor, upon the moft trifling occafions, and other things not belonging to his office, not only pillaged the poor, but alfo many of the rich, who rather than lofe time in appearing before the magiftrate, gave money to get rid of this
common

common pest of the citizens, which, together with his numerous quarterages from the brokers, &c. enabled him to amafs annually a confiderable fum of money. But by thefe and other mercenary practices, he fo incurred the hatred and ill-will of the citizens of all ranks and denominations, that the perfons who attended his funeral obfequies, with great difficulty faved his corpfe from being joftled off the bearers fhoulders in the church, by the enraged populace, who feized the bells, and rang them for joy at his unlamented death.

It is farther remarkable of this Mr. Bancroft, that he entertained a notion that he fhould rife from the dead, after a certain number of years, and ordered his body to be preferved within a fhow-glafs, in the church of St. Helen's, Bifhopfgate-ftreet, where it ftill lies, and the door is, by his directions in his laft will, fet open, during the time that the annual fermon is preached in that church in memory of himfelf. But notwithftanding thefe precautions, and the many opportunities that have been given him of changing his quarters, Mr. Bancroft ftill continues very peaceably in the place wherein he was originally depofited.

S T E P N E Y

Is a village near Mile-end, of great antiquity. This parifh was of fuch vaft extent, and fo amazingly increafed in buildings, as to produce the parifhes of St. Mary Stratford at Bow, St. Mary Whitechapel, St. Ann's Limehoufe, St. John's at Wapping, St. Paul's Shadwell, St. George Ratcliff Highway, Chrift Church Spitalfields, and St. Matthew's Bethnal Green; all which have been feparated from it, and yet it ftill remains one of the largeft parifhes within the bills of mortality, and contains the hamlets of Mile-end, Old and New Towns, Ratcliff and Poplar.

The village of Stepney is remarkable for its church, and the great number of tomb-ftones, both in that edifice and its fpacious cemetery. It has alfo an independant meeting houfe, and an alms-houfe. The village however is but fmall, and confifts of few houfes befides thofe of public entertainment; many people of both fexes reforting thither on Sundays, and at Eafter and Witfun-holidays, to eat Stepney buns, and to regale themfelves with ale, cyder, &c.

There was a church here fo long ago as the time of the Saxons, when it was called the church of all Saints, *Ecclefia omnium Sanctorum*; and we read of the manor of Sepney
under

under the reign of William the Conqueror, by the name of Stibenhede, or Stiben's-Heath; but it does not appear when the church changed its name by being dedicated to St. Dunstan, the name it now bears.

When the present church was erected is not recorded; the wall and battlements are built of brick and wrought stone, plastered over; and the roof is covered with lead. It is of a very considerable extent, for it is an hundred and four feet long, though it is no more than fifty-four broad; the height of the roof is thirty-five feet, and that of the tower, with its turret, ninety-two feet. The pillars, arches and windows, are of a modern Gothic, and the west porch, built in 1610, has no resemblance to the rest of the building, it being of the Tuscan order. The tower, which is plain and heavy, is supported at the corners by a kind of double buttresses; it is crowned with square plain battlements, without pinnacles, and with a small mean turret; and the same kind of battlements are carried round the body of the church.

On the inside are three galleries and an organ, and the altar-piece is adorned with four Corinthian pilasters, with their entablature and a pediment; these have gilt capitals; with the arms of Queen Anne carved; but what is most singular is a stone on the east side of the portico, leading up to the gallery, on which is the following inscription.

Of Carthage great I was a stone,
   O mortals read with pity!
Time consumes all, it spareth none,
   Men, mountains, towns, nor city:
Therefore O mortals! all bethink
   You where unto you must,
Since now such stately buildings
   Lie buried in the dust.

It is probable this stone was really brought from Carthage, otherwise this inscription would scarcely be permitted to be there; but as a modern author observes, it is to be hoped, that he who ordered it to be fixed there did not go to Carthage on purpose to fetch it.

Among the great number of tomb-stones in this church-yard, there is a very handsome one to the memory of Sir John Leake, an eminent English Admiral. And at the east-end of the church-yard, near the church, is a monument of

3   white

white marble, adorned with a cherub, urn, palm-branches and a coat of arms, under which is the following inscription:

·Here lieth interred the body of Dame Rebecca Berry, the wife of Thomas Elton of Stratford Bow, Gent. who departed this life April 16, 1696, aged 52.

> Come ladies, you that would appear
> Like angels fair, come drefs you here;
> Come drefs you at this marble ftone
> And make that humble Grace your own,
> Which once adorned as fair a mind,
> As e'er yet lodg'd in woman kind.
> So fhe was drefs'd, whofe humble life
> Was free from pride, was free from ftrife:
> Free from all envious brawls and jars
> (Of human life the civil wars)
> Thefe ne'er difturb'd her peaceful mind,
> Which ftill was gentle, ftill was kind.
> Her very looks, her garb, her mien,
> Difclos'd the humble mind within.
> Trace her through ev'ry fcene of life,
> View her as widow, virgin, wife,
> Still the fame humble fhe appears,
> The fame in youth, the fame in years;
> The fame in low and high eftate,
> Ne'er vex'd with this, ne'er mov'd with that.
> Go, ladies, now, and if you'd be
> As fair, as great, as good as fhe,
> Go learn of her humility.

Near the fouth fide of the church on a marble tomb-ftone, adorned with a coat of arms, are the following lines on Capt. Thomas Chevers, his wife, and a fon, who died at five days old.

> Reader, confider well how poor a fpan,
> And how uncertain is the life of man:
> Here lie the hufband, wife, and child, by death
> All three in five days time depriv'd of breath.
> The child dies firft, the mother on the morrow
> Follows, and then the father dies with forrow.
> A Cæfar falls by many wounds, well may
> Two ftabs at heart the ftouteft captain flay.

On

On a ftone near the foot path on the north weft fide, is the following infcription :

> Whoever treadeth on this ftone,
> I pray you tread moft neatly,
> For underneath the fame doth lie
> Your honeft friend Will. Wheatly.

The laft infcription we fhall mention is the following fhort one, on the fouth-weft fide of the church.

> Here lies the body of Daniel Saul,
> Spittlefields weaver, and that is all.

POPLAR.

This is a hamlet of Stepney, fituated on the Thames, and obtained its name from the great number of poplar trees that anciently grew there. The chapel of Poplar was erected in the year 1654, when the ground upon which it was built, together with the church yard, were given by the Eaft India company, and the edifice erected by the voluntary contributions of the inhabitants and othe.s; fince which time that Company has not only allowed the Minifter a convenient dwelling houfe, with a garden and field containing about three acres, but has allowed him 20l. per annum during pleafure.

Poplar Marfh, called the Ifle of Dogs, from the great noife made by the King's hounds that were kept there during the refidence of the royal family at Greenwich, is rather an ifthmus than an ifland, and is reckoned one of the richeft fpots of ground in England; for it not only raifes the largeft cattle, but the grafs it bears is efteemed a great reftorative of all diftempered cattle.

Here are two alms houfes, befides an hofpital belonging to the Eaft India company

Blackwall is chiefly noted for fhip carpenters, and other artifts employed in making utenfils for the navy, and is one of the greateft rendezvous of the Eaft-India fhips.

STRATFORD-LE-BOW.

This is a village in Middlefex, commonly known by the name of Bow, a little to the eaft of Mile end, and is divided from Stratford in Effex by the river Lea, over which there is a ftone-bridge, of which we have already made men-

VOL. I.   Y   tion*.

tion*. The church is very ancient, being built by Henry II. adjoining to which is a good free-school. In the reign of Queen Elizabeth this village was noted for bakers; for it is said that all the persons of that profession who supplied London with bread, then resided here. From hence it was carried to London in carts, and sold to the people at their own doors. There is at present a considerable manufactory carried on here, for making of porcelain, which is brought to such perfection as to be little inferior to that of China. There are also great numbers of scarlet dyers and callico printers reside here, for the conveniency of water and grounds to dry their clothes. There is a fair held here in Whitsun-week.— A little to the south of this village is another named *Bromley*, which is pleasantly situated, wherein there are many handsome houses.

─────────────────────────

HAVING described the most remarkable places, public edifices, royal palaces, and feats, within the distance of twenty miles round London, we shall now proceed to treat of other parts of the kingdom, and to give an account of such other places, elegant feats, and splendid edifices, and other curious particulars, as may be most deserving the attention of the inquisitive reader.

C H E L M S F O R D.

This is a considerable town in the county of Essex, which is situated at the confluence of two rivers, the Chelmer and the Cann; from the former of which it derived its name. It is the county town, and is distant from London twenty-nine miles. The town consists but of four streets, but is regular and well built. The entrance to it from the London road is over an old stone bridge, built by Maurice, Bishop of London in the reign of Henry the First. As soon as this is passed over, a spacious street presents itself to the view of the traveller, at the upper end of which, upon a little ascent, stands the shire-house. Each street lies with an easy descent towards the centre, and is washed with a current of clear water. The Chelmer and the Cann form here an angle; along which lie many pleasure gardens, and some of them are agreeably laid out.

In an open place nearly a square, adjoining to the shire-house,

* See page 55, 56.

The South East View of Chelmsford Church, in the County of Essex:

houfe, ftands a conduit. It is of a quadrangular form, about fifteen feet high, built with ftone and brick : it has four pipes, on each fide, from which the pureft water is perpetually flowing. The following infcription is on the fide that fronts the part from whence the fpring rifes. ' This conduit in one '. minute runs one hogfhead and a half, and four gallons and a ' half. In one day 2262 hogfheads and 54 gallons. In one ' month 63,360 hogfheads. And in one year 825,942 hogf-' heads and 54 gallons.'

The affizes, general quarter feffions, and other county courts, are held at Chelmsford ; and likewife are held the elections for the knights of the fhire; and here ftands the county gaol. The great road from London to Colchefter, to Harwich, to Suffolk, and many parts of Norfolk, lies through this town ; fo that it is furnifhed with feveral good inns. Adjoining to the fhire-houfe is a good market place; where a market is held every Friday, fupplied with corn, meat, fifh, fowls, &c. The church is an handfome ancient ftructure, fituated at the end of the town. There are feveral handfome monuments in it erected in memory of the Mildmay family ; one in particular for Benjamin Mildmay, Earl of Fitz-walter.—There is a good free-fchool in this town, which was founded by King Edward the Sixth, befides two other charity-fchools.

Sir William Mildmay, Bart. has a very handfome feat near this town, known by the name of MOULSHAM HALL. It is pleafantly fituated on an eafy afcent, about a quarter of a mile on the eaft fide of Chelmsford. The grand front commands Danbury-hill. It is a very regular edifice, and on the top of it are three ftatues, reprefenting Diana, Apollo, and Mercury : under thefe are the family arms in baffo relievo, carved in free-ftone. The other parts of the houfe have a view of the London road, of the town of Chelmsford, and of the park and gardens. It was rebuilt by the late Earl of Fitzwalter, and was fo conftructed as to be at once elegant and commodious. The pilafters, cornices, entablatures, and other decorations, are of ftone. In the infide is a quadrangular court flagged. It has a gallery on each floor round it, by which means an eafy accefs is obtained to all the different apartments, without the inconveniency of making any of them a paffage.

The principal rooms are large and well difpofed. The grand hall at the entrance is lofty, and the cieling curioufly wrought

wrought with fret-work. In the breakfaſt room are many
pictures of the Mildmay family, ſome of which are well executed. Among theſe are Sir William Mildmay, who was
chancellor of the exchequer in the reign of Queen Elizabeth,
and founder of Emanuel College, Cambridge. The great
picture room contains ſeveral family portraits ; and here is alſo
a good piece of the old Duke of Schombergh on horſeback,
attended by a black who carries his helmet. In the little
picture room contiguous to this, are ſome good paintings : on
the right hand the door, is ſeen an half length of an old woman
in a white hood, whoſe diſtorted features ſhew the utmoſt diſ-
treſs. Upon her ſhoulder a caterpillar is ſeen crawling, which
is ſaid not only to have cauſed the violent agitation apparent
in her face, but alſo her death. Here is alſo an antique
painting of Matilda, daughter to the Lord Robert Fitzwalter,
who was ſaid to be poiſoned in the abbey of Dunmow by King
John. And in another room here, is a picture of one Sir
Henry Mildmay, a branch of this family, repreſenting him
as dead and laid out, covered with a black velvet pall. It is
ſaid that he died abroad, and that a faithful ſervant, who accompanied him, employed a limner to draw him after his
deceaſe. It is ſo well done, as to ſtrike the beholder with ſome
degree of horror ; and for this reaſon has been removed from
the collection to an anti chamber.—The gardens belonging to
this ſeat are neatly laid out, and here is alſo a park prettily diſpoſed.

Facing Moulſham hall are ſix alms-houſe, which were
founded by Sir Thomas Mildmay, Bart. and Anne his wife,
for ſix poor people. And at a little diſtance from hence
there was formerly an houſe of Dominican friars. The building was very ſtrong, being a compoſition of brick, flint, and
free-ſtone. The kitchen remained till within theſe few years,
and was eſteemed a great curioſity ; the room being ſupported
and decorated in the manner of the theatre in Oxford. The
ſite of it is now called *the Friars.*—In a field called Long-
ſtumps, between Moulſham hall and Gallywood common,
formerly ſtood a chapel, which belonged to the abbey of St.
Oſyth.

N E W - H A L L.

This ſeat is now the property of Lord Waltham, and is
ſituated in the pariſh of Boreham, which is three miles from
Chelmsford. It is not certainly known by whom this edifice
was erected ; but it is ſuppoſed to have been built by Butler,

Earl

Earl of Ormond, in the reign of King Henry VII. It was once made a place of royal refidence by King Henry VIII. who in 1524 kept the feaft of St. George here. It afterwards came into the poffeffion of George Monk, Duke of Albemarle, famous for the fhare he had in bringing about the Reftoration, who lived here in great pomp. The late Lord Waltham took down a confiderable part of this great edifice, and yet referved enough of it to make a noble and commodious country feat for himfelf, to which he added feveral new offices. It muft, indeed, in its primitive grandeur, have been a houfe of extraordinary fize, if what is very confidently faid be true, namely, that what is now left is only one tenth part of the original building.

The great hall is one of the nobleft in the kingdom. At the entrance of it the beholder is ftruck with its grandeur, it being upwards of forty feet high, ninety in length, and fifty wide. Oppofite to the grand entrance, is another door, which formerly led into a fpacious court: over this are the arms of Henry VIII. done in baflo relievo in free ftone, and well executed. The prefent Lord Waltham has greatly improved this feat, and is now laying out the gardens and park with much tafte. He has made a noble piece of water in the new gardens behind the houfe, and erected near it a good green-houfe. He has likewife added to the other buildings a new wing for ftables and coach-houfes. The avenue which leads from the great road to the houfe is near a mile long, and has double rows of lofty trees on each fide. It is reckoned the fineft in England, and gives a very venerable air to this magnificent manfion.

In the fame parifh, Richard Hoare, Efq. an eminent banker in London, has a fine feat. It is beautifully fituated at the top of an avenue of trees, between which is a fine piece of water, extending from the road nearly to the houfe. The houfe itfelf is not very large, but of an elegant conftruction, built of white brick: the infide is adorned with marble chimney pieces, and other decorations, the fpoils of the ancient manfion of New-hall. The gardens are prettily difpofed behind it; from thefe runs a delightful lawn down to the banks of the Chelmer, which, together with Danbury-hill, and various other beautiful objects that here meet the eye, furnifh a moft agreeable landfcape.

Boreham church is an ancient edifice, and there are here the remains of a fine monument in the Suffex chapel, which

was

was erected to perpetuate the memory of the noble family of that name. There are three alabaster figures of Robert Radcliff, Henry Radcliff, and Thomas Radcliff, Earls of Sussex; and in the vault, which is very neat, are twelve coffins, containing the remains of these noblemen, and others of the same family. Some of them have inscriptions on one fide, and a star and garter on the other. Others are cast in a human shape, with eyes, nose, mouth, &c. This ancient chapel and monument were for many years in a ruinous state; it being a subject of dispute to whom it belonged to preserve and repair them. But Richard Hoare, Esq. having obtained a faculty to convert the chapel in to a place of interment for his family, has repaired it for that purpose at a considerable expence.

In the church-yard is erected a Mausoleum for the Waltham family, in the imitation of the Temple of the Winds at Athens. It was built with white brick and stone: the remains of the late Lord Waltham are here deposited.

About three miles from Chelmsford is the parish of *Widford*, wherein John Richard Comyns, Esq. has an handsome seat. It is a neat modern built house, surrounded by a good park and pleasant gardens, well watered. It is called *Highlands*, from the loftiness of its situation; which circumstance renders it very delightful, from the several pleasing prospects it commands. It was erected by the late Sir John Comyns, Chief Baron of the Exchequer.

I N G A T E S T O N E.

This is a market-town in Essex, six miles from Chelmsford, and twenty three from London. It consists chiefly of inns, being a post town, and the great thoroughfare to Norfolk, Suffolk, Harwich, and Colchester. A considerable market for live cattle is held here every Wednesday; and a very large fair is annually held here on the first of December, the principal commodity of which is also live cattle.

Ingatestone Hall, the property of Lord Petre, is a venerable stately pile of building, having within a spacious court, and before it is another, round which are the offices. It lies very low, but upon that account is well supplied with water, and stored with fish-ponds; and the gardens are laid out in an elegant manner.—In the same parish is also a very good modern built house, called *the Hide*; which was built

by

by the late Timothy Brand, Efq; who was high-fheriff of the county of Effex in 1721, and it is now in poffeffion of Thomas Brand, Efq.——Ingateftone church is a good brick edifice, and contains fome handfome monuments in memory of the Petre family.

In the parifh of *Margaretting*, which joins to Ingateftone and Widford, Richard Holden, Efq; has a pleafant manfion-houfe, known by the name of *Cold Hall*. It is an elegant modern building, fituated on an eminence, with gardens well laid out.——There is alfo in this parifh, on the left hand fide of the road leading from Chelmsford to Ingateftone, a very good houfe belonging to Humphrey Sidney, Efq. Before the houfe is a pleafant avenue of ftately trees.——There is a manor in this parifh, named Shenfield, which is faid to be one of the houfes of pleafure where King Henry VIII. ufed to refort to his miftreffes. The houfe lay in a bottom, had many large buildings about it, and was furrounded by a moat. It had a draw bridge, at the extremity of which were two ftrong watch-towers, of brick; and there was a chapel adjoining to the houfe. But moft of the original buildings, if not all, are now pulled down, and it is become the habitation of a private gentleman.

Tradition fays, that there was more than one place in the county of Effex, to which Henry VIII. ufed occafionally to retire with his miftreffes. At fome diftance from hence is the parifh of Blackmore, which he is reported to have made ufe of for his amorous retreats. The manor houfe of Blackmore is alfo called Jericho; and we are told, that when Harry chofe to retreat from public bufinefs, and indulge himfelf in the embraces of his courtezans, the cant phrafe among the courtiers was, "He was gone to Jericho," He is alfo faid to have made ufe of Newland-hall in this county for the fame purpofe. But, in truth, much more is faid of Henry's miftreffes by the traditionary reports of the people of Effex, than is to be met with in our hiftorians.

In the parifh of *Great Waltham*, which is about four miles from Chelmsford, John Jolliff Tuffnel, Efq; has an handfome feat, about a quarter of a mile from the church, known by the name of *Langleys*. It ftands on a pleafant eminence; the foot and fides of which are wafhed by the river Chelmer on the north, and a brook on the fouth. There is a good park around it and pleafant gardens. Great Waltham church is

2   a ftrong

a ftrong brick building, and contains fome handfome monuments.

WITHAM.

This is a neat and pleafant town, about thirty-feven miles
from London, and between eight and nine from Chelmsford.
It is a poft-town, and contains fome good inns.   It has a market for grain on Tuefdays, and two fairs are held here annually, one on the Monday before Whitfunday, and the other
on the 14th of September.—Edward, the fon of King Alfred,
commonly called Edward the Elder, built this town in the beginning of his reign, and refided at Malden during the time it
was building.———Witham church ftands upon an eminence,
about half a mile weft from the town.   The walls both of the
church and fteeple are of Roman flint, except the top of the
tower, which is brick.   There are fome monuments in the
church, two of which are ancient.

At the entrance into Witham from the Colchefter road,
upon the left hand, is a good houfe and gardens belonging to
the Earl of Abercorn ; and General Douglas has alfo an handfome houfe in the fame parifh.

In the parifh of *Great Bracktead*, which is about three miles
from Witham, Peter Du Cane, Efq; has an elegant feat,
called *Braxted Lodge*.   It is furrounded by a park, and ftands
upon an eminence which commands an agreeable profpect of
the neighbouring country.——Charles Buxton, Efq; has alfo
a good houfe in the fame parifh, with fpacious gardens well
watered.

Kelvedon is four miles from Witham, and about a mile
from the former is *Fælix Hall*, the feat of Daniel Matthews,
Efq.   It is a handfome edifice, fituated on an eminence,
and around it is a fmall park.   The gardens are laid out with
elegance, and have in them green-houfes, and hot houfes,
and every other requifite to render them ufeful as well as
pleafing.

COGGESHALL.

This is a market-town in Effex, about feven miles from
Witham, and forty-four from London.   It ftands partly on
the declivity of a hill, and is pleafantly fituated; and is

pretty

Felix Hall in Essex the seat of Danl. Matthews Esqr.

pretty large and populous. Here is a market on Thurſday for corn, and an annual fair on Whitſun Tueſday. The church is a ſpacious and lofty edifice, and ſtands pleaſantly at the upper end of the town, having a good proſpect ſouthward.

Hereabouts have been found the remains of ſome antient little Roman ſtation, or villa, adjoining to the road which leads to the town. An arched vault of brick was diſcovered, and in it a burning lamp of glaſs, covered with a Roman tile, about fourteen inches ſquare, and an urn with aſhes and bones, and other antiquities.—Oſgood Hanbury, Eſq; has a good ſeat, with a park, near this town, known by the name of *Oldfield Grange.*

An Abbey was founded at Coggeſhall, in the year 1142, by King Stephen, and his Queen Maud, for Ciſtercian or White Monks, and dedicated to the Virgin Mary. The remains of the abbey ſtands within the precincts of Little Coggeſhall, near the river: it was a Gothic edifice, but is now moſtly demoliſhed.

In the pariſh of *Markſhall,* which is two miles from Coggeſhall, General Honeywood, who is Lord of the Manor, has a fine ſeat. It is an handſome edifice, pleaſantly ſituated near the church, on a riſing ground. The gardens, park, and fiſh-ponds, contribute to make it a very pleaſant retirement. In the dining-room is an original painting of Mrs. Mary Waters, or Honeywood, in a widow's habit. This memorable perſon was born at Lenham, in Kent, and is ſaid to have continued forty-four years a widow, and then arriving at the age of ninety-three, ſaw 367 children lawfully deſcended from her, 16 of her own body, 114 grand-children, 228 in the third generation, and nine in the fourth.

BRAINTREE.

This town is about ſix miles from Coggeſhall, and forty from London; and is a great thoroughfare from London into Suffolk and Norfolk. The buildings are moſtly old, and of timber; but ſomewhat improved of late by a few new ones of brick and plaiſter. Here is a market every Wedneſday, well ſupplied with all kinds of neceſſaries, and at which vaſt quantities of corn, malt, and hops, are ſold by ſample. Two fairs are held here annually; one on the ſecond of October, which holds three days; and the other on the eighth of May, which

Z   laſts

lasts the same time; the principal traffic of which is live cattle, butter, and cheese.

In the parish of *Black Notley*, which is at a little distance from Braintree, there is a handsome monument in the church-yard, in memory of that celebrated naturalist, Mr. John Ray, which was erected at the expence of Henry Compton, Bishop of London. Mr. Ray was born at Black Notley, being the son of a blacksmith there, and was also interred there in 1706.

B O C K I N G.

This is one of the most considerable villages in the county of Essex: it consists chiefly of one street, in which the baize-trade is carried on to a very great amount. The church is a spacious building, situated upon an eminence. Here is also a large meeting-house, and another belonging to the Quakers.——An urn of old coins, mostly Vespasion's, was some time since found in the grounds belonging to High Garret, in this parish.

In the parish of *Gorsfield*, Lord Clare has a very handsome seat, known by the name of GORSFIELD HALL. It is situated at a small distance from the church, and is surrounded by an extensive park, and has also elegant gardens.

D U N M O W.

This is a very antient town, situated pleasantly on a hill, at the distance of thirty-seven miles from London. The trade of this place is inconsiderable, but a manufacture of bays and blankets is carried on here. In the center of the town stands what is called the market-cross, which is a very antient edifice: and over against this is the guildhall, in which the town officers meet to transact the corporation-business. The market is on Saturday, and here are two fairs held, for toys only, one of which is on the sixth of May, and the other on the eighth of November. The church stands near a mile north from the main street, in a bottom, and is a large neat building.

In the parish of *Little Dunmow*, which is two miles from the town of Dunmow, there was formerly a priory. It stood in a delightful situation, but is now entirely decayed. In this priory were maintained a prior, and ten or eleven canons regular, of the order of St. Augustine.——Amongst the

Gosfield Hall the Seat of the Right Hon:ble Lord Viscount Clare.

'held 7 June, 1701, before Thomas Wheeler, gent. stew-
'ard, the homage being *five fair ladies*, spinsters, namely,
'Elizabeth Beaumont, Henrietta Beaumont, Annabella Beau-
'mont, Jane Beaumont, and Mary Wheeler; they found
'that John Reynolds, of Hatfield Broad Oak, gent. and
'Anne his wife, and William Parsley, of Great Easton,
'butcher, and his wife Jane, by means of their *quiet* and
'*peaceable, tender* and *loving* cohabitation for the space of
'three years last past and upwards, were fit and qualified
'persons to be admitted by the court to receive the an-
'cient and accustomed oath, whereby to entitle themselves
'to have the Bacon of Dunmow delivered to them accord-
'ing to the custom of the manor. Accordingly having taken
'the oath, kneeling on the two great stones near the church
'door, the bacon was delivered to each couple.'——The
last who received it were John Shakeshanks, wool comber,
and Anne his wife, of Wethersfield, on the twentieth of June,
1751.

T H A X T E D

Is an ancient town in Essex, six miles from Dunmow,
and forty-two from London. There is but little trade in this
place; but here are two fairs annually, one held on the 10th
of August and the other on the Sunday after the Ascension.
This town is chiefly remarkable for its church, which is the
finest in the county. It is a noble Gothic building; and the
length of it is an hundred and eighty-three feet, and the
breadth eighty-seven feet, in the inside, exclusive of the thickness of the walls, and the projection of the buttresses. It is
three hundred forty-five feet in circumference. It is built ca-
thedral-wise, with a cross isle; and consists of a spacious and
lofty body with north and south isles. At the west end stands a
noble tower, and spire, all of free-stone, the perpendicular
height of which, from the summit of the vane to the ground-
floor, is sixty yards, and one foot.

S A F F R O N   W A L D E N.

This is a large and populous town, seven miles from
Thaxted, and forty-two from London. The neighbouring
fields were formerly chiefly appropriated to the cultivation of
saffron, from which circumstance it derived part of its name;
but that plant is now chiefly cultivated more westward, in
　　　　　　　　　　　　　　　　　　　　　　　　　and

and about the confines of Cambridgeshire. Saffron is said to have been first brought into Essex in the reign of King Edward III. and Essex and Cambridgeshire saffron is accounted the best in the world. There is a great deal of the malting businefs carried on at Saffron Walden; here is likewife a manufacture for bolting cloths, and for checks and fustians. Many of the poor are employed in the making of facks, and in spinning of fine yarn, for the manufactories in Norwich. Many of the inhabitants are Diffenters, who have a meeting-houfe for the Independents, another for the Baptifts, and a third for the Quakers. It has a large market weekly on Saturday, and two fairs annually; one on the Sunday in Mid-lent, for horfes, &c. and the other on the firft of November, for cows, &c.— The church is an ancient and ftately ftructure, fituated nearly in the center of the town. On the fouth fide of the chancel are fteps which lead to a vault, the burial place of the Suffolk family. The remains of fix Earls of Suffolk are depofited here, and of others of the fame noble family. And under the fouth arch of the chancel is an elegant altar monument, erected to the memory of Lord Audley, High Chancellor of England, in the reign of King Henry the Eighth.

There was a priory founded here in 1136, by Geoffrey de Mandeville, Earl of Effex; and in the year 1190, it was converted into an abbey. The fcite of it was near the great pond by the bowling green at Saffron Walden, where foundations and bones have been dug up.

About a mile fouth of Saffron Walden is AUDLEY HOUSE, or as it is more frequently called, AUDLEY END, which is at prefent the feat of Sir John Griffin Griffin, who is Colonel of the thirty-third regiment of foot, and a Lieutenant-General. It was built by Thomas Lord Audley of Walden, who was created Earl of Suffolk by King James the Firft, to whom he was Treafurer. The Earl defigned it as a Palace for his Majefty, and when it was finifhed prefented it to him; but the King, when he faw its vaft extent and magnificence, faid that " it would fuit very well a Lord Treafurer, but was too " much for a King." It remained therefore in the poffeffion of the Earls of Suffolk during that and the fucceeding reign, but it was afterwards purchafed by King Charles the Second; who, not being able to pay for it, mortgaged the hearth tax to the then Earls, as a fecurity for the money. This tax was taken off foon after the Revolution, but the ftate not being

2   then

then in a condition to pay the money for which it had been pledged, the house was granted back again to the family. It was then the largeft royal palace in the kingdom ; the expence of building it is faid to have amounted to ninety thoufand pounds. The mere model of it in wood is faid to have coft five hundred pounds. It confifted of two courts, one of which, and part of the other, including a gallery 226 feet long, 32 wide, and 24 high, were taken down by Henry Earl of Suffolk between fixty and feventy years ago. The part of it which is now remaining is only a fourth of its original extent. Before the weft front of it are many lawns, rifing to the view, and watered by the river Cam, cut in the form of a fine canal, over which are two elegant bridges. The eaft front commands an extenfive park, walled in, and a view of the church and town of Saffron Walden. The fouth fide looks into a curious piece of clumped pleafure ground, called the Mount Garden ; and the north into a lawn, feveral plantations, and a neighbouring village.

At *Afhdon*, about three miles north-weft of Saffron Walden, there are four barrows, or pyramidical hills, which were erected by Canute the Dane, over the bodies of thofe who were killed in a battle which was fought here, and in which Canute totally defeated the army of Edmund Ironfide, and took moft of the nobility who attended him prifoners. One of thefe hills being dug into or opened, there were found, in a ftone coffin, two bodies, one of which lay with his head towards the other's feet; alfo two other ftone coffins were found with pieces of bones in them, and many chains of iron, about the fize of thofe belonging to horfes bits.

At *Chefterford*, a village four miles north of Saffron Walden, fome years ago the ruins of a Roman city were difcovered ; the foundation of the walls take in a compafs of about fifty acres ; and the foundations of a Roman temple were not long fince very vifible.

In the parifh of *Hadftock*, which joins to that of Afhdon, is a very antient church, the north door of which is much adorned with thick bars of iron work, of an irregular form, underneath which is a fort of a fkin, faid to be that of a Danifh King : it is nailed on with large nails.

There is a tradition about the church door of Copford parifh, which is about five miles from Colchefter, of which Mr. Newcourt gives us the following account. He fays,

it

A View of the Hills near Ashdon, in Essex, raised over ÿ bodies of those slain in a Battle fought there.

it was ' taken notice of in the year 1690, when an old man
' at Colchefter hearing Copford mentioned, faid, that in his
' young time, he heard his mafter fay, that he had read in
' an old hiftory, that the church of Copford was robbed by
' the Danes, and their fkins nailed to the doors ; upon which,
' fome gentlemen being curious, went thither, and found a
' fort of tanned fkin, thicker than parchment, which is fup-
' pofed to be human fkin, nailed to the door of the faid church,
' underneath the faid iron-work, fome of which fkin is ftill to
' be feen.'

CASTLE HEDINGHAM.

This place, which is about forty-eight miles from London, was the caftle and chief feat of the noble family of
De Vere, Earls of Oxford, on which account the appellation
of caftle is prefixed to it. The greater part of the caftle is
demolifhed ; but the remaining tower is one hundred and ten
feet, from the ground to the top of the four-fquare turrets at
the corners. It is faid there were three other towers, and in its
perfect ftate this caftle appears to have been very lofty and magnificent.

Queen Maud, wife of King Stephen, died in this caftle.
It was reckoned a place of great ftrength before the invention
of gunpowder. It held out fome time againft King John,
in 1215 ; and againft the Dauphin Lewis, who had been in-
vited over by fome of the Barons in 1217.—It was at this caftle that King Henry the Seventh, whofe avaricious character is
well known, made John De Vere, Earl of Oxford, pay fo
extravagantly for having had the honour of entertaining him:
The King having been feafted in a very fumptuous manner by
the Earl, at his going away the Earl's fervants and tenants ftood
in their livery coats, with cognizances, ranged on both fides,
and made the King a lane to pafs through them. Upon
this Henry called the Earl to him, and faid, " My Lord, I have
" heard much of your hofpitality, but I fee it is greater than
" the fpeech. Thefe handfome gentlemen and yeomen, which
" I fee on both fides of me, are fure your menial fervants."
The Earl fmiled and faid, " It may pleafe your Grace,
" that were not for mine eafe. They are moft of them my
" retainers, who are come to do me fervice at fuch a time as
" this, and chiefly to fee your Grace." The King ftarted a
little, and faid, " By my faith, my Lord, I thank you for my
" good cheer, but I may not endure to have my laws broken

" in

" in my fight. My attorney muſt ſpeak with you."
And accordingly the King obliged him to pay a fine of
fifteen thouſand marks, for a breach of the ſtatute againſt
retainers.

Hedingham Caſtle is now the property of Sir Harry Hoghton, Bart. who lately diſtinguiſhed himſelf ſo honourably in the
Houſe of Commons, in the promotion of religious liberty ; and
who has a handſome modern edifice here, in which he occaſion-
ally reſides. The village is a neat and healthy place, and there
are three fairs held here, one on the 3d of May, another on
the 23d of July, and the third on the 6th of December.—Sir
Harry Hoghton has erected a ſtrong bridge of brick here, conſiſting of three arches, at his own expence.

A religious houſe was founded in this pariſh, for black-veiled
nuns, of the Benedictine order, by Alberic de Vere, the firſt
Earl of Oxford. , The nunnery-houſe is ſtill in being, but converted into a farm-houſe, and moſt of the church or chapel belonging to it, is ſtill ſtanding.

In the middle of the chancel of Caſtle Hedingham church,
is an handſome and curious marble tomb, containing the remains of John de Vere, the fifth Earl of Oxford of that
name. There are alſo ſome other handſome monuments in the
church.—There is a meeting-houſe in this pariſh, and Peter
Muilman, Eſq; has a good ſeat here, known by the name of
Kirby Hall.

The pariſh of *Hedingham Sible* joins to this, and in the wall
of the ſouth iſle of the church there, is part of a ſuperb arch,
which formerly contained a magnificent monument in memory
of Sir John Hawkwood, who was a very remarkable perſon,
and who was born here. He was the ſon of Gilbert Hawkwood, a tanner of this place ; and was bound apprentice to
a taylor in the city of London, where being preſſed into the
ſervice of King Edward the Third, then about to make war
in France, he behaved himſelf ſo gallantly, that he was firſt
made a Captain, and then Knighted by that Prince. When
the French war was at an end, he offered his ſervice to the
ſtates of Florence, in which he ſignalized himſelf ſo much,
that Barnaby Galeazo, Duke of Milan, gave him his daughter
Domnia to wife, by whom he had a ſon, who was born in Italy,
but naturalized and Knighted in England, in the reign of Henry
IV.—Sir John Hawkwood died in a very advanced age in
1394, and was buried in the cathedral church of Santa Maria
. Florida

Hedingham Castle in Essex, the seat of Sr. Harry Hoghton Bart.

Kirby Hall in Essex, the Seat of Peter Muilman Esq.

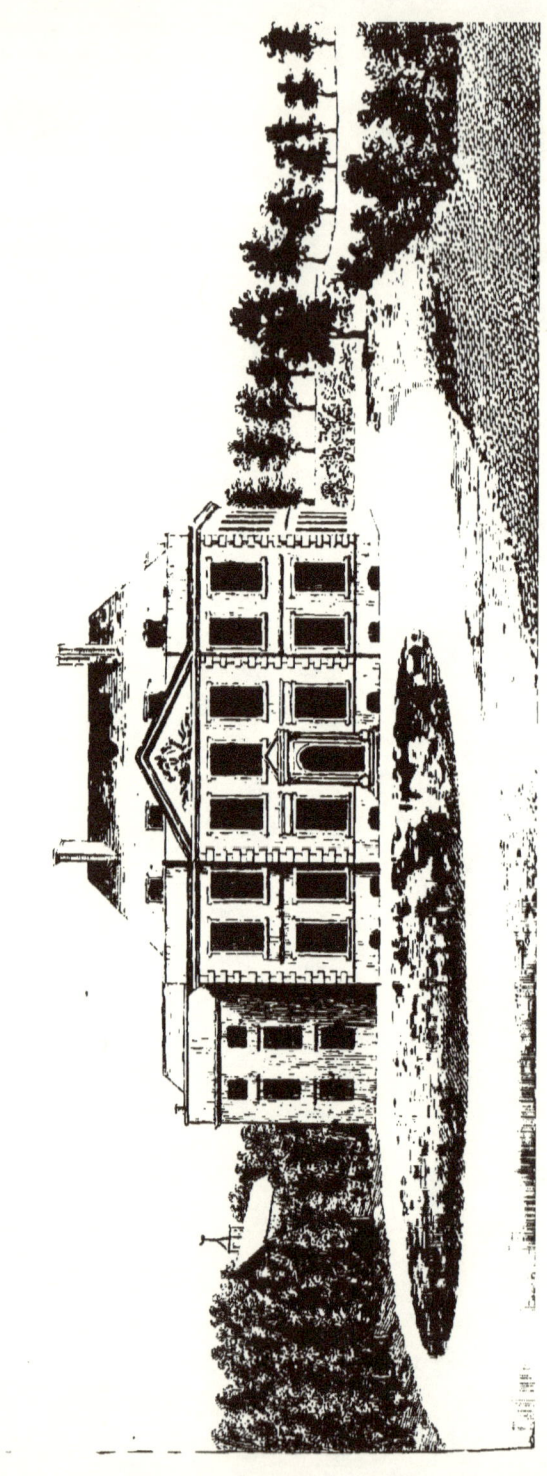

Florida at Florence, where that republic, out of gratitude to his memory and extraordinary deferts, have honoured him with a ftatue on horfeback, and a noble monument.—A manor in the parifh of Sible Hedingham, called *Hawkfwood's* manor, derives its name from this eminent man.

In the parifh of *Bulmer*, which is at a ſmall diftance, Robert Andrews, Efq; has an handfome feat, known by the name of AUBERIES. It is a modern, regular, and uniform brick building, and is fituated upon an eminence, which commands a delightful profpect of the borough of Sudbury, and of fome part of Cambridgefhire. It is adorned with gardens laid out in a pleafing tafte, and has feveral ponds belonging to it, well ftocked with fifh.

H A L S T E A D.

This is a pleafant and healthy town in Effex, at the diftance of forty-feven miles from London, fituated on the fide of a hill, the foot of which is watered by the river Colne. There are many hops produced here, for the excellency of which this town is famous ; and a manufactory for bays is eftablifhed here. A market is held every Friday, and two fairs annually, one on the 6th of May, and the other on the 29th of October, for cattle, hops, and toys. Here is a grammar-fchool, which was founded in the reign of Queen Elizabeth.

In the parifh of *Great Maplejtead*, which is about three miles from Halftead, Henry Sperling, Efq; has an handfome feat, known by the name of DYNES HALL. The houfe is an handfome edifice, a mile fouth of the church, and fituated upon an eminence, commanding a beautiful profpect. The gardens belonging to it are elegant.

C O L C H E S T E R.

This is a very ancient town, in the north-eaft part of the county of Effex, at the diftance of about fifty-one miles from London. It ftands upon the north fide of a fine eminence, rifing gradually from the river Colne, which waters the north and eaft fides. It is the moft confiderable town in the county, and is governed by a mayor, high-fteward, recorder, eleven aldermen, eighteen common council-men, and other corporation officers. It was laft incorporated by King William the Third, and is a liberty of itfelf, having four wards and fixteen parifhes, eight of which are within the walls, and eight without. It is a populous place, and is

A a   about

about three miles in circumference; the ftreets are fpacious, and though not in general remarkably well built, yet there are a great many good houfes in it, befides the guild-hall, adjoining to which is the town-gaol, and a hall called Dutchbaize-hall, belonging to a corporation for the fupport of the bays and fay manufactures, both which are fine buildings. Here are ten parifh churches, and three meeting-houfes, of which one is for the Quakers. Here are two charity-fchools, one for feventy boys, and the other for fifty boys and girls, a work-houfe, and two free grammar-fchools; and there are three bridges upon the river Colne, which was made navigable by act of parliament for fmall craft up to a long ftreet next the water-fide, called the Hithe, where there is a quay, and for fhips of large burthen, to a place called the Wyvenhoe, within three miles of the town, where there is a cuftom-houfe.

Colchefter had formerly the greateft manufactory of bays and fays of any in England; but that trade has of late years confiderably declined here. This place is alfo remarkable for candying eringo roots, but much more for its oyfters, for which it is particularly famous. . They are taken near the mouth of the Colne, upon fands called the Spitts, and are carried up to the Wyvenhoe, where they are laid in beds or pits on the fhore to feed; after they have continued in thefe pits fome time, they are barrelled and brought to Colchefter, from whence they are fent in great quantities to London and other places. Such fhoals of fprats are caught here, and confumed by the woollen manufacturers, that the common name for this fifh is the weavers beef of Colchefter.

This town has fent members to parliament from the 23d of Edward I. to the prefent time; and upwards of fifteen hundred perfons are entitled to votes here. There are three marketdays in every week in this town, viz. on Wednefday, Friday, and Saturday; and here are five fairs held, one on the fecond Tuefday in April, another on the 5th of July, another on the 23d of July, another on the 2d of Auguft, and the laft on the 20th of October.

Colchefter is fuppofed by fome to be the ancient *Camuludunum*; and it has been obferved, that there are a greater quantity of Roman remains here than in any other part of *Britain*; vaft quantities of Roman bricks and tiles being to be feen incorporated, and which are indeed the principal ingredients in all the moft antient edifices; the town wall, the caftle, and the churches being half built with them. The *Suppellex Romana*

of

of all kinds ftill abounds, fcarcely any places being dug up without difcovering urns, vafes, and *poterie*, of all forts, or at leaft
fragments; among which is a great deal of the fine glazed and
red ware, refembling the moft beautiful of that which comes
from China. Lamps, rings, intaglias, ftyles, chains, and fe-
pulchral urns, with the afhes therein, are likewife frequently
found. A remarkable urn in particular was taken up a few
years ago; it contained twenty gallons, having in it another of
two gallons, with the afhes, as is fuppofed, of a Roman lady,
becaufe there were alfo with it two bottles of clay for incenfe,
two clay lamps, one metal veffel for ointment, and a fpeculum
of polifhed metal, anciently ufed for a looking-glafs. And
there are here a great number of Mofaic or teffelated pave-
ments, about three feet under ground, having black, white,
red, and yellow tefferæ, and looking like a beautiful carpet.
Some of thefe are preferved, being inclofed and covered. But
as to Roman coins and medals, it is faid that even bufhels have
been found in and about this town, and amongft them many
gold ones.—The walls of this town are ftill ftanding, but very
much decayed in fome places, particularly on the north fide.
Where the walls remain perfect, it is faced either with Roman brick, or fquare ftones, about feven or eight inches in
diameter.

Colchefter-caftle ftands on the north fide of what is called the
High-ftreet, and is a fquare of about two hundred and twenty-
four yards in circumference on the outfide. The whole building
is a mixture of ftone and Roman bricks; but moft of the Roman bricks are in broken pieces, taken from the ruins of more
ancient edifices formerly ftanding in the town. The corners of
the walls, and fides of doors and windows, are of free ftone.—
In 1631, Dr. Harfnet, archbifhop of York, gave to the town
of Colchefter all his library of books, and they are depofited
in the caftle. Several additions have fince been made to this
library; and a very capital addition of valuable books would
have been made to it by the late Bifhop Compton; but the love
of learning was then fo prevalent at Colchefter, that the Bifhop's benefaction was neglected, in order *to fave the expence of
carriage!*

D E D H A M

Is fituated feven miles from Colchefter. This was anciently a famous cloathing-town, fo early as the reign of King
Richard the Second; and the bay-trade extended into it afterwards; but is now greatly on the decline. The town

is

is tolerably well built, and there are some very large houses in it. Here is a grammar-school, the governors of which were incorporated by a charter granted by Queen Elizabeth; and that princess particularly enjoined the parents of the boys who were educated at this school, that they should furnish their sons with bows, shafts, bracers and gloves, in order to train them to arms.—Dedham church is an handsome and spacious building, and the roof of an arch underneath the steeple is finely adorned with the arms of the two families of York and Lancaster, and red and white roses; and at the east side of the battlements there is a statue of Margaret, Countess of Richmond, and coronets all round.

MANINGTREE

Is a market-town in Essex, at the distance of about sixty miles from London. It is situated on the south side of the river Stour, and a considerable trade is carried on here in deals, coals, iron and corn; and from hence the best whitings, and a quantity of other fish, are carried to Colchester. The market is held here on Thursday, and here is a fair on the 15th of June.— Richard Rigby, Esq; has an handsome seat near this town, known by the name of MISTLEY HALL, which is pleasantly situated on an eminence. It is adorned with extensive gardens, and plantations, laid out in much taste.

At *Mistley Thorn*, the late Richard Rigby, Esq; (father of the present gentleman of the same name, who is well known in the political world) built a village of about thirty brick houses, convenient for tradesmen, and well inhabited. He also built several granaries, warehouses, a large malting office, and made good quays and coal-yards, and there is now a large trade carried on here.—Maningtree church is a neat edifice, and was built at the expence of Mr. Rigby.

HARWICH.

This town is at the distance of seventy-two miles from London, and is situated on a cliff or point of land, at the north east corner of the county of Essex. It is bounded on the east by the sea, and on the north by the mouth of the river Sour, and the haven of Orwell. The washing and underming of the tides, and the falling of large pieces of the cliff, have made this point a peninsula, and it is apprehended in a course of years, will make it quite an island. The town

is

Mistley Hall, in Essex, the Seat of Richard Rigby, Esqr.

is not large, but well built, and populous. It was formerly walled round, and had four gates; it had also a castle, and an admiralty house. It was first made a borough by King Edward the Second, and was afterwards incorporated by King James the First. Between this town and a high hill, called Beacon-hill, not far distant, there is a cliff consisting of a kind of clay, parts of which are continually falling down into a petrifying water at the bottom, which they imbibe, and being afterwards taken out and dried, they become an impenetrable and durable stone, and with this stone the town is paved.

The harbour is very safe, and so spacious, that an hundred sail of men of war, and their tenders, besides three or four hundred sail of colliers, have sometimes been seen here at the same time. The mouth of the harbour at high water, is near three miles wide, but the channel, by which alone the ships can come into the harbour, is deep and narrow, and lies on the Suffolk side; so that all the ships that come in or go out, are commanded by a strong fort, called *Landguard Fort*, which was built by King James the First, on a point of land, so surrounded by the sea at high water, that it looks like an island, lying about a mile from the shore. The town was formerly fortified on the land side, but in the reign of King Charles the First, the fortifications were demolished.—There is a guildhall, and a tolerable good exchange at Harwich; and as it is a sea port, here is a custom-house, called the King's-house, with a collector, comptroller, land-surveyor, tide-surveyor, two land-waiters, and four tide-waiters.

For the guidance of vessels into the harbour, in a room over the chief gate there is a light kept every night with a coal-fire, to which answers a light-house on the town-green below the cliff, with lamps supplied with oil. By means of them ships are conducted clear of a sand called the Andrews, into the rolling grounds, where there is a good anchorage. The shortest and safest passage between England and Holland being from this port, it brings a considerable number of travellers this way, especially in time of war; for whose conveniency, and the carrying of the mails, there are four pacquet boats, and in war-time two Dover pacquet boats. King William, and King George I. and II. usually embarked and landed at this place, in their journies to and from Holland and Hanover.

Here is a good yard for building ships, with store-houses, cranes, launches, and other necessaries.——The town-hall and

gaol

gaol were lately pulled down, and rebuilt with brick ; and the private buildings and pavement of the streets, are of late years much improved. The fishery here is so much increased of late years, that there are now upwards of sixty fishing sloops belonging to this town, of about fifty tons burthen. The copperas works, which were formerly carried on here, have been dropped for some years, and very little copperas is now picked up here; neither are there many lobsters taken on the shore, as formerly. But a number of fishing sloops from hence are employed to fetch lobsters from Norway to London, and other markets, each of them bringing on an average about twelve or fourteen thousand on a single voyage, and most of them making two voyages from hence between February and July. As many, or rather a larger number of vessels, sail every winter from hence to the Dogger bank, and there fish for Dogger cods, which are very large and much esteemed. This fishery, till within these five or six years, was not understood by our fishermen; but they are now become so expert therein, that hopes are entertained of establishing the turbot-trade here likewise, which will be a great saving to the nation, as the Dutch carry a great quantity of ready specie from London markets every season, for that kind of fish.

Part of a Roman castra or camp, still remains at Harwich; and here and there are found mutilated parts of a large stone pavement, which are supposed to be a sufficient proof of its having been a Roman military way; or, in the Saxon stile, a Stane-street. Several coins have been found here ; and a tesselated pavement was also discovered, and a wall pulled down about twenty years ago, built entirely of Roman materials.— At a Roman castle called by Camden, Walton, otherwise Felixstow-castle, many fragments of urns, and other antiquities have been dug up. An elephant's tooth was likewise found near the remains of this castle ; and it is said that more of them have been found in Harwich cliff, which were probably buried here by the Romans. Dion Cassius says, that elephants were brought into Britain by Claudius, who landed his army in Kent, and crossed the Thames with it into Essex, where he conquered the natives. This happened A. D. 43. So that these teeth are supposed to have lain in the earth 1700 years.

Harwich church is only a chapel of ease to the mother church of Dover-court. It was founded by Roger Bigod, Earl of Norfolk.—Harwich sends two members to parliament.—

Here

St. Osyth Priory, the Seat of the Earl of Rochford.

Here are two fairs held, one on the feaft of St. Philip and St. James, and the other on the feaft of St. Luke the Evangelift.

Dover-court is a mile diftant from Harwich. In this parifh grows ftrong knotted and crooked elms, famous for their feveral ufes in hufbandry, which are faid to be very durable, and to wear like iron. Here are two fairs held, one on the 1ft of May, and another on the 18th of October.

There are three iflands fouth-weft of Harwich, called Pewet, Horfey, and Holmes, which however are feparated from the main land only by the winding of a ftream, and the influx of the fea into that ftream. Upon thefe iflands there is found a fea-fowl, which, when fat, is very delicious food; fouth of thefe iflands there are three villages, which are included within a liberty or lordfhip, anciently called the liberty of the Soke, in which the Sheriff of the county has no power, and in which no writ can be executed but by the bailiff of the liberty, nor by him without the confent of the lord.

St. O S Y T H.

This is a parifh in Effex, at the diftance of twelve miles from Colchefter. It derived its name from the lady Ofgyth, or Ofyth, who was obliged by her father, againft her will, to marry Sighere, King of the Eaft Angles. She found means, however, to prevent the marriage being confummated; and, in the abfence of her hufband, took the veil. He at length confented to her living in a ftate of celibacy, and gave her a village which was fituated at this place, called Chich, or Cice, and permitted her to found here a church, and a nunnery. But Ingua and Hubba, we are told, fpoiled the nunnery, and caufed her head to be cut off, at a fountain where fhe ufed to wafh herfelf with her virgins; fhe was buried, it is faid, before the door of the church erected by herfelf.

Richard de Beauveis, bifhop of London, founded a monaftery here about the year 1118, for canons of the order of St. Auguftine. The revenues of this monaftery were very large, and there are two parks belonging to it. At the diffolution of the monafteries, this place was granted to the famous Thomas Cromwell, Earl of Effex. It afterwards became the property of Lord Darcy, who converted it into a feat for himfelf. Part of it only is ftanding, yet it is a noble

pile

pile of building, and is now the seat of the Earl of Rochford.

MALDEN

Is a very ancient town in Essex, at the distance of thirty-seven
miles from London. It stands on an eminence or side of a
hill, south of Blackwater bay. It consists of one wide street,
extending from west to east near a mile, which is crossed
near the top by another. On the west side of the town are the
remains of a camp, through the middle of which is the road
to Chelmsford; three sides of the fortifications are visible, being
a square or oblong, inclosing about twenty-two acres; the rest
is built upon and defaced. The bay here makes a convenient
harbour for ships, and the merchants carry on a considerable
trade in coal, iron, deals, and corn. Malden has sent burgesses to parliament from the third year of the reign of Edward
III.—The market here is on Saturday, and a fair is held three
weeks before Michaelmas, and another on Lady-day, and two
days after.

A shopkeeper of this town, whose name was Edward
Bright, was rendered famous by his extraordinary bulk and
weight. He is mentioned in the Philosophical Transactions, and
prints were published of him. Another instance of so vast a size
is scarcely to be met with in ancient or modern history. At the
age of 12 years he weighed 144 pounds; at 19 he weighed
336 pounds; about thirteen months before he died, his neat
weight was 41 stone 10 pounds, or 584 pounds; at the time
of his death he was manifestly grown bigger since his last weighing, in that proportion by which he had encreased on an average, viz. of about two stone a year; so that he was nearly
44 stone, or 616 pounds neat weight. He measured five feet
nine inches and an half in height; his body round his chest
was five feet six inches, and round his belly six feet eleven inches. His arm in the middle was two feet two inches about, and
his leg two feet eight inches. After his death seven men were
buttoned in his waistcoat. He died in 1750, aged twenty-nine.
He was an active man till a year or two before his death, when
his corpulency so overpowered his strength, that his life began
to be a burthen to him. He left a widow big with her sixth
child. His coffin was of an enormous size, and they were
obliged to cut a way through the wall and staircase, to let
his corpse down into the shop. It was drawn upon a carriage

to the church, and let down into the vault by the help of a sli-
der and pullies.

R O C H F O R D

Is a town in Effex, at the diftance of forty miles from London, fituated on a fmall ftream that falls into a river called the
Crouch. It gives its name to the hundred in which it lies. The
market is on Thurfday, and here are two fairs annually, one on
Eafter Tuefday, and the other on the Wednefday after Michaelmas day.—At King's-hill, about half a mile north-eaft of
Rochford church, is held what is called the *Lawlefs-court*, a
whimfical cuftom, the origin of which is not known. On the
Wednefday morning next after Michaelmas-day, the tenants
are bound to attend, upon the firft cock-crowing, and to kneel
and do their homage, without any kind of light but fuch as the
Heavens will afford. The fteward of the court calls all fuch as
are bound to appear, with as low a voice as poffible, giving no
notice when he goes to execute his office; however, he that gives
not an anfwer is deeply amerced. They are all to whifper to
each other, nor have they any pen and ink, but fupply that deficiency with a coal; and he that owes fuit and fervice, and appears not, forfeits to the Lord of the Manor double his rent
every hour he is abfent. A tenant of this manor forfeited, not
long ago, his land for non-attendance, but was reftored to it,
the Lord only taking a fine.

At the diftance of five miles from Rochford, is HADLEY,
or HADLEY AD CASTRUM, as it has been ftiled ever fince
the reign of King Henry the Third, when Hubert de Burgh,
Earl of Kent, built a caftle here. The ruins ftill extant, fhew
its ancient grandeur. It is near a mile fouth from the church,
and about three quarters of a mile from the road, facing
the Channel or Canvey-ifland. It is fituated on the brow of
a fteep hill, there is from thence a delightful profpect acrofs
the Thames into Kent. It is built of ftone almoft of an
oval form; the entrance is at the north-weft corner, between
two towers, and there are alfo two towers at the fouth-eaft
and north-eaft corners, which are embattled, and have loop
holes on the fides; the walls in the bottom of the towers are
nine feet thick, and the reft five feet; and on the north and
fouth fides, the walls are ftrengthened with buttreffes. The ce-
ment or mortar, which is almoft as hard as the ftones themfelves,
hath in it a mixture of fhells of fea-fifh, &c. At the entrance,

the

the earth lying very high near the towers, a very deep ditch is cut behind them which runs along the north side of the caflle ; the ruins are now greatly over-grown with bufhes.

***

ROCHESTER.

This is a very ancient city in the county of Kent, at the diftance of thirty miles from London. It is fituated on an angle of land formed by the current of the river Medway, which coming from the fouth runs northward till it has pafled by the city ; and then, turning, proceeds nearly to the eaft. This city has fent members to parliament from the earlieft times, and is the fee of a Bifhop, and next to Canterbury, the moft ancient fee in England. It is but a fmall city, though it is fuppofed to have been walled round before the conqueft ; and great part of the walls ftill remain. The town is well fupplied with provifions of every kind, and with plenty of fifh from the Medway. The buildings are lately much improved, and in feveral parts of the town are fome agreeable refidences for fmall genteel families. On Boley Hill, which is a retired and pleafant fituation, is an ancient feat, which is the property of Jofeph Brooke, Efq; wherein Queen Elizabeth was entertained in 1573. Part of the houfe has been new-built by Mr. Brooke. And near to this, on a delightful eminence, is the refidence of —— Gordon, Efq; from many parts of whofe houfe is a pleafing view of the Medway and the furrounding hills. This gentleman is poffeffed of a collection of fine paintings, many of them by the firft mafters in that polite art; particularly two capital drawings of Rubens, viz. the Crucifixion and the Penticoft.

There are three capital and fpacious inns in this city, which will vie with moft in England, as well for their good accommodations, as for their antiquity. Nearly on the fame fpot where the Crown now ftands, has been an inn diftinguifhed by that name upwards of four hundred and fifty years, it having been kept by Simon Potyn, the founder of St. Catharine's hofpital, A. D. 1316. It alfo appears from court rolls, that on the fame fpots where the Bull and the King's-head now ftand, there have been houfes of public entertainment diftinguifhed by the fame figns for above three hundred years.—In the neighbourhood of this city are feveral very rural and pleafant walks, particularly on the banks of the Medway.

Rochefter

A View of Rochester Castle & Bridge.

Rochester Castle, which is supposed to have been erected about 700 years, is placed on a small eminence, near the river Medway, just above Rochester bridge, and consequently is in the south-west angle of the walls of the city. It is nearly of a quadrangular form, having its sides parallel with the walls of the city. It is about three hundred feet square within the walls, which were seven feet in thickness, and twenty feet high above the present ground, with embrasures. Three sides of the castle were surrounded with a deep broad ditch, which is now nearly filled up; on the other side runs the Medway. In the angles and sides of the castle were several square towers, some of which are still remaining which were raised above the walls, and contained lower and upper apartments, with embrasures on their tops.

But what chiefly attracts the notice of a spectator, is the noble tower, which stands in the south east angle of this castle, and is so lofty as to be seen distinctly at twenty miles distance. It is quadrangular in its form, having its sides parallel with the walls of the castle. And from the top of it is a very pleasing prospect of the city and adjacent towns, with their public buildings, the dock-yard at Chatham, the meanders of the Medway, and the surrounding country.

There is an antient stone *Bridge* at Rochester, over the Medway, which was erected in the reign of Richard II. Sir Robert Knolles is celebrated for being the founder of this bridge. He was distinguished both by his courage and military preferments, being raised by degrees from the rank of a common soldier to that of a General. He attended Edward III. in his succesful campaigns in France; and when the King's affairs declined by the ill state of health of Edward the Black Prince, Sir Robert was sent over to the continent with an army of thirty thousand men. He advanced into the heart of France, and extended his conquests as far as the gates of Paris. In this, and many other expeditions, he acquired great riches, and returned to his country laden with wealth and honour.

Lombard says, Sir Robert built this bridge with " the " spoils of towns, castles, churches, monasteries and cities, " which he burnt and destroyed; so that the ruins of houses, " &c. were called Knolles's Mitres."—This bridge, for height and strength, is allowed to be superior to any in England, excepting the bridges at London and Westminster. It is above five hundred and sixty feet long, and fourteen feet broad, with

a stone

a ftone parapet on each fide, ftrongly coped and crowned with
an iron balluftrade. It has eleven arches, fupported by ftrong
and fubftantial piers, which are well fecured on each fide
with fterlings.   The river has a confiderable fall through
thefe arches.——At the eaft end, and fronting the paffage
over the bridge, a chapel was originally erected by Sir John
Cobham, who gave fome affiftance to Sir Robert Knolles in
building the bridge; but a neat ftone building has fince been
erected on the place where the chapel ftood, wherein the
perfons to whom the care of the bridge is entrufted, hold their
meetings.

A bifhopric was founded at Rochefter, in the reign of Ethelbert, King of Kent, foon after Auguftine the Monk had landed in the ifle of Thanet, and preached at Canterbury. The
firft church at Rochefter was finifhed in the year 604, but this
building having fuffered confiderably by time and the ravages
of foreign enemies, bifhop Gundulph rebuilt the cathedral about
the year 1080. It confifts of a body and two ifles, one on
each fide; its extent, from the weft door to the ftep afcending
to the choir, is fifty yards, and from thence to the eaft windows
at the upper end of the altar, fifty-two yards more, in all one
hundred and two yards, or three hundred and fix feet. At the
entrance of the choir is a great crofs ifle, the length of which,
from north to fouth, is one hundred and twenty-two feet. At
the upper end of the choir, between the Bifhop's throne and
the high altar, is another crofs ifle, which extends from north
to fouth, ninety feet.

The weft front extends eighty-one feet in breadth; the arch
of the great door is doubtlefs the fame which Gundulph built;
and is a moft curious piece of workmanfhip, every ftone being
engraved with fome device. It muft have been very magnificent in its original ftate, its remaining beauties being fufficient
to excite the attention of the curious; it is fupported by feveral columns on each fide, two of which are carved into ftatues
reprefenting Gundulph's royal patrons, Henry I. and his Queen
Matilda. The capitals of thefe columns, as well as the whole
arch, are cut into the figures of various animals and flowers.
The key ftone of the arch feems to have been defigned to reprefent St. Andrew, the apoftle and tutelar faint of the church,
fitting in a niche, with an angel on each fide, but the head is
broke off: under the figure of St. Andrew, are twelve other
figures, fuppofed to be defigned for the twelve apoftles, fome

few

few of which are perfect; but in general the whole arch is much injured by time.

On each side of the west door is a square tower ; that on the north side has lately been rebuilt, and has on the centre niche, on the west front, a very ancient figure, supposed to be the statue of Bishop Gundulph.

A priory was founded at Rochester about the year 600. A chapter of secular priests was first placed here, but they were afterwards removed, and Gundulph, bishop of Rochester, already spoken of as the builder of the cathedral, established here sixty black monks.—There are some ruins still remaining of the ancient chapter house, which shew it to have been a building of elegance, considering the age in which it was erected.—A skeleton was dug up, in December, 1766, by the workmen employed in digging a new cellar for the deanery of Rochester, in an area under the old chapter-house, or secretarium of the priory. This skeleton was full seven feet in length, and the skull very entire, with fine teeth quite firm in the jaw.

The town-hall of Rochester is an handsome brick structure, supported by coupled columns of stone, in the Doric order. At the upper end of the hall are the original portraits of King William III. and Queen Anne, by Sir Godfrey Kneller. Here are also the portraits of Sir Cloudesley Shovel, Sir John Leake, and other persons of note, well executed by eminent masters.— The clock-house, which is a neat building, was erected by Sir Cloudesley Shovel, who represented this city in four parliaments.—This city is governed by a mayor, eleven aldermen, and twelve common councilmen.

Sir Joseph Williamson, who was one of the plenipotentiaries at the treaties of Nimeguen and of Ryswick, and who was one of the representatives of this city, founded a mathematical school here. There is also a grammar school here, called the King's school, consisting of twenty scholars on the royal foundation, who have their education free, and each 9s. 4d. per quarter. They wear surplices, and with the choristers, are always obliged to attend divine service at the cathedral. A market is kept in this city on Fridays, and two annual fairs are held here, one on the 30th of May, and the other on the 11th of December.

There is in the river Medway at Rochester, and in several of its creeks and branches within the jurisdiction of the city, an oyster fishery ; which is free to every one who has served seven years apprenticeship to any fisherman or dredger, who

is

is free of the said fishery; and the Mayor and citizens of Rochester hold a court once a year, or oftner, when occasion re-
quires it, for the regulation of this fishery, and to prevent
abuses in it.

Rochester, Stroud, and Chatham, though they are three
distinct places, yet are so contiguous, as to appear in a manner
but one city; and these three towns form a continued street,
extending above two miles in length. Stroud is separated from
Rochester only by a bridge. There is an hospital here for sick
and lame soldiers; and an annual fair is held here on the 26th
of August.

CHATHAM

Is a suburb to Rochester, and perhaps the completest naval
arsenal in the world. It affords a sight equally noble and pleasing, to every one who is sensible how much the safety and pros-
perity of this nation depends on its maritime strength. It has
been brought to its present state of perfection by degrees, the
dock having been begun by Queen Elizabeth, and continually
improved by her successors.—This celebrated dock-yard, including the ordnance wharf, is about a mile in length; it is ranged
on the south east side of tthe river, and is adorned with many
elegant buildings, inhabited by the commissioner and principal
officers belonging to the yard, which well become the opulence
of the nation, and the importance of the navy. Here are many
neat and commodious offices for transacting the business of the
yard; also spacious storehouses (one of which is six hundred and
sixty feet in length) and work rooms, which, by their ampli-
tude, manifest their prodigious contents, and the extensive works
carried on within them; the sail-loft, in which the sails are
made, is two hundred and nine feet in length; in these magazines are deposited amazing quantities of sails, rigging, hemp,
flax, pitch, tar, rosin, oil, and every ingredient necessary for
the building and equipping of ships; the coils of cordage, and
heaps of blocks, with innumerable other articles, are arranged
with such order, that on any emergency they may be taken out
without the least confusion. To every apartment proper officers
and attendants are assigned, for the more expeditious dispatch
of business, so that even a first or second rate is often equipped
for sea in a few weeks.

The masts are carefully deposited in storehouses peculiarly adapted for them, one of which, in this yard, is two
hundred and thirty-six feet in length, and one hundred and
twenty

twenty feet wide ; fome of thefe mafts are near one hundred and twenty feet long, and thirty-fix inches in diameter : theie are alfo two fpacious bafons of water, in which thefe mafts are kept continually floating. The fmith's fhop contains twenty-one fires ; here the anchors are made, fome of which weigh near five tons. In an extenfive rope houfe, which is upwards of feven hundred feet in length, large quantities of hemp are twifted into cables one hundred and twenty fathoms long, and fome of them twenty-two inches round. In this yard are four deep and wide docks, for docking and repairing large fhips ; in one of thefe docks was built the Victory, a firft rate, the largeft fhip in the univerfe, carrying one hundred and ten guns, which is now moored in this river near Gillingham ; there are alfo four flips and launches, on which new fhips are conftantly building.

The ordnance wharf is fituated to the fouth of the dock-yard, between Chatham church and the river, and was the original naval yard. The guns belonging to the fhips in this river are depofited in long tiers ; fome of thefe guns weigh fixty-five hundred weight each ; large pyramids of fhot are to be feen on different parts of this wharf ; there are alfo capacious ftorehoufes, in which are depofited prodigious quantities of offenfive weapons, as mufkets, piftols, cutlaffes, pikes, poleaxes, &c. &c. The armory is a curious affemblage of hoftile weapons, arranged in admirable order. To defend this large naval magazine, there is a ftrong garrifon at Sheernefs, the entrance into the Medway. A fort is alfo erected at Gillingham. For the further fecurity of this yard, in the beginning of the laft war, ramparts were thrown up.

That which is called the Cheft at Chatham, was inftituted in 1588, the memorable year of the defeat of the Spanifh Armada ; when with the advice of Sir Francis Drake, Sir John Hawkins, and others, the feamen in the fervice of Queen Elizabeth voluntarily affigned a portion of each man's pay, to the relief of their wounded fellows ; which method being confirmed by the Queen, has been continued ever fince. Two annual fairs are held at Chatham, one on the 15th of May, and the other on the 19th of September.

About four miles from Rochefter ftands the pleafant village of *Shorne*, the church belonging to which has feveral ancient monuments in it, efpecially of the Cobham family. Near this

place

place is Cobham-hall, an ancient and noble ftructure, the original manfion of the Cobham family, but now the refidence of the Earl of Darnley. In a large room in this houfe are the arms of Queen Elizabeth, and a memorandum of her having been entertained there by the then proprietor of this feat; here is an extenfive park well ftocked with deer. In Cobham church are feveral ancient and curious monuments of the Cobham family. Near the church is a college, founded about the year 1389, by John de Cobham, and fuppreffed by Henry VIII. But it was founded anew on a reformed plan, by Sir William Brooke (lord Cobham) A. D. 1597. Twenty poor perfons with their families, are admitted into this college, from the adjacent parifhes.

On the other fide of the London road, is the parifh of *Higham*, where was a nunnery of the Benedictine order. Near this place are the remains of the ancient town of Clive at Hoo, now called Cliff, by many writers fuppofed to have been the Clovefhoe, where fo many councils were held during the Saxon heptarchy. Not far from Cliff is Cooling caftle, erected by John, Lord Cobham, about 1380; it being granted to him by Richard II. which grant he caufed to be cut on a large ftone, and placed on the front of the caftle; part of it is ftill vifible. This caftle was a place of confiderable ftrength, and furrounded by a deep moat. Two round towers which formed the entrance, are ftill ftanding, as are fome fragments of towers erected for its defence in different parts of the walls. The pious and intrepid Sir John Oldcaftle, who in the reign of Henry V. fell a victim to papal cruelty, refided in this caftle; part of it is now a farm-houfe, in the occupation of Mr. Comport.

About three miles from Rochefter, on the road towards London, is *Gad's Hill*, fuppofed to have been the fcene of the robbery mentioned by Shakefpear in his play of Henrv IV. At a fmall diftance to the left, appears on an eminence the Hermitage, the feat of the late Sir Francis Head, Bart. and clofe to the road, on a fmall afcent, is a neat building lately erected by Mr. Day.

M I L T O N.

This is an ancient town in Kent, about twelve miles from Rochefter, and forty-two from London. It is in a manner fituated on the waters of a fine rivulet, at the head of a creek that runs into the Swale, which feparates the ifle of Shepey from the main. Antiquity has dignified it by calling it,

" The

" The royal town of Middleton." When king Alfred divided his kingdom into hundreds and ſhires, Milton was in his poſſeſſion, and therefore was ſo denominated ; it was honoured with a royal palace, which was ſituated near where the church at preſent ſtands, about a mile north-eaſt of the town : It was a flouriſhing place until the reign of Edward the Çonfeſſor ; nor do we read of its being injured by the Danes, although it muſt have been viſited by them : in the ſame reign A. D. 1053, Earl Godwin, who had been baniſhed, came hither and burnt the palace and town to aſhes. Milton church is a large handſome building ; there was a church in this place very early, for Sexburga, the foundreſs of the nunnery at Minſter in Shepey, is ſaid to have expired in the church porch of Milton, about the year 680. It contains ſeveral ancient monuments of the Norwood family. The town is governed by a portreeve, who is annually choſen on St. James's-day. There is a good oyſter fiſhery in the Swale, belonging to this town : the oyſters are much eſteemed in London. A market was granted by King Edward I. A. D. 1287, and continues on Saturdays. A fair is held on the 24th of May. Within a mile to the eaſt of the church is a large open field or marſh, called Kelmſley-down, derived, it is imagined, from Campſley-down, or the place of camps, becauſe there the Danes under Haſting, in 892, encamped on their arrival from France with eighty ſhips. On the eaſt ſide of the down are the remains of a caſtle, ſaid to have been built at that time by thoſe free-booters ; it is now called Caſtle Ruff. All that appears of this fortreſs at preſent, is a ſquare piece of ground ſurrounded by a large moat. On the oppoſite ſide of Milton creek, and about half a mile north of Sittingborn, are the poor remains of Bayford caſtle, ſaid to have been raiſed by the good and vigilant King Alfred, to ſecure the country from the excurſions of the Danes, while they rendez-vouſed on Kelmſley downs. The moat and a ſmall part of the eaſt wall are ſtill viſible.

FEVERSHAM

Is forty eight miles from London, and is a town of great antiquity. In a charter of Kenulph, King of Mercia, dated 812, it is called the King's little town, and ſeems to have been a royal reſidence at that time. King Stephen founded an abbey here in 1148, but there are no remains of it, except an inner gate and ſome walls. The church is large and handſome. Feverſham is now in a flouriſhing ſtate, being the chief port for

C c   this

this part of the country; it is fituated on a rivulet which fa'ls into the mouth of the Swale, and has an oyfter fifhery. The dredgers have a peculiar law among them, which obliges a perfon to marry before he can be free of the grounds. The town is an appendage of the town and port of Dover. It is governed by a mayor, jurat, and commonality; has a market on Wednefdays and Saturdays; and two fairs, one on the twenty-fifth of February, and the other on the twelfth of Auguft. A large powder manufactory fubfifted near this town as early as the time of Queen Elizabeth: it has been lately purchafed by government. To the north-weft of the town, on the other fide of the rivulet, is the chapel of Davington, where was an eminent nunnery. It was founded foon after the abbey of Fever-fham, in the reign of King Stephen, A. D. 1153. The chapel of this ancient religious houfe is now the parifh church. To the fouth of the town, near the road, is the fmall, but neat church of Prefton, in which are fome monuments three hundred years old.

At a little diftance from hence, Lord Sondes has an elegant feat, known by the name of LEES COURT. And in this neighbourhood is alfo NASH COURT, the handfome and pleafant feat of the Hawkins's family, with a balluftraded terrace on its top, fronted with a green park, in which are beautiful plantations.—At Broughton-hill, which is between Feverfham and Canterbury, there is a beautiful profpect on every fide from the fummit, and the high fteeple of Canterbury cathedral appears directly in the road.

About three miles from hence is the ancient village of *Har-bledown*, the church of which is fituated on an hill weft of the ftreet. Oppofite to the church is the hofpital and chapel, originally built and endowed by archbifhop Lanfranc, about the year 1080: it was for the benefit of poor lepers. This was the place that formerly held the precious relick, called St. Thomas Becket's flipper, neatly fet in copper and chryftal, mentioned by Erafmus. The numerous pilgrims to the fhrine of St. Thomas ufed to ftop here, and kifs his flipper, as a preparation for their more folemn approach to his tomb. Since the reformation, this hofpital is continued for the relief of poor perfons.

C A N T E R B U R Y.

This famous and ancient city, the chief of the county of Kent, and the metropolitan fee of all England, ftands at the

distance

distance of fifty-six miles from London. It is situated in a beautiful and fruitful valley, with the river Stour running through it, in two clear and useful streams. It is supposed to have been walled in the time of King Ethelbert, about the year 600; and when the walls were repaired in 1400, they are said to have been nearly two miles in compass. There were twenty-one small towers on the walls, and seven gates, besides posterns. There are now only six, and a great part of the wall is in a ruinous state. The *castle* is a venerable structure, and was built about the time of the conquest. It is situated on the south side of the city, but is in ruins. Besides the cathedral, there are sixteen parish churches in this city; the whole of which is divided into six wards, which are named after the six city gates. Here were also a priory, a nunnery, and three religious houses for the Augustine, black, and grey friars. The knights templars had a mansion in this city. It likewise contained nine hospitals, three of which are dissolved. Here is a free-school, and three charity schools.

The cathedral, called Christ's Church, is a fine piece of Gothic architecture; it is situated in a spacious square towards the east side of the city, and is built in the form of a cross; about five hundred feet long, seventy-four broad, exclusive of the cross isle, and eighty feet high. From the middle of the building rises a beautiful tower two hundred and thirty-five feet high, called Bell Harry.—There are many antient monuments in this church, some in very good condition; among which are those of Henry the Fourth, and his Queen, built A. D. 1413; and Edward the black prince. There was also a famous monastery belonging to this cathedral, containing, it is said, one hundred and fifty Benedictines; the cloysters and chapter house belonging to it, are on the north side of the church, and are of the same age with the body of it. In this chapter room, A. D. 1171, King Henry the Second, either through piety or policy, suffered the Monks to scourge him, by way of penance, on account of the murder of Thomas Becket. This monastery was dissolved in 1539; and there are now belonging to this cathedral, a dean, archdeacon, twelve prebendaries, six preachers, six minor canons, twelve lay clerks, ten choristers, two masters, fifty scholars, and twelve alms men. In the windows of this fabric are some fine remains of painted glass, and underneath it the French and Wallooon congregation have a church.

This

This was firft given by Queen Elizabeth to the Walloons, who fled hither from the Netherlands, to efcape the Duke of Alva's perfecution ; and this congregation has fince been much encreafed, by numbers of Proteftants who were driven from France in the reign of Lewis XIV. Thefe foreign Proteftants were extremely ferviceable to Canterbury, by introducing here the art of weaving broad filks, which has been brought to great perfection.

The ruins of St. Auguftine's monaftery, or abbey, are without Burgate, to the eaft of the city. The abbey was built by Ethelbert, and given to Auguftine, and richly endowed by the donations of many Kings and Queens. At the weft end of the abbey is Ethelbert's tower, which is thought to have been ufed as a belfry and fteeple, and to have been fo called from a large bell named from that King. It was built about the year 1047, and is now much decayed. Near the ruins of this abbey, are thofe of Pancrafs chapel, which was an idol temple, and probably built by the Romans, or foon after their time, from the Roman bricks ftill to be feen. Auguftine confecrated it for Chriftian worfhip. This abbey and chapel with its precincts, occupied a large compafs of ground, which is furrounded by a high wall, the two grand entrances into which are ftill remaining. To the eaft of this monaftery is St. Martin's church, famous for its antiquity, it being built by the believing Romans, and rebuilt and ufed by Bertha, Ethelbert's Queen, for Chriftian worfhip, before Auguftine came into England; and was the firft place that miffionary faid mafs in, after his arrival. Bertha is faid to have been buried in the porch with her hufband Ethelbert. There are rows of Roman bricks yet to be feen in it ; it had a bifhop before the conqueft.

This city was formerly governed by the archbifhop ; the King had a præfect, who poffeffed but very little authority. It is now governed by a mayor, recorder, a fheriff, twelve aldermen, and twenty-four common-council-men. A court is held every Monday in the Guildhall, for civil and criminal caufes, and every other Thurfday for the government of the city. Here is a market on Wednefdays and Saturdays, and a fair for toys on the 29th of September.

ISLE OF THANET.

This is in the north-eaft part of the county of Kent, and lies open to the fea on the north and eaft, with the river Want-

fam

fam on the weft and fouth. It is about nine miles long, and eight broad, and in general very fertile. The fmall village of Sarre is the firft place a traveller comes to in this ifland : this was formerly a large town, endowed with the privileges of the cinque ports, and ftill belongs to Sandwich ; the paffage into this ifland is at this place, over a narrow ftream. To the left of the road, and fix miles from Margate, is the church of St. Nicholas, which is a handfome building, but there are no monuments in it prior to the year 1500. About the fame diftance from Margate, to the right of the road, is the fmall town of Monkton or Monktown, fo called from its being the property of the Monks, who ufually refided in this place. There are collegiate ftalls in the church, and the heads of feveral priors in the remains of painted glafs in the windows. The church has been larger than it now is. Birchington is a member of the town and port of Dover. The church is a neat building, and contains feveral antient and modern monuments of the Queke and Crifpe families, who refided at the ancient manfion in this parifh, called Quekes or Quex. At this houfe King William III. ufed to refide, until the winds favoured his embarking for Holland. A room, faid to have been the bedchamber of this royal gueft, is ftill fhewn, together with an adjacent inclofure in which his guards encamped. On the right hand, near the marfhes, about four miles from Margate, is the ancient but fmall town of Minfter. Domneva, daughter of Ercombert, King of Kent, built and founded an abbey at this place, about the year 670, and furnifhed it with vield virgins to the number of feventy ; herfelf becoming the firft abbefs: Mildred, her daughter, fucceeded her : and fo far excelled her mother in piety, that fhe was canonized a faint, and the nunnery ever after was called by her name. It was deftroyed by the Danes about the year 990. Minfter church, which is the moft ancient in the ifland, is a handfome ftructure, confifting of three ifles : it has eighteen collegiate ftalls in the choir. On the floor, and in the church porch, are feveral flat grave-ftones, which are very ancient. In the laft century a pot of Roman filver coins was ploughed up near Minfter ; the coins were chiefly of Lucius Aurelius Verus. Between Minfter and Margate is Cleve-court, an elegant building belonging to I. Farrer, Efq. Beyond Minfter are fome downs, which are much celebrated for affording extenfive and delightful profpects. Canterbury cathedral, the ifle of Shepey, the Effex fhore, Dover cliffs, and the town of Sandwich, may be each diſtinctly diſcerned from this pleaſant ſpot. From theſe downs (as the Monks inform us) ſtarted Domneva's deer, which ran in an irregular courſe, quite acroſs the iſland, in the ancient map of which this tract is marked. King Egbert gave Domneva ſo much ground as the deer would run over at one courſe; which cut off the eaſt end of the iſland, where ſhe built her nunnery. This tract, from the name of her daughter, was called St. Mildred's Lynch, and was a bank of earth thrown up deſcribing the ancient bounds of the two great manors of Monkton and Minſter : and is yet viſible in ſome places.

Eaſt Kent, and the Iſle of Thanet, have long been reckoned the beſt cultivated part of England, and this tract of country has no ſlight pretenſions to that character. The drill huſbandry is very general here, and is carried on in a very complete and judicious manner. The culture of hops throughout Eaſt Kent, is a very important branch of huſbandry ; and madder is here cultivated by farmers more than in any other part of the kingdom.

M A R G A T E

Is ſituated on the north-ſide of the iſle of Thanet, within a ſmall bay, in a breach of the cliff, where is a gate to the ſea, from whence it has its name : it is ſeventy-two miles from London, and about ſixteen from Canterbury. In ſummer it is a pleaſant and agreeable ſituation. Its principal ſtreet runs north and ſouth near a mile in length, and terminates at the pier; with a gentle deſcent, by which means the ſtreets are always neat and clean. But what has given Margate ſo great an eclat in the beau monde, is its conveniency for bathing : the ſhore being level and of fine ſand, is extremely well adapted to this purpoſe. On the wharf are ſeveral bathing rooms, where the company reſort to drink the water, and from whence they enter into the machines, which are afterwards drove out two or three hundred yards into the ſea, under the conduct of careful guides. There is a door in the machine, which being opened, they deſcend into the water, by means of a ladder ; an umbrella of canvas is let down which conceals them from public view.

Since Margate has been ſo much frequented by the nobility and gentry, many conſiderable additions and improvements have been made to the town. A large new ſquare has been lately erected, conſiſting of very convenient houſes

for

for the accommodation of the nobility and gentry who refort to this place; the fquare is paved after the fame manner as the ftreets in London; in the fquare is a noble and commodious affembly-room, finifhed with great elegance and tafte; and being eigthy feven feet in length, and forty-three in breadth, is fuppofed to be the largeft in England, and commands a delightful profpect of the fea. Adjoining to this are very convenient apartments for cards and tea; on the lower floor is a billiard-table, and a large room for public entertainments, with a piazza which extends the whole length of the building; in the upper floor are ranges of bed-chambers. The number of fubfcribers to thefe rooms have amounted to near a thoufand in a feafon, The amufements are conducted with great regularity by Mr. Walker, mafter of the ceremonies, who has the happinefs to give general fatisfaction. In the fquare is an elegant tavern, now kept by Rumfey, which communicates with the room for public entertainments.

Befides the tavern in this fquare, there is another called the New Inn, fituated on the parade; where are two hot faltwater baths, which are faid to have a very falutary effect. There is alfo a playhoufe here. Provifions are very plentiful, and great quantities of fifh are daily caught. In fhort, here is every requifite to render this place a genteel and delightful fummer refidence.

Two machines fet out for Canterbury every morning, to meet the coaches from London, and return to Margate the fame evening. The hoys fail from Wool-key near the Cuftom-houfe, London, on Wednefdays or Thurfdays, and with a weft-northweft wind, fail to Margate in twelve hours; but when it is unfavourable, may be three days in their paffage. They go from Margate on Fridays or Saturdays; the fare is half a crown. They bring great quantities of goods from London, for the town and country. As a proof of the fafety of this paffage, there has not been a hoy loft for upwards of one hundred and forty years.

This town is under the fame jurifdiction as the port of Dover, the mayor being reprefented here by a deputy. Its church is dedicated to St. John the Baptift, which was the ancient name of the parifh. It was formerly a chapel to Minfter church, and fuppofed to have been built about the year 1050, and made parochial fince the year 1290. It contains feveral ancient monuments.

At

At a little diftance from Margate, is a feat built by Lord Holland, in imitation of an Italian villa, with a noble portico fronting the fea. It contains feveral elegant apartments, with a variety of marble columns, bufts, vafes, &c. brought from Italy. His Lordfhip has alfo erected with chalk ftones feveral buildings refembling Gothic towers, convents, &c. in ruins, and planted ivy round them to encreafe the deception. Near this feat are Hackendown banks, or the field of battle axes, being the place where a fierce battle was fought in the year 854, between the Danes and Anglo-Saxons, which conflict was fo near the cliff, that many fell into the fea ; and fome hiftorians fay, that both Commanders were flain, and the victory doubtful. Here are two barrows or hills of earth, thought to have been the tombs of certain great officers killed in that battle. Thefe barrows were lately opened, and found to contain bodies bent together and thurft into graves dug out of the chalk, a little below the furface, but not above three feet long. Several earthern urns, containing about two or three quarts, were alfo found, in which were afhes and charcoal, but they would not bear the air. Lord Holland has erected a monument, with an infcription in the ftyle of antiquity, to perpetuate this action.

About half a mile to the fouth of King's gate, is the north Foreland lighthoufe, for the direction of fhips by night, to fecure them from the Goodwin fands, and this head land. It was formerly built of wood, but being burnt down, the prefent ftrong flint octagon was erected about the beginning of this century ; at its top is an iron grate, on which a large coal fire blazes all night : for the fupport of this light, the owner of every fhip belonging to Great Britain, that fails by this Foreland, pays two-pence per ton, and every foreigner fourpence.

SANDWICH

Is one of the Cinque Ports, and is at the diftance of eight miles from Margate, and fixty-feven from London. The walls of the town, which were made by throwing up the earth, are nearly in the form of a parallelogram, and are about five furlongs in length from eaft to weft, and two and a half from north to fouth ; at the foot of which is a wet ditch of confiderable breadth. They command a pleafant and extenfive view of the adjacent country. In thefe walls are feveral femicircular projections which overlook the ditches,

there

there were alfo fome pieces of ordnance, which being quite un-
ferviceable, have been lately removed. The river and quays are
on the north fide of the town. There are feveral gates belonging to it, fome of which are in a ruinous condition.

It appears from the remains of fortifications about this town,
that it was anciently a place of great ftrength ; and, before the
ufe of cannon, was capable of enduring a vigorous fiege. Sandwich has been efteemed the moft famous of all the ports in England; and is thought, by many refpectable authors, to have
been the landing place generally ufed by the Romans, and inhabitants of the ancient city Rhutupiæ.

In Sandwich are three parifh churches, St. Clement's, St.
Mary's, and St. Peter's. There was formerly a fourth in the
fouth-weft part of this town, dedicated to St. James, but there
are no remains of it at prefent. The church-yard is ftill inclofed, and is ufed for the interment of ftrangers. St. Clement's church is in the eaft part of the town, and fituated upon
higher ground than the reft. It is a large and ancient ftructure,
and much refembles the Norman ftyle of architecture; particularly the tower, which is confiderably older than the reft of
the building.

There is a good bridge here, which was erected in 1757. It
is built with ftone, having an arch on each fide, and a paffage
between for the larger veffels, that ufe this port. The middle arch is of wood, divided into two parts, which are eafily
drawn up or let down. The paffage over the ftone part of
the bridge is fecured by a parapet wall on each fide, and the
wooden arch by Chinefe rails. It is a work of confiderable utility, not only to the inhabitants of Sandwich and the ifle of Thanet, but to the eaftern part of the county of Kent, and to the
public in general.

The ftreets of Sandwich are narrow and irregular ; but
there are fome good houfes, and an handfome fquare called
the fifh-market, which confifts principally of fhops. Here is
alfo another fquare called the corn-market ; and near the
weft fide of this is the Town-hall, which is a very antient
ftructure.——Sandwich claims jurifdiction over Deal, Ramfgate, Fordwich, Sarre, and Brightlingfea, in Effex, which are
members of this cinque port. It ufed to furnifh five fhips compleat for fervice. This town was anciently incorporated by
the name of the barons of the town and port of Sandwich ;
but at prefent is incorporated by the name of the mayor, ju-

D d

rats, and commonalty. It fends two members to parliament, who ftill retain the antient name of barons of the cinque port of Sandwich. The freemen of the cinque ports have the privilege of fending a certain number of their own members to fupport the royal canopy at a coronation. Befides the mayor, there are twelve jurats and twenty-four common council men, a town-clerk, two treafurers, and other inferior officers.—The trade of this town chiefly confifts in coals, fir, timber, deals, &c. with which the country is fupplied. Here alfo are fhipped corn, malt, fruit, and feeds, for London and other markets. The feeds raifed from this foil are in much repute.

Sandwich is for the moft part fupplied with water from a narrow ftream called the Delph, which runs through it. Here is a market on Wednefdays and Saturdays, and a fair on the 4th of December, which continues two days. The fhrimps which are caught near this town are remarkably excellent. There are feveral good inns in Sandwich, and many wealthy inhabitants. Here is alfo a large and elegant affembly-room, which has been bu'lt within thefe few years. Since the conftruction of the bridge, and the refort to Margate as a bathing-place, the town has been more frequently vifited by ftrangers; a tour from thence to Sandwich, Deal, Dover, &c. being a pleafant and agreeable excurfion.

Between Sandwich and Deal is a large tract of land called the Downs, part of which is level, and part mountainous. Here are thofe remarkable eminences which Mr. Camden fays, were in his time called Rome's work; now they are known by the name of Sand Hills; commencing near Sandown Caftle, and ftretching toward Sandwich, along the fea fhore. The furface is in general a fine white fand, or thin covering of heath. On this coaft it is generally fuppofed that Cæfar landed in both his expeditions to Britain. Sandown Caftle is a regular fortification, erected on the fhore within a mile of Deal. There is another to the fouth of the town, called Deal Caftle, and beyond that is Walmer Caftle: they were built on this coaft by Henry VIII. to fecure it from the hoftile intentions of his enemies. They are kept in good repair, and are under the government of the Lord Warden of the cinque ports.

About a mile from Sandwich, at a fmall diftance from the road which leads to Dover, is the village of Wodenfborough; the church contains memorials of the Paramour and Heyre families.

milies. Near the church is a remarkable eminence, fuppofed to have been raifed by the Saxons as a pedeſtal for their idol Woden, which ſtood upon it, and from which the place derives its name.

In the parifh of *Walderſhire*, which is ſix miles and an half from Sandwich, the Earl of Guildford has a very elegant and pleafant feat. To the weſt of the houfe is erected a high Belvidere, which commands a beautiful and extenſive view of the country. Oppoſite to Lord Guildford's feat, half a mile to the left of the road, are the remains of *Weſt Langdon Abbey.*

D E A L.

This town is about five miles ſouth-weſt of Sandwich, and ſeventy-two from London. It is divided into upper and lower Deal; the former is the moſt ancient, the latter having had its exiſtence from the great increafe of trade. The trade of the inhabitants chiefly conſiſts in fupplying the fhips which rendezvous in the Downs. This town is a member of the port of Sandwich, and is governed by a mayor, and jurats fubordinate to that town. Here is a market on Wednefdays and Saturdays, and two fairs annually on the 5th of April, and 10th of October.

D O V E R

Is at the diſtance of feventy-one miles from London, and is ſituated on the fea-fhore, in the narroweſt part of the channel that divides England from France; the cliffs of Calais on the French coaſt, being only thirty miles diſtant. It is a very agreeable fea-port, the fituation being very romantic, at the foot of feveral bold hills; and the harbour in the center of the town, quite built round, is furrounded by quays, that are very pleaſing to the view. From the caſtle, and the hills near the town on the road to Hythe, are noble views down on the town, the harbour, and the fhipping; and over the channel, the high lands in France are diſtinctly feen.

Dover is a place of great antiquity, and was undoubtedly one of the Roman ports in this country. It was a town of great repute in the time of Edward the Confeſſor, when it was the principal of the cinque ports. It was formerly walled in, having ten or eleven gates; and the walls are faid to have been built by the Emperor Severus; but there are now but fmall re-

mains

mains either of the walls or gates.   There were alfo formerly feven churches in Dover, but there are now only two.

Dover Caftle is built on the extremity of the ftupendous cliffs which form the eaftern barrier to Dover town and harbour, and is fo large as to contain thirty-five acres of ground.   There has been a fortification on this fpot ever fince the Romans poffeffed this ifland, and it was of great repute among the Saxon Kings : it was thought a very important object by William the Norman ; and through a courfe of ages fucceeding Kings built new towers, and increafed its natural ftrength to fuch a degree, that in Henry the Third's time it was called the key and barrier of the whole realm.   This caftle contains a curious fpecimen of anci- ent fortification, and is well worthy of attention.   St. Martin's le Grand is faid to have been fituated here, for the fervice of the royal palace, which was in the caftle ; here is a tower at the weft end, which with the church bears evident marks of great antiquity.   The bells which were in it were removed to Portf- mouth by Sir George Rook.   There is a well in this caftle three hundred and fixty feet deep, lined to the bottom with free-ftone. In the caftle they fhew two very old keys, and a brafs trumpet, faid to have been ufed in the time of Julius Cæfar.   Here is a brafs gun, fuppofed to be the longeft in the world, it was prefent- ed to Queen Elizabeth by the States of Utrecht ; it carries a ball of fifteen pounds weight, is twenty-two feet long, and is faid to throw a ball feven miles.   It is commonly called Queen Eliza- beth's pocket piftol.

Dover is incorporated by the name of the mayor, jurats, and commonality of the town and port of Dover, and fends two members to parliament ; it has received many favours from dif- ferent Princes, one of which was the privilege of a licenfed packet-boat to France ; on account of the narrownefs of the channel, it is become the general place of embarkation for that kingdom, and arrival from thence.   In the reign of Richard II. the fare from France for a fingle paffenger, in fummer time, was fettled at fix-pence, and a fhilling in winter.   A market is kept here on Wednefdays and Saturdays, and a fair on the 22d of November.

As Dover is one of the *cinque ports*, it may not be improper here to obferve, that this phrafe is derived from *quinque portus*, *five havens*, that lie over againft France, and were thus called by way of eminence, on account of their fuperior importance. Our Kings have thought them worthy a particular regard ; and

2   the

the better to fecure them againſt invaſions, have granted them a peculiar form of government. They are governed by a keeper, who has the title of Lord Warden of the Cinque Ports. They had a particuliar juriſdiction granted them by King John, and ſeveral other privileges which have been confirmed by moſt of his ſucceſſors. Their Warden, who was firſt appointed by William the Conqueror, has the authority of an Admiral among them, and iſſues out writs in his own name. The five original cinque ports, are Dover, Rumney, and Sandwich, in Kent; and Winchelſea and Rye, market-towns, of Suſſex: and to theſe five original ports, there were afterwards added Haſtings and Seaford, two other market-towns of Suſſex; and Hithe in Kent. When the ſervice which was required of the cinque ports towards their preſervation became too burdenſome, each was allowed a certain number of other towns in its neighbourhood, as auxiliaries, that they might bear a part in this public charge. The cinque ports claim the honour of ſupporting the canopy, which at a coronation is borne over the Sovereign, and afterwards to dine at the uppermoſt table on the King's right hand: the canopy, ſtaves, &c. are their fee. Thirty-two barons or inhabitants of the ports uſed to be ſummoned for this purpoſe, whoſe expences were borne by the ports; but at preſent they uſually depute their members of parliament to that office.

Near Dover Caſtle there is a head of land called *South Foreland*, by way of diſtinction from another head or promontory, which forms the north-eaſt point of the Kentiſh ſhore, and is therefore called *North Foreland*. Theſe two points lying at the diſtance of ſix miles from each other, are the two moſt eaſterly in Kent; the coaſt between them is ſheltered by them on the ſouth and north, and by a bank of ſand, running parallel to the ſhore for three leagues together, and at the diſtance of a league and an half from it, called Godwin Sands, on the eaſt. Thus the South Foreland, North Foreland, Godwin Sands, and the Coaſt, form a tolerable good road for ſhips, which is called *the Downs*, and which would otherwiſe be very dangerous, for the Godwin Sands, which are dry at low water, break all the force of the ſea on the eaſt, ſouth, and ſouth-weſt; yet when the wind blows exceſſive hard at ſouth-eaſt, eaſt-by-north, and eaſt-north-eaſt, ſhips are driven from their anchors, and

forced

fored afhore on the Godwin Sands, or fent into Sandwich bay, or Ramfgate pier, near Sandwich.

North Foreland is a point declared by act of parliament to be the moft fouthern part of the port of London, which by the fame act is extended north in a right line, forming the mouth of the Thames, to the point called the Nafe, on the eaft of Effex. All the towns or harbours between London and thefe places, whether on the Kentifh or Effex fhore, are called members of the port of London. As foon veffels have paffed the North Foreland, out of the port of London, or any of its members, they are faid to be in the open fea; if to the North they enter the German Ocean; if to the fouth, the Britifh Channel.

BARHAM DOWNS,

Which are about fixty-two miles from London, are celebrated at prefent for the annual horfe races which are there exhibited. Several villages, and elegant gentlemen's feats, are fituated on the right and left of the Downs; on the right is an eminence, on the left a beautiful vale, in which runs a fmall branch of the river Stour. On the right is *Denhill Houfe* and gardens, the feat of Lady Gray; near which is *Netherfole Houfe*, the manfion of ────── Winchefter, Efq; which is fituated in the finall village of Wymlingfwold. To the left of the downs, is the village of Barham, which gives name to this delightful fpot. The church has in it fome monument of the Diggs family, who refided at *Diggs-Court*, in this parifh.

On Barham Downs is a fcite of an antient camp, with three ditches round it, which fome conjecture to be the work of Julius Cæfar, on his fecond expedition to this ifland. About the year 1212, King John encamped here with an army of fixty thoufand men, to oppofe the French, who threatened him with an invafion. Simon Montford, Earl of Leicefter, alfo drew up a large army on thefe downs in the reign of Henry III.

Near Beakefborne, which is about fixty miles from London, Sir Thomas Pym Hales, member of parliament for the port of Dover, has a fine feat, known by the name of *Howlets*.

FOLKSTONE

Is fituated between Dover and Hythe, and is a member of the cinque port of Dover. It is feventy one miles from

London,

London, and appears to have been a very antient place, from the
Roman coins and other antiquities which have been found in it.
Here was formerly a nunnery; but so near the coast, that it was
often pillaged by the Danes, and at last swallowed up by the
sea. However, after the conquest, a priory was founded here.
Here is a charity-school for twenty boys, nominated by the
mayor and jurats, who, with the commonalty, constitute the
corporation. A copious spring runs through the town; but it
is chiefly noted for the multitude of fishing boats that belong to
its harbour, which are employed at the proper season in catching
mackrell for London. And about Michaelmas the Folkstone
barks, with others from the Essex shore, sail away to the coasts
of Suffolk and Norfolk, to catch herrings.

In going from Dover to Folkstone, the traveller meets with
six or seven very romantic miles; the road runs along the edge
of vast precipices, the shore very high and bold, and nobly
varied. From the hill, going down into Folkstone, the view is
extremely fine: you look down on a fine sweep of inclosures,
many of them grass, of the most pleasing verdure. The town,
with its church on a point of land close to the sea. The edge of
the lower grounds describe as beautiful an outline as can be imagined: the union of the land and sea compleat. As you descend
the hill, the prospect extends to the right: the vale opens, and
spreads to the view a fine range of inclosures, bounded to the
land by many hills, rising in a great variety of forms: the whole
scenery is very magnificent.

H I T H E

Is situated in the south-east part of the county of
Kent, and is sixty-nine miles from London. It is a cinque
port and corporation, governed by a mayor, jurats and commonalty. This town had anciently five parish churches, though
now it has only one. Here are two hospitals, and a charity-school
for thirty-eight boys.

A remarkable pile of dry bones has been preserved in
this town, and kept in a vault under the church, consisting of several thousand heads, arms, legs, thigh bones, &c.
some of which are very gigantic, and appear by an inscription to be the remains of the Danes and Britons
killed in a battle near this place, before the Norman Conquest.

RUM.

R U M N E Y

Is often called *New Rumney*, to diſtinguiſh it from an incon
ſiderable town within a mile and a half of it, called Old Rumney.   New Rumney is ſeventy miles from London, and is one
of the cinque ports, and a corporation, governed by a mayor,
jurats, and commonalty.   The town ſtands on a high gravelly
hill, in the middle of Rumney Marſh.—*Old Rumney* was once
a large town, containing twelve wards, and five churches ; and
had a ſafe and commodious haven, when the ſea came ſo cloſe to
it, that ſhips uſed to anchor in one of the church-yards ; but the
ſea deſerted it in the reign of King Edward I. and it has now
but one church.   It is ſaid that by a ſtorm which happened here
in 1334, above 300 windmills and houſes were carried away ;
which, together with the withdrawing of the ſea, ſo impoveriſhed the place, that it could never recover it.

Rumney Marſh is the richeſt tract of grazing land in this part
of the kingdom.   It contains between 40,000 and 50,000 acres
of fruitful land, on which vaſt flocks of ſheep, and herds of
black cattle, are fattened, which are ſent hither from other parts,
and ſold in the London markets.   The ſheep are reckoned rather larger than thoſe of Leiceſterſhire and Lincolnſhire ; and
their bullocks the largeſt in England, eſpecially thoſe they call
ſtalled oxen, from being kept all the latter ſeaſon within the farmer's yards, or ſheds, where they are fed for the winter ſeaſon.
This Marſh is the place from whence a ſet of ſmugglers, called
Owlers, from their going out in the duſk of the evening, have
for many ages exported our wool to France.   It is ſuppoſed to
have been once covered by the ſea ; and, as it is very unwhole
ſome, is but thinly inhabited.

T E N D E R D E N

Is an ancient town in Kent, at the diſtance of fiftyeight miles from London.   It is governed by a mayor and
jurats.   The beacon of the church here is remarkably lofty,
and is proverbially ſaid to have been the cauſe of ſome
dangerous ſands in the channel, called Godwin Sands, of
which we lately made mention.   Theſe ſands were a tract
of ground near the Iſle of Thanet, belonging to Godwin,
Earl of Kent, which lying low, were defended from the ſea
by a great wall, that required a conſtant care to uphold
it.   This tract was afterwards given to St. Auſtin's monaſtery

naſtery, near Canterbury; and the abbot neglecting the wall, while he was taken up in building Tenterden ſteeple, the ſea broke in and overflowed the ground, leaving the ſands upon it. At the time of the alarm of the Spaniſh invaſion, in the reign of Queen Elizabeth, a beacon was placed upon Tenterden ſteeple.

CRANBROOK

Is ſituated in a woody part of the county of Kent, and is the place where the firſt woollen manufacture in the kingdom was erected, by thoſe Flemings who were encouraged to ſettle here by King Edward III. in order to teach the art to his ſubjects; and excellent cloth uſed to be made here formerly; but that trade has long ſince decayed, and this is now only an inconſiderable place.

TUNBRIDGE.

This is a market town, at the diſtance of thirty miles from London, ſituated upon the river Medway, which here branches out into many little ſtreams, over all which there are bridges: from thence it derives its name, which is compounded of *Ton*, the Saxon word for Town, and *Bridge*. It conſiſts of one broad ſtreet, adorned by ſome very good modern houſes. Here is a good free-ſchool, which was erected and endowed about two hundred years ago, by Sir Andrew Judd, Lord Mayor of London, who veſted the care of it in the Skinners Company. It is kept in excellent repair, and is at preſent in a very flouriſhing condition. There is nothing remarkable in the church, which is a neat modern building. Here is a market on Fridays, and fairs held on Aſh-Wedneſday, the 5th of July, and the 29th of October.

At the further end of the town, on the right hand, as you come from London, the noble ruins of an old caſtle ſtrike you with awe and veneration. It was built by Richard de Clare, on a piece of ground which was given him by Langfranc, Archbiſhop of Canterbury, in exchange for as much land in Normandy, the meaſurement being on both ſides made with thongs of raw hides. It ſtands upon an eminence cloſe upon the banks of the Medway, and has been very ſtrong, and was anciently a place of conſiderable importance. Edward I. was nobly feaſted here in the ſecond year of his reign, by Gilbert de Clare, Earl of Gloucester and Hertford. In the reign of Edward IV.

this

this caftle was in the poffeffion of Henry, Duke of Buckingham; but in the reign of Henry VIII. both the town and caftle
were forfeited to the crown by the attainder of Edward Stafford, Duke of Buckingham; and the latter has not been in the
leaft repaired fince that time.   Queen Elizabeth gave it to her
kinfman, Henry, Lord Hunfdon; from whofe heirs it paffed
into private hands.

Five miles from the town of Tunbridge, at the very edge of
the county, are *Spelhurft Wells*, more commonly called *Tunbridge Wells*, which are much frequented on account of their
mineral waters.   Thefe wells are at the bottom of the walks,
which are handfomely paved : on one fide is the affembly-room,
the coffee-rooms, the bookfellers fhops, jewellers and milliners
fhops, and fhops for china, and for Tunbridge-ware, which is
made here to great perfection out of holly, cherry-tree, and
fycamore ; of which a great quantity grows hereabouts.   On
the other fide of the walks are coffee-rooms, another affembly-
room, and taverns, and lodging-houfes.   The mufic gallery is
in the middle of the walks, which are beautifully fhaded with
trees : a piazza extends from the upper end to the bottom, quite
down to the wells.   The houfes and lodgings are very neat and
commodious ; moft of them on the hills contiguous, called
Mount Sion, Mount Ephraim, and Mount Pleafant.   Here is
a decent chapel, which was built by fubfcription, and where
divine fervice is performed every day : the Clergyman is paid
by public contribution for his attendance.   Here is alfo a diffenting meeting-houfe.

The high rocks are about a mile from the walks, of which
there are a vaft number adjoining to each other, and feveral of
them are feventy or eighty feet high ; and at many places there
are cliffs and cavities, that lead through them by narrow dark
paffages ; and their being fituated among the woods, by a little
winding brook, makes them afford a moft retired and delightful
fcene.

P E N S H U R S T

Is three miles fouth-weft of Tunbridge, and was the antient feat of the noble family of Sidney, but at prefent of William Perry, Efq.   Penfhurft was forfeited to the crown by
the attainder of one of the Vane family, who followed the
fortune of the unhappy Somerfet in the reign of Edward VI.
That monarch beftowed it upon the father of Sir Henry Sidney,

in

in whofe arms he expired. This fact is mentioned in an infcription over the gate of the Tower, through which you pafs
into the court-yard, which is a very large ancient quadrangle
of hewn ftone, and was fortified in old times, being reckoned
a place of no fmall ftrength. Here are many more rooms
than are fhewn to ftrangers; thofe that are opened are well
furnifhed, and contain good pictures, tables, pillars, and vafes
of fine marble brought lately from Italy, well worth the in-
fpection of the curious. The houfe lies very low, and clofe
to a mean village, of great antiquity, of the fame name. A
powerful family, called Penfhurft, or Penchefter, was fettled here in the time of the Conqueror, which has been long
extinct. The park, which was formerly very confiderable,
is at prefent but fmall, being inclofed and divided into
farms.

The famous Sir Philip Sidney was born here; and it
was here the celebrated Waller wrote many of his beft
pieces, under the aufpices of Lady Dorothy Sidney, whom he
has immortalized by the name of Sacchariffa. This Lady
was daughter to Sidney, Earl of Leicefter, to whom Penfhurft then belonged; and wife to Henry, Lord Spencer,
created Earl of Sunderland by King Charles the Firft, in
whofe defence he was flain, gallantly fighting at Newbury.

Not far from Penfhurft is a noble ftructure, mouldering
into ruins, called *Somerhill*, which ftands very high, and has a
moft extenfive command of country. It antiently belonged to
the Earls of Hertford and Gloucefter. Somerhill being forfeited to the Crown by Stafford, Duke of Buckingham, was
given by Queen Elizabeth to Sir Francis Walfingham, with
whofe daughter it paffed into the hands of three great families;
for fhe was married to three different hufbands. Her firft was
the renowned Sir Philip Sydney; her fecond the unfortunate
Earl of Effex; and her third, Ulick de Burgh, Marquis of
Clanrickard, Earl of St. Alban's, Vifcount Tunbridge, and
Baron Somerhill, one of the moft remarkable and accomplifh-
ed Noblemen of King Charles the Firft's reign. Charles II.
who ufed to come fometimes to Tunbridge, kept his retinue
at Somerhill.

MAID

MAIDSTONE

Is situated on the river Medway, and is thirty-six miles from London. In the time of the Britons it was their third chief city, it was also a station of the Romans, and has been a confiderable town in all ages since. It is a large, pleasant, and populous place; and is a corporation, governed by a mayor and commonalty. The chief trade of Maidstone is in thread, which is made here in great perfection, and in hops, of which there are vast plantations, besides orchards of fine cherries. From this town, and the adjacent country, London is said to be supplied with more necessaries of life, than from any other market-town in England, particularly with large bullocks, timber, wheat, hops, and apples. The county courts are held in this town, and generally the assizes. Here is a fine stone bridge over the Medway, erected by one of the archbishops of Canterbury. At this place the river Len falls into the Medway, and the tide flows quite up to the town, and carries barges of sixty tons.—The weekly market on Thursday is reckoned the best frequented of any in the county, and is toll-free for hops. There are four annual fairs here, viz. on the 13th of February, the 12th of May, the 20th of June, and the 17th of October.

West Malling is a market-town of great antiquity, thirty miles from London, and where there was formerly a nunhery of the Benedictine order; but it is now an inconfiderable place.

MEREWORTH CASTLE.

This fine seat is situated two miles south-east of Malling; it was formerly the seat of the Earl of Westmoreland, but is now in the possession of Lord Despenser. It is esteemed a very fine piece of architecture, and was designed by Colin Campbell, in imitation of a palace in Italy, built by the famous Palladio. It is a square extending eighty-eight feet, and has four porticos of the Ionic order. In the middle there rises above the roof a semicircular dome, which has two shells; the one forms the stucco-cieling of the saloon, being thirty-six feet diameter; the outward shell is carpentry covered with lead. Between these two shells is a strong brick arch, that brings twenty-four funnels to

the

Mereworth-Castle in front, the Seat of Lord Despenser.

the lantern, which is finished with copper ; but by this contrivance there is occasioned an inconvenience ; the chimnies often smoke.

SEVENOKE.

This town, which is twenty-four miles from London, in the road to Tunbridge, is said to have derived its name from seven very large and high oaks which stood near it, when it was first built, but which have been long since cut down. Here is an hospital for maintaining poor old people, and a school for educating poor children, which was built and endowed by Sir William Sevenoke, who was Lord Mayor of London in 1418, and who is said to have been a foundling, brought up by some person of this town, from whence he took his name. John Potkyn, who lived in the reign of King Henry the Eighth, was a great benefactor to the school ; and the revenue being augmented by Queen Elizabeth, it was from thence called Queen Elizabeth's free-school. It was rebuilt in 1727.

At *Knowle*, in the neighbourhood of Sevenoke, the Duke of Dorset has a fine seat, the park and gardens belonging to which are laid out in a very elegant manner.

EAST GRINSTEAD.

This is a town in Suffex, thirty miles from London, and which is so called to distinguish it from a small place of the same name in the county, called West Grinstead. It is an antient borough by prescription, and has sent members to parliament from the time of Edward II. The town is but small, though it is the place where the county assizes have been frequently held. There is an hospital here, which was built in the reign of King James I. by Robert Sackville, Earl of Dorset, who endowed it with 33ol. a year, for the maintenance of thirty-one poor persons of this town. The weekly market is on Thursday, and there are two fairs held here, one on the 13th of July, and the other on the 11th of December.

Between East Grinstead and Lewes, near Newick, Mr. Holyroyd has a very pleasing seat, known by the name of SHEFFIELD PLACE, and which is situated in one of the most agreeable parts of the county of Suffex. The park is fine,

forming

forming varied lawns well wooded, fhelving into winding vales, and commandig very noble fweeps of richly cultivated country. One vale takes an irregular courfe through the park and grounds; and the boundaries of which are well contrafted. In fome places thick woods of oak hang to the bottom; in others copfes, inclofures, and fcattered trees; in one fpot the hills rife in a bold manner, intermixed with rocks and pendent woods. A fmall river takes its courfe through the vale, which is formed into two lakes, one of them at the foot of the romantic ground abovementioned; the other partly environed by a large wood, which on one fide is thick to the very water's edge; but on the other the underwood againft the water is cleared away, and the land converted to lawn, but the trees left in it, which forms a m.ft agreeable retired fcene, backed by the thick wood. The lawn breaks away among the woods, and rifes to the houfe, which ftands on higher ground. This winding vale, fo rich in wood, water, and hanging fides of hills, is feen to great advantage from a feat in the park, from whence the view is truly picturefque. Near the houfe is a wood of fixty acres, full of very fine timber, and cut into agreeable walks, one of which, that winds by the fide of the river in a fequeftered part of the valley, is very beautiful.

L E W E S.

This town is fifty miles from London, and is a place of great antiquity, as appears from King Athelftan's having appointed his royal mint to be kept here. It is a pleafant place, fituated in an open country, on the edge of the South Downs, and is one of the largeft and moft populous towns in the county of Suffex. The affizes are often held here. Though it is a borough town by prefcription, and fends two members to parliament, it is not under the direction of a corporation; but is governed by two conftables, who are affifted by the principal inhabitants of the town. The town is large, and has fix parifh churches in it, and contains many handfome houfes; and there are two large fuburbs adjoining to it; one called South-over, on the weft fide of the town; and the other called Cliff, from its fituation on a chalky hill, on the eaft fide of the river Oufe. There are many gentlemen of fortune who refide in this town, and its neighbourhood.

There are feveral iron works in Lewes, particularly a
foundery

foundery for cannon. There are feveral diffenting meetings here; and a charity-fchool for boys, fupported by voluntary fubfcription. In the neighbourhood of this town horfe-races are often held.

B A T T L E.

This is a town in Suffex, fifty-fix miles from London, which derives its name from the battle in which William the Norman defeated King Harold, and obtained the crown of England. This battle was fought in a field called Heathfield, near this town: Heathfield is alfo near Haftings, and this battle is there-fore fometimes called the battle of Haftings. On the fpot where the body of the brave Harold was found, the Conqueror erected a ftately abbey in memory of that event; to which was given the name of *Battle Abbey*; and he placed in it a number of Benedictine monks, to pray for the fouls of the flain. Not long after, feveral houfes were erected round it, and it at length became a town.

Some of the remains of this abbey are yet ftanding, but the town has gradually fallen to decay from the time of the reformation. The parifh church is a low Gothic ftruc-ture. The trade of the town confifts principally in making gunpowder, and that made here is efteemed the beft in Eng-land. The weekly market is on Thurfday, and there is a fair held here on Whit-Monday, and another on the 22d of November.

About eight miles fouth-weft of Battle, are the remains of an ancient caftle, called *Hurfimonceux*, which was a place of great repute at the time of the Norman conqueft.

R Y E.

This town is fixty four miles from London, and is an ap-pendage to the cinque port of Haftings. It is a peninfula, wafhed on the weft and fouth by the fea, and on the eaft by the river Rother. The town ftands on the fide of a hill, and has a delightful profpect of the fea. In the reign of King Edward the Third, Rye was walled and fortified by William D'Ypres, Earl of Kent; and there is a tower yet ftanding, which bears his name, and is ufed for the town gaol. Here is one of the largeft parifh churches in England, an handfome Gothic ftruc-ture; and there is a free grammar fchool here, founded and endowed

dowed on a very benevolent and expensive plan; for it is open for the reception of every child in the town who chuses to go to it. This place formerly had one of the most considerable harbours between Portsmouth and Dover; but for a considerable time it has been so choaked up with sand, that the smallest vessel could scarcely enter it; and a considerable part of the harbour, gained from the sea, was turned into arable land. Some endeavours have since been used to make it again a commodious harbour; and an act of parliament was passed to promote that design in 1762. There is a market here on Wednesdays and Saturdays: and two fairs, one on Whit-Monday, and another on the 10th of August.

WINCHELSEA

Is three miles from Rye, and sixty-seven from London. This town was built in the reign of King Edward the First, when an older town of the same name, two or three miles to the south-east, which is said to have been very large, was swallowed up by the sea in a tempest. The town enjoys the privileges of a cinque port, sends two members to parliament, and is governed by a mayor and three jurats. It is, however, a very inconsiderable place; for it was not long after it was built, before it was deserted by the sea, after which it lost all its trade. There now remains little more than the skeleton of a town; for the ground where most of the streets were formerly, is now turned into corn fields, or pasture grounds; and of three parish churches, there remains only the channel of one, which is used for divine service. There is a fair held here on the 14th of May.

HASTINGS.

This town is sixty-three miles from London, and is supposed to have derived its name from one Hasting, a Danish pirate, who generally built a small fort wherever he landed to pillage, in order to cover his men, and secure his retreat. This is the chief of the cinque ports, and is governed by a mayor, jurats, and commonalty. The town lies between two high cliffs, one on the sea, and another on the land-side. Great quantities of fish are taken upon this coast, and sent to London. It is a populous place, and contains two parish churches. The weekly markets are on Wednesdays and Saturdays; and there are three annual fairs
here,

here, namely on Whit-Tuefday, the 26th of July, and the 23d of October.

At *Afhburnham*, which is eight miles from Haftings, the Earl of Afhburnham has a fine feat.

At *Pevenfey*, which is fouth-weft of Haftings, are the remains of a caftle, which was built by William the Conqueror, and which appears to have been a very venerable ftructure.

Beachy-head is a famous promontory, near Pevenfey, and is reckoned the higheft cliff of all the fouth coaft of England; for it projects over the beach to a greater perpendicular height, than the monument in London. Many fhips have been loft here in ftormy weather, and in the rock are many caverns formed by the violence of the waves. As this is reckoned the higheft beach on the fouth coaft of this ifland, and is divided into feven points or cliffs, it is well known to our mariners, who call it the Seven Cliffs.

Seaforth is a fmall fifhing town, near Beachy-head. It is a place of confiderable antiquity, and enjoys the privileges of a fea port.

Newhaven is a fmall, but populous town, in the neighbourhood of Seaforth. It has a convenient, though little harbour, and fome veffels are built here; and the trade of the place is not inconfiderable.

B R I G H T H E L M S T O N E.

This town is fifty eight miles from London, and is a place of fome antiquity; but it is at prefent chiefly celebrated for the concourfe of nobility and gentry who vifit it, during the fummer feafon, for the benefit of bathing in the fea. The town is pleafantly fituated on a rifing ground, near the fea, and the air is efteemed healthy. Before the civil wars in the laft century, this was efteemed the greateft fifhing town in the county of Suffex; but it has declined in that branch of trade ever fince, its chief dependence now being on the number of perfons who refort here for the purpofe of bathing; though indeed many come here rather becaufe it is confidered as a genteel place of diffipation, than from any defire of benefitting their health by bathing in the fea.

The town is divided into feveral fmall ftreets, between which there are lanes, wherein the poorer fort of people refide. The town hall ftands near the fea, and under it is a

F f

prifon

prifon for felons, and a warehoufe in which the ftores are kept, they having a fmall battery for guns, although they are not mounted but in time of war. The parifh church ftands at a little diftance from the town, and there are meeting-houfes for diffenters and quakers. The Countefs of Huntingdon has alfo erected a chapel here at her own expence. There is a free-grammar fchool here, and two charity-fchools.

There is every neceffary accommodation and convenience provided, for thofe who come here for the purpofe of bathing; and a perfon is appointed to act as mafter of the ceremonies, in the fame manner as at Bath, and who regulates the public meet-ings and diverfions. There is a weekly market on Thurf-day, well fupplied with all forts of provifions; and there are two fairs held here, one on Holy Thurfday, and the other on the 4th of September.

On the weft fide of Brighthelmftone, a great number of human bones have been found, from whence it is concluded that a battle was fought here. Many are of opinion that Cæfar, in one of his expeditions into Britain, landed at this place. In the neighbourhood of this town an urn was dug up fome years ago, containing a thoufand filver denarii, and fome of all the emperors, from Antoninus Pius to Philip; and the altars of the Druids have no where been met with in greater numbers than about Brighthelmftone.

NEW SHOREHAM

Is nine miles from Brighthelmftone, and fifty-eight from London. It took its rife from the decay of *Old Shoreham*, now a fmall village north weft of it. Though moft of this town has been wafhed away by the fea, it is ftill a large populous place. The parifh church is a noble Gothic ftructure. The harbour here is but indifferent, though fhips of confiderable burthen can come into it. Many artificers are conftantly employed here, in building fmall veffels for the coafting trade. There is a fair here on the 25th of July.

Bramber, which is not far diftant from New Shoreham, was formerly a place of confiderable repute, but is now fallen to decay. *Findon* is a village between Bramber and Arun-del; and from this place, round by Houghton-bridge, along the edge of the Downs, towards Arundel, are very noble views over the wild. At one fpot in particular, where the road leads very near a precipice, the flope of the hill is fo
fteep,

Arundel Castle, in Sussex, one of the Seats of the Duke of Norfolk.

steep, that a boy could not crawl it, and so high, that the immense country open to you, is seen below in such a manner, that almost every enclosure is distinct, in a vale ten miles long by three broad. A bold wave of the hill to the right and left, forms a dell at your feet at the foot of the down; a thick clump of wood fills it, and forms a romantic scene. The wave of the hill to the left is finely fringed with wood; groves that skirt the fields break from it, and diversify the view: a farm with stacks, and a large water, under the shade of a noble wood, form a complete picture: other woods spreading about the vale, are broken by innumerable inclosures, of which you have an admirable view. To the right, the down hills bear away one beyond another, forming very striking projections. The whole is a scene extremely magnificent.

A R U N D E L

Is so called from its situation in a dale, or valley, upon the bank of the river Arun. It is 56 miles from London, and is a borough by prescription, having sent members to parliament from the thirteenth year of King Edward the First, and is so antient as to be mentioned in King Alfred's will. It is governed under a charter of Queen Elizabeth, by a mayor, twelve burgesses, a steward, and under officers. The mayor is invested with confiderable powers, and no writ can be executed within the borough without his permission.

This town is pleasantly situated on the side of a hill, and has an ancient castle, said to be a mile in compass, and to have been built in the time of the Saxons. William the Conqueror conferred this castle on Roger de Montgomery, who repaired it, and was created Earl of Arundel and Shrewsbury; but he took his title from Arundel Castle, where he resided; and his successors long enjoyed it as a local dignity, together with the castle; but the title being disputed, it was declared by act of parliament in the reign of King Henry the Sixth, that all persons who had been, or should be possessed of the castle and honour of Arundel, were, and should be, Earls of the same, without any other creation; and the title, manor, and castle, still continue inseparable. Arundel Castle is in a better condition than might be expected from its age, and is now one of the feats of the Duke of Norfolk, who enjoys the title of Earl of Arundel.

Arundel church is a venerable Gothic structure, and was formerly a collegiate.—There is a good wooden bridge here

over

over the river.—Four fairs are held here yearly, viz. on the 14th of May for cattle, on the 21st of August for hogs, on the 25th of September for sheep, and on the 17th of December for pedlary wares.

C H I C H E S T E R.

This City, which is sixty-three miles from London, is supposed to derive its name from the Saxon words *Ciffanceafter*, which signifies the City of Cissa; and it was thus called from Cissa, the second king of the South Saxons, who rebuilt it after it had been destroyed by some Saxon and Norwegian pirates, and made it the royal residence, and the capital of his kingdom. This city has been the see of a bishop ever since the time of William the Conqueror. It is a county of itself, and is governed under a charter of King James the Second, by a mayor, a recorder, aldermen, and common council.

Chichester is surrounded by the river Lavant on every side but the north, and is a neat compact city, inclosed by a stone wall, with four gates, answering to the four points, east, west, north, and south. From each of these gates there is a street, which is denominated from its gate, and terminates in the market-place, which is the center of the city, and is adorned with a stone piazza. In the middle is a stately cross, erected by Bishop Story, about the beginning of the sixteenth century. The streets in general are broad, and the houses uniform and well built.

There is a cathedral in Chichester, and five parish churches. The cathedral is a neat, though small building, and is adorned with a spire, much admired for its strength and curious workmanship. There is an episcopal palace here, which was rebuilt some years ago, but it is rather large than elegant. This edifice, with the cathedral, and houses of the prebendaries, takes up all that quarter of the city between the west and south gates. The market house is a handsome structure, and over it is a large room, in which the gentry have balls and public assemblies.

Much of the trade of this city consists in making of malt; and here is also a considerable manufactory of needles. The river is not deep enough near the city to make a good harbour; but here is some foreign trade; and a collector, with other officers of the customs, at Dell Key, a small harbour, about four miles from the sea, where vessels come in at high water, and go out with wheat, flour, timber, and coals,

for

for London and other ports.——There are five annual fairs here; viz. on the third of May, Whit-Monday, the fifth of August, the tenth of October, and twentieth of the same month.

In the year 1723, a stone was dung up at Chichester, with an inscription, which, though somewhat defaced, plainly intimated, that it was the foundation stone of a temple erected here in the reign of the emperor Claudius, and dedicated to Neptune and Minerva. In this city there have been also found, at different times, a great number of Roman coins. And when the episcopal palace was re-built, the workmen dug up several antient coins; and in the garden was discovered a curious piece of Roman pavement.

On the west side of Chichester is a large Roman camp called the Brill. It is an oblong square, being about half a mile in length, and a quarter of a mile in breadth. It lies in a flat low ground, with a great rampart and a single graff, and is generally thought to have been the first camp of the emperor Vespasian, after his landing in Britain. Not far from Chichester, on the same side, is another camp, called Gonshill, which is also supposed to have been thrown up by the Romans, it being likewise an oblong square.—On a hill, north of the city, called Rook's Hill, or Roche's Hill, is an ancient camp of an orbicular form, something more than a quarter of a mile in diameter, supposed to have been thrown up by the Danes.

At a little distance from Chichester, the Duke of Richmond has a fine seat, known by the name of GOODWOOD. It formerly belonged to the noble family of Piercy; but being purchased by the late Duke of Richmond, he pulled down the antient Gothic structure, and erected a fine mansion, according to a plan drawn by Mr. Campbell, author of the Vitruvius Britannicus. It is a most excellent structure, and the prospect from it is extremely delightful.

Near Goodwood was an antient castle, now converted into a dwelling house, surrounded by fine gardens, from the windows of which there are some admirable views. And near it is a small delightful village, called Boxgrove, where a monastery was founded in the reign of King Henry I. for monks of the Benedictine order. The church which belonged to this monastery, is now used by the inhabitants of the parish for divine service.

About

About five miles from Chichester, is STANSTED PARK, a fine seat which belonged to the late Earl of Hallifax; who left it by will, to his natural daughter. It is a most agreeable place; and from the dining room windows there is a complete prospect of the Isle of Wight, together with a view of the royal navy in Portsmouth harbour, St. Helen's, and Spithead. The gardens are delightful, and the walks in the park extremely rural.

At *Bosham*, a village south-west of Chichester, now chiefly inhabited by fishermen, a monastery was founded before the year 681. And the parish church here is a stately Gothic edifice, which was built at the sole expence of William Warelwast, Bishop of Exeter, in the reign of Henry I. It was made collegiate for a dean and prebendaries; and the stalls for the prebendaries are yet standing, over which are carvings of very antient workmanship. The daughter of Canute the Great was buried here, and there is in the church an ancient monument, said to be in memory of that Princess.

M I D H U R S T.

This town is fifty-two miles distant from London, and is a borough by prescription, governed by a bailiff, chosen annually by a jury at the court leet, It has sent members to parliament ever since the year 1311, the fourth of Edward II. and is a pretty large town, pleasantly situated on a hill, surrounded with several other hills. There is a fair held here on Ladyday.

Lord Viscount Montacute has a very handsome seat at COWDRY, near Midhurst. It is one of the most agreeable places in the county of Sussex. The situation is in a beautiful valley, and the late Lord Montacute was at great expence in adorning the house, and making improvements in the park and gardens. The wars of Henry VIII. are painted on different parts of the rooms by Hans Holbein; and here are portraits of several noble persons of this antient family by that artist. The new improvements in this seat are executed in the Gothic taste; so that the house, although modern, has all the appearance of antiquity.

There are several agreeable villages in the neighbourhood of Midhurst, particularly *Charlton*, where the country gentlemen have houses to keep their dogs and horses for the

chace;

chace; and amongst others, there is one belonging to the Duke of Richmond, executed on a design of the Earl of Burlington.

P E T W O R T H

Is forty-nine miles from London, and is a large, populous, handsome town, situated on a fine dry ascent, in a healthy air. The church here is an indifferent structure, though the rectory is the richest in the county, being said to be worth seven hundred pounds a year. There is a fair held at this place for black cattle on Holy Thursday, and another for sheep and hogs on the 20th of November.

The Earl of Egremont has a noble seat here, which formerly belonged to Algernon, Duke of Somerset. The front is of free-stone, and adorned on the top with statues: the great stairs and apartments are magnificent; the offices are very commodious, and there is one vault near four hundred feet in length. This seat originally belonged to the noble family of Piercy, and there is a sword in the armoury here, which is said to have been the weapon of the famous Henry Hotspur, Lord Piercy, who was killed in the battle of Shrewsbury, fighting against King Henry IV.

H O R S H A M.

This town derives its name from Horsa, brother of Hengist the Saxon, who is supposed to have had his residence here. It is thirty-seven miles from London, and is a borough by prescription, governed by two bailiffs, chosen yearly at the courtleet. The county assizes are sometimes held here; and here is the county goal. This is one of the largest towns in Sussex, and has a fine church, a large venerable Gothic structure, and a well endowed free-school. The country round Horsham is well cultivated, and there is a quarry of excellent free-stone in the neighbourhood. The weekly market on Saturday, is well supplied with provisions, particularly poultry, of which the greatest part is bought up by the dealers in London — There are three fairs held here, viz. on the Monday before Whitsunday, on the 18th of July, and the 27th of November.—On the north-east of Horsham is the forest of St. Leonard, where the neighbouring gentry enjoy the diversion of hunting.

HASLE-

HASLEMERE.

This is a borough-town in the county of Surrey, at the distance of forty-four miles from London. It is pleasantly situated on the borders of Suffex, and is a place of confiderable antiquity; but is now greatly decayed. It is governed by a bailiff, and is faid to have had feven parifh churches formerly, though it has now no more than one chapel of eafe to Chidingfold, a village about two miles to the eaft of it. There is a fair held here on the firft of May, and another on the 25th of September.

GODALMIN

Is an ancient town fituated on the river Wey, thirty-four miles from London, and ten from Haflemere. It is faid to have derived its name from Goda, a Saxon lady, who was the foundrefs of a religious houfe. It is a flourifhing place, particularly for the manufactory of woollen cloth, and worfted ftockings, of which laft great quantities are made here. It is faid, that in 1739, the fmall-pox carried off above five hundred perfons here in three months, which was more than a third of the inhabitants. There are feveral paper-mills in this town, which have continued here ever fince the reign of King James I. There is a fair held here on the 13th of February, and another on the 10th of July.

FARNHAM

Is fuppofed to have derived its name from the plant called *Fern*, with which this place formerly abounded. It is forty miles from London, and was given by Ethelbald, King of the Weft Saxons, to the fee of Winchefter; the Bifhops of which fee have generally refided here in the fummer, ever fince the reign of King Stephen, in a Caftle built by that King's brother, who was then Bifhop of Winchefter. This Caftle was a magnificent ftructure, with deep moats, ftrong walls, and towers at proper diftances, and a fine park; but it is much decayed.

This is a large and populous town, and here is one of the greateft wheat-markets in England: a great quantity of hops, faid to be as good as any in the kingdom, is produced in the neighbourhood of this place. This town fent members to parliament in the reign of Edward II. but never fince.

GUIL.

The South West View of Guildford, in Surry.

GUILFORD.

This town is situated on the river Wey, at the distance of thirty miles from London. In the time of the Saxons, as well as afterwards, it was a royal villa, where many of our Kings used to pass the festivals; and in particular King Henry II. King John and King Edward III. kept their Christmas here. This town is governed by a mayor, a recorder, seven aldermen, sixteen bailiffs, and other officers. The assizes for the county are held often here, and always the election of knights of the shire. The town is large, handsome, and well built; and has always been famous for good inns, and excellent accommodations for travellers. There were three churches in this town, but one of them, being an ancient building, fell down in April 1740. Here is a free school, founded by King Edward the Sixth, and an handsome alms-house, called Trinity-hospital, founded by George Abbot, archbishop of Canterbury, and endowed by him with lands worth 300l. a year, for the maintenance of a master, twelve brethreen, and eight sisters. It consists of a handsome quadrangle, built of brick, with a tower and four turrets over the gate. It has a chapel, in which are two windows well painted. Here also are two charity-schools, one for thirty boys, and the other for twenty girls.

In the neighbourhood of Guilford, there is a fine circular course for horse races, which begin when the Newmarket races end; and King William III. left a plate of 100 guineas to be run for here every May. On the south side of this town there is a chalky hill, called St. Catharine's Hill, from which there is an exceeding fine prospect to the north and north west; and on this hill stands a gallows, which is in such a position, as to be seen from all the shop doors in the High-street of Guilford, so that the inhabitants can see the executions there without going from home.—At a little distance from Guilford is *Clandon-Park*, a fine seat belonging to Lord Onslow; and at *Horsley* is a seat of Lord Bingley's.

OCKLEY, OR OAKLY.

This is a village in Surry, which is said to have derived its name from the vast number of oak trees, growing in the neighbourhood. There was a castle here formerly, which was besieged by the Danes in the reign of King Ethelwolf, and the moat which surrounded it is still to be seen near the church. The church-yard here is remarkable for rose bushes planted

G g

at

at the head of several graves, in conformity to an ancient custom observed here among lovers; for if either of any two lovers dies before marriage, the survivor plants a rose tree at the
head of the deceased's grave; and some are at the expence of
keeping up such trees for many years. This practice is supposed to have been derived from the ancient Greeks and Romans,
who, according to Anacreon and Ovid, imagined that roses,
planted or strewed upon the graves of the dead, perfumed and
protected their ashes.

D A R. K I N G.

This is a market town in Surrey, twenty-four miles from
London, pleasantly situated on the banks of the river Mole.
It is a place of considerable antiquity, and is built on a soft rock
of sandy stone; and the cellars under the houses being cut out
of the same materials, are extremely cold even in summer.
Some of our most eminent physicians have esteemed the air at
this place the most healthy in England; and many of the citizens of London have country seats in and near the town. The
streets are broad, open, well-paved, and kept extremely clean;
so that the whole has a very agreeable appearance. The town
is famous for its great corn trade, and vast quantities of corn,
poultry, and other necessaries of life, are sold here for the use
of the London markets; and the town is well supplied with
butchers meat, fresh water fish from the Mole, and sea fish from
the coast of Sussex.—At the entrance of the town is *Shrub-hill*,
the seat of Lord Cathcart.

Box-hill, in this neighbourhood, had its name from its being
planted for the most part with box trees, cut out into a great
number of arbours, and formed into Labyrinths. This hill,
from whence there is a most enchanting prospect, is much the
resort of gentry from all parts of the county.

About five miles from Darking, is the village of *Wotton*;
and in opening the ground in the church-yard here, to en-
large the vault of the Evelyn family, in the reign of King
Charles the Second, a human skeleton was found, which measured nine feet three inches in length.—Not far from Wotton is
Leith-hill, which is celebrated for its extent, and the uncommon fineness of its prospect. It consists of one continued, and
almost imperceptible ascent from Wotton, for near three miles
to the south; and from the summit sinks, on the south side,
with a gentle declivity of about eight miles, as far as Horsham
in Sussex. This is by much the highest hill in the county of
Surrey,

Surrey, and from the top of it may be seen, in a clear day, all Surrey and Suffex, parts of Hampshire, Berkshire, Oxfordshire, Buckinghamshire, Hertfordshire, Middlesex, Essex, and Kent; and by the help of a telescope, some part of Wiltshire; so that the whole circumference of the view is thought to be near 260 miles.

R Y E G A T E.

This town is twenty-three miles from London, situated in the vale of Holmsdale, and is surrounded with hills. It is an ancient borough by prescription, and is governed by a bailiff, chosen annually at the manor-court. Here is a handsome church, built of free stone, a charity-school, and a market-house, which was formerly a chapel, dedicated to Thomas a Becket; and here are some inconsiderable remains of a very antient castle.—There is a fair held here on Whit Monday, and another on the 14th of September.

In the reign of King Henry III. William Warren, Earl of Surrey, founded a priory of Black Canons, at the bottom of a hill, adjoining to Ryegate, which is now converted into a dwelling-house, and a few years ago was the residence of the late Alderman Parsons.

On the south-side of Ryegate is a fine park full of little groves; and under this there is a wonderful vault of arched work, made of free-stone, and hollowed with great labour.

WOKING is a small market-town, twenty-eight miles from London, which was once a considerable place, but is now much decayed. Two miles to the north by east of Woking, is PURFORD, or PYRFORD, a village, in which is a fine seat which belonged to the late Denzil Onslow, Esq. It is situated near the banks of the Wey, and is rendered extremely pleasant by the beautiful intermixture of wood and water, in the park, gardens, and adjoining grounds. By the park is a decoy, the first of the kind in this part of England.

Four miles to the east of Woking, is OAKHAM, the seat of Lord King, whose park extends to the great road. This was purchased by Sir Peter King, afterwards Lord Chancellor. The house was greatly repaired and beautified by the late Lord, and the present Lord King has made great improvements in the park and gardens.—The inhabitants of this village have a tradition, that at Ockham Court was formerly a nunnery, and that a subterraneous passage went from it to Newark abbey, (which stood in the neighbouring parish of

Send).

Send) by which there was a communication between the monks and nuns.

B A G S H O T.

This is a village in Surrey, twenty-seven miles from London, in the great Western road, and chiefly remarkable for its affording good accommodations for travellers. At a little distance is *Bagshot Park*, a fine seat belonging to the Earl of Albemarle. *Bagshot-heath* is a large barren tract of country, but appears to be capable of great improvement.

M A I D E N H E A D.

This is a market-town in Berkshire, at the distance of twenty-eight miles from London. It stands in two parishes, Cookham and Bray, and was raised out of obscurity by a bridge, which about three centuries ago was built over the Thames at this place, and brought hither the great north-west road, which used to cross the Thames at a place called Babham end, about two miles to the north, where there was a ferry. After this bridge was built, Maidenhead began to be accommodated with inns, and the town is now pretty large, and tolerably well built. The bridge is maintained by the corporation, for which they are allowed the tolls both over and under it; and the crown gives three trees a year out of Windsor forest towards repairing it. The barge pier divides Berkshire from Buckinghamshire. There is a great trade here in malt, meal, and timber, which are carried in barges to London. Here is a gaol both for debtors and felons, a chapel dedicated to St. Andrew the apostle and St. Mary Magdalen, but no church, and an alms house, consisting of dwellings for eight poor men and their wives; each man has six pounds a year, and every second year each person has a new gown. It was endowed by James Smith, citizen and salter of London, and his wife, about 1589, and the Salters company of London are trustees.

The village of *Bray* is about a mile from Maidenhead, and is very famous, both on account of its antiquity, and a former vicar, who was twice a Papist, and twice a Protestant, in the reigns of Henry VIII. Edward VI. and the Queens Mary and Elizabeth.

READ-

R E A D I N G.

This town is fuppofed to derive its name from *Redin*, the Britifh word for Fern, which is faid to have grown here in great abundance. It is thirty-nine miles from London, is the county-town, and is governed by a mayor, twelve aldermen, and twelve burgeffes. It contains three parifh churches, and the ftreets of this town are well built, and it is more fpacious and populous than many cities. It is partly encompaffed by the Thames, which juft by it receives the river Kennet, that paffes under feven bridges in the town and neighbourhood, and abounds with pike, eel, dace, and fine trout. It had anciently a caftle, of which the Danes are faid to have been in poffeffion, when they drew a ditch between the Kennet and the Thames; and they retreated hither, after they had been routed, at a little diftance from hence, by the Saxon King Ethelwolf; but in 872, they quitted it to the Saxons, who plundered and de-ftroyed the town, which they repeated in 1006. But it re-covered itfelf, and is faid to have been a borough in the reign of William the Conqueror. Its caftle afterwards having been a refuge for King Stephen's party, was demolifhed by King Henry II.

A magnificent abbey of flint-ftone was founded here by King Henry I. which is faid to have equalled moft of the abbies in England for its ftructure and wealth; and its abbots fat in the houfe of lord. It was fuppreffed foon after the Reformation; but the gate-houfe is ftill pretty entire, and there are fome re-mains of its walls eight feet thick.

Reading has a confiderable trade in the country, but its chief traffic is with London; whither it fends malt, meal, and tim-ber, and receives back coals, falt, tobacco, grocery wares, and other commodities. The largeft barges come up to the town-bridge, where there are commodious wharfs for clearing and loading them. The Kennet, which runs through the town, will bear a barge of more than an hundred tons, and is naviga-ble almoft to Newbury.—This town fends two members to par-liament; and there are four annual fairs held here; viz. on the 1ft of February, the 25th of July, the 21ft of September, and the 6th of November.

As fome peafants were digging fome years ago, on a rifing ground, not far from Reading, they difcovered a ftratum of oyfter fhells, lying on a bed of green fand, and covered with a ftratum of bluifh clay. Many of the fhells when they are

2   taken

taken up, have both the valves lying together, and when the upper and under shell or valve are found separate, it appears, upon comparing and joining them, that they orginally belonged to each other. This stratum has been found to extend through five or six acres of ground.

N E W B U R Y.

This town is fifty-six miles from London, and is pleasantly situated on the river Kennet, which runs through the town; the streets are spacious, and the market-place, in which there is a guild-hall, is large. The town is supposed to have risen out of the ruins of the antient *Spinæ*, a town mentioned by Antoninus in his Itinerary : for there is a little village within less than a mile, that is still called *Spene*, which the inhabitants of Newbury own to be the mother-place, and part of Newbury itself is called Spenham Land.

The town has been very famous for the manufacture of broad cloth, but that trade is now much on the decline here. So much broad cloth was made here formerly, that in the reign of Henry VIII. here flourished John Winscomb, commonly called Jack of Newbury, one of the greatest clothiers that ever was in England. He kept an hundred looms in his house ; and in the expedition to Flodden-field against the Scots, he marched thither in defence of his country at the head of an hundred of his own men, all cloathed and armed at his own expence. He behaved in that engagement with distinguished bravery ; and afterwards returned to his native place, and at his own expence re-built the greatest part of the parish-church of this town. The house in which he lived remained till about a century ago, when it was divided into tenements, and let out to different tenants.

The town-hall at Newbury is an ancient edifice, built of brick, and supported by pillars; and in this hall the inhabitants have fixed up a fine historical picture of the surrender of Calais, which was painted by Mr. Pine in the year 1762, and for which he received the first premium of one hundred pounds given by the Society of Arts.——There is an alms-house here, said to have been originally founded by King John, for six poor men, and six poor women ; each person is allowed twenty one pence per week, four shillings each on the fair day, thirteen shillings and four pence at Christmas, an hundred faggots of wood yearly, and a new coat or gown every two years.

There

There are several agreeable villages in the neighbourhood of Newbury, particularly *Enbourne*, which is remarkable for the following singular and whimsical custom of the manor. The widow of every copyhold tenant is intitled to the whole copyhold estate of her husband so long as she continues unmarried and chaste ; if she marries, she loses her widow's estate without remedy; but if she is guilty of incontinence, she may recover her forfeiture, by riding into court on the next court day, mounted on a black ram, with her face towards the tail, and the tail in her hand, and repeating the following lines :

" Here I am, mounted on a black ram,
" Like a whore as I am ;
" And for my *crincum crancum*
" Have lost my *bincum bancum,*
" And for my tail's game,
" Am brought to this worldly shame,
" Therefore, good Mr. Steward, let me have my lands again."

At *Hamstead Marshall,* which is not far from Newbury, Lord Craven has a handsome seat and park. And at a little distance from hence is the castle of Donnington, pleasantly situated, at the brow of a hill, near the small river Lambourn, and celebrated for being the residence of our fomous English poet, Geoffrey Chaucer. Since the beginning of the present century, there was a tree in the park, under which, according to a traditionary report, he used to compose his poems.

HUNGERFORD

Is a small market-town, about eight miles from Newbury, and sixty-four from London. It is governed by a constable, who is chosen yearly, and is lord of the manor, which he holds immediately of the King, for the time being. The church is an handsome Gothic structure. They have a horn here that holds about a quart, and which appears by an inscription on it, to have been given to this town by the famous John of Gaunt, son of K. Edward III. together with a grant of the royal fishery, in a part of the river which abounds with good trout and craw-fish.

LAM.

L A M B O U R N E.

This is a fmall town, fixty-eight miles from London, which derives its name from the little river Lambourne which rifes near it. It is not a place of much note, but the adjacent country is pleafant. There is an hofpital here for ten poor men, which was founded in 1502. This town is moſt remarkable for its rivulet, which is always higheſt in ſummer, but ſo low in winter, as to be almoſt entirely loſt.

At a little diſtance from hence, is the moſt remarkable curiofity in Berkſhire. This is the rude figure of a White Horſe, which takes up near an acre of ground, on the ſide of a green hill. A horſe is known to have been the Saxon ſtandard; and ſome have ſuppoſed that this figure was made by Hengiſt, one of the Saxon Kings; but Mr. Wife, the author of a letter on this ſubject to Dr. Mead, publiſhed in the year 1738, brings ſeveral arguments to ſhew that it was made by the order of Alfred, in the reign of his brother Ethelred, as a monument of his victory gained over the Danes, in the year 871, near Aſhdown, now called Aſhen or Aſhbury Park, which is at preſent one of the ſeats of Lord Craven, and at a little diſtance from this hill. Others however ſuppoſe it to have been partly the effect of accident, and partly the work of ſhepherds, who obferving a rude figure, ſomewhat reſembling a horſe, as there are in the veins of wood and ſtone many figures that reſemble trees, caves, and other objects, reduced it by degrees to a more regular figure. But however this be, it has been the cuſtom immemorial for the neighbouring peaſants to aſſemble on a certain day about Midſummer, and clear away the weeds from this white whorſe, and trim the edges to preſerve its colour and ſhape; after which the evening is ſpent in mirth and feſtivity.— The hill on which this ſtands is called White Horſe Hill; and to the north of this hill there is a long valley reaching from the weſtern ſide of the county, where it borders upon Wiltſhire, as far as Wantage, which from this hill is called the Vale of White Horſe, and is the moſt fertile part of the county.

F A R R I N G D O N

Is a neat clean town, fixty-eight miles from London, and pleaſantly ſituated on a hill near the river Thames. The church is a venerable Gothic ſtructure, and has painted

glaſs

glaſs in the windows, beſides many antient monuments.—
Henry Pye, Eſq; has an handſome ſeat here.

W A N T A G E.

This is an agreeable market-town, ſixty miles from London, and eight from Farringdon; and is pleaſantly ſituated in
a fine ſporting country. This place was formerly a royal villa,
and is ſaid to have been the birth place of King Alfred.—The
country adjoining to Wantage is extremely pleaſant.

E·A S T - I L S L E·Y.

This is a ſmall market town, fifty-four miles from London,
agreeably ſituated in a ſporting country. The houſes in the
town are neat, and the adjoining lands well cultivated. The
market, which is held on Wedneſday, is ſaid to be the greateſt
for ſheep of any in England.

About three miles eaſtward of Ilſley is a village called *Ald-
worth*, a place of great antiquity, where was formerly a caſtle,
which was deſtroyed in the reign of King Edward III. The
pariſh church is a venerable Gothic ſtructure, and has in it ſeveral
antient monuments; among theſe are nine, with the figures
of the deceaſed cut in ſtone, and lying in a ſleeping poſture;
five of which are ſuppoſed to have been knights templars. The
church-yard is extremely rural, and has in it one of the fineſt
yew-trees in England, being no leſs than twenty-ſeven feet in
circumference.

W A L L I N G F O R D

Is forty-ſix miles from London, and is a large town, and
makes a good appearance. It is ſituated on the river Thames,
over which it has a ſtone bridge, that is 309 yards long, having
nineteen arches, and four draw-bridges. It has a market-houſe,
over which is the town-hall. The chief ſupport of this town
is the malt trade. There was formerly a famous caſtle here,
ſome remains of which are yet to be ſeen.

Within a mile of this town is a farm called *Choſely*, the lands
belonging to which lie all together, and are let at one thouſand
pounds per annum; and there is one barn on the eſtate, the
roof of which is three hundred and ſix feet long.—This uſed
to be conſidered as the largeſt farm in England, but it is probably not ſo now, ſince the pernicious practice of engroſſing
and enlarging farms has become ſo prevalent. Some artful
reaſoners have, indeed, endeavoured to prove, that large farms

are

are moſt advantageous to the community ; but the arguments brought in ſupport of this opinion, appear to be extremely ſophiſtical ; and it is certain, that an equitable and benevolent government would chuſe to encourage that mode of cultivating the earth, that was moſt favourable to population, and by which the greateſt number of induſtrious families might be comfortably ſupported ; which cannot be the caſe when the monopolization of farms becomes general, and which therefore may juſtly be conſidered, for this and various other reaſons, as a moſt pernicious practice.

A B I N G D O N

Is ſituated on a branch of the Thames, at the diſtance of fifty-ſix miles from London. It is a large, populous, and flouriſhing town : the ſtreets are well paved, and center in a ſpacious area, where the market is held. In the center of this area is the market-houſe ; which is a curious building of aſhler-work, ſupported on lofty pillars, with a large hall of free-ſtone above, in which the aſſizes are frequently held, and other public buſineſs tranſacted. There was formerly a very magnificent abbey here, which was deſtroyed at the general diſſolution of the monaſteries. Here are two pariſh churches, both of which are ſaid to have been built by one of the abbots of Abingdon. There is alſo here a well endowed free-ſchool, and two alms-houſes for poor people of both ſexes. The trade carried on by the inhabitants of this town chiefly conſiſts in dealing in corn, and preparing malt, which is conveyed down the river in barges to London.

O X F O R D.

This famous city is fifty-five miles from London, and is a place of great antiquity, but is chiefly diſtinguiſhed for its illuſtrious univerſity. It is ſituated on the banks of the Thames, near its confluence with ſeveral other rivers, in a beautiful plain, and a ſweet air. It is encompaſſed by meadows and corn-fields. The meadows, which are chiefly to the ſouth and weſt, are about a mile in extent ; beyond which are hills of a moderate height, bounding the proſpect. The eaſtern proſpect is likewiſe bounded by hills at a little diſtance. The north is open to corn-fields and encloſures for many miles together, without an hill to intercept the free current of air, which purifies it from noxious vapours. When this city
was

was firſt fortified does not appear; but the walls now remaining are ſuppoſed to have been raiſed upon ſome former
foundation about the time of the Norman invaſion.   Robert D'Oilie erected the caſtle, at the command of William
the Norman in 1071.   Its maſſy ruins ſhew its ſtrength and
extent.

Oxford, including the ſuburbs, is a mile in length from
eaſt to weſt, and almoſt as much in breadth from north to ſouth,
being three miles in circumference; but it is of an irregular
figure, and ſeveral void ſpaces are comprehended within theſe
limits, beſides the many courts and gardens belonging to the re-
ſpective colleges.   The city, properly ſo called, which was
formerly ſurrounded by a wall, with baſtions, at about one
hundred and fifty feet diſtance from each other, is of an oblong form.   There are ſtill ſome conſiderable remains of the
old walls.

The ſtreets of Oxford are ſpacious, clean, and regular;
the private buildings in general are neat, and the public ones
ſumptuous.   There is a cathedral here, and thirteen pariſh
chutches.   The city is governed by a mayor, a high-ſteward,
a recorder, four aldermen, eight aſſiſtants, a town-clerk, other
officers, and twenty-four common councilmen.   The mayor,
for the time being, officiates at the coronation of our Kings, in
the buttery, and has a large gilt bowl and cover for his fee.
The magiſtracy of this city is ſubjected to the chancellor or
vice-chancellor of the univerſity, in all affairs of moment, even
relating to the city; and the vice-chancellor every year admini-
ſters an oath to the magiſtrates and ſheriffs, that they will maintain the privileges of the univerſity.   And on the 10th of February annually, the mayor and ſixty-two of the chief citizens
ſolemnly pay each one penny, at St. Mary's church here, in lieu
of a great fine laid upon the city, in the reign of King Edward III. when ſixty-two of the ſtudents were murdered by the
citizens.

The town-hall here is a neat modern edifice, in which the
aſſizes for the county, and the city and county ſeſſions are held;
and there are in this city five or ſix charity ſchools, in which
about three hundred children are taught and cloathed.   There
are two ſtone bridges here over the Thames, which is navigable
by barges to the city, from whence large quantities of malt are
ſent by barges to London.

The

The UNIVERSITY

Is one of the nobleſt in the world, eſpecially for the opulency of its endowments, and the conveniency of its manſions for ſtudy. It conſiſts of twenty colleges, and five halls, and is a corporation governed by a chancellor, a high-ſteward, a vice-chancellor, two proctors, a public orator, a keeper of the archives, a regiſter, three eſquire-beadles, carrying ſilver maces gilt and wrought, and three yeomen beadles, with plain ſilver maces, and a verger with a ſilver rod. The chancellor is uſually a peer of the realm, he is the ſupreme governor of the univerſity, and is choſen by the ſtudents in convocation, and continues in his office for life. The high-ſteward is named by the Chancellor, but muſt be approved by the univerſity. His office, which continues alſo for life, is to aſſiſt the chancellor in the government of the univerſity, and to hear and determine capital cauſes, according to the laws of the land, and the privileges of the univerſity. The vice-chancellor, who is always in orders, and the head of ſome college, is appointed by the chancellor, and approved by the univerſity; he is the chancellor's deputy, and exerciſes the power of his ſubſtituent, by governing the univerſity according to its ſtatutes; he chuſes four pro-vice-chancellors out of the heads of colleges to officiate in his abſence. The two proctors are maſters of arts, and are choſen annually in turn out of the ſeveral colleges and halls. Their buſineſs is to keep the peace, puniſh diſorders, inſpect weights and meaſures, appoint ſcholaſtic exerciſes, and the taking of degrees. The public orator writes letters in the name of the univerſity, and harrangues princes and other great perſonages who viſit it. The keeper of the archives has the cuſtody of the charters and records; and the regiſter records all the public tranſactions of the univerſity in convocation.

Beſides the public officers of the univerſity which have been mentioned, there are particular and private officers in all colleges and halls, to ſee that due order and diſcipline be obſerved and kept up, lectures read, diſputations performed, and all the liberal ſciences read and taught, as logic, phyſics, ethics, metaphyſics, aſtronomy, geography, and geometry, &c. of which alſo there are public lecturers and profeſſors.

The degrees taken in the univerſity are in divinity, law, phyſic, and arts; four years are required for taking a bachelor of arts degrees; ſeven years for a maſter of arts;

fourteen

fourteen years for a bachelor of divinity ; eighteen years for a doctor of divinity ; seven years for a bachelor of laws, phyfic, or mufic; and twelve years for a doctor of laws, phy-fic, or mufic.

As to the antiquity of Oxford, it is fuppofed to have been a confiderable place even in the time of the Romans ; and Camden fays, that " wife antiquity did, even in the Britifh " age, confecrate this place to the mufes." Before the time of King Alfred it was ftiled an univerfity ; and the beft hiftorians admit, that this moft excellent prince was only a reftorer of learning here. Alfred built three colleges here ; one for divinity, another for philofophy, and a third for grammar.

The number of officers, fellows, and fcholars, maintained at prefent by the revenues of this univerfity, is about 1000, and the number of fuch fcholars as live at their own charge is ufually about 2000 ; the whole amounting to 3000 perfons, befides a great number of inferior officers and fervants, belonging to the feveral colleges and halls, which have each their ftatutes and rules for government; under their refpective heads, with fellows and tutors. Here are four terms every year for public exercifes, lectures, and difputations, and fet days and hours when the profeffors of every faculty read their lectures, and in fome of the colleges are public lectures, to which all perfons are admitted.

The Public Schools.

Thefe, with one fide of the Library on the weft, form within a fpacious fquare of 105 feet. The principal front of the fchools on the outfide is about 175 feet in length, in the middle whereof is a great gate, with a magnificent tower over it, which is Sir Henry Savile's library ; and the higheft apartments of the tower are ufed for aftronomical obfervations, and fome experiments in philofophy ; and from thence called the Obfervatory.

The Schools are as follows, 1. the Divinity fchool ; 2. the Anatomy fchool ; 3. the Natural Philofophy fchool ; 4. the Moral Philofophy fchool ; 5. the Law fchool ; 6. the Hiftory fchool ; 7. the Language fchool ; 8. the Geometry fchool ; 9. the Metaphyfic fchool ; 10. the Logic fchool ; 11. the Mufic fchool ; a new one was built in Holywell, in 1747 ; 12. the Aftronomy fchool ; 13. the Rhetoric fchool.

In thefe public fchools the profeffors are to read their lectures in the feveral fciences every day in the week during

term-

term-time, except Sundays. In which schools likewise all scholars are obliged, by the statutes of the university, at such and such certain times to perform such and such exercises for their several degrees, as disputations, declamations, examinations, lectures, &c.

Three sides of the upper story of the Schools, form one entire room, which is called the PICTURE GALLERY. It is furnished with the portraits of many learned and famous men, several large cabinets of medals, and some cases of books; being intended as a continuation of the Bodleian library. Among the paintings, are portraits of King Alfred, William of Wykeham, Bishop of Winchester, Sir Thomas Bodley, Dr. Wallis, Sir Henry Savile, Sir Hans Sloane, Dr. Halley, Samuel Butler, Archbishop Usher, Hugo Grotius, Joseph Scalagier, Isaac Casaubon, Meric Casaubon, Erasmus by Hans Holbein, Franciscus Junius by Vandyke, John Selden, Montaigne, Father Paul, Dr. Edward Pococke, Galilæo, Chaucer, Dr. Henry Hammond, Sir Thomas More, Dr. Samuel Clarke, Samuel Bochart, Sir William Dugdale, Michael Angelo, Ben Jonson, Pope, Prior, Swift, the Earl of Clarendon, Dr. Radcliffe, Lord Falkland, Mr. Locke, and many other eminent and learned persons.

The *Arundel marbles* are placed to advantage in a large apartment on the north side of the schools. They consist of some very antient monuments, both Greek and Latin, procured from the Levant, and were most of them the gift of Henry Howard, Earl of Arundel.——In the Logic and Moral Philosophy school is also placed a fine collection of statues, bustos, and marble sculptures, which were many years at Easton, the seat of the Earl of Pomfret, and were presented to the University of Oxford by the late Countess of Pomfret.

The UNIVERSITY LIBRARY, usually called the BODLEIAN LIBRARY, from Sir Thomas Bodley its principal founder, is a large, lofty structure, in the form of a Roman H, and is said to contain the greatest number of books of any library in Europe, (except perhaps the Vatican) a catalogue whereof is printed in two volumes, folio. The original library has been prodigiously increased by many large and valuable collections of Greek and Oriental manuscripts, as well as other choice and curious books.——Among a great number of most valuable books in this library, are the following :——The four Gospels in Greek, above 1000 years old, in large capital
letters.

letters.—The four Gospels, a Latin manuscript, one thousand four hundred years old, supposed to have been one of those books which were brought over into Britain by St. Augustine. The Acts of the Apostles, in Latin and Greek, thought to be as old as the last, and to have formerly belonged to Venerable Bede.

The RATCLIFFE LIBRARY is situated between St. Mary's church and the public schools, and was built at the sole expence of that eminent physician Dr. John Radcliffe, who bequeathed forty thousand pounds for this purpose. It is a sumptuous pile of building, standing upon arcades, which circularly disposed, inclose a spacious dome, in the center of which is the library itself, and into which there is an ascent by a flight of spiral steps, well executed. The library, which is a compleat pattern of elegance and majesty in building, is adorned with fine compartments of stucco. It is inclosed by circular series of arches, beautified with festoons, and supported by pilasters of the Ionic order; behind these arches are formed two circular galleries above and below, where the books are disposed in elegant cabinets; the compartments of the cieling in the upper gallery are finely stuccoed; the pavement is of two colours, and made of a peculiar species of stone brought from Hart's Forest in Germany; and over the door is a statue of the founder. The finishing and decorations of this Attic edifice are all in the highest taste imaginable.

The THEATRE at Oxford is another most magnificent structure, which was erected by Sir Christopher Wren, at the expence of Archbishop Sheldon. The building is in the form of a Roman D; the front of it, which stands opposite to the divinity school, is adorned with Corinthian pillars, and several other decorations. The greatest curiosity of this theatre is its flat roof, which has no pillars to support it, being entirely kept up with braces and screws, and whose main beams are made of several pieces of timber, from side wall to side wall, eighty feet over one way, and seventy the other, whose lockages are in several respects perhaps not to be paralleled in the world; and is the subject of an excellent mathematical treatise, written by the learned Dr. Wallis. The inside of this flat roof is decorated with allegorical painting. In this edifice are kept the public acts, called the *Comitia* or *Encænia*; at which solemn times, for the preservation of order, there are appointed, besides the curators of the theatre, several proctors of it, who

are

are to take care that the public peace is kept undifturbed, and that all perfons be placed in their proper ftations. When the theatre is properly filled, the vice-chancellor being feated in the center of the femi-circular part, the noblemen and doctors on his right and left hand, the proctors and curators in their robes, the mafters of arts, batchelors, and under graduates, in their refpective habits and places, together with ftrangers of both fexes, it makes a moft auguft appearance.

On the weft of the Theatre is the ASHMOLEAN MUSEUM, which is an handfome edifice, that was finifhed in 1682, by Sir Chriftopher Wren, and is remarkable for its fymmetry and elegance. The eaftern portico is highly finifhed in the Corinthian order, and adorned with variety of characteriftical embellifhments. This Mufæum is a famous repofitory of natural and artificial rarities, and of feveral Roman antiquities, as altars, lamps, medals, &c. and the building was erected at the expence of the Univerfity, at the requeft of Elias Afhmole, Efq; who placed here the large collection of rarities which he had collected and purchafed. And this collection has been fince greatly enriched by feveral ample and valuable benefactions. The principal natural curiofities confift of the bodies, horns, bones, &c. of animals, preferved dry, or in fpirits; curious and numerous fpecimens of metals, minerals, fhells, ores, and foffils. On the firft floor of this building lectures are read in experimental philofophy; and, in proper apartments underneath, is an elaboratory for courfes of chemiftry and anatomy. There are three fmall libraries in this edifice, the firft called Afhmole's ftudy, which contains his printed books and manufcripts relating to heraldry and antiquity, and the manufcripts of. Sir William Dugdale; the fecond contains Dr. Lifter's library; and the third that of Anthony Wood, with his laborious collections, chiefly relating to this city and univerfity.

On the other fide of the theatre, and north of the fchools, ftands the CLARENDON PRINTING HOUSE, built in the year 1711, with the profits arifing from the fale of Lord Clarendon's Hiftory; the copy of which was given to the Univerfity by the Lords Clarendon and Rochefter, fons of that nobleman. It is a grand edifice. one hundred and fifteen feet in length; and confifts of two lofty ftories. Towards the ftreet, is a magnificent portico in the Doric order; the height of the columns being equal to the two ftories. This is anfwered on the oppofite fide, next the fchools, by a frontifpiece fupported by three

. quarter

quarter columns of the same dimensions; and the Doric entablature encompasses the whole building. On the top, are statues of the nine Muses; and over the entrance on the south
side a statue of the Earl of Clarendon. As we enter on this
side, on the right hand, are the apartments where bibles and
common prayer-books are printed, under the privilege and ap-
pointment of the university. On the left, is the university-
press. Besides the apartments assigned for the compositors, press-
men, &c. there is one with a lobby, or ante chamber, where
the heads of houses and delegates meet which is well proportioned and highly finished. In this room is a very good picture
of Queen Anne, by Sir Godfrey Kneller.

The PHYSIC GARDEN is situated on the south of Magdalen college, and was given to the university by Henry D'An-
vers, Earl of Danby, who purchased the ground, containing
five acres, of Magdalen college, surrounded it with a lofty wall,
and erected, next to the street, a parapet, with iron palisades
thereon. The piers which support these and other iron-work,
are properly ornamented with vases of fruits and flowers of various kinds, serving as a fence to the green-court, through
which we pass to the gateway; the design of which is attribu-
ted to Inigo Jones, and is justly esteemed an elegant piece of
architecture. In the center over the arch is a bust of the
founder, Lord Danby; and on the left hand of the entrance is
a statue of Charles I. and on the right hand, one of Charles
II. The garden is divided into four quarters, with a broad
walk down the middle, a cross walk, and one all round.
Near the entrance, are two elegant and useful green-houses,
one on the right, the other on the left, built by the university
for *Exotics*, of which there is a considerable collection. In the
quarters, within the yew hedges, is the greatest variety of such
plants as require no artificial heat to nourish them, all ranged
in the proper classes, and numbered. Eastward of the garden,
without the walls, is an excellent hot-house; where tender
plants, such whose native soil lies between the Tropics, are
raised and brought to great perfection; viz. the anana or pine
apple, the plantain, the coffee shrub, the cinnamon, the
creeping cereus, and many others. This useful foundation
has been much improved by the late Dr. Sherrard, who
brought from Smyrna a valuable collection of Botanical Books,
and a valuable *Hortus Siccus*. The east end of the building
is the apartment for the professor, whose salary is paid out
of the interest of three thousand pounds, given by Dr. Sher-

I i

rard

rard for that purpofe. An affiftant to the profeffor is provided by the univerfity.——We now proceed to give fome account of the feveral Colleges and Halls of this famous univerfity.

MAGDALEN COLLEGE is fituated without the eaft gate of the city, on the bank of the river Cherwell ; a Doric portal, (decorated with a ftatue of the founder, and other figures,) leads to the weft front of this college, which is a ftriking fpecimen of the Gothic manner. The firft court is a venerable old quadrangle, furrounded by a cloifter, on the fouth fide of which are the chapel and hall ; the windows of the chapel are finely painted ; the hall is a ftately Gothic room, adorned with fine paintings. From this court there is a narrow paffage on the north, that leads to a beautiful opening, one fide of which is bounded by a noble and elegant edifice, in the modern tafte, confifting of three ftories, and three hundred feet in length. This college is remarkable for a moft beautiful fituation, and a charming profpect. It was founded in the reign of Henry VI. by William Patten, commonly called William of Wainfleet, Bifhop of Winchefter. It confifts of a prefident, forty fellows, thirty demies, fchool-mafter, and ufher, four chaplains, an organift, eight clerks, and fixteen chorifters, and three readers of divinity, and natural and moral philofophy. The whole number of ftudents, including gentlemen commoners, is about one hundred and twenty.

The Grove belonging to this College, which is laid out in walks, and well planted with trees, feems perfectly adapted to indulge contemplation ; it has in it about forty head of deer. Befides the walks which are in the grove, there is a very delightful, and much frequented one, round a meadow containing about thirteen acres, furrounded by the feveral branches of the Cherwell, from whence it is called the *Waterwalks*. It is fhaded with tall trees, and there is an agreeable view of the adjacent country.

QUEEN's COLLEGE is fituated on the north fide of the High-ftreet, oppofite Univerfity College. The front of this College is in the ftile of the palace of Luxemburgh, and is at once elegant and magnificent : in the middle of it a cupola, under which is a ftatue of the late Queen Caroline. This beautiful college is one entire piece of well executed modern architecture ; the whole area on which it ftands is an oblong fquare, 300 feet in length, and 220 in breadth ; which area
being

being divided by the hall and chapel, is formed into two courts ; the first, or south court, is one hundred and forty feet in length, and one hundred and thirty in breadth ; it is surrounded by a beautiful cloyster, except upon the north side, which is formed by the chapel and hall, and finely finished in the Doric order : in the center, over a portico leading to the north court, stands a handsome cupola, supported by eight Ionic columns ; the north court is 130 feet long, and 90 broad. On the west stands the library, which is a fine pile of building, of the Corinthian order, upwards of one hundred feet in length. This college was founded by Robert de Eglesfield, chaplain to Queen Phillippa, wife to King Edward III. That princess was a benefactress to this college, and it was in compliment to her that it was stiled Queen's College. Its revenues have been much increased by several benefactors ; and its members are one provost, sixteen fellows, two chaplains, eight taberdars (so called from *Taberdum*, a short gown which they formerly wore) sixteen scholars, two clerks, and forty exhibitioners ; eight fellows, and four scholars, supported by an estate left to the college by Mr. Mitchell, of Richmond ; besides a great number of masters, bachelors, gentlemen commoners, and other students ; in all about 110.—Among other singular customs in this college, one is, that of calling the students to dinner or supper every day by the sound of a trumpet ; and another is, having a Boar's head on Christmas day, ushered in very solemnly with an old Monkish song.

UNIVERSITY COLLEGE is a spacious, superb, and uniform structure, began in 1634, at the expence of Charles Greenwood, formerly a fellow here, and carried on by Sir Simon Bennet, and completed by Dr. John Radcliffe. The magnificent north front of this college is extended two hundred and sixty feet along the south side of a street called the High-street, having two stately portals with a tower over each ; the western portal leads to an handsome Gothic quadrangle, one hundred feet square ; on the south side of the eastern quadrangle are the chapel, and hall ; there is also a third court of three sides, each of which are about eighty feet.—The Hall, at the entrance of which is a statue of King Alfred, has been lately fitted up in a very beautiful Gothic style, and is a most complete room of the kind.

The colleges, or halls, which were erected by King Alfred in the year 872, were situated near, or on the spot where this college now stands ; and that excellent Prince gave the

students

ſtudents in his ſeminaries certain penſions iſſuing from the Exchequer. But theſe halls were ſoon alienated to the citizens of Oxford, and their penſions were ſuppreſſed about the reign of William the Norman. But in 1219, William archdeacon of Durham purchaſed of the citizens, one of the halls which had been originally erected by Alfred, and endowed it with lands. A ſociety being thus eſtabliſhed, many other benefactors improved the revenues and buildings. This college now has a maſter, twelve fellows, ſeventeen ſcholars, and many other ſtudents, amounting in the whole to above ſeventy.

ALL SOULS COLLEGE was founded in 1437, by Henry Chicheley, archbiſhop of Canterbury; and conſiſts chiefly of two courts. The firſt court is a Gothic edifice, 124 feet in length, and 72 in breadth; the chapel on the north ſide is a ſtately pile; and the hall, which forms one ſide of an area to the eaſt, is an elegant modern room, adorned with many portraits and buſts. Adjoining to the hall is the buttery, which is a well proportioned room, of an oval figure, and an arched ſtone roof, ornamented with curious workmanſhip. The ſecond court is a magnificent Gothic quadrangle, 172 feet in length, and 155 in breadth; on the ſouth are the chapel and hall, on the weſt a cloiſter, with a grand portico; on the eaſt two Gothic towers, in the center of a range of fine apartments, and on the north a library of uncommon magnificence. It is 200 feet in length, 30 in breadth, and 40 in height, and finiſhed in the moſt ſplendid and elegant manner. It was built at the expence of Colonel Codrington, who laid out in it ſix thouſand pounds, and alſo gave his own library to be depoſited in it, and four thouſand pounds to purchaſe new books. This college maintains a warden, forty fellows, two chaplains, and nine ſcholarſhips.

BRAZEN-NOSE COLLEGE was founded in the year 1507, by the joint benefaction of William Smith, Biſhop of Lincoln, and Sir Richard Sutton. There is a brazen-noſe on the top of the College gate, which gives denomination to the college. The refectory is neat and convenient, adorned with pictures of the principal benefactors, and good paintings in glaſs of the two founders. It ſtands on the ſouth ſide of the firſt quadrangle, in the center of which is a ſtatue of Cain and Abel; the figures of which are very ſtriking. Through a paſſage on the left hand of the gate of the firſt quadrangle

we

A View of All Souls College in Oxford.

we enter the second. This is a more modern structure than
the other, and supposed to have been erected by Sir Christopher
Wren. This college maintains a principal, twenty fellows,
thirty-two scholars, and four exhibitioners; and there are about
forty students besides.

HERTFORD COLLEGE stands opposite to the grand gate of
the public schools, and consists of one irregular court, which
has been lately beautified, from a fund raised for that purpose.
Part of this court consists of a few modern buildings, in the
stile of which the whole college is to be rebuilt, according to
a plan consisting of one quadrangle, projected in the year
1747. This college consists of a principal, two senior fellows
or tutors, junior fellows or assistants, thirty under-graduate-
students, and four scholars.

NEW COLLEGE was founded by the famous William of
Wykeham, Bishop of Winchester, in the year 1375. It has
been called New College from its first foundation, being at that
time highly regarded for its extent and grandeur. The first
court is 168 feet in length, and 129 in breadth; in the center
of which is a statue of Minerva. The north side, which consists of the chapel and hall, is a venerable specimen of Gothic
magnificence; the two upper stories of the east side form the
library, and on the west are the lodgings of the warden.
The chapel, for beauty and grandeur, exceeds all in the
university; and near it is a cloister, 146 feet in length on two
sides, and 105 the other two. Contiguous to it on the north,
is a large and lofty tower, with ten bells. From the first
quadrangle there is a passage into another, called Garden-
court, the beautiful area of which, by means of a succession of
retiring wings, displays itself gradually in approaching the garden, from which it is separated by an iron palisade, 136 feet in
length.

On the north side of the chapel is preserved the crosier of
the founder, which is usually shewn to strangers; a well preserved piece of antiquity, and almost the only one in the kingdom. It is of silver gilt, and near seven feet hight, finely worked and embellished in the Gothic taste; and though it is near
four hundred years old, it has lost little of its original beauty.—
In the garden of the college, there is a lofty artificial mount,
encompassed with several hedges of juniper, adorned with trees
cut into several shapes, with stone steps and winding walks
up to the top, and the top encompassed with rails and seats,
and

and a tree growing in the middle. Here are also shady walks, arbours, and a bowling green.—The members of this college are one warden, seventy fellows, ten chaplains, three clerks, sixteen choristers, and one sexton, together with many gentlemen commoners.

WADHAM COLLEGE was founded by Nicholas Wadham, Esq; and built, in pursuance of his will, by Dorothy his widow, in 1613. It is one of the most regular, uniform, and beautiful colleges belonging to this university; and consists of one noble quadrangle, which is near one hundred and thirty feet square. The windows of the chapel, which stand on the east side of the court, are beautifully painted; the east window is admirably drawn by one Van Ling, a Dutchman; it represents the passion of our Saviour, and is said to have cost one thousand five hundred pounds. The present members of this college are the warden, fifteen fellows, two chaplains, fifteen scholars, and sixteen exhibitioners; the whole number of students being usually about eighty. The scholars, out of whom the fellows are to be chosen, to be taken three out of Somersetshire, and three out of Essex; the rest out of any county in Great Britain.

TRINITY COLLEGE was founded by Sir Thomas Pope, who was privy counsellor to Queen Mary, and an intimate friend to Sir Thomas More. It consists of two courts; in the first court are the chapel, hall, library, and lodgings of the president. The chapel, which was built in 1695, is a fine structure, richly and beautifully finished. The second court is an elegant pile, erected by Sir Christopher Wren. The gardens of this college are extensive, well laid out, and kept in good order. This college consists of a president, twelve fellows, and twelve scholars. These, with the other members, gentlemen commoners, commoners, &c. amount to near seventy.

BALIOL COLLEGE was founded in 1262, by Sir John Baliol of Brenard Castle in Yorkshire, father of John Baliol, King of Scotland, and Devorguilla his consort, daughter of Alexander III. King of Scotland. The college consists chiefly of one court, which we enter by an handsome gate with a tower over it. The buildings about this court are antient, except the east end. The members of this college are a

master,

master, twelve fellows, fourteen scholars, and eighteen exhibitioners; the whole number of students amounting to about fifty.

St. JOHN's COLLEGE is situated north of Baliol and Trinity colleges, having a terrace, with a row of lofty elms before it. The buildings of this college chiefly consist of two large quadrangles, uniformly and elegantly built. In the first court are the chapel and hall on the north side, and the president's lodgings on the east. The east and west sides of the second court are supported by stately and beautiful piazzas. In the hall, which is very handsome, is a picture of St. John the Baptist, by Titian. The gardens belonging to this college are extremely agreeable, very extensive, and well laid out. The college was founded by Sir Thomas White, Alderman of London; and the members of it are a president, fifty fellows, two chaplains, an organist, five singing-men, six choristers, and two sextons; the number of students of all sorts being usually about sixty.

WORCESTER COLLEGE is situated on an eminence on the banks of the Thames. At entering into the college, we have the chapel and hall on each side, both of which are twenty-nine feet in breadth, and fifty five in length; these are just built. The library, which is furnished with a fine collection of books, is a magnificent Ionic edifice, on the west of the chapel and hall, and is one hundred feet in length, supported by a spacious cloister. According to a plan proposed, this college is to consist of a very spacious and elegant building; but it is not yet completed.—This was formerly called Gloucester college, being a seminary for educating the novices of Gloucester monastery. But being suppressed at the Reformation, it was converted into a palace for the Bishop of Oxford; but was soon after turned into an academical hall by Sir Thomas White, the founder of St. John's college; in which state it continued, till Sir Thomas Cookes, a Worcestershire gentleman, procured for it a charter of incorporation, by the name of Worcester college, and endowed it with fifteen thousand pounds, for the maintenance of a provost and six fellows.—There are now a provost, twenty fellows, and eleven scholars; and the whole number of students is about forty.

EXETER COLLEGE was founded by Walter Stapleton, Bishop of Exeter, in the reign of King Edward the Second:
The

The building confifts chiefly of a handfome quadrangle; in the center of the front, which is 220 feet in length, there is a beautiful gate of ruftic work, with a handfome tower. This college has a rector, twenty-five fellows, one fcholar who is bible clerk, and two exhibitioners; the whole number of members about eighty.

Jesus College was founded by Hugh Price, L. L. D. who began to build, and competently endowed it in 1571. But Queen Elizabeth is alfo fometimes termed the founder of this college, becaufe fhe granted the charter for it, and alfo timber for erecting it out of two adjoining forefts. The buildings confift of two courts, in the firft of which is the hall, the chapel, and the principal's lodgings. The library is on the weft fide of the inner court, and the other three fides are finifhed in a decent and uniform manner. This college is chiefly for Welchmen, and confifts of a principal, nineteen fellows, and eighteen fcholars, befides a confiderable number of exhibitioners.

Lincoln College was founded by two of the Bifhops of Lincoln; one completing what the other left imperfect. It confifts of two quadrangular courts, and maintains a rector, fifteen fellows, twelve exhibitioners, and eight fcholars, with a bible-clerk, befides the independent members.

Oriel College chiefly confifts of one regular, uniform, well-built quadrangle. On the north fide are the library and the provoft's lodgings; on the eaft the hall, and the entrance into the chapel, which runs eaftward from thence and on the fouth and weft fides are the chambers of the fellows and other ftudents. King Edward II. was the titular founder of this college, but Adam de Brome, his almoner, was the real founder of it: for that prince did little more than grant licence to his almoner to build it. King Edward III. gave this fociety a tene-, ment called *Le Oriel*, on which ground the college now ftands, and from whence it derives its name. The prefent members of this college are a provoft, eighteen fellows and fourteen exhibitioners; the whole number of ftudents of all forts being about eighty.

Corpus Christi College was founded by Richard Fox, Bifhop of Winchefter, in 1516; and confifts of one quadrangle, an elegant pile of modern building, in which are

pleafant

Merton College, in Oxford, seen from the Meadows.

pleasant and commodious rooms, and a cloister adjoining ; and also a neat structure, which looks eastward towards Merton college grove, in which are apartments appropriated to gentlemen commoners.

MERTON COLLEGE was founded by Walter de Merton, Lord High Chancellor of England in the reign of Henry the Third, and afterwards Bishop of Rochester. This college is situated east of Corpus Christi, and consists of three courts, The largest, or inner court, is about 100 feet long, and 100 broad. The chapel is at the west end of the first court, and is likewise the parish church of St. John Baptist de Merton. It is one of the largest, and best proportioned Gothic structures in the university. The gardens are very pleasant, having the advantage of a prospect of the adjacent walks and country from the south terrace. This college maintains a warden, twenty-eight scholars, fourteen other scholars upon a different foundation, termed post-masters, two chaplains, and two clerks ; the whole number of students of all sorts being about eighty.

CHRIST-CHURCH COLLEGE is the largest and most august of all the collges in Oxford. It was first began to be founded by Cardinal Wolsey, on the scite of the priory of St. Fridefwide, but his disgrace and death hindered him from compleating it. It was afterwards settled and endowed by King Henry VII. The front is very stately, extending to the length of 382 feet, and terminating at each end by two corresponding turrets. In the center is a grand Gothic entrance, the proportions and ornaments of which are remarkably magnificent ; over it is a musical tower, in which are ten musical bells, and a great bell, and a great bell called Tom, that weighs near 17,000 pounds, and on the sound of which, every night at nine o'clock, the students of the whole university are enjoined by statute to repair to their respective societies. This college consists of four quadrangles, one of which, distinguished by the name of the Grand Quadrangle, is 264 by 261 feet in the clear. The greatest part of the south side is formed by the hall, which is considerably elevated above the rest of the building ; and, taken as a detached structure, is a noble specimen of antient magnificence. This room is one of the largest and most superb of any in the kingdom ; it contains eight windows on each side, is 123 feet in length, 40 feet in breadth, and its cieling is 30 feet high. The church of this college is situated at the east end of the Grand Quadrangle, and is the cathedral of the diocese : it is an antient venerable structure ; the roof of the choir is a beautiful piece of stone work, and some of the windows are finely painted.

Peck-

Peckwater-court, to the north-east of the Grand Quadrangle, is p rhaps the moſt elegant edifice in the univerſity ; it has three uniform ſides, each of which has fifteen windows in front ; and on the fourth ſide of this court is a magnificent library. Eaſt of Peckwater court is Canterbury-court, originally Canterbury college. It is a ſmall court, and chiefly remarkable for its antiquity. The fourth quadrangle is Chaplain's-court, which ſtands north-eaſt of Canterbury-court. This college maintains a dean, eight canons, one hundred and one ſtudents, eight chaplains, eight ſinging men, and as many choriſters, a ſchool-maſter, an uſher, an organiſt, and a teacher of muſic. There is a gravel-walk belonging to this college, planted on each ſide with elms, which is a quarter of a mile in length, and of a proportionable breadth. In the lower departments of the ilbrary of this college is depoſited a fine collection of paintings, the donation of General Guiſe. There is elſo a fine ſtatue of Mr. Locke, by Roubilliac.

PEMBROKE COLLEGE derives its name from the Earl of Pembroke, who was chancellor of the univerſity at the time it was erected. It was founded by Thomas Tiſdale, Eſq; and Richard Whitwicke, B. D. The building conſiſts of two courts ; the firſt is a ſmall quadrangle, but neat and uniform ; the ſecond court is an irregular area, and on one ſide of it ſtands the chapel ; which is an elegant modern edifice of the Ionic order. In the garden, which is weſt of the chapel, is a pleaſant common room, and a terrace-walk. The preſent members of this college are a maſter, fourteen fellows, and thirty ſcholars and exhibitioners ; the whole number of ſtudents being uſually about ſixty.

Having thus diſtinctly deſcribed the ſeveral Colleges of this celebrated univerſity, we now proceed to the Halls, which are five in number. There were formerly a great number of theſe academical Halls, or *Hotels*, where profeſſors or tutors reſided ; but ſince the colleges were founded, they have been reduced to the preſent number. Theſe Halls are now endowed with eſtates and revenues as colleges are ; yet ſome of them have exhibitions, or yearly ſtipends given towards the maintenance of certain ſtudents therein. The ſtudents pay an annual rent to the principals, and live at their own charge, as at the inns of court at London.

ST. ALBAN HALL adjoins to Merton College on the eaſt. It derives its name from Robert Abbot de St. Albans, a citizen
of

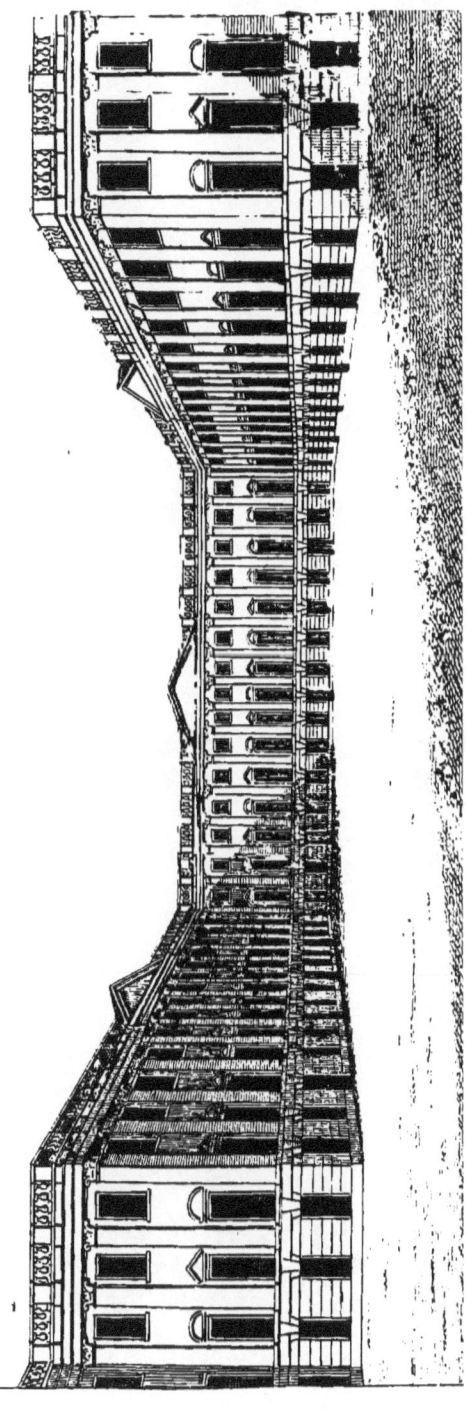

A View of the remains of Godstow's Nunnery in Oxford shire.

of Oxford, who conveyed this tenement to the nuns of Little-more in Oxfordshire, in the reign of King Henry the Third.

St. Edmund Hall is opposite to the east side of Queen's college, to which it is dependant, and has about twenty-five students. The buildings were completed, and other considerable improvements made by Dr. Shaw, the late principal.

New-Inn Hall stands at the west side of Oxford. Opposite to this Hall is the gateway of a college of monks of the Augustine order, in which Erasmus resided two years. He left an elegant Latin poem on his manner of living there.

St. Mary Hall is situated north of Oriel college, near the High-street of Oxford. It consists of one quadrangle, with a garden inclosed in the middle of it. It is formed by the principal's lodgings on the north, the hall and chapel on the south, and on the east and west by the chambers of the students.

Magdalen Hall is adjoining to Magdalen college, to which it is an appendage. The number of exhibitions given to this Hall, supplies it with many members; and it has in it a large grammar-school as a nursery to Magdalen college. The famous Lord Clarendon was educated at this Hall.

Before we quit Oxford, we shall observe, that at the north side of the city is the Radcliffe Infirmary, which was erected by Dr. Radcliffe's trustees, and is supported by voluntary contribution. Such an institution here has a natural tendency to be productive of very extensive advantages; as, while it relieves the poor, it serves as a school to those who study the medical art.

G O D S T O W.

This village is about two miles north from Oxford, and here are the ruins of a famous nunnery, which was founded in the reign of King Stephen for Benedictine nuns. Fair Rosamond, who was seduced by King Henry II. spent much of her time with these nuns, before her amour with that Prince, and afterwards ended her days with them. She is said to have been the most beautiful woman of that age, and was the daughter of Lord Clifford, who was a great benefactor to this nunnery. There is great reason to believe that King Henry promised her marriage before he seduced her, though for political reasons he afterwards espoused Eleanor of Guinne. He had two sons by Rosamond, but that lady shook off all connexions with the King, after he brought his Queen to England, and retired to Godstow nunnery,

K k 2   where

where she spent the remainder of her days in penitence. Part of her monument in the church is still standing; and from the remains of the inscription, it appears that she lived to a considerable age; so that the story of her being secreted in a bower near Woodstock, and poisoned by Queen Eleanor, seems to have been a mere fable.

WOODSTOCK.

This is a town of great antiquity in Oxfordshire, sixty three miles from London. It is pleasantly situated, and a town-house has been lately built here; and the place is noted for its manufactory of fine wash leather gloves, and polished steel watch chains, which are esteemed all over Europe for the goodness of the workmanship. This is a corporation governed by the mayor, a recorder, four aldermen, and sixteen common councilmen. It being on a great road, contains some very good inns; and there are here three alms-houses, and a school, which was founded in the reign of Queen Elizabeth, by Richard Cromwell, citizen and skinner of London. This town sends two members to parliament, who are elected by the burgesses and freemen. There is a house in this town which is said to have been the birth-place of our celebrated Poet Chaucer; but this seems to be an erroneous tradition, as there is the greatest reason to believe that he was born in London.

BLENHEIM HOUSE

Is the magnificent seat of the Duke of Marlborough, and is one of the most stately edifices in the kingdom. It is situated a little to the west of Woodstock, about four miles and a half from Oxford. In the reign of Queen Anne, the honour and manor of the town and hundred of Woodstock, were settled by parliament upon that illustrious General, John Duke of Marlborough, as a reward for his signal military services. A palace was also built for him at the public expence, and which, to commemorate the important victory he had obtained at Blenheim over the French and Bavarian forces, was called BLENHEIM HOUSE. It was built by Sir John Vanburgh, and is extremely magnificent, though many objections have been made to it by the connoisseurs in architecture.

From the town of Woodstock we enter the park, through a spacious portal of the Corinthian order; from whence a noble prospect is opened to the palace, the bridge, the lake with its
valley,

A View of Blenheim House, the Seat of the Duke of Marlborough.

valley, and other beautiful scenes of the park. The house in particular, which we survey from this point obliquely, is no where viewed to greater advantage. The front is 138 feet from wing to wing: the roof is adorned with a stone balustrade, and statues. The south front is not so highly ornamented; but on the pediment of it is a noble busto, larger than life, of Lewis XIV. taken from the citadel of Tournay. The common entrance is at the east gate, which leads us into a quadrangle, consisting of offices. From thence, opposite the entrance, we proceed into the grand area.

In the centre of the front, a superb portico, elevated on massy columns, admits us to the HALL; which is the height of the house, supported by Corinthian pillars. It is one of the largest and finest rooms in England. The cieling is adorned with an allegorical piece, painted by Sir James Thornhill, representing the Duke of Marlborough crowned with Victory, who points to the plan of the battle of Blenheim. In the recesses, are well-finished casts from the antique statues of the Venus of Medicis, the Roman Slave, the *Atacetæ*, and Saltator. Over these is a series of paintings, called the Loves of God, which are ascribed to Titian, and which were a present to the Duke from the King of Sardinia. In the arcades on the right and left, is a fine arrangement of marble *termini*. And over the door that leads into the saloon, is a bust of the great Duke of Marlborough, with a Latin inscription.

Strangers are usually conducted from the Hall into the apartments on the left; and in the *first* apartment, the hangings begin a suit of tapestry, representing the victories and atchievements of Alexander the Great, which are continued in some succeeding rooms. There are also in this room paintings of St. Austin when young, and of Pope Gregory, both by Titian, of the woman taken in adultery by Rembrandt, and of Mary of Medicis by Rubens.

In the *second* apartment are some pieces of beautiful tapestry, the subjects taken from classical allegory: there are also some fine paintings in this room, one of which is a Holy Family by Rubens. In the *third* apartment is a picture of Rubens's family, painted by himself; portraits of the Duchess of Portsmouth, and Eleanor Gwyn, mistresses to Charles II. by Vandyke; and also Lord Stafford dictating to his Secretary, by the same. This last is perhaps one of Vandyke's principal portrait pieces. The earnestness of the speaker, and the attention of his amanuensis, heighten each other in the most expressive manner.

In

In the *fourth* apartment, is a portrait of Rubens's wife, by Rubens; of Catharine of Medicis, by the same; and of Mary Queen of Scots, by Vandyke. In the *fifth* apartment, are four sculpture pieces, a head, and an unfinished piece, all by Rubens; two Madonnas, in different attitudes, by Titian; Herod's cruelty, and Queen Esther, by Paul Veronese; and some other pieces by capital masters.

In the *sixth* apartment begins the tapestry of the Duke of Marlborough's battles, which are introduced by a most lively representation of a suttling booth, foragers, a battle, and a siege. Here are also three good paintings, one of which is a picture of Dobson, an English Painter, in the reign of King James I. with his family, by himself. This last is an admirable piece, in the old correct manner. In the *seventh* apartment, the tapestry represents the battles of Wynendale, Bouchain, and Oudenard, with the siege of Donawert. Here are also three fine pictures, one of which is Jupiter and Europa, by Paul Veronese. The *eighth* apartment contains the three Graces cloathed; Venus and Adonis, and two other pieces by Rubens; the Egyptian fortune-teller, by Angelo Carravaggio, and some other pictures of great merit.

The SALOON is nobly decorated, and is proportioned to the grandeur of the other rooms. The door-cases are of marble, and exceedingly magnificent; the floor is also of marble. The walls are adorned with paintings of the different habits, and modes of dress of all nations, by La Guerre. The cieling, which is executed by the same hand, is an allegorical piece, representing John Duke of Marlborough in the midst of his victories stopt by Peace, and Time reminding him of the rapidity of his own flight.

In the *ninth* apartment, the tapestry of the Duke's battles is continued, with the battles of Blenheim, Malplaquet, and the siege of Lisle. In the *tenth* apartment, the tapestry contains the conclusion of the Duke's battles; with a picture of Isaac blessing Jacob, by Rembrandt; a portrait of John Duke of Marlborough, by Sir Godfrey Kneller; and a fruit-piece, by Michael Angelo. The *eleventh* apartment contains two pieces of still-life, by Maltese; and a portrait of the Duchess of Marlborough, by Sir Godfrey Kneller.

The LIBRARY is a most noble room, upwards of 183 feet in length, and proportionably broad and lofty. The Doric pilasters of marble, with the complete columns of the same, which support a rich entablature, the window-frames, the surrounding basement of black marble, and the stuccoed compart-

ments

ments of the vaulted cieling, are in very high tafte both with refpect to defign and finifhing. It was originally intended as a gallery for paintings; but the late Duke of Marlborough has added utility to elegance, having furnifhed it with a noble collection of books, made by Lord Sunderland, his grace's father. Their number is faid to amount to 24,000 volumes, which have been allowed to be worth 30,000l. and are faid to be the beft private collection in England. They are kept under gilt-wire lattices. On the top of the cafes is a feries of bronzes; and that no affiftance to learning might be wanting, the late Duke placed here a fine Orrery and Planetarium.

At the upper end of the room is a highly finifhed ftatue of Queen Anne, by Ryfbrack; and over the book-cafes are copies of the Cartoons, by Le Blond; Lot and his daughters, by Rubens; and a Crucifixion by Vandyke, with other paintings. From the bow-windows of the library we have a delightful profpect of the declivity defcending to the river, and of the gradual afcent of the venerable groves which cover the correfponding hills.

The CHAPEL is one of the wings of this ftately building, in which is a fuperb monument to the memory of the old Duke and Dutchefs of Marlborough, by Ryfbrack. They are reprefented with their two fons, who died young, as fupported by Fame and Hiftory. Beneath in a baffo-relievo, is the taking of Marfhal Tallard.

The *Gardens* are fpacious and agreeable; they originally confifted of about 100 acres, but the prefent Duke has made very large additions, and many elegant improvements. The noble defcent to the water on the fouth and weft, covered with flowering fhrubs, and embellifhed with other natural beauties, are not eafy to be paralleled. About the middle of the grand approach, is a magnificent *Bridge*, confifting chiefly of one arch, in the ftyle of the Rialto at Venice. The water is formed into a fpacious Lake, which covers the whole extent of a capacious valley, furrounded by an artificial declivity of a prodigious depth, and has been confidered, both with regard to its accompaniments and extent, as the moft capital piece of water in the kingdom.

The *Park* is between ten and eleven miles in circumference, and contains many beautiful fcenes. The lover of rural variety will be entertained here with every circumftance of beauty, which he can expect from diverfified nature; from hills and vallies, wood, and water. In this park originally ftood a royal palace, and here Ethelred called a parliament. King

Alfred,

Alfred, while he was refident here, tranflated *Boetius de Confo-latione Philofophiæ.* Henry I. enclofed the park with a wall, the greateft part of which is now remaining. His fucceffor, Henry II. principally refided at this feat, and is faid to have erec-ted in the park a houfe, encompaffed with a Labyrinth of ex-traordinary contrivance. We have before obferved, that the ftory of Fair Rofamund's being fecreted here, with a view of fecuring her from the rage and jealoufy of Queen Eleanor, is a tradition not well founded; but it is not improbable, that while the amour between this Lady and that Prince fubfifted, fhe might refide here. For it is faid that the romantic retreat, which was called Fair Rofamond's Bower, was fituated here in the valley, to the north-weft of the Bridge, near a remarkable bath, or fpring, called at prefent Rofamond's Well.

The grant of the park and manor of Woodftock, and of this palace, to the Duke of Marlborough, and his important fervices to the nation, are enumerated on the pedeftal of a ftately column, 130 feet in height, on the top of which is a ftatue of the Duke. This column is fituated in the grand avenue to Blenheim-Houfe, and part of the infcription, which is admirably well written, is as follows:

The Caftle of BLENHEIM was founded by Q. Anne,
In the fourth Year of her Reign,
In the Year of the Chriftian Æra 1705.
A Monument defigned to perpetuate the Memory of the
Signal Victory
Obtained over the French and Bavarians,
Near the Village of BLENHEIM,
On the Banks of the Danube,
By JOHN, Duke of MARLBOROUGH,
The Hero, not only of his Nation, but of his Age;
Whofe Glory was equal in the Council and in the Field;
Who by Wifdom, Juftice, Candour, and Addrefs,
Reconciled various, and even oppofite, Interefts;
Acquired an Influence
Which no Rank, no Authority can give,
Nor any Force, but that of fuperior Virtue:
Became the fixed important Centre,
Which united in one common caufe,
The principal States of Europe;
Who by military Knowledge, and irrefiftible Valour,
In a long Series of uninterrupted Triumphs,
Broke the Power of France,

When

Ditchley, the Seat of the Earl of Litchfield, near Woodstock, in Oxfordshire

When raifed the higheft, when exerted the moft ;
   Refcued the Empire from Defolation ;
Afferted and confirmed the Liberties of EUROPE.

Blenheim Houfe itfelf was finifhed at the public expence, but
the Bridge, the Column juft mentioned, and the portal contiguous to the town, were erected at the expence of Sarah, Dutchefs
Dowager of Marlborough.

D I T C H L E Y,

Is the noble feat of the Earl of Litchfield, fituated about four
miles from Blenheim, on the north-weft. It is a lofty edifice,
built of hewn ftone, fituated on a hill, which commands all the
country, having Blenheim, Oxford, and the hills beyond it, in
full view. The fouthern front is very elegant, and the offices,
which form two beautiful wings, have a communication with the
principal building by circular colonnades.

The *Hall* is elegantly decorated, and finely proportioned.
The cieling contains an affembly of the Gods, painted by Ken .
Two of the compartments are filled with hiftorical pieces from
the Æneid, by the fame hand ; one of which reprefents Æneas
meeting Venus, his mother, in the wood, near Carthage ; and
the other, Venus prefenting Æneas with the new armour. The
fciences are introduced as ornaments, with bufts of the poets
properly difpofed ; and a ftatue of the Venus de Medicis. The
chimney-piece is fuperb and lofty, decorated with a portrait of
the late Earl of Litchfield, by Akerman.

The conftruction of the *Mufick Room* is well adapted to the
ufe for which it is intended ; and its elegance cannot fail to have
the moft pleafing effect on the fpectator. There is a painting
in this room of Rubens and his family hunting wild beafts ; and
fome other good pictures. The *Dining Room* is executed with
much fimple elegance ; and here are the capital portraits of
Henry VIII. and Prince Henry, by Hans Holbein, executed
with much ftrength and freedom. There are alfo fome other
good pictures here, particularly a family-piece of Charles I.
with Charles II. at his knee, by Vandyke ; and two fine portraits
by Jonfon.

The *Damafk Bed-Chamber* is adorned with tapeftry, reprefenting boys fqueezing grapes, and engaged in other fports ; and
contains fome fine portraits. The *Tapeftry Drawing-Room* is
alfo adorned with tapeftry, reprefenting the Mufes and Apollo,
a vintage, and Bacchanalian fcenes ; and there are alfo fome
good portraits here. From this apartment we have an entertaining view of a winding valley, with a ferpentine canal, over

which is thrown an elegant Bridge from a design of Palladio's.

The cieling and walls of the *Saloon* are richly stuccoed; and in the middle compartment of the roof is a representation of Flora and the Zephyrs. Here is also an excellent antique of the Goddess Health, about thirty inches in height, purchased from Dr. Mead's collection. On its pedestal is a bass-relief of the head of Æsculapius, cut with remarkable boldness.

In the *Green Damask Drawing Room*, the chimney-piece is finely executed by *Scheemaker*, and finished with two small Corinthian columns. In the middle, is a landscape, by Wootton. Over the doors, are two striking pictures brought from Italy, of ruins, rocks, and cascades. Here is also a table of Italian marble, having a greenish ground interspersed with white veins.

In the *Gilt Drawing-Room*, is a full-length portrait of Charles II. and the Dutchess of Cleveland, by Lely; with two other portraits by Kneller, and two curious tables of Egyptian marble. In the *Velvet Bed-chamber* both the bed and hangings are of rich figured Genoa velvet. The chimney-piece is elegantly finished by Scheemaker, and adorned with a prospect of a ruin by Paul Panini.

The *Tapestry-Room* is curiously ornamented in the Chinese taste. Here are two pieces of tapestry, one of which represents the Cyclops forging the armour of Æneas; the other, Neptune, with his proper attendants, giving directions about re-fitting a vessel, which has just been ship-wrecked. Over the chimney-piece, which is finely finished in white marble, is a capital picture of the Duke and Dutchess of York, and the Princesses, Mary and Anne, by Sir Peter Lely; and over the doors are two masterly landscapes, by an Italian hand.

On the whole, this seat is a repository of valuable portraits, executed by the most eminent artists in that species of painting; Rubens, Vandyke, Sir Peter Lely, and our ingenious countryman and rival of Vandyke, Jonson. As a piece of architecture, this seat is inferior to none for the justness of its proportions, and the convenient disposition of its apartments. With regard to its furniture and decorations, it is finished with taste rather than with splendour; and adorned with that elegance which results from simplicity,

WHITNEY

Is a town in Oxfordshire of great antiquity, sixty-nine miles from London. It appears to have been a place of considerable repute before the time of William I. and increased in the number of inhabitants so much afterwards, that it received summon-

ses

ſes to ſend members to parliament in the reign of Edward I. but that privilege has been long ſince taken away. The town chiefly conſiſts of one ſtreet, about a mile in length; and has a great manufacture of rugs and blankets, and the latter are for their whiteneſs preferred to thoſe made at any other place. It is computed, that ſeven thouſand packs of wool are wrought into blankets here every year; and beſides five hundred weavers, there are ſeldom fewer than three thouſand perſons employed in carding and ſpinning, with many others who dreſs the goods afterwards. The town is populous. Here is a free-ſchool, which was founded and endowed by Mr. Henry Box, a druggiſt in London, with a good library adjoining: the grocers company in London are governors of this ſchool. There is alſo a charity-ſchool here for fifty children, and an hoſpital for ſix poor blanket-makers widows.

BURFORD is an antient market-town, in the ſame county, and eighteen miles from Oxford. It has a great market for ſaddles; and on a heath near it, called the Seven Downs, there are frequent horſe-races.

CHIPPING NORTON

Is a place of great antiquity, and appears to have been a market-town in the time of the Saxons. Roman coins have been frequently found here; and the church is a building after a curious model, in which there are monuments, with ſo many names of merchants on braſs plates, as ſhew it to have been once a place of great trade. This town is pleaſantly ſituated, and formerly ſent members to parliament, but that privilege is now taken away.

In the neighbourhood of this town are what are called *Roll-rick's ſtones*, or *Roul-rich ſtones*, which ſome ſuppoſe to be the remains of an old Britiſh temple, whilſt others imagine they were ſet up in memory of Rollo, the famous Daniſh Commander. They are very lofty, and placed in a circular direction, with one taller than the other, which is vulgarly called the King.

At a little diſtance from Chipping Norton is a village named *Hook-Norton*, which is ſaid to have been an antient ſeat of the Saxon kings. About the beginning of the tenth century there was a great battle fought here between the Danes and the Engliſh, in which the latter were defeated; and there are here ſeveral barrows, or ſepulchral monuments of the antient Britons. Camden ſays, this place was formerly inhabited by ſuch clowns and churls, that it was from that circumstance called *Hog's-Norton*, a name which is now frequently given to it.

BANBURY

It a town of great antiquity, and pleasantly situated on the river Cherwell. It is seventy four-miles from London, and twenty-three from Oxford. It is a pretty large town, with a handsome church, a meeting house, a free-school, and two charity-schools. The trade of this town is considerable; and great quantities of cheese are made here, which is noted for its goodness. This place has also been famous for a particular kind of cakes, called Banbury cakes. The lands in the neighbourhood are remarkable for their fertility. Several remarkable battles have been fought near this place, and at a little distance from hence is an ancient castle called Broughton-castle, built before the reign of King Henry the Sixth.

HANWELL-PARK, near Banbury, is the seat of Sir Jonathan Cope, Bart. There is here a clock which is esteemed a great curiosity. It moves by water, and shews the time by the rising of a new gilded sun for every hour, moving in a hemisphere of wood, each sun having in its center a figure for the hour. For instance, One, which, ascending half way to the zenith of the arch, shews it to be a quarter past One, at the zenith half an hour; whence descending half way towards the horizon, three quarters; and at last absconding under it, there arises another gilded sun above the horizon at the other side of the arch bearing the figure 2; and so of the rest.

DEDDINGTON is a place of great antiquity, and sent members to parliament in the reigns of Edward I. and III. but never since. The town is small, though it is pretty populous.

BICESTER is thirteen miles from Oxford, and is a long straggling town, chiefly remarkable for excellent malt liquor.—Near this town is an old castle, called Alchester, which is situated on the Roman highway, called *Akeman-street*. That this was a place of great strength, and even a flourishing city, is supposed to be evident from the vast number of coins that have been dug up, and because it is no uncommon thing for the husbandmen to break their ploughs against the ruins of the foundation.

THAME, or TAME, is so called from the river of that name, which runs by the town. It is forty-six miles from London, and the situation is extremely pleasant; and being on an eminence, the prospect over the neighbouring country is delightful. It is a large town, with a fine church, and one great street, in the middle whereof is the market-place, which is well furnished

with

with live cattle, and all kinds of provifions, and the river is navigable to it by barges. It has an handfome free-fchool, and an alms-houfe.

DORCHESTER, which is forty nine miles from London, was a town of note among the Romans, and afterwards a bifhop's fee; but it is now an inconfiderable place. It has, however, a very large old church, and a good ftone bridge over the Thames.

HENLEY UPON THAMES.

This is fuppofed to be the oldeft town in Oxfordfhire, and is pleafantly fituated on the fide of the Thames, which is navigable to it by barges. It is a corporation governed by a warden, burgeffes, and other officers. The buildings are generally good; and here are two free-fchools, one a grammar-fchool, founded and endowed by King James the Firft, and the other called the Blue-coat fchool, founded by the Lady Elizabeth Periam, for teaching and cloathing poor children. Here is alfo an alms-houfe, founded by Dr. Longland, Bfhop of Lincoln; and a wooden bridge over the Thames, where, it is faid, there was antiently one of ftone. The greater part of the inhabitants of this town are maltfters, mealmen, and bargemen, who enrich themfeves and the neighbourhood, by fending corn, malt, and wood to London; and it is faid that 300 cart-loads of malt and corn are often fold here on a market-day.

GREAT MARLOW

Is a borough-town in Buckinghamfhire, thirty-one miles from London, which derives its name from the marly foil in which it ftands. It is a confiderable town, with a bridge over the Thames, not far from the place where it receives the Wycombe river; and has an handfome church and town hall. The chief manufacture of the town is bone-lace, but it is of more account for the navigation carried on by the Thames for meal, malt, and beech timber. There are feveral corn and paper-mills in its neighbourhood, particularly on the little river Loddon; and alfo three remarkable mills called the Temple Mills, or the brafs mills for making kettles, pans, &c. befides a mill for making thimbles; and another for preffing oil from rape and flax feed.

HIGH

This town is thirty-two miles from London, in the road to Oxford. It is suppofed to derive its name from a fmall ftream, which glides through the low grounds near this place into the Thames. The town has on each fide of it pleafant hills fhaded with woods, and may for antiquity, extent, and beauty, compare with the greateft and beft in the county. It is a corporation, governed by a mayor, aldermen, common-council, recorder, and other officers. It has two principal ftreets, one of which is fpacious, and well-built with good brick houfes, and full of large inns. Queen Elizabeth gave lands for the maintenance of a free-grammar-fchool in this town. The affizes are fometimes held here, and this town fends two members to parliament.

This place is fuppofed to have been a Roman ftation; for in the year 1724, a Roman pavement was difcovered by fome workmen, who were digging in a neighbouring meadow belonging to Lord Shelburne. It was about nine feet fquare, and confifted of ftones of various colours, wrought with exquifite art; but the largeft was not broader than the fquare of a die.

BEACONSFIELD is another market-town in the road to Oxford, and contains fome good inns, but has nothing in it that is very remarkable.

AMERSHAM is an antient borough town, fituated in a valley between two woody hills, near the river Coln. It confifts of two ftreets, a long one and a fhort one, which crofs each other at right angles in the middle. In the area where thefe ftreets interfect each other, ftands the church, which is the beft rectory in the county. Here is a handfome town-hall and a free-fchool.

MONK'S RISBOROUGH is only remarkable for the antiquities in its neighbourhood; particularly an old fortification, called Bellinus's caftle; and fome trenches and fortifications fuppofed to have been made when the Romans were in Britain. And not far from Monk's Rifborough, there is a high fteep chalky hill, on the fouth-weft fide of which there is the figure of a crofs, an hundred feet long, formed by trenches cut into the chalk about two feet deep, which is fuppofed to be the work of the Saxons. —Near Monk's Rifborough is *Prince's Rifborough*, where on the top of a hill are the traces of a camp; and it is faid that thirteen counties may be feen from hence.

AYLES-

AYLESBURY.

This is a very ancient town, forty-four miles from London, and stands on a rising ground, at the east end of a rich valley, called *Aylesbury Vale*, which feeds incredible numbers of cattle and sheep, remarkable for their size and fine fleeces; and extends almost from Thame on the edge of Oxfordshire, to Leighton in Bedfordshire. The town-hall of Aylesbury is an handsome fabric, in which the county assizes and sessions are often held, and stands in the middle of the market-place, which is a large handsome square. This is a neat, compact, and populous town, the best and largest in Buckinghamshire, and consists of several fine streets. It sends two members to parliament.

In the reign of William the Norman, Aylesbury was a royal manor, several parts of which that King gave to his favourites, to hold of him by the following odd tenure; namely, that they should find litter or straw for the King's bed and chambers, and provide him three eels in winter, and three green geese in summer, besides herbs for his chamber; and this they were to do thrice a year, if the King came thither so often.

Some of the principal public edices in this town were erected at the expence of Sir John Baldwin, Lord Chief Justice of the Court of Common Pleas in the reign of Henry VIII. He was otherwise a great benefactor to this town, and had a causeway made from the market-place towards London for the distance of three miles, at his own cost.

BUCKINGHAM.

This is the county town, and is sixty miles from London. It is washed on all sides but the north, by the river Ouse, over which it has three stone bridges. The castle of the town, now in ruins, was built in the middle of it, and divides it into two parts. In the north part stands the town hall, a very handsome convenient structure, in which are kept the weights and measures of the county. This town was for many years a staple for wool, and several of its wool-halls are yet standing; but that trade is now lost here. It is very populous; and the church, which is in the west part of the town, is a very large building, and, when its spire was standing, might be reckoned the best in the whole county, and was as high as most in England; but in 1698 was in part blown down, and has never since been rebuilt. In the year 1725, many of the old buildings in this town were destroyed by fire, which burnt out 138 families, and did near 33,000 pounds damage. The county-gaol was kept in the

castle

castle here, till it fell to decay; but a new one has been built; and by a late act the summer affizes, which had been sometimes held at Aylesbury, are always to be held here. This town sends two members to parliament.

S T O W,

The celebrated feat of Earl Temple, is about two miles north-west from Buckingham, well situated in a fine spot, which is much more beautiful than any of the surrounding country. The houfe is large; it extends in one line of front in nine hundred feet. A grand flight of steps, defigned by Signior Borra, ornamented with baluftrades, leads us to the *Saloon*, which is a grand apartment hung with tapestry, reprefenting the functions of the cavalry. The dimensions of this room are 43 feet by 22; the furniture is crimfon, ornamented with two marble bufts, a rich cabinet, and fine china jars.

The *Hall* is a fpacious room, 36 feet by 22 and half, defigned and painted by Kent. Its cieling is enriched with the figns of the Zodiac, and the walls are adorned with feftoons of flowers, &c. Over the chimney is a curious piece of alto relievo, the ftory of which is Darius's tent. Here are also eleven marble bufts properly difpofed.

The *Dining Room* is a well proportioned apartment, 43 feet by 25, in which are fome fine paintings, particularly a dancing at the Duke of Mantua's marriage, by Tintoret, a landfcape by Claude Lorraine, the marriage at Cana by Baffan, and Mofes burying the Egyptian by Pouffin. There are also in this room three pieces of ftatuary that deferve attention; a Narciffus, whofe attitude is eafy, and the figure elegant; Vertumnus and Pomona, by Scheemacher; and a Venus and Adonis by Delveau. The Venus is very delicate and beautiful.

The Grand *Stair Cafe* is ornamented with iron work, and enriched with three cieling pieces, painted by Sclater; namely, Juftice and Peace, Fame and Victory, Plenty and Conftancy.

The *Chapel* is wainfcotted with cedar, and has a gallery of the fame, hung with crimfon velvet. Its dimenfions are 37 feet by 20 feet 10 inches, and 26 feet high. Over the communion table is a fine painting of the refurrection, by Tintoret; and over that is the King's arms, richly carved and ornamented. Above the cedar wainfcot, are the following paintings at full length, viz. Mofes and Aron, St. Peter and St. Paul, the four Evangelifts, the afcenfion, baptifm, and the falutation of the Virgin Mary. The cieling is the fame as in the chapel royal

at

at St. James's, and the cedar wainscot enriched with elegant carving, by Gibbons.

In Lady Temple's *Dressing room*, the hangings, chairs, and window curtains, are of fine printed cotton; and there is here a fine old japan cabinet, ornamented with china jars; and a fine view of Pekin over the chimney-piece, by Iolli

In her ladyship's *Bed-chamber*, the hangings, chairs, &c. are the same as the Dressing-room; with a picture of a Chinese Temple over the chimney, by Iolli.

The *Chinese Closet* is the repository of her ladyship's valuable china. The japan and ornaments were a present from the late Prince and Princess of Wales. From hence we enter a colonnade adorned with paintings by Sclater. It is embellished with exotics and flowering shrubs. The *Grenville Room* is 29 feet 8 inches by 26 feet 3 inches, and 19 feet 4 inches high, is hung with green velvet, and ornamented with portraits at full length of the Grenville family.

The *Gallery* is a magnificent apartment, 74 feet by 25 feet, and 20 feet high, with gobelin tapestry chairs, and is hung with three fine pieces of tapestry, viz. a beautiful representation of a Farm, A Dutch Wake from Teniers, and a Dutch Fishery, from the same. The two chimnies have pictures of Roman ruins over each, by Pannini. The four doors have rural pictures over each, viz. Plowing, Reaping, Hay-making, and Sheep-shearing. And a rich cabinet at each end containing books; and 10 marble busts of Roman Emperors.

In the *Waiting-Room* are some fine pictures, particularly Cymon and Iphigenia, by Guerchino; gold pouring into the mouth of Crassus, by Poussin; and a very curious piece by Albert Durer, the subject Joan of Arc musing on her expedition.

In the private *Drawing-Room* is a fine picture of Samson, by Rembrandt, the expression of which is very great; a landscape by Claude Loraine; Rubens's first wife, by Rubens; Sileno, by the same; the Duke of Sully, by Vandyke; Samson and Dalilah, by Guerchino; and a portrait of Oliver Cromwell, by Old Richardson.

The *State Gallery* is seventy feet long, and twenty two high, and is a very beautiful room. It is hung with Brussels tapestry, representing the triumphs of Diana, Mars, Venus, Bacchus, and Ceres. The cieling is stuccoed in compartments, and ornamented with medallions, and paintings in obscura.

The *State Bed-chamber* is extremely magnificent, the bed and cieling by Signor Borra; and is finely furnished with crimson damask and gold ornaments. The *State Closet* is hung with blue damask, finely ornamented with carving and gilding; out of which we go into a colonnade, where is a beautiful view of

M m

the

the gardens and the country. The paſſage is ornamented with marble buſts.

The GARDENS at Stow have long been conſidered as the moſt magnificent in England, and have always been admired by perſons of taſte ; and have therefore a natural claim to a particular deſcription in our work. The ſouthern entrance of the gardens is formed by two pavilions of the Doric order, deſigned by Sir John Vanbrugh ; the walls of which are adorned with paintings, in freſco, the ſtories taken from Paſtor Fido. Almoſt the firſt ſtriking object that occurs in the gardens, is, an obeliſk near ſeventy feet high, deſigned for a jet de eau, and placed in the middle of a large octagon piece of water. At ſome diſtance we perceive two rivers, which are at laſt united, and enter the octagon in one ſtream. Over one of theſe is a Palladian bridge. From this point a *Gothic Temple*, 70 feet in height, appears on the top of an hill. On the left is an Egyptian pyramid ; from whence we are conducted to the Cold Bath. Here we have a proſpect of a natural caſcade, falling from the laſt-mentioned octagon, in three diſtinct ſheets, into an extenſive lake. One of the ſheets paſſes through the arch of an artificial ruin, covered with ever-greens.

Theſe noble gardens contain a great variety of elegant edifices and decorations. The building called the *Hermitage* is built of rough ſtone, and agreeably ſituated in a riſing wood on the banks of the lake ; not far from which are the ſtatues of Cain and Abel, finely executed. The *Temple of Venus* is a ſquare building, with colonnade wings. It was deſigned by Kent, and is painted with the ſtory of Hellenore and Malbecco, from Spenſer's Fairy Queen. The room is adorned with a naked Venus ; and the ſmaller compartments with a variety of intrigues. Upon the frize is the following motto from Catullus:

Nunc amet qui nunquam amavit ;
Quique amavet, nunc amet.

Let him love now, who never lov'd before :
Let him, who always lov'd, now love the more.

Underneath the *Belvidere*, or Gibbes's Building, is an icehouſe ; at ſome diſtance from which are the Roman boxers, admirably copied. Here are alſo two *Pavilions*, one of which is uſed as a dwelling houſe ; and the other is ornamented with the ſtatues of Julius Cæſar, Cicero, Portia, and Levia.

The *Egyptian Pyramid*, which was before-mentioned, and which is ſixty feet in height, has a Latin inſcription to the following purpoſe: " To the memory of Sir John Vanbrugh, by

2   whom

" whom feveral of the buildings in thefe gardens were defigned,
" Lord Cobham erected this pyramid."

In a field, enclofed with a fence of ftakes, after the military
manner, are the ftatues of Hercules and Antæus. *St. Auguftine's Cave* is a monaftic cell, built with mofs and roots : within
is a ftraw couch, and feveral Latin infcriptions, in the ftile of
the old Monkifh Latin verfe. The *Temple of Bacchus* is an
edifice of brick, the infide of which is adorned with Bacchanalian fcenes, painted by Nollikins; and here are two vafes in a
very mafterly tafte. The *Saxon Temple* is an aitar fituated in an
open grove, about which the feven Saxon Deities, which deno-
minate the feveral days of the week, were formerly placed;
but thefe have fince been removed to the Gothic Temple.

Nelfon's Seat is an elegant little building, from whence there
is an agreeable opon profpect. In the infide are fome paintings,
with infcriptions. At the head of the canal, oppofite the north
front of the houfe, is an equeftrian ftatue of King George I. in
compleat armour. There is alfo a ftatue of his late Majefty,
King George II. raifed on a Corinthian pillar. And in a rural
amphitheatre is a ftatue of Queen Caroline, erected on four Ionic
columns.

Dido's Cave is a retired dark building with this infcription from
Virgil :

> *Speluncam Dido, Dux et Trojanus, eandem,*
> *Deveniunt.*

" Repairing to the fame dark cave are feen,
" The Trojan Hero, and the Tyrian Queen."

The *Rotunda*, which was defigned by Sir John Vanbrugh, is
fupported by Ionic pillars. Within, is a ftatue of Venus de
Medicis on a pedeftal of blue marble. Scarcely any object in
the whole garden fhews itfelf to more advantage, than this
ftructure; or makes a more beautiful figure, from feveral different points of profpect.

The *Sleeping parlour* is a fquare building, with an elegant
Ionic portico, fituated in a clofe wood, with this Epicurian infcription : *Cum omnia fint in incerto, fave tibi*; i. e. Since all
things are uncertain, indulge thyfelf. The *Witch Houfe* is a
kind of hut, on the walls of which are roughly painted the mid-
night merriment of hags.

The *Temple of ancient Virtue* is a compleat and beautiful rotunda of the Ionic order, defigned by Kent. Over each door
on the outfide, is this motto : *Prifcæ Virtuti*; to ancient Virtue.
It is adorned with ftatues of Lycurgus, Socrates, Homer, and
Epaminondas, under which are Latin infcriptions to the following purpofe.

LYCURGUS,

LYCURGUS, having planned with confummate wifdom a con-
ftitution, fecured againft every inroad of corruption, this truly
great Father of his country bequeathed to his citizens a lafting
liberty ; luxury being kept out by this difufe of wealth.

SOCRATES, innocent amidft corruption, an encourager of
good men, a worfhipper of one God, the wifeft of men delivered Philofophy from an idle fcholaltic life, and introduced her
into fociety, to amend mankind.

HOMER, the firft as well as beft of Poets, whofe genius fub-
fervient wholly to the caufe of virtue, inftructed mankind, by a
language univerfally known, in the godlike arts of daring and
fuffering heroically.

EPAMINONDAS, by whofe courage, prudence, and moderation, the Theban commonwealth obtained liberty and empire,
an happy eftablifhment as well civil as military ; and by whofe
death it loft them.

Over one of the doors of this edifice is alfo the following infcription : " Charum effe civem, bene de republica mereri,
" laudari, coli, diligi, gloriofum eft : metui vero, & in odio
" effe, invidiofum, teteftabille, imbecillum, caducum ;" i. e.
To be dear to our country and to deferve well of the ftate, to be
honoured, reverenced, and loved, is truly glorious ; but to be
dreaded and hated of mankind is bafe, deteftable, weak, im-
politick.

Over the other door is as follows : " Juftitiam cole et pieta-
" tem, quæ cum fit magna in parentibus et propinquis, tum in
" patria maxima eft. Ea vita via eft in cælum, et in hunc cætum
" eorum qui jam vixerunt ;" i. e.   An affection for our friends
and relations is amiable ; but for our country divine.   This is
the path to future happinefs, and the affembly of thofe who have
already lived.

From the Temple of *Ancient Virtue*, you look down on a very
beautiful winding hollow lawn, fcattered with fingle trees in the
happieft manner, through the ftems of which, the water breaks
to the eye in a ftile admirably picturefque.   Near to this temple
in a thicket, is the *Temple of Modern Virtue*, fatirically reprefented
in ruins.

The gardens continue extremely various and beautiful, till
you cometohe Princefs Amelia's arch, from which you at once
break upon a fcenery truly enchanting ; being more like a rich
picturefque compofition, than the effect of an artful management of ground and buildings.   The lawn from the arch, falls
in various waves into the water, at the bottom of the vale : it is
fcattered with trees, whofe fpreading tops unite, and leave the
eye an irregular command among their ftems of a double wave
on the lake.   The fmooth green of the lawn, obfcured in fome

places by the shade of the trees, in others illuminated by the sun, forms an object as beautiful as can be imagined ; nor can any thing be more picturesque than the water appearing through the fore-ground of the scene, thus canopied with trees. A break in the grove presents a compleat picture above these beautiful varieties of wood and water : first, the Palladian-bridge, backed by a rising ground scattered with wood ; and at the top of that a castle. The objects of the whole scene, though various, and some distant, are most happily united to form a compleat view, equally magnificent and pleasing; indeed it is the richest that is seen at Stow.

The *Palladian Bridge* is adorned with several antique marble bustos. The roof on the side facing the water, is supported by Ionic pillars. The back wall is covered with a fine piece of Alto Relievo, which represents the four quarters of the world bringing their various products to Britannia. Here are also paintings of Sir Walter Raleigh with a map of Virginia; and of William Penn, presenting the laws of Pennsylvania.

After crossing the Serpentine River, we pass into the *Elysian Fields*, a most delicious retreat, consisting of beautiful waves of close shaven grass ; breaking among wood, and scattered with single trees ; bounding on one side by thick groves, and shelving on the other down to the water, which winds in a very happy manner ; and commanding from several spots, various landscapes of the distant parts of the gardens.

The *Temple of British Worthies*, is a semi-circular wall, adorned with the following bustos and inscriptions :

Sir THOMAS GRESHAM, who by the honourable profession of a merchant having enriched himself and his country, for carrying on the commerce of the world, built the Royal Exchange.

IGNATIUS JONES, who, to adorn his country, introduced and rivalled the Greek and Roman architecture.

JOHN MILTON, whose sublime and unbounded genius equalled a subject that carried him beyond the limits of the world.

WILLIAM SHAKESPEARE, whose excellent genius opened to him the whole heart of man, all the mines of fancy, all the stores of nature, and gave him power, beyond all other writers, to move, astonish, and delight mankind.

JOHN LOCKE, who, best of all philosophers, understood the powers of the human mind, the nature, end, and bounds of civil government ; and with equal courage and sagacity, refuted the slavish systems of usurped authority over the rights, the consciences, and the reason of mankind.

Sir ISAAC NEWTON, whom the God of nature made to comprehend his works ; and from simple principles, to discover

the

the laws never known before, and to explain the appearance never understood, of this stupendous universe.

Sir Francis Bacon, Lord Verulam; who, by the strength and light of a superior genius, rejecting vain speculation, and fallacious theory, taught to pursue truth, and improve philosophy by the certain method of experiment.

King Alfred, the mildest, justest, most benificent of kings; who drove out the Danes, secured the seas, protected learning, established juries, crushed corruption, guarded liberty, and was the founder of the English constitution.

Edward, Prince of Wales, the terror of Europe, the delight of England; who preserved unaltered, in the height of glory and fortune, his natural gentleness and modesty.

Queen Elizabeth, who confounded the projects, and destroyed the power that threatened to oppress the liberties of Europe; took off the yoke of ecclesiastical tyranny, restored religion from the corruptions of Popery: and, by a wife, a moderate, and a popular government, gave wealth, security, and respect to England.

King William III. who by his virtue, and constancy, having saved his country from a foreign master, by a bold and generous enterprize, preserved the liberty and religion of Great Britain.

Sir Walter Raleigh, a valiant soldier, and an able statesman; who, endeavouring to rouse the spirit of his master, for the honour of his country, against the ambition of Spain, fell a sacrifice to the influence of that court, whose arms he had vanquished, and whose designs he had opposed.

Sir Francis Drake, who, through many perils, was the first of Britons who ventured to sail round the globe; and carried into unknown seas and nations the knowledge and glory of the English name.

John Hampden, who with great spirit and consummate abilities, began a noble opposition to an arbitrary court, in defence of the liberties of his country; supported them in parliament, and died for them in the field.—There are also in this temple busts of Mr. Pope, and Sir John Barnard.

In the niche of a pyramid is placed a Mercury, with these words inscribed, *Compos ducit ad Elysios*; i. e. Leads to the Elysian-Fields. And below this figure is fixed a square of black marble, on which are the following lines:

> *Hic manus ob patriam pugnando vulnera passi,*
> *Quique pii vates, et Phœbo digna locuti,*
> *Inventas aut qui vitam excoluere per artes,*
> *Quique sui memores alios fecere merendo.*

Hero

A View of the two Shell Temples in Stow Gardens.

The Serpentine River and Grotto in Kew Gardens.

Heroes are here, who for their country bled,
And bards whofe pure and facred verfe is read ;
Thofe who, by arts invented, life improv'd,
And public merit made their mem'ries lov'd.

The *Chinefe Houfe* is fituated, after the Chinefe manner, upon a large piece of water. We enter it by a bridge, decorated with Chinefe vafes. It is a fquare building, with four lattices, and covered with fail cloth. The windows and roof, together with its cool fituation on the lake, afford us a juft fpecimen of the manner of living in a hot country. Within is the figure of a Chinefe lady afleep. The outfide of the houfe is painted in the Chinefe tafte, and the infide is India Japan work.

The *Grotto*, fituated at the head of the Serpentine river, is furnifhed with a great number of looking-glaffes, both on the walls and cielings, fixed in frames of plaifter-work, ftuck with fhells and flints. It has a marble ftatue of Venus, on a pedeftal adorned in the fame manner. On each fide is a pavilion ; one of which is ornamented with fhells, the other with broken flints and pebbles.

The *Ladies Temple* is fupported by arches, with Venetian windows. The infide is beautified with the following paintings by Sclater. On the right fide, Ladies employed in needle and fhell-work. On the oppofite fide, Ladies employed in painting and mufic.

The late Anne, Vifcountefs Cobham, erected in thefe gardens fluted column, to the memory of her hufband Lord Cobham ; on one fide of which are the following lines :

Quatenus nobis denegatur diu vivere,
Relinquamus aliquid,
Quo nos vixiffe teftemur.

As we cannot live long,
Let us leave fomething behind us,
To fhew that we have lived.

Paffing by this column, from whence is a view through the wood of the temple of Concord, you come by winding walks to the banquetting-room, from whence is a fine varied profpect ; and the Corinthian arch appears to advantage. From hence you are conducted to the temple of *Concord* and *Victory*, and in the way, pafs a moft beautiful winding hollow lawn ; the brows of all the furrounding flopes, finely fpread with woods, thick in fome places, and others fcattered fo as to open for the eye to follow the bends of the lawn, which is every where different. The temple is excellently fituated on the brow of one of the hills: it is a very fine building ; an oblong totally furrounded by a colonnade of well-proportioned pillars. The architecture is

light

light and pleafing. There is a room here, ornamented with a ftatue of liberty, and feveral medallions in the walls.

From hence the walk leads next to a fequeftered winding vale, finely furrounded with wood ; and a fmall water takes its courfe through it, broken by woody iflands, and a various obfcured fhore.   At the head, the grotto of fhells looks down on the water in a pleafing manner; and muft be particularly beautiful when the woods and waters are illuminated ; which they are when Lord Temple fups in it.   Here is a ftatue of Venus rifing from the bath ;   a pleafing ftatue, and the attitude naturally taken.

The *Imperial Clofet* is a fquare room, in which are painted in frefco, the Emperors Titus, Trajan, and Antoninus ; each of whom is refpectively diftinguifhed by a memorable faying of his own, fixed over him, as follows :

Imp. Titus Cæf. Vefpafian.

Diem perdidi—I have loft a day.

Imp. N. Trajan Cæf. Au.

Pro me : fi merear, in me.

For me—if I deferve it, againft me*.

(Alluding to his fword.)

Imp. Marcus Aurelius Cæfar Antoninus.

Ita regnes imperator, ut privatus regi te velis.

So govern being an Emperor, as you would wifh to be governed if a fubject.

A grand terrace, near three hundred feet long leads us to the *Temple of Friendfhip* ; which is a well proportioned ftructure of the Doric order.   The emblemn of friendifhip over the door, thofe of Juftice and liberty, with the reft of the decorations, are elegantly touched.   Britannia is feated upon the cieling.   On one fide are exhibited the glory of her annals, the reigns of Edward III. and Queen Elizabeth.   On the other is offered the reign of * * * *, which fhe covers with her mantle, and feems unwilling to accept.—Here are alfo the bufts of the late Lord, and his illuftrious friends; viz. Frederick Prince of Wales ; the Earls of Chefterfield, Weftmoreland, and Marchmont ; the Lords Bathurft and Gower ; the prefent Earls of Chatham Temple, and the late Lord Lyttelton.

There is likewife in thefe gardens a monument erected 'to the memory of Congreve ; the embellifhments of which are emblematical of that celebrated Poet's comic genius.   And alfo another monument erected by Lord Cobham, in honour of his
nephew

* This noble fentiment of Trajan's, that the fword of juftice ought to be employed *for* him if he governed well, but *againft* him if he governed ill, is what few modern Princes would have the magnanimity to affent to.

nephew Captain Thomas Grenville, who was killed bravely fighting againſt the French, in a fleet commanded by Admiral Anſon.

There is in STOW GARDENS ſo great a variety of beauties, that the ſpectator, whoſe mind is capable of being moved, either with grace or majeſty, cannot, without reluctance, leave a place ſo properly calculated to inform the judgement, and intereſt the fancy ; where art appears without affectation, and nature without extravagance.

STONEY STRATFORD.

This town is ſuppoſed to derive its name from the ſtoney ſtreet that runs through it, and the ford where travellers uſed formerly to paſs the Ouſe. It is diſtant from London in the road to Cheſter, fity-two miles. The town is rather large, and the houſes in general are built of free-ſtone, which is dug from a quarry very near the town. The Ouſe is now croſſed by a ſtone bridge at the ford, and ſometimes ſwells ſo high, that it breaks into the neighbouring fields with great violence, eſpecially on that ſide next the town, the banks on the other ſide being ſomewhat higher. This town has two pariſh churches, and alſo two chapels, and a ſmall charity ſchool. In 1743, a fire broke out here, which conſumed one hundred and fifty houſes, but that damage has been ſince repaired, and the town in general makes an handſome appearance. The chief manufacture of the place is bone-lace.

FENNY STRATFORD is an ancient market-town, in which there are many good inns, and ſeveral fine houſes. It is at preſent a pleaſant and thriving town.

NEWPORT PAGNELL is a well built and populous market-town, and has two ſtone bridges over the Ouſe. It is a kind of ſtaple for bone lace, of which, it is ſaid, more is made in this town, and in the neighbouring villages, than in any other town in the kingdom.

OULNEY is but an inconſiderable town, and has hardly any thing remarkable in it beſides its church, which has a very fine ſpire.

WINSLOW is a ſmall town, ſurrounded with woods, but has nothing in it remarkable.—In the manor of Crendon near this town, there was an abbey, or priory, for regular canons of the order of St. Auguſtine, called *Noctele*, or *Nuttley*. It was built and endowed by Walter Giffard, the ſecond Earl of Buckingham, and Ermengard his wife, in the year 1162. Some of the ruins of this abbey are ſtill ſtanding, and near it are the remains of an ancient caſtle. N n IVINGO

Ivingo was formerly a town of great repute, and had a convent of Benedictine nuns, but it is so reduced at present as to be little better than a village, though it has a kind of weekly market.—About four miles from Ivingo is the pleasant village of *Ashbridge*, which is delightfully situated. The Duke of Bridge-water has a fine house and gardens here, with parks well stored with all sorts of game. Vast numbers of cattle are fed in the neighbourhood of Ashbridge, particularly sheep, whose fleeces are equal, if not superior, to any other in England.

T R I N G.

This is a market town in Hertfordshire, thirty-one miles from London, situated at the western extremity of the county, where it joins with Buckinghamshire. It is a place of considerable antiquity, as appears from Doomsday book, wherein it is men-tioned as a royal demesne, and as such it was given by William the Norman to his favourite, Robert Earl of Ewe. The town, though small, is extremely neat, with some very handsome houses in it; and the church is a venerable Gothic structure, the inside of which has been neatly wainscotted, at the expence of Mr. Gore. This gentleman, who is lord of the manor, has enclosed a park, near the town, containing three hundred acres of land, and in it is a fine plantation of trees, resembling a wood. Here is a charity-school for teaching and cloathing twenty boys, supported by subscription. At a village called *Little Tring*, in this parish, rises one of the heads of the river Thames. Tring is a considerable market for corn, of which there are here very large granaries.

In 1751, John Osborne, and his wife Ruth, both poor aged people, were dragged to a deep pond near this town, and there ducked, by a large mob assembled for that purpose, who had ig-norantly supposed that this couple were a witch and wizzard. They stripped them both naked, tied their thumbs and great toes together, and in that manner threw them three different times into the pond; but the poor woman who was seventy years of age, died in the water. They then took John Osborne to a neighbouring house, where they laid him in a bed, and the body of his murdered wife beside him, after which they dispersed to their own homes. But Thomas Colley, the ringleader of the mob, was afterwards apprehended, and tried for murder at Hertford. He was found guilty, and executed at Tring, his body being hung in chains.

BERK-

, was
n dug
held
fwore
laws
Corn-
ins of

town
pafs
:qui-
·uted
ly by
arket
tants
n the
:enth
here
anor,
o pay
there
and
t, to
{ion,
eter;
lerk,
ifhed
Irop-

)eing
et of
ifice,
vhere
ars of
em a
e kil·
Say e
nance
free-
{ruc-
war-

grainmar-....
ture, and is well ... *born's his Wife on a chance*
den of All Souls colle...

HEM

IVINGO was formerly a town of great repute, and had a
conve ...... but it is so reduced at present as to
be lit
m rke
Ajhbr
water
w th
neigh
are e

——

T
Lon
it joi
antic
:ione
the l
thou
houf
infid
Mr.
encle
of la
Here
fupp
this
is a
large
I
peop
duck
n ra
The
toes
time
year:
to a
body
to tl
the
Hert
body

BERK-

BERKHAMSTED.

This town, which is twenty-feven miles from London, was anciently a Roman town, and Roman coins have often been dug up here. Some of the Saxon kings kept their courts, and held their great councils at this place. William the Norman fwore here to the Englifh nobility, that he would preferve the laws made by his predeceffors. Robert de Morton, Earl of Cornwall, built a caftle on the north fide of this town, the remains of which are converted into a gentleman's feat.

King Henry II. kept his court here, and granted the town feveral privileges, particularly that its merchandize fhould pafs free of toll and cuftom through England, Normandy, Acquitain, and Anjou, and that no judicial procefs fhould be executed by any of the King's officers, within its liberties, but only by its own high fteward, coroner, and bailiffs; that no market fhould be kept within feven miles of it, and that the inhabitants fhould not be obliged to attend at any affizes or feffions. In the reign of Henry the Third, it was a borough, and in the fourteenth of King Edward the Third fent members to parliament. There are no lefs than fifty three townfhips belonging to the manor, which derives its name from the town, which are obliged to pay homage, and chufe conftables here. Of thefe townfhips there are eleven in this county, fifteen in Buckinghamfhire, and twenty-feven in Northamptonfhire. King James the Firft, to whofe children this place was a nurfery, made it a corporation, by the name of bailiff and burgeffes of Berkhamftead St. Peter; the burgeffes to be twelve, to chufe a recorder and town clerk, and to have a prifon: but the corporation was fo impoverifhed by the civil wars, in the next reign, that the government dropped, and has not fince been renewed.

The fituation of Berkhamfted is extremely pleafant, being built on the fide of a hill, chiefly confifting of a good ftreet of confiderable length. The church is a fpacious Gothic edifice, dedicated to St. Peter, and has many chapels and oratories, where mafs ufed to be faid in the times of Popery. On the pillars of the church are eleven of the apoftles, and over each of them a fentence of the creed; and on the twelfth pillar is St. George killing the dragon. Here is an alms-houfe built by Mr. John Say e and his wife, who endowed it with 1300l. for the maintenance of fix poor widows. Here is alfo a charity fchool, and a free-grammar-fchool; the grammar fchool is a handfome brick ftructure, and is well endowed, the King being patron, and the warden of All Souls college in Oxford, vifitor.

HEM

HEMPSTED

Is four miles from Berkhamſted, and twenty three from London. It was incorporated by King Henry VIII. It is governed by a bailiff, and the inhabitants are empowered to have a common ſeal, and a pye powder court, during its market and fairs. It is pleaſantly ſituated on a ſmall river, called the Gade, and ſurrounded with hills. The church, which ſtands at a little diſtance from the the town, is an ancient gothic ſtructure, with a ſquare tower, and a fine ſpire. The market here is the greateſt in Hertfordſhire for wheat ; and 20,000l. is ſaid to be often returned weekly for meal. There are eleven mills ſtand within four miles of the place, which bring a great trade to it.

About four miles from Hempſted is *King's Langley*, which is a large and pleaſant village, where King Edward III. built a fine palace, wherein he often reſided, of which ſome part ſtill remains. And here his fifth ſon Edmund, commonly called De Langley, was born ; and this prince, with his wife Iſabel, daughter of Don Pedro, King of Caſtile, lies buried in this church, which is a venerable Gothic ſtructure.

Abbots Langley is another agreeable village in this neighbourhood, which belonged to the abbey of St. Albans. The church is an handſome edifice, ſituated in the middle of the village, and at the end is a fine tower. This was the birth place of Nicholas Breakeſpeare, who was elected pope under the name of Adrian IV.

Redburne is a village on the high road leading to Dunſtable, which contains many handſome houſes, and ſeveral good inns ; for being a great thoroughfare, the waggons from Birmingham, Shrewſbury, Wolverhampton, and many other places, put up at it the night before they reach London. It is an agreeable place, and was formerly much frequented by dovotees, on account of the pretended relics of Amphibalus, a martyr, who is ſaid to have preached the goſpel here in the third century.

Flamſtead, on the left hand of the road, about four miles beyond Redburne, was formerly a market town, and had ſeveral fairs ; but, they are diſcontinued. The church is a venerable Gothic ſtructure, ſituate on a hill, with a ſquare tower and a lofty ſpire, which are ſeen at a great diſtance. The church has three iſles, and in them are ſeveral ancient monuments.

STEVENAGE is a ſmall, but ancient market-town in Hertfordſhire, in the great north road. The church was built upon
a dry

a dry fandy hill; the houfes in the town are but indifferent; but there is a good free-fchool, with an ancient hofpital, and feveral alms-houfes.—A little to the fouth of this town are the remains of an ancient camp, by fome fuppofed to have been made by the Romans, although others have afcribed it to the Danes; and there is a place near it ftill known by the name of Danes-end.

STANDON is a fmall town on the river Rib, which has an handfome church, and feveral endowments for a fchool, and for the poor.

BISHOP's STORTFORD

Is thirty miles from London, and thirteen from Stevenage. It derives its name from a ford over the river Stort, at the bottom of the town, which, ever fince the time of William the Norman, has belonged to the bifhops of London. King John made this a corporation town, with power to chufe its own officers, and it formerly fent members to parliament, but has long ago loft that privilege. The bifhop of London appoints a bailiff here, for what is called his liberty, and to him are directed fheriff's warrants, to be executed in this and feveral of the neighbouring parifhes. The bifhop holds his courts leet and baron at the manor of Padmore, at the north end of the town.

This is a confiderable, well-built place, full of good inns, being a thoroughfare to Cambridge, Newmarket; and feveral towns in Suffolk. It confifts of four ftreets, in the form of a crofs, pointing eaft, weft, north and fouth. It has a church, which ftands on a hill, in the middle of the town, with an handfome tower, a fine ring of eight bells, and a fpire, covered with lead, fifty feet high. This church had an organ fo long ago as the time of Henry the Seventh, and is thought to be very ancient, becaufe in one of the windows were the names and pictures of king Athelftan, St. Edward, and king Edward. Here are two alms-houfes and a grammar-fchool; the fchool was built about half a century ago, by the contribution of the gentry, both of this county and Effex. It ftands in the high ftreet, upon arches, under which are fhops and a market; it fronts the church-yard, and confifts of three rooms, which, with the ftair-cafe, make a fquare building; the front to the ftreet is the grammar-fchool, and the two wings are the writing-fchool and library, to which every fcholar, when he leaves the fchool, gives a book.

The river of *Hunfdon*, which is fituated on the river Stort, was fo much efteemed in former times for its healthy fituation, that

King

King Henry VIII. erected a houfe here, to which he often reforted, and in which he had his children brought up. It ftands
on a high hill, from whence there is a moft delightful profpect ;
and underneath are meadows, with the river winding in the moft
agreeable manner. Near it is the houfe where the royal children
received their education, which is now the feat of a private gentleman. The gardens are laid out with great tafte, and there is
a large bafon, from whence water is conveyed to the different
plantations in the gardens.

B U N T I N G F O R D

Is a fmall town, fituated at the ford of a fmall river, called
the Rib, in the poft-road to Cambridge, at the diftance of thirty-
one miles from London. It ftands in four parifhes, in one of
which, called Layfton, it is a chapelry. The chapel is an handfome brick ftructure, finifhed in 1626. Here is a fumptuous
alms-houfe, founded and endowed by Dr. Seth Ward, Bifhop
of Salifbury, for four ancient men, and as many ancient women,
who, from a ftate of affluence, were reduced by misfortunes to
poverty. Each man and each woman has an apartment confifting of four rooms, two above and two below, with every
convenience that can be reafonably wifhed for or expected. An
eftate was alfo left for their fupport, by the fame prelate. There
is a free-grammar fchool in this town, wherein Bifhop Ward
was educated, he being a native of this place ; he gave four fcho-
larfhips, of twelve pounds a year, to Chrift's college in Cambridge, to be enjoyed by four fcholars, natives of Hertfordfhire, who were educated at this fchool, till they are mafters of
arts.

The village of *Braughing*, which is at a little diftance from
hence, was confidered as a place of great importance when the
Romans were in Britain ; and by many is fuppofed to be the
Cafferomagum of Antoninus. There are near it the ruins of
a Roman camp, which appears to have been ftronglv fortified,
and many coins have been dug up near it. The church in this
village a very handfome edifice. Near the church-yard is an old
houfe, at prefent inhabited by poor families, but which was originally defigned for a very different purpofe. Some centuries ago,
a perfon of fortune, whofe name is not at prefent known, built
this houfe, and endowed it with a fufficient falary, to defray the
expences attending the weddings of the poorer fort of people in
the parifh. It contained all forts of neceffary furniture, with
a large kitchen, a cauldron for boiling meat, and fpits for what
they intended to roaft. Here was alfo a large room for merriment

mei t, a lodging-room with a bride-bed, and good linen; some of which furniture was in being a few years ago.

BARKWAY is a flourishing and populous town, at the distance of thirty-five miles from London, and being a considerable. thoroughfare in the north-road, contains some good inns. The church in this town is an handsome Gothic structure, and several of the windows in it are painted; and in one of them is an absurd and superstitious representation of the Deity creating the world, which is a disgrace to a Protestant church.

BALDOCK is thirty-seven miles from London, and stands between two hills, in a chalky soil, fit for corn It is a pretty large town, and in the middle of it is an handsome church, with three chancels, and a beautiful tower: among other benefactions to the poor of the place, Mr. John Winne gave 11,000l. to build six alms-houses, and purchase lands to raise an annuity of forty shillings a piece to every poor person settled in them. Here are many maltsters, and the market of this town is very considerable both for corn and malt.

HITCHING

Is one of the best built, and most populous towns in the county of Hertford. It stands in a pleasant valley, at the distance of thirty-four miles from London; and is governed by a bailiff and four constables, two for the town, and two for the out-parts. It is divided into the three wards of Bencroft, Bridge, and Tilthouse. It is said to have been formerly one of the greatest places of inland trade in England, and many merchants both from France and Flanders resided here, to purchase our commodities, and to dispose of their own. Here is an handsome church, 153 feet long, and 67 broad, with three chancels. Here is a free-school, a charity-school, and eight alms-houses. Large quantities of malt are made in this town, and it is a great market for all sorts of grain. There is a meeting here for Protestant Dissenters.

The village of *Hexton*, near Hitching, is remarkable for a bloody battle fought between the Saxons and Danes, wherein it is supposed some persons of considerable note were slain, because there are several funeral monuments near the place. There is also at a little distance from hence a very strong camp, which is conjectured to have been thrown up by the Danes, to defend themselves in case of their being defeated, until they received fresh succours from their countrymen. It is raised in an oblong manner, and so strongly fortified both by nature and art, that a thousand men might defend themselves in it against a considerable

able

able army.—A little to the fouth of Hexton, is a fine piece of ground, called *Liliho*, on a rifing ground, where horfe-races are held, and from whence there is an extenfive and beautiful pro-fpect.

L U T O N.

This is an handfome town in Bedfordfhire, fituated between two hills, at the diftance of thirty-two miles from London. The inhabitants carry on a confiderable manufactory of ftraw hats. In the middle of the town is a good market-houfe, which on the market-day, which is Monday, is well furnifhed with corn, poultry, and other provifions; and there are two fairs held here, one on the 25th of April, and the other on the 18th of Octo-ber.

At a little diftance from hence is LUTON HOO, a fine feat belonging to the Earl of Bute. It is an elegant pile of building, and that nobleman, who feems to underftand decorating a coun-try feat, much better than governing a kingdom, has expended very confiderable fums of money in ornamenting this retreat. The entrance to it is through a lodge facing the town of Luton, and the walk up to the houfe is along a fine artificial river, which was formerly nothing more than a fmall ftream. On the right hand is a rifing ground, whereon are fome exceeding fine plan-tations, and on the left are a vaft number of trees, planted fo as to imitate nature, along the banks of the ftream. The Earl has caufed an artificial lake to be made, and in the middle of it is a fmall ifland, to which you pafs by a pleafure boat, and from whence the profpect is extenfive and delightful.

On the ifland are fine plantations of young trees; and as you advance towards the houfe, you pafs through a fine row of elms, and on each fide are large clumps of beech, which add greatly to the beauty of the fcene. Through thefe trees there is a fine profpect of the neighbouring hills, fields, and cottages; whilft the towers and fpires of fteeples, lead the fpectator into a plea-fing deception, by caufing him to imagine, that what he beholds is actually a rural city. In a pleafing valley, near the houfe, is a monumental pillar, elegantly executed in the Tufcan order, and feen to the greateft advantage through the trees, on the pede-ftal of which is the following infcription, " In memory of Mr. " Francis Napier."

3

A View of Flitwick Church in Bedfordshire taken from the Garden of J. Fisher Esq.

DUNSTABLE

Is a populous town, thirty-four miles from London, built on the spot where two Roman ways, called Watling-street, and Icknild-street, cross each other; and Roman coins have sometimes been found here. The town is situated on a hill of chalk, just at the end of a long ridge of hills, called the Chiltern. Here are four streets, answering to the four cardinal winds; and because of the dryness of the foil, where they cannot find springs, have each a pond, which though only supplied by rain water, is never dry. There are several good inns here. King Henry the First built and endowed a Priory of Black Canons here; and the church of Dunstable is part of that which belonged to the Priory, and is a noble Gothic structure. There is a tomb-stone in this church, from which it appears, that a woman in the town had nineteen children at five births, having been delivered twice of five, and three times of three. There is a large manufactory of straw hats carried on in this town, and another of lace, by which almost all the poor women and girls are employed. There was formerly a royal palace here, which stood over against the church, and there are still some remains of it, which have been repaired and converted into a farm house, still called Kingsbury. At the weekly market, which is on Wednesday, vast quantities of corn are sold; and there are four fairs held here annually, namely, on Ash-Wednesday, the 22d of May, the 12th of August, and the 12th of November.

In a plain upon the top of the chalk-hills, near Dunstable, is an area, of about eight or nine acres of land, vulgarly called " the Maiden's Bower." Some have imagined it to have been a British camp, and others a work thrown up by the Danes. The rampart is high, and the Icknild street runs along the bottom of the hill. The road along the chalk-hill is extremely dangerous in frosty weather, and has occasioned many fatal accidents, both to men and horses. But some years ago the gentlemen of Bedfordshire entered into a subscription, for sloping the hill, near the town, for the benefit of the road, and there are constantly employed a certain number of hands to keep it in order.—Dunstable is remarkable for larks, which are said to be in greater plenty, and of a larger size, near this town, than any where else in the kingdom.

LEIGHTON BUZZARD is a small market town, seven miles and an half from Dunstable, which has little in it that is remarkable; but its market is well stored with cattle, and its Whitsuntide fairs with horses.

O o   WO.

WOBURN

Is a small market-town, forty-three miles from London, and being situated on the road to Northampton, &c. contains many good inns. The whole town belongs to the Duke of Bedford, and that noble family have endowed here two charity-schools. In 1724, about one hundred houses were burnt down, which are since neatly re-built; and a fine market-house has been erected, at the expence of the Duke of Bedford; so that the town now makes an handsome appearance. The principal trade of this place consists in the making of jockeys caps, and digging fuller's earth, of which there are great quantities in the neighbourhood.

WOBURN ABBEY, the noble seat of the Duke of Bedford, is in the neighbourhood of this town; and was originally built by Hugh Bolebec, a powerful baron in the reign of King Stephen. It was intended for the use of the monks of the Cistertian order, who came in great swarms into this kingdom in the twelfth century. At the dissolution of the monasteries, the lands and manors belonging to this abbey were given to Sir John Russel, ancestor of the present Duke; and this spacious and elegant house, which is situated in the middle of the park, is erected where the convent formerly stood.

The house forms a large quadrangle, with an handsome court in the center, fronting which is a large bason, supplied with water from its own springs. Behind are two large quadrangles of offices distinct from the house, which are very beautiful buildings; plain and simple, but extremely proper for their destination. They are built like the house, of white stone; and in the center of their principal front is a small dome, rising over a porticoed center, supported by Tuscan pillars, which have a very good effect.

In the house you enter first the *Hall*, which is an handsome room, the cieling of which is supported by eight pillars. The *Green Drawing Room* is extremely elegant: between the windows are fine glasses, and two very noble slabs of Egyptian marble. The chimney-piece is of white marble polished, and very handsome. In this room are pictures of the plagues of Egypt, David and Abigal, and a very fine landscape. What is called the *Decker-worked Room* contains a bed of uncommon elegance, of decker work lined with green silk. The work is exquisite, and the representation of the birds and beasts in it admirable. The chimney-piece is very elegant; the scroll of polished white marble in a light and elegant taste.

The

The *Dining Room* is a very noble room. The chimney-piece is elegant, with a festoon of flowers carved in white marble, and finely polished. In the room are four large pictures of the battles of Alexander. In the *Yellow Drawing Room* are two fine portraits by Sir Joshua Reynolds, one of the late Marquis of Taviftock, and the other of the present Dutchefs of Marlborough. The chimney-piece is very elegant, and the pier-glafs frame finely carved of plated filver. Here is alfo a portrait of the late Duke of Bedford.

In the *Coffee Room* is a fmall portrait of Francis, Earl of Bedford, which is exceedingly fine, the face and hands admirably painted. The *Grotto* is pretty of its kind; with bafs relief figures of ruftic in fhells, and fine china jars. The *Billiard Room* is hung with very fine tapeftry, defigned from Raphael's cartoons. The *Dutchefs's Dreffing Room* is extremely elegant, hung with emboffed work on white paper, which has a very pleafing effect. The chimney-piece has a carved fcroll in wood, the marble black and veined. The pier-glafs is large, and the frame very elegant; and over the chimney-piece is a portrait of Lady Offory, by Hudfon. The chairs and fofas are of painted taffeta.

The *French-Bed-chamber* is exceedingly elegant; the bed and hangings are of a very rich belmozeen filk. The chimney-piece is light and beautiful; the cornice feftoons of gilt carving on a white ground, and the cieling of the fame on a lead ground; the pier-glafs and frame, and the frame of the landfcape over the chimney are very elegant.

The *Dreffing Room* is likewife hung with the fame filk, the cieling and cornice richly ornamented with fcrolls of gilding on a white ground: the chimney-piece is all of white marble polifhed. The doors, door-cafes, and window-fhutters, &c. are all ornamented like the cieling, in white and gold. In this room are four very large blue and white china jars; the two by the windows are uncommonly fine.

The *State Bed-chamber* is moft magnificently furnifhed. The bed and hangings are of very rich blue damafk; the cieling ornamented in compartments of rich gilding on a white ground. The chimney-piece, of marble polifhed, is very elegant; and the carved and gilt ornaments around the landfcape over it in a beautiful tafte: the toilette is all of very handfome Drefden work, the glafs frame, and boxes of gold. An India cabinet on each fide of old japan, with coloured china jars exquifitely fine.

The *Dreffing Room* is hung with green damafk; the chimney-piece is very handfome, and the pier-glafs fine. The *Drawing Room* is exceedingly elegant; the cieling a Mofaic pattern of rich carving on a white ground; the chimney piece exceffively

hand-

handsome, the cornice supported by double pillars, of very fine Siena marble. The pier-glasses immensely large, and in one plate; under them most noble slabs of Siena marble. In this room are several exquisite paintings, particulary a landscape by Claude Lorraine, representing a ship partly appearing from behind a building amazingly beautiful; the diffusion of light, the general brilliancy, and the harmony of the whole, are admirable. A holy family, very fine, the turn of the boy's head is inimitable. A virgin and child; the hair of the virgin's head, and her attitude are most sweetly elegant and expressive. A Magdalen; very fine. The inside of a church; the minute expression of the architecture, and the rays of light are finely done. A rock, with the broken branches hanging from its clefts, supposed to be by Salvator; the expression is very noble, and the romantic wildness of the scene most excellently represented. A holy family; the child standing in the cradle; a very pleasing picture. Joseph interpreting the dreams of Pharaoh, by Rembrandt; most admirably executed; in a greater stile than is common with this master. Rembrandt by himself; inimitably done. The Duchess of Bedford, presenting Lady Caroline to Minerva, by Hamilton; this is a very large picture, and some of the figures not inelegantly done for this master.

The *Saloon* is most magnificently fitted up, and elegantly furnished; the cieling beautiful, of gilt carving on white; the door case finely carved and gilt, the cornices supported by Corinthian pillars in a noble, but light and pleasing stile; the chimney-piece of white marble, beautifully polished: in the center hangs a magnificent lustre. Here is a fine picture representing the last supper; the drawing is in a free and bold stile; and a fine piece of angels, supposed to be painted by Albano.

The *Second Dining-room* is a very noble room, the cieling white and gold, and the chimney piece very elegant, over which is a fine landscape. *The Second Drawing-room* is very elegantly fitted up; and among other pictures contains two capital landscapes, morning and evening, by Marrat; two paintings of battles; and one of lyons, by Rubens. The *Picture Gallery* is ornamented by a vast number of elegant portaits of the Russel family; and among those which are most finely executed, are the portraits of William, Earl of Bedford, the Countess of Somerset, and Lady Catharine Brooke. The ornaments of this room are all carving painted white. There are four statues here, one of which is a Venus of Medicis, and another Venus plucking a thorn from out of her foot.

WOBURN PARK is one of the largest in the kingdom, being ten miles round, all walled in, and contains a great variety of hill and dale, with fine woods of the noblest oaks. We pass
from

from the houfe through them towards the fouth, and look up the great glade, which is cut through the park for feveral miles, at the end of which appears a Chinefe temple. Then winding through the woods we come to the Duchefs's Shrubbery, which contains fixteen acres of land beautifully laid out in the modern tafte, with many venerable oaks in it. From whence we advance to the hill at the north end, from which is a vaft profpect into Buckinghamfhire, Hertfordfhire, and Bedfordfhire. Turning down the hill to the left, the riding leads to the ever-green plantation of above two hundred acres of land, which little more than thirty years ago was a barren rabbit warren, but is now a very beautiful winter's ride, on a dry foil, with all kinds of ever-greens of a noble growth. About the middle on the left hand fide, is an handfome temple, retired and pleafing; at the end of this plantation, we come to the lower water, which is about ten acres, and in the center is an ifland with a very elegant and light Chinefe temple, large enough for thirty people to dine in; and in the adjoining wood is a kitchen, and other accommodations for making ready the repafts the Duke takes in the temple. And in the front of the houfe is a large bafon of water, in which are feveral handfome boats.

A M P T H I L L

Is a fmall market-town, forty-four miles from London, pleafantly fituated between two hills, almoft in the heart of Bedfordfhire. Here is a charity-fchool, and an hofpital for ten poor men, who have each a confiderable weekly allowance.—This place is chiefly remarkable for a large manfion-houfe, which belongs alfo to the Duke of Bedford. It was repaired and fitted up in 1765, for the ufe of the late Marquis of Taviftock. It was firft built by Sir John Cornwall, in the reign of King Henry VI. out of the fpoils taken from the French; but afterwards came by forfeiture to the crown. Queen Katherine of Arragon, fometimes refided in this houfe, after her divorce from Henry VIII. The hall is adorned with a capital collection of paintings by the beft Italian mafters, which the late Marquis of Taviftock collected whilft he was abroad on his travels.

At *Houghton Park*, near Ampthill, the Earl of Upper Offory has a fine feat, which was firft built by the Countefs of Pembroke. The houfe is a noble and venerable edifice, containing many fine rooms; and the gardens are laid out with much tafte and magnificence. There is ftill a large pear-tree here, under which the celebrated Sir Philip Sydney is faid to have written part of his Arcadia.

Weftoning

Westoning is a pleasant village, which has a venerable church, that stands in an agreeable and rural situation. The Earl of Pomfret has a seat here.

Near Silsoe is WREST-HOUSE, a magnificent seat, with a large park, which belonged to the ancient family of De Grey, Dukes of Kent. It now belongs to the Earl of Hardwicke, who acquired it by his marriage with Jemima Marchioness Grey, and Baroness Lucas, who is a peeress in her own right. In an hermitage here is the following inscription, which was written by a person who came on a visit to this agreeable retreat.

" Stranger, or guest, whome'er this hallow'd grove
" Shall chance relieve where sweet contentment dwells,
" Bring here no heart that with ambition swells,
" With av'rice pines, or burns with lawless love.
" Vice-tainted souls will all in vain remove
" To sylvan shades, and hermits peaceful cells ;
" In vain will seek retirement's lenient spells,
" Or hope that bliss, which only good men prove
" If heav'n-born truth, and sacred virtue's love,
" Which chear, adorn, and dignify the mind,
" Are constant inmates of thy honest breast ;
" If, unrepining at thy neighbour's store,
" Thou count'st as thine the good of all mankind,
" Then, welcome, share the friendly groves of *Wrest*."

At a little distance from hence is the village of *Cophill*, which is a pretty rural place, not far from which is a fine seat belonging to Earl Granville, known by the name of *Hawnes*.

SHEFFORD is a small market-town, pleasantly situated between two rivulets, over each of which there is a bridge.—At a little distance from hence is *Chicksand Priory*, the seat of Sir George Osborne, Bart.

At *Southill* in this neighbourhood, is a fine seat of the Lord Torrington's.

At *Northill*, there is a very fine window in the chancel of the church, painted by Oliver ; and the rector of that church has two small pieces of painted glass by the same master, which are of uncommon excellence.—The parish of *Sandy*, near Northill, is much noted for its gardens ; there are above one hundred and fifty acres of land occupied by many gardeners, who supply the whole country, for many miles, with garden stuff, even to Hertford.

Cardington is a very neat and agreeable village ; most of the houses and cottages are new-built, all of them tiled, and many of brick ; which, with white pales, and little plantations, have a most pleasing effect.

B E D-

A View of Westoning Church in Bedfordshire.

T. Oliver del.

BEDFORD

Is forty-eight miles from London, and is the county-town, being a clean, well-built, and populous place. The town, as well as the county, is divided into two parts by the river Ouse, which crosses it in the direction of east and west; the north and south parts of the town are joined by a stone bridge, which has two gates. The assizes are always held here; and the town is governed by a mayor, recorder, two bailiffs, twelve aldermen, two chamberlains, and other officers. There are five churches here, three on the north, and two on the south side of the river. The chief of them, and indeed the principal ornament of the town, is St. Paul's, which had once a college of prebendaries. There was a famous castle here, which was demolished in the reign of Henry VIII. and the scite is now a bowling-green: it stands high and pleasant, and is reckoned one of the finest in England.

There is a good free-school in this town, which was founded by Sir William Harpur, Lord Mayor of London in the reign of Queen Elizabeth. This gentleman was a native of Bedford, and now lies buried in one of the churches. Near the free-school are two ancient hospitals, for lazars, and an alms house for eight poor persons, besides a charity-school for forty children, partly endowed, and partly supported by voluntary subscription. But the most considerable provision made for the poor of Bedford was, a field where Bedford-Row stands, behind Gray's Inn, London, which at the time the donation was made, produced only a small rent, but now, by the encrease of buildings, and the expiration of leases, is become extremely valuable. It was given to the town, that the rents might be applied to the portioning young women, when they entered into the marriage state, and to put out poor children as apprentices. If this large estate be managed with judgment and integrity, it may be rendered a charitable institution of a very extensive and beneficial nature.

Bedford sends two members to parliament, who are chosen by all the freemen, the mayor being the returning officer. The liberties of the corporation extend about nine miles round the town. There are some good inns here, and provisions of all sorts are in great plenty. There is a lace manufactory here, which employs about five hundred women and girls.

The *Vale of Bedford*, which is a perfect flat tract of land for some miles round the town, is very rich in soil, and excellently cultivated, producing noble crops of wheat, barley, and turnips.

2 At

At *Clapham*, about two miles from Bedford, is a fine feat belonging to the Earl of Afhburnham; and near it is *Oakly*, a feat belonging to the Duke of Bedford. At *Brumham*, which is on the weft fide of the river Oufe, Lord Trevor has a fine feat.

Harewood, or *Harold*, is a place of confiderable antiquity, but is now reduced to a village. Here was formerly a nunnery of the order of St. Auguftine. Part of the church is ftill remaining, and appears to have been a very elegant Gothic building.

BIGGLESWADE

Is a market-town, five miles from Bedford, and forty-five from London. It is pleafantly fituated on the banks of the river Ivel, over which there is a good ftone bridge ; and lighters come up with coals to the town. There was formerly a fmall college for fecular priefts here. At prefent the town is in a flourifhing condition, and has fome good inns in it, being a great thoroughfare in the road from London to York. Its weekly market is on Tuefday, and it is reckoned one of the greateft in England to barley.

There is a village called *Wardon*, near *Bigglefwade*, where a monaftery was founded for the monks of the Ciftertian order, in the latter end of the reign of King Henry I. which was endowed with lands to a confiderable value.

BEFORE we conclude this Volume, we fhall make fome general remarks on the feveral COUNTIES, in which thofe places are fituated which we have already defcribed.

SURREY is bounded by the river Thames, which parts it from Middlefex, on the north ; by Suffex on the fouth ; by Kent on the eaft ; and by Berkfhire and Hampfhire on the weft. It is about thirty-four mile in length, twenty-one in breadth, and one hundred and twelve miles in circumference ; and contains thirteen hundreds, one hundred and forty parifhes, thirteen market towns, four hundred and fifty villages and hamlets, and about five hundred and ninety-two thoufand acres. It lies in the province of Canterbury, and diocefe of Winchefter.

The air and foil in the middle and extreme parts of this county are very different. Towards the borders of the county, efpecially on the north-fide, near the Thames, and on the south side, in and near a vale called Holmsdale, that stretches for several miles from Darking to the county of Kent, the air is mild and healthy, and the soil fruitful in corn and hay, with a fine mixture of woods and fields; but in some parts of the county the air is rather bleak. Surrey contains many delightful places, though some parts of it consist chiefly of open and sandy ground, and barren heaths. The air of Cotcman Dean, near Darking, has been reputed the best in England. The principal commodities of this county are corn, box-wood, wallnuts, and fullers earth. There is a kind of wild black cherry, that grows about Darking, of which the inhabitants make considerable quantities of red wine, which is said to be little inferior to French claret, and much more wholesome. The county in general is well provided with river fish, and the Wandle is famous for plenty of fine trout.

The rivers of this county are the Thames, the Mole, the Wey, and the Wandle. The *Mole* rises near Oakley, south-west of Darking, and running eastward for several miles, along the borders of Suffex, forms an angle, and directs its course north-west. At the bottom of a hill called Boxhill, near Darking, the stream disappears, and passes under ground in a place called the Swallow, probably from the river being swallowed up there. From this circumstance the river is also sometimes called the Swallow; and it appears to have derived the name Mole from working its way under ground; for it is generally believed, that from the bottom of Box-hill, where it is swallowed up, it works a passage for more than two miles to Leatherhead, where it is supposed to spring up anew; and from whence it continues its course northward, till it falls into the Thames, over-against Hampton-Court, in the county of Middlesex. Some late writers have, however, been of opinion, that the stream of the Mole is altogether lost at the Swallow, and is not the same that rises at Leatherhead; but rather that the waters issue from a new spring, and that the river formed by them is another river; though from a belief of its being the same river, it obtained the same name. The *Wey* rises not far from Alton, a market-town of Hampshire, and directing its course eastwards, enters this county at Farnham, from whence it passes in the same direction to Godalming, and there forming an angle, it runs northward by Guildford, from thence to Woking, and running north-east, empties itself by a double mouth into the Thames, about a mile from Chertsey. This river is navigable to Godalming, and its navigation is of great benefit to the south-west parts of Surrey, by supplying the inhabitants with coals, and many other necessaries, from London. The *Wandle*, or *Vandal*, rises at Carshalton, near Croydon, and running north,

with

with a fmall, but clear ftream, falls into the river Thames at Wandfworth.

MIDDLESEX derives its name from its having been inhabited by the Middle Saxons, who were thus diftinguifhed, on account of their fituation in the Middle, between the three antient kingdoms of the Eaft, Weft, and South Saxons, by which they were furrounded. This county is bounded by Hertfordfhire on the north; by the river Thames, which divides it from the county of Surrey, on the fouth; by the river Colne, which feparates it from Buckinghamfhire, on the weft; and by the river Lea, which divides it from the county of Effex on the eaft. It extends fcarcely twenty four miles in length, about eighteen in breadth, and is not more than ninety-five miles in circumference; but as it comprehends the cities of London and Weftminfter, which ftand in the fouth eaft part of the county, it is by much the wealthieft and moft populous county in England. It is divided into fix hundreds, and two liberties; and contains two cities and five market-towns. It lies in the province of Canterbury, and diocefe of London; and exclufive of London and Weftminfter, has feventy-three parifh churches, befides chapels of eafe.

The air of Middlefex is very pleafant and healthy, to which a fine gravelly foil contributes not a little. The foil produces plenty of corn; and the county abounds with fertile meadows and gardeners grounds; for the art of gardening, affifted by the rich compoft from London, is brought to much greater perfection in this county than in any other part of England.

The rivers of this county are the Thames, the Colne, the Lea, and the New River. The *Thames* is one of the fineft and moft beautiful rivers in the world; and at London, the depth of it is fufficient, not only for the navigation of large fhips, but for making it, what it really is, one of the greateft ports for trade in the univerfe. Its water is extremely wholefome, and fit for ufe in the longeft voyages, during which, it will work and ferment itfelf like ftrong liquor, till it becomes perfectly fine. It abounds with a great variety of fifh, among which, its falmons, fmelts, and flounders are particularly admired.

ESSEX is bounded by Suffolk and Cambridgefhire on the north; by the German Ocean on the eaft; by the river Thames, which feparates it from the county of Kent on the fouth; and by the counties of Midlefex and Hertford on the weft. It is about fifty miles in length, thirty-five in breadth, and one hundred and forty in circumference; and contains twenty hundreds, twenty-two market towns, four hundred and fifteen parifhes, and

and one million two hundred and forty thousand acres. It abounds with corn, cattle, and wild fowl; and the north parts of it, especially about Saffron-walden, produce great quantities of saffron. Abundance of oxen and sheep are fed in the marshes near the Thames, and sent to the markets of London. The inhabitants of this county have plenty of fish of all forts from the sea and rivers; and by the sea side are decoys, which in the winter season produce great profit to their owners. Towards the sea, the air of this county is aguish, though it is more so in regard to strangers than the natives. The principal manufactures of this county are cloths and stuffs, but particularly bays and says, of which, not half a century ago, such quantities were exported to Spain and the Spanish colonies in America, to cloath the nuns and friars, that there has often been a return from London of 30,000l. a week, in ready money only, to Colchester and a few small towns round it.

The principal rivers in this county are the Stour, the Lea, the Coln, the Blackwater, and the Chelmer. The *Stour* rises in the north-west part of Essex, and running south east, separates it from Suffolk, and falls into the German Ocean at Harwich. The *Lea* rises in the north-west part of the county, runs almost directly south, and separating Essex from the counties of Hertford and Middlesex, falls into the Thames at Blackwall. The *Coln* rises also in the north-west part of Essex, and running south-west to Halsted, runs parallel to the river Stour, and passes by Colchester, where, forming an angle, it runs south-south east, and falls into the German Ocean, about seven or eight miles south-east from that town. The *Blackwater* rises also in the north-west part of Essex, and running south-east, passes by Braintree and falls into the Chelmer at Malden. The *Chelmer* rises within two or three miles of the source of the river Blackwater, and running nearly parallel to it, passes to Chelmsford, where, forming an angle, it runs directly east, and receiving the Blackwater, falls into the German Ocean near Malden.

KENT is bounded by Sussex and the English channel on the south, by the river Thames and the German sea on the north, by the same sea on the east, and by Surrey on the west. This county is divided into five lathes, which are subdivided into fourteen bailiwicks, and these again into sixty eight hundreds. A lathe is a division peculiar to Kent and Sussex, and consists of two or more bailiwicks, as a bailiwick does of two or more hundreds. Kent contains two cities, and twenty-nine market-towns, e even hundred and eighty villages, and about one million two hundred and forty eight thousand acres. It lies in the province

of

of Canterbury, and partly in that diocese, and partly in the diocese of Rochester, and has four hundred and eight parishes.

The county is nominally divided into three districts, East-
Kent, West-Kent, and South-Kent; or Upper-Kent, Midde-
Kent, and Lower-Kent. Upper-Kent, or East-Kent, which
is in the north-east division, is said to be healthy, but not wealthy; Lower-Kent, or the south parts, called also the Weald of
Kent, are said to be wealthy, but not healthy; and Middle Kent,
bordering upon London and Surrey, is said to be both wealthy
and healthy. In general, as great part of this county lies upon
the sea, the air is thick, foggy, and warm, though often puri-
fied by south, and south-west winds, and the shore being generally cleaner than that of Essex, the marshy parts of Kent do
not produce so many agues in the same degree as the hundreds of
Essex; and the air in the higher parts of Kent is reckoned very
healthy. The soil is generally rich, and fit for plough, pasture,
or meadow; and that part of the county which borders upon
the river Thames abounds with chalk-hills, from whence not
only the city of London, and parts adjacent, but even Holland
and Flanders, are supplied with lime and chalk; and from these
hills the rubbish of the chalk is carried in lighters and hoys to
the coasts of Essex, Suffolk, and Norfolk, where it is sold to
the farmers as manure for their lands.

This county affords some mines of iron, and in general abounds
with plantations of hops, fields of corn, and orchards of cherries, apples, and other fruit; it produces also wood and madder
for dyers; and in the cliffs between Dover and Folkstone, there
is found plenty of samphire; hemp and St. Foin grow here in
great abundance; and the south and west parts of Kent, especially that called the Weald, are covered with woods of oak,
beech, and walnut trees, which afford great quantities of timber for shipping and other uses; here are also many woods of
birch, from which the broom-makers in and about London are
abundantly supplied. The cattle here of all sorts are reckoned
larger than they are in the neighbouring counties; and the
Weald of Kent is remarkable for large cattle; here are several
parks of fallow deer, and warrens of grey rabbits; and this
county, abounding in rivers, and being almost surrounded by
the sea, is well supplied with all manner of fish, and in particular is famous for large oysters.

BERKSHIRE is bounded by Hampshire on the south; by
Wiltshire and Glocestershire on the west; by the river Thames,
which divides it from Buckingham———— and Oxfordshire on
the north; and on the east by Middlesex and Surrey.
is about thirty-nine miles long, twenty-nine broad, and one
                                                    hundred

hundred and twenty in circumference ; and contains four parliamentary boroughs, twenty hundreds, twelve market-towns,
one hundred and forty parishes, and six hundred and seventy-one
villages.

The air of this county is healthy even in the vales, and tho'
the soil in general is not the most fertile, yet · the appearance of
the country is remarkably pleasant, being delightfully varied
with wood and water, which are seen at once in almost every
prospect. This county is well stored with timber, particularly
oak and beech ; and some parts of it produce great quantities of
wheat and barley. The whole of this county is in the province
of Canterbury and diocese of Salisbury.

The river *Thames* washes more of this county than any other
it touches; and from this circumstance Berkshire derives both
fertility, and convenience for the carriage of its commodities
to London, of which it sends a great many, particularly malt,
meal, and timber. There are four other rivers in the county, the *Kennet*, great part of which is navigable, the *Lod-*
den, the *Ocke*, and the *Lambourne*, a small stream, which
contrary to all other rivers, is always highest in summer, shrinks
gradually as winter approaches, and at last is nearly, if not
quite, dry.

BUCKINGHAMSHIRE is bounded by the Thames, which
divides it from Berkshire on the south ; by Oxfordshire on the
west ; by Northamptonshire on the north; and by Bedfordshire, Hertfordshire, and Middlesex on the east. It is thirty-
nine miles in length, eighteen in breadth, and one hundred and
thirty-eight in circumference ; and contains eleven market-
towns, eight hundreds, one hundred and eighty-five parishes,
six hundred and fifteen villages, and about four hundred and for-
ty-one thousand acres. It lies in the province of Canterbury,
and diocese of Lincoln.

This county is diversified with pleasant woods, and fine streams,
which render it a charming retreat. Its chief rivers are the
Thames, the Ouse, and the Coln. The soil is very fruitful, both
in corn and pasture, and abounds with physical plants.

HERTFORDSHIRE is bounded by Cambridgeshire on the
north ; by Middlesex on the south; by Bedfordshire and Buckinghamshire on the west, and by Essex on the east. It measures twenty eight miles from east to west, thirth-six miles from
north to south, and one hundred and thirty miles in circumference ; and is divided into eight hundreds, in which are eighteen
market-towns, one hundred and twenty parishes, and about
four hundred and fifty-one thousand acres. This county is watered

tered by feveral rivers, the chief of which are the **Lea**, the Coln, the Stort, the Ver, and the New River.

The air of this county is very pure, and confequently healthy, and is often recommended by phyficians to valetudinarians, for the prefervation or recovery of health. The foil is for the moft part rich, and in feveral places mixed with a marle, which produces excellent wheat and barley. The chief produce of this county is wood, wheat, barley, and all other forts of grain ; and the wheat and barley of Hertfordfhire are generally held in very high eftimation. This county lies in the province of Canterbury, and partly in the diocefe of London, and partly in that of Lincoln.

SUSSEX derives its name from a Saxon word which fignified *the county of the South Saxons*. This county is bounded on the north by Surrey; on the eaft and north-eaft by Kent ; on the fouth by the Britifh channel ; and on the weft by Hampfhire. It is about fixty-five miles in length, twenty-nine in breadth, and one hundred and feven in circumference. It is divided into fix rapes, or lathes, each of which is faid to have had its particular caftle, river and foreft. It is alfo fubdivided into fixty-five hundreds, wherein are reckoned three hundred and twelve parifhes, one city, eighteen market-towns, and one thoufand and fixty villages and hamlets.

The air of this county along the fea coaft, is aguifh to ftrangers ; but the inhabitants in general are very healthy. In the north part of the county, bordering upon Kent and Surrey, the air is foggy, but not unhealthy ; and upon the Downs it is exceedingly fweet and pure. The foil is various, the hilly parts lefs fruitful than the others ; the vales, efpecially in that part of the county called the Weald, are dirty but very fertile. On the fea-coaft are very green hills, called the South Downs, well known to travellers for their beautiful profpect, but better to thofe who deal in wool or fheep, there being great numbers bred here, whofe wool, which is very fine, is too often exported clandeftinely to France. The middle part of the county is delightfully chequered with meadows, paftures, groves, and corn-fields, which produce great quantities of wheat and barley. The north quarter is fhaded with woods, from whence great quantities of excellent timber are carried to the dock-yards, and of charcoal to the iron-works, in the eaftern part of the county.—The principal rivers are the *Arun*, the *Adur*, the *Oufe*, and the *Rother*. Other lefs confiderable rivers in this county are the *Lavant*, the *Cuchmeer*, the *Afhburn*, and the *Aften*. Suffex lies in the province of Canterbury, and diocefe of Chicefter.

O X-

OXFORDSHIRE is bounded on the east by Buckinghamshire; on the west by Gloucestershire; on the north by Northamptonshire and Warwickshire; and on the south by Berkshire.
It is about forty-two miles in length, twenty-six in breadth,
and one hundred and thirty in circumference; and contains one
city, fifteen market-towns, two hundred and eighty parishes,
fourteen hundreds, and about five hundred and thirty-four thousand acres.

The air of Oxfordshire is as good as that of any other county
in England; for the soil is naturally dry, free from bogs, fens
and stagnant waters, and abounding with quick limpid streams,
that necessarily render the air sweet and healthy. The soil is in
general very fertile, both for corn and grass; but there is a
great variety in it, and consequently several degrees of fruitful-
ness. There is plenty of river fish here, of various kinds, The
productions of this county are cattle, fruit, free-stone, and several sorts of earth used in medicine, dying, and scouring; but it
is thinly strewed with wood, and fuel is consequently very
scarce. The principal rivers of this county are the Thames or
Isis, the Evenlode, the Windrush, the Tame, and the Char-
well. This county lies in the province of Canterbury, and diocese of Oxford.

BEDFORDSHIRE is bounded on the south by Hertfordshire; on the north by Northamptonshire and Huntingdonshire;
on the east by Cambridgeshire; and on the west by Bucking-
shire. It is about twenty-two miles in length, fifteen in breadth,
and seventy-three in circumference. It contains nine hundreds,
ten market-towns, and one hundred and twenty four parishes,
five hundred and fifty villages, and about two hundred and sixty
thousand acres. This county, on the north side of the river Ouse
is fruitful and woody, on the south side it is less fertile. It produces wheat and barley in great abundance, and of an excellent
kind, and it has forests and parks well stocked with deer, and
fat pastures with cattle. The air is pure and healthful, and the
soil in general a deep clay. The principal rivers of this county
are the Ouse and the Iwell. It lies in the province of Canterbury and diocese of Lincoln.

THE END OF THE FIRST VOLUME.